Philosophy, Public Policy, and Transnational Law

Series Editor
John Martin Gillroy
Lehigh University
Bethlehem
Pennsylvania, USA

Philosophy, Public Policy, and Transnational Law seeks, uniquely, to publish new and innovative arguments about global law and policy that transcend realist/positivist assumptions and the conventions of current legal/policy discourse. This series means to encourage the application of systematic philosophical and theoretical arguments to practical policy and legal issues that combine domestic, comparative or international law. We will pursue scholarship that integrates the superstructure of the positive law with its philosophical and public policy substructure, and which, in this way, produces a more three dimensional understanding of transnational law and its evolution, meaning, imperatives and future. We seek dissertations, solo and edited volumes, as well as innovative reports that integrate new methods, epistemologies and interdisciplinary perspectives with practical issues on the full range of policy and legal dilemmas challenging transnational relations.

More information about this series at
http://www.springer.com/series/14550

Giada Girelli

Understanding Transitional Justice

A Struggle for Peace, Reconciliation, and Rebuilding

palgrave
macmillan

Giada Girelli
London, United Kingdom

Philosophy, Public Policy, and Transnational Law
ISBN 978-3-319-53605-7 ISBN 978-3-319-53606-4 (eBook)
DOI 10.1007/978-3-319-53606-4

Library of Congress Control Number: 2017940426

Printed on acid-free paper

This Palgrave Macmillan imprint is published by Springer Nature
The registered company is Springer International Publishing AG
The registered company address is: Gewerbestrasse 11, 6330 Cham, Switzerland

Acknowledgements

The writing of this book has been a long journey, started in Italy almost four years ago, passing through London, and concluded under the sun of South-East Asia, and I would have never reached my destination without the incredible help and support I received.

First of all, I must thank Professor Sergio Dellavalle, for the constant trust and support provided, for offering his insightful and constructive advice throughout this elaboration and for inspiring me to always strive for (at the very least) perfection. Without his guide, his patience and his wisdom this book would have never become reality.

I am also indebted to my professors at the Centre for Transitional Legal Studies and at the School of Oriental and African Studies, for teaching me that my opinion counts, and for training me to approach every subject and every opinion, especially my own, with a critical and open mind. In this context, I would like to express my deepest appreciation to Professor David Luban, not only for reading the first version of this book, and responding with much-needed words of encouragement, but also for being such a model of competence, kindness and passion.

A big thanks goes to my family, whom despite the distance I have never felt so close.

Finally, I want to thank Elia, for having accompanied me, with astonishing patience, through this and many other journeys, and for sharing with me his strength and determination.

To him this book is dedicated.

Contents

List of Abbreviations

(I)NGOs	(International) Non-Governmental Organisation
AC	Amnesty Committee (South Africa TRC)
AFRC	Armed Forces Revolutionary Council (Sierra Leone)
ANC	African National Congress (South Africa)
CDF	Civil Defence Forces (Sierra Leone)
CEH	Comisión para el Esclarecimiento Histórico (Commission for Historical Clarification, Guatemala)
CONADEP	Comisión Nacional sobre la Desaparición de Personas (Argentina)
DDR	Disarmament, Demobilisation and Reintegration
DRC	Democratic Republic of Congo
ECCC	Extraordinary Chambers in the Courts of Cambodia
ECHR	European Convention on Human Rights
ECtHR	European Court of Human Rights
HRVC	Committee on Human Rights Violations (South Africa TRC)
IACHR	Inter-American Commission on Human Rights
IACtHR	Inter-American Court of Human Rights
ICC	International Criminal Court
ICTR	International Criminal Tribunal for Rwanda
ICTY	International Criminal Tribunal for Former Yugoslavia
IMT	International Military Tribunal (Nuremberg tribunal)
IMTFE	International Military Tribunal for the Far East (Tokyo tribunal)
PAC	Patrulla de Autodefensa Civil (Guatemala)
PRN	National Reparation Program (Guatemala)
RRC	Reparation and Reconciliation Committee (South Africa TRC)
RUF	Revolutionary United Front (Sierra Leone)
SCSL	Special Court for Sierra Leone
SFRY	Socialist Federative Republic of Yugoslavia

TRC	South Africa's Truth and Reconciliation Commission
UN	United Nations
UNAMSIL	United Nations Mission in Sierra Leone
UNSC	United Nations Security Council
URNG	Unidad Revolucionaria Nacional Guatemalteca

CHAPTER 1

Introduction: Building Justice in the Wake of Atrocities

A few days before submitting the final draft of this book, I had the chance to visit the Tuol Sleng Genocide Museum in Phnom Penh (Cambodia), a former school turned detention centre under the Khmer Rouge regime (one of the most efficiently run among a network of dozens of prisons), and now preserved as a museum and memorial.

Having visited a few other similar sites, and having researched and read extensively on conflicts and their aftermath, I thought I would approach the museum with a clinical eye, as a researcher seeking answers to the many academic questions I encountered in the past years, and looking for elements of confirmation – or questioning – of my beliefs with regards to conflicts and transitions. Among others, I was planning to investigate how the memorial had been established, and how was it funded; whether (and how) survivors were involved in the process, and whether memorials can really be instrumental to the healing process; what is the country's attitude towards the Extraordinary Chambers. Heading there, I thought I would experience – like I had in Auschwitz, in its resemblance to a quiet countryside village, waiting for its inhabitants to come back from a day of work – the infamous banality of evil. Instead, I found nothing banal in the barbed wire still hanging outside the buildings to prevent prisoners from committing suicide; nothing banal in the crying eyes of a museum guard, struggling – more than 30 years later – to cope with what had happened to his

G. Girelli, *Understanding Transitional Justice*,
Philosophy, Public Policy, and Transnational Law,
DOI 10.1007/978-3-319-53606-4_1

country, nor in the blood stains still stubbornly covering the ceiling of the interrogation room.

It took me just two minutes, the time required to listen to the introductory recording and hesitantly step into the first prison cell – my heart pounding, while retracing the steps of the many who had entered these rooms, never to leave them – to forsake my objectivity and forget about my well-thought enquiries, assaulted by dozens of questions, many of my strongly held beliefs about conflicts and peace processes problematised or shattered by a relentless flow of emotions. Who bears ultimate responsibility for the horrors these walls witnessed? Is it the prison guards and the interrogators, many of whom were handpicked in the villages when just teenagers, indoctrinated and then induced to carry out acts of violence? Was it the prison director, as the agent of a paranoid regime pursuing a delusional project of ill-conceived communist revolution? Or does the ultimate guilt lie with the French colonisers, together with the American forces that since the late 1960s carpet-bombed Cambodia, destroying the country and energising the Khmer Rouge rebels?

At the same time, I could not help but ponder what my role in these rooms was, staring at the pictures and skulls of unidentified victims, as a white privileged woman who never witnessed – let alone experienced – war or poverty or despair: was I paying tribute to the victims, educating myself to prevent "this" from happening again – to become myself a victim, a silent and complicit bystander or, who knows, maybe a perpetrator? Was I acknowledging and honouring these subjects' pain and suffering? Or rather, was I just satisfying, paraphrasing Mahmood Mamdani, my pornographic lust for violence?

And also, how was it even possible to talk about reconciliation in the aftermath of such a crude experience? What was there left to reconcile, for people who had lost, or since childhood were denied, everything, forced to sacrifice their lives for a country that disappeared and killed their own families?

***

This book describes and critically analyses some of the defining themes and foundational experiences of the field of transitional justice, primarily aiming not at providing answers to this kind of questions, but rather at being a guide, a useful tool for navigating this complex and evolving field, which is extraordinarily fascinating precisely because it is a field of tensions. Indeed, transitional justice strives towards identifying – and realising – the necessary, ideal and practical interventions required in post-conflict situations, while operating in the most challenging of circumstances: the country needs to be rebuilt from scratch, often through structural reforms refashioning the political, economic and social systems, but at the same time resources are scarce; the administrative structure is destroyed or rotten; people have fled the country or have been murdered, perhaps by the very subjects that should have granted peace and security, sometimes by their own neighbours. In seeking solutions, this discipline goes beyond ordinary legal problems, or it casts a new light on them, while looking for viable ways to reconcile tensions between its different goals.

Clearly, the main objective is justice. However, the very significance and connotations of this term are debated: while sometimes understood in the traditional sense of punishment, another approach is increasingly promoted which envisages, alongside the classical retribution and deterrence, a less traditional conception of justice as addressing and redressing of those socio-economic inequalities and abuses which often constitute the root causes of violence. Another core purpose of transitional projects, whose relationship with justice is however a source of discussion, is truth: for justice to be done, the responsibilities of the wrongdoers need to be ascertained and stated, names must be made, and the suffering of the victims and survivors needs to be acknowledged and dignified. However, when focusing on the specific contexts this longing for truth at any cost, for telling and being told, is called into question by diverging approaches to peace and healing. Furthermore, in the aftermath of conflicts and authoritarianism the reconstruction of the state is necessary, in all its dimensions. First, there is a need for a physical reconstruction, for the (re)building of streets, bridges, houses and courts of justice. Second, the political and administrative structures must be reformed, through the development of new institutions, a new government, sometimes even a new foundational charter. Third – and here lies the most peculiar and unordinary feature of transitional justice projects – a symbolic reconstruction is called for. Indeed, conflicts, atrocities and dictatorships disrupt the relationships among individuals, and between individuals and the state; families and communities are wrecked, their members turned against each other by the very organisms that were supposed to protect them, and/or by entrenched prejudices. Reconstructing the social fabric, at the very least in a way that allows for peaceful coexistence, requires rebuilding trust and fostering dialogue.

All these (together with other) objectives and needs, which are essential, intrinsic to the discipline, are however also in tension with each other:

it results almost impossible to pursue them concurrently without at the same time sacrificing or compromising them, at least in part. Here lies the difficulty, and here lies the very substance of transitional justice: in striking a delicate balance between essential but seemingly irreconcilable goals. This volume, ideally divided into two parts, considers these issues.

The first part explores some foundational topics informing the transitional justice discourse, starting with the victims, as its ideal protagonists. In particular, after reflecting on how to define and delimitate this category in the extraordinary context of a transition, specific attention will be reserved to the relation between gender and conflict. Subsequently, some of the key justifications in favour of the involvement of victims in transitional processes will be outlined, while also considering possible shortcomings. Finally, an introduction is provided to the different approaches adopted by the principal transitional instruments, retracing an evolution that ranged from a substantial marginalisation to a strong (although not always unproblematic) focus on this cathartic figure, thanks to the development of mechanisms that define themselves as victim-centred. The third chapter delves into the issue of truth, considered both in its theoretical dimension and in its relevance in post-conflict scenarios. Accordingly, some of the main philosophical approaches to this elusive notion will be retraced, building largely upon the Habermasian elaboration of a discursive conception of truth. After assessing the development and scope of a legal human right to know the truth, the potential benefits, and some of the shortcomings will be described, that are normally attached to truth-recovery and truth-narration processes in post-conflict scenarios, as phases in which truth and history are particularly contested; a critical reflection upon these issues will lead to the conclusion that truth, with its inevitably political and contested character, should mainly be pursued as a dynamic, long-term process, embracing – rather than resisting – its limitations and tensions. The fourth chapter is dedicated to reconciliation, a term which is as dominant in the transitional justice discourse as it is unclear in its significance. The chapter begins with an attempt to define the term, considering how this problem has been tackled in the literature and in the practice and pausing on the term ideological and religious underpinnings, as well as on its relation with the concept of forgiveness. Furthermore, some key factors and mechanisms are explored, which are identified as instrumental in pursuing reconciliation among former enemies, together with obstacles and potential shortcomings related to the establishment of reconciliation as a central theme of post-conflict initiatives. Chapter 5 concludes this ideal first part, considering a practical instrument – amnesties – as the living embodiment of the many dilemmas emerging in post-conflict scenarios; not only those between peace, truth and memory, and reconciliation, but also those between the Western individualistic approach to justice, and non-Western, holistic perspectives. This chapter provides a working definition of the mechanism, while also retracing its evolution and typical legal effects. Further on, the main advantages and disadvantages will be outlined, typically attached to its adoption in the aftermath of conflicts and grave violations of rights, pausing on the issue of the compatibility of amnesties with international law. The phenomenon will then be considered in the practice, by differentiating between different kinds of amnesties and focusing on the archetypical experiences of Argentina and South Africa.

The second part is reserved to the reconstruction and critical assessment of those mechanisms which are most commonly adopted in order to provide accountability post-conflict,[1] analysing how – in the specific context in which they were implemented – these dealt with the issues and dilemmas introduced in the first part. Proceeding chronologically, and in line with the development of the field, criminal tribunals as typical retributive instruments will be first considered, distinguishing among three stages of their evolution in the international realm. Chapter 6 is therefore dedicated to the Post-World War II Nuremberg and Tokyo tribunals, as the first specimens of adjudicatory bodies established supra-nationally and specifically to deal with the faults and legacies of dictatorial regimes. After briefly analysing their creation and foundational charters, attention will be devoted to some dilemmas emerging in many debates around these institutions – such as the spectre of victors' justice and alleged violations of the non-retroactivity principle, and the impact of these experiments on the evolution of international law. In the conclusions, the results of the operations of the courts will be outlined, highlighting lessons as well as missteps. These experiments have been repeated, with several adjustments, in the 1990s, with the creation of the ad-hoc international tribunals for Rwanda and former Yugoslavia, which are the subjects of Chapter 7. After reconstructing the events unravelling in former Yugoslavia and Rwanda, which led to the establishment of these bodies, their statutes will be introduced, together with their strengths and weaknesses, in light of the Nuremberg experience. In this context, particular attention is paid to the lack of outreach capacity – and a general detachment from the population – and to the denounced tension between law and politics. The third phase, considered in Chapter 8, is represented by "hybrid" or "mixed" courts, best exemplified by the Special Court for Sierra Leone. The main peculiarity of these instruments consists in their incorporating, at least ideally, the best characteristics of the local and international legal systems, in such a way overcoming the main limitations of international instruments while involving more substantially the victims and the local population. This chapter thus briefly reconstructs the civil war in the African country and the establishment of the court, also outlining its most significant characteristics, merits, and limitations, which largely reflect those of most hybrid courts. This reflection will also allow to pause on the concept of hybridity, and to consider potential issues related to its uncritical adoption as an objective of transitional justice processes.

Shifting from the retributive to the restorative approach to justice post-conflict, Chapter 9 is dedicated to truth commissions, which differently from tribunals were specifically created to operate in transitional scenarios (although they are increasingly being adopted beyond strictly transitional contexts). The discussion is informed by an analysis of the South African experience (although with an eye also to the Argentinian example), due not only to its prominence, but also to its being appreciated as the most successful and inspiring example of truth commissions, as well as to its peculiar characteristics (such as the unique amnesty process envisaged). A familiar pattern is followed: an analysis of the historical background, with specific attention to the origins of Apartheid, precedes a reconstruction of the institution and the structure of the Truth and Reconciliation Commission (TRC), whose most iconic qualities and shortcomings will be assessed.

Following, Chapters 10 and 11 adopt a more critical approach towards this dominant paradigm of transitional justice which hopefully emerged, retraced and outlined in the previous eight chapters. They follow a common thread and introduce similar arguments – denouncing both tribunals and truth commissions as expressions of a "one-size-fits-all" approach to accountability and justice developed at the international level, and specifically focusing on the perceived imperialistic influence of foreign actors, and on the uncritical preference for purely legal instruments – but they also adopt two different focuses. In particular, Chapter 10 reflects on the perceived colonising tendency of transitional initiatives and considers grassroots initiatives, often praised as the key solution to this problem, thanks to their close relation to the local context and culture: their main potential or actual benefits are outlined, while also accounting for their limitations. Chapter 11, on its part, delves into the theme of development, reflecting on the continuities between pre- and post-conflict violence and inequality. Hereby the issues of the ownership and context-sensitivity of the process are more thoroughly addressed, by focusing on the experiences of indigenous peoples post-conflict. After an introduction to key defining features of indigenous peoples, some typical characteristics of the traditional paradigm of transitional justice will be re-evaluated according to their indigenous understandings. Following, the case of Guatemala will be considered, through an overview of the armed conflict, its root causes and their impact on indigenous communities. The final paragraph is dedicated to investigating whether transitional processes are, or hold the potential to be, an adequate forum in which to address the plight of indigenous peoples and provide a meaningful justice, as basis for lasting peace and more equitable social relations.

Continuing on the path undertaken in the last chapter, in the conclusions a review of the main themes and findings will be offered, together with some final thoughts concerning the past, the present, and the future of transitional justice, as a field operating in a world in which conflicts and abuses become more complex, transnational and challenging to eradicate.

Note

1. The field of "transitional justice" nowadays encompasses much more than the mere accountability, and it is organically concerned with a plethora of issues faced by countries in the aftermath of conflicts and authoritarian regimes, such as constitutional reform, disarmament and demobilisation, and memorialisation, just to cite some. However, aiming this book at reconstructing and critically assessing the dominant paradigm of transitional justice as developed on the ashes of Nuremberg, the focus has been restricted primarily, although not exclusively, on instruments providing accountability.

CHAPTER 2

A Fight for Inclusion: The Transforming Role of Victims in Transitional Justice Processes

Introduction

Victims are nowadays a primary subject of the transitional justice enterprise, in their roles as beneficiaries, participants, advocates, increasingly identified as the only true ratio of post-conflict mechanisms. Engaging victims in the transitional machinery is, beyond all the technicalities, a matter of dignity and respect[1]; however, it is only since the last 30 years that victims have become truly involved in transitional initiatives as more than mere symbolic addressees. This evolution in the approach towards victims, which is the result of hard-won battles for acknowledgement and inclusion, is however not unproblematic; indeed, the identification, in the practice, of the "worthy victim" raises several issues, which call into question traditional legal and socio-political categories; also, some authors believe this shift in attitude to be substantially nothing more than an instrumentalisation of the survivors' suffering for the pursuit of ulterior goals, such as political stability, deterrence, or legitimisation of the new order.[2]

In the following paragraphs the issue of defining and delimitating the category of victims will be addressed, which implies several dilemmas, such as with regards to the discerning criteria, the possibility and necessity to identify different categories of victims or the desirability of considering society as a whole as a victim. Notably, victims can be considered from different perspectives, as every person can be described by reference to

G. Girelli, *Understanding Transitional Justice*,
Philosophy, Public Policy, and Transnational Law,
DOI 10.1007/978-3-319-53606-4_2

several factors, such as age, gender and sexual identity, religious belief, nationality, employment and so on: each element, and all of these combined, have an effect on our identity at the point of defining it; as such, these factors also influence the way conflicts (as well as peace, and justice) are perceived and experienced, and the responses we seek. In this chapter, specific attention will be reserved to the relation between gender and conflict, in particular reflecting upon how the two influence each other; adopting the lens of gender, indeed, allows to perceive how blurred the lines are, between peace and conflict, victims and non-victims. Subsequently, some of the key justifications in favour of the involvement of victims in transitional processes will be outlined, while also considering possible shortcomings. Finally, an introduction is provided to the different approaches adopted by the principal transitional instruments, retracing an evolution that ranged from a substantial marginalisation to a strong (although not always unproblematic) focus on these subjects, thanks to the development of mechanisms that define themselves as victim-centred.

Who Is a Victim? Between Categorisations and Ambiguities

The literature offers different sociological and legal definitions of victims and victimhood,[3] proving how these concepts are less straightforward than it might appear at first glance. With specific regards to transitional scenarios, among the most debated issues are: whether one or more categories of victims can be identified, and which are the criteria to discern among them; whether the whole society should be treated as a victim; who is entitled to express the victims' perspectives and needs. Identifying the victims is not merely a theoretical problem; on the contrary, it has several practical consequences, for example concerning the entitlement to receive reparations or to participate in transitional projects, while also affecting the identification of the subjects criminal prosecutions will (not) focus on.[4] Furthermore, the criteria according to which a society recognises victims are indicative of the sanctioned version of the past.[5]

One possibility is to define victims as the subjects whose rights have been violated.[6] However, while such an approach is particularly welcomed by legal professionals, grave abuses such as those experienced during wars inevitably affect not only the person directly hurt, but also his loved ones, as well as, more indirectly, society as a whole. For this reason, authors such as Ruth Rubio-Marin and Pablo de Greiff suggest to move beyond the concept of *right* as discerning factor, in favour of the notion of *harm*, which "allows initiatives to go beyond the right-holder and incorporate both the social tissue and the relationships disrupted by violations, especially in a family context".[7] In this way a more comprehensive understanding of victimhood is envisaged, which avoids artificial distinctions between subjects who have all been impacted, although in different ways, by the hostilities. However, this shift in approach does not solve the core issue of identifying victims in practice, as in post-conflict societies this harm can be so widespread to be potentially claimed by anyone. Thus, another concept that is sometimes referred to in order to define victims (in negative) is that of *blame*.[8] Indeed, according to the most traditional approach to conflicts, as well as in the general, popular perception, victims are (blameless) "saints, martyrs and heroes"[9] struck by an absolute (blamed) evil. The concept of blame is also a key tenet of the social dimension of retribution, as widespread demand, witnessed in the aftermath of hostilities, for punishment as civilised revenge; this in turn impels the identification of a right and a wrong side, of clearly defined and distinguishable harmed and harming subjects, precisely through the act of establishing blame, by identifying the one that is responsible for the disruption of the social harmony, which will be restored through his punishment and neutralisation.[10] This act of tracing clear lines between victims and wrongdoers through the concept of blame is linked to what Kieran McEvoy and Kirsten McConnachie define as the "urge to blame"[11]: the innate necessity of the human being to identify someone or something (other men, bad luck, a god) responsible for one's own suffering.

However, while for many subjects their identity as victims is obvious and unproblematic, there are also cases in which the line between good and bad can prove to be blurred, making the identity of a survivor and a resister as victim much more complex to assess.[12] For example, in several situations the same subject could be considered as much a victim as a perpetrator, depending on the authority charged with the task of defining him or her, the time-frame taken into account, the ideological justifications behind his actions and the dominant social reaction towards them. This resonates especially with regards to complex scenarios such as prolonged internal conflicts, in which group identities – as well as social tensions – are exacerbated, and individual choices are affected by factors such as ideology and radicalisation, poverty and lack (or denial) of means of subsistence, a partial and often abusive legal system and widespread impunity.[13] Indeed, in these contexts the concepts of right and wrong are strongly contested and relativised, and the issue of establishing blame is, ultimately, the core dilemma around which the whole conflict revolves. In such circumstances a "double victimhood"[14] is often experienced, with each group defining itself as the victim, and consequently perceiving and blaming the other as perpetrator. This conflicting narrative about who is to be acknowledged as a worthy victim is problematic, as each group expects the other to admit its responsibilities for the conflict[15]: this obstacles dialogue and reconciliation, as well as the implementation of inclusive state-building initiatives, thus potentially impinging on the effectiveness of the transitional process as such, which in these scenarios inevitably entails calling into question deep-rooted narratives about personal and social identities.[16]

As a consequence, acknowledging that all sides of a conflict have been responsible for wrongdoings might often prove more useful than the a priori adoption of an unrealistic Saint-versus-Evil (blameless-versus-blamed) discourse, which can provoke a denial of the experiences and struggles of those subjects harmed by the faction generally identified as "good" (which most of the times coincides with the winning side).[17] At the same time, however, a more sensitive approach should not translate into the uncritical equating of very different experiences and struggles, as this would result in excessive homogenisation, and potentially lead to further victimisation.[18]

A related issue is whether victims constitute a unique and cohesive category, or whether lines of demarcation between different sub-groups are traceable (and, in cases, necessary). Indeed, despite the tendency to perceive communities as a monolithic group, these are in fact constituted of subjects with different approaches and ideologies, experiences, material and psychological needs.[19] As a consequence, numerous distinctions have been made between different categories of victims, such as direct and indirect, first- and second-generation victims.[20] However, less attention is reserved (often for practical reasons, and because of a need to follow clearly defined parameters) to the person's self-perception, and to its correspondence with the cultural and social understanding of victimhood; indeed, while some persons consider themselves as victims, and are treated accordingly by the society, there are subjects whose self-perception as victims is rejected by the larger community: this is often the case of persons, or groups, commonly deemed responsible for acts of violence, who however identify themselves as victims because of the highly contested nature of the historical and ideological narratives, or because of a psychological need to justify their actions.[21] Also, some individuals refuse to be labelled as victims (such as some Argentinian children of those who have disappeared, who reject the grandmothers' narrative about their past or refuse to rethink their identity according to it),[22] or prefer to be identified as survivors or resisters,[23] due to a tendency to conceive of victims as passive and weak subjects, to be pitied and rescued, thus ignoring the experiences of struggle and resistance many of them share.

The issue of categorisation and identification of victims is also strictly linked to that of the representation of victims. Indeed, subjects affected by conflicts and atrocities often lack resources, and/or are physically and culturally distant from the epicentres of power. Therefore, their involvement in the transitional experience and in the state-building process is mediated by victims' associations or other organisations, which speak and act on their behalf. Furthermore, also in those cases in which victims play an active role (as witnesses in trials, or by narrating their experiences in front of truth commissions) their participation is usually preceded by a selection of the most "relevant" victims or experiences. The result can be not only an essentialisation of complex events and roles, but also an instrumentalisation of victims' voices, and the development of a "hierarchy" of victims, in which some experiences and subjects are given central relevance, while others remain essentially ignored. For example (as described further on with regards to gender-based violence), most post-conflict mechanisms limit their focus to particular crimes or categories of victims, often influenced by a partial understanding of violence and/or by the need to capture the public attention; this provokes an underestimation of other crimes, and consequently the silencing or denial of the victimhood of other subjects.[24] This kind of dynamic is reported in criminal trials, where "victims' voices are picked out, appropriated and then re-presented to suit the aims of the prosecution".[25] Such appropriation, however, can also be witnessed in the field of research, or by the part of NGOs and media, because of a (sometimes unconscious) tendency to select the voices and experiences to which to give more relevance, for advocacy reasons or to support a certain narration of the events.[26]

Indeed, victimhood and suffering are particularly successful in attracting the almost voyeuristic attention of the public – as stressed by authors such as Mahmood Mamdani, who, with reference to the

Darfur crisis, denounced a "pornography of violence", as fixation on gruesome details, on the faces and scars of the victims, whose result is to obscure the politics behind violence, the larger effects of the conflict, as well as the responsibilities of a plethora of local and international actors.[27] Additionally, victims hold a strong justificatory, legitimising potential within the transitional justice enterprise: because of their painful past and their being the most direct beneficiaries of the intervention, denying or opposing victims' perspectives or priorities proves extremely delicate. In other words, suffering and loss tend to provide victims, and therefore their representatives, with an unconditional entitlement, almost to the limit of un-disputability.[28] An interesting contribution on the phenomenon is provided by Thorsten Bonacker, who connects the growth of the relevance of the victim in the transitional justice discourse with the emergence of a "global victimhood".[29] More precisely, the author pauses on a relatively recent shift in perception, as a result of which victims are now appreciated not merely as passive subjects and recipients of justice, but rather as actors – subjects with the ability to act, to pursue independently determined goals and actively fight for them; however, their peculiarity lies in their being an "injured actor"[30] and for this very reason a charismatic one, who is able to persuade other actors to advocate for them, while their condition "makes it seem illegitimate to refuse to recognize the victim and deny the validity of their testimony".[31]

In conclusion, the definition and identification of the victims in a post-conflict context is an extremely complicated process: it entails several difficult, even problematic choices, and it carries numerous – sometimes unpredictable – consequences, both practical and symbolic; it is thus a political act, which also inevitably implies a moral judgement, concerning the righteousness of one's (often violent or illegal) acts and ideological stand.[32] Post-conflict processes are therefore built on difficult and sometimes precarious balances between competing identities and needs; for a more sensitive understanding, victims should be acknowledged as a unified and differentiated category at the same time. Indeed, by recognising victimhood as a unifying character, the overcoming of past categorisations is promoted (such as those based on race or gender) that fostered the conflict, hence identifying a new basis on which to rebuild society, meaning the sharing – by the part former enemies – of a painful and transformative experience.[33] At the same time, the different constituencies of the category need to be taken into account, as every group has peculiar grievances, priorities and assets. In sum, transitional programmes should be differentiated, context-sensitive, and constituted of mechanisms able and willing to focus on different crimes, violations of rights and subjects.

An Unbreakable Cycle of Violence? Looking at Conflicts and Victims through the Lenses of Gender

As introduced earlier, investigating conflicts, as well as their aftermath, through the lenses of gender allows to critically rethink many seemingly uncontroversial concepts typical of the transitional justice discourse, such as "victims" and "perpetrators", "conflict" and "security", while also perceiving the partialities and, more in general, the intrinsic biases of law, which inevitably affect the design and implementation of post-conflict processes.

Gender can be defined as a "social construct and as a system of power which shapes the lives, opportunities, rights, relationships and access to resources of women, men, boys and girls"[34]; as such, everything is gendered, and everything can be analysed through gender lenses. Importantly, gender norms and dynamics are not something natural, or innate; rather, gender identities are essentially constructed, and as such plural, dynamic, and necessarily contextual, as informed by the religious, cultural and historical background of the community.[35]

Gender dynamics are therefore fundamentally an issue of power, which influences, if not determines, dominant perceptions of men and women, of their "natural" behaviours and characteristics, and of their mutual interactions.[36] As such, they also influence understandings of conflict and violence[37]: every culture (and in a globalised world the international community as such) has a perception, thought of as innate, of how men and women participate in conflict, and how they are affected by it; of who will perpetrate atrocities, and against whom. At the same time, gender norms also influence peace negotiations, as well as the design and implementation of peace processes. Therefore, exploring and reconstructing these dynamics and gender norms is not just an academic exercise; rather, it is fundamental in understanding the conflict and its origins, as well as in designing a transitional process which is effective and responsive to local needs and priorities.

This issue is complex, and the subject of much study and reflection; the following paragraphs will therefore just outline some of the key issues encountered, with a focus on victimhood, and especially with an eye to revealing biases intrinsic to legal and humanitarian initiatives, also introducing the not rarely overlooked issue of the relationship between conflicts and masculinities.

Violations of Women in Conflict: Between Stereotypes and Hard-Fought Conquests

Women suffer numerous gender-specific violations in contexts of conflict, and increasing attention has been reserved, in the literature as well as by the part of the media and the actors on the ground, to sexual abuses, as well as to violations such as forced abortion, slavery and forced marriage.[38] Particularly dominant has become the debate around rape and its instrumentality as a weapon of war: this now ubiquitous term expresses how in conflict rape is often not merely an "accident", or the brutal effect of a culture of violence and impunity, but rather part of calculated strategies of terror and annihilation, a tool for the destruction of the enemy. Women's bodies therefore become fields of combat, while the final target is the enemy's very manhood, its ability to protect "his" woman (and "his" country).[39]

These abuses provoke long-lasting physical and psychological scars, and wound women in their most intimate dimension – a dimension that is rarely spoken about, especially in public. Underreporting is therefore rife, also caused by a patriarchal ideology that marginalises and ostracises the woman who suffered sexual abuses, thus causing a second victimisation.[40] This happens especially, but not only, within those societies that accord a strong relevance to marriage as basis of the community, and consequently to the purity of the woman. For example, Alison Crosby and Brinton Lykes, discussing the situation in Guatemala after the signing of the peace agreements, recall how

> After the rapes [. . .] they were not seen as survivors of genocide, as human beings who had lived the brutality of the state scorched earth policy, but rather as women who, because they were raped, had broken internal community structures, ordering and power.[41]

The international system has reserved increasing attention to rape and violence against women in war especially thanks to the activism of feminist groups, local community leaders and human rights organisations,[42] as well as international and ad hoc tribunals. In particular, while the Nuremberg and Tokyo trials essentially ignored the issue of rape,[43] the innovative approach of bodies such as the International Criminal Tribunal for the Former Yugoslavia (ICTY) and the International Criminal Tribunal for Rwanda (ICTR) shaped international law. More specifically, these and other courts gradually expanded the definition of rape to include acts which were before excluded, thus restricting spaces for impunity[44]; in addition, rape and other forms of sexual violence have been recognised as grave violations of humanitarian law and as elements of crimes under international law, such as genocide and crimes against humanity.[45] This growing attention to the phenomenon marks a fundamental shift in the approach of international law to rape and violence against women, which were traditionally considered as almost inevitable contingencies of conflicts, and it is thus critically important in promoting a debate on these crimes' underlying causes, on the structural factors that enable and perpetuate the oppression and violation of women, and on the characteristics that tailored post-conflict programmes should have, in order to satisfy victims' needs and prevent more violations from occurring.[46] However, the strong focus on this kind of violations has also been a subject of criticisms, on several grounds.

For example, according to some voices this almost voyeuristic focus on sexual violence would reflect a more general limited preoccupation of international criminal law and transitional justice with violations of civil and political rights, and violations of physical integrity committed in the public sphere.[47] This approach would have the effect of essentialising women's experiences in times of wars, in this way diverting attention (and resources) away from a broader set of violations women suffer (as well as from other categories of victims, as discussed further on). Concurrently, this almost obsessive preoccupation with rape as a weapon of war too often causes to overlook how violence against women in times of conflict is neither exceptional nor temporary, but rather constitutes an embittered perpetuation, in a more public and more visible sphere, of ongoing violence women suffer in apparently ordinary times,[48] which are ultimately rooted in a patriarchal ideology which devaluates and sexualises women.[49]

Similarly, focusing on violations of physical integrity often comes at the expenses of the socio-economic dimension of female victimhood. During conflicts women suffer from the lack of basic and fundamental goods and services, for them and for the children they are predominantly in charge of; additionally, they often represent a substantial portion of the refugee and internally displaced population, and as such they find themselves forced to live in precarious conditions.[50] In the aftermath of conflicts, women also face several obstacles in securing resources, because of traditional limitations to their entitlements in favour of the male members of the family (this also informed by unequal gender dynamics); for example, in situations in which their husband or father died or disappeared during the hostilities, women often struggle to gain access to bank accounts or forms of credit, inheritances, land property, which can be crucial for their survival.[51]

The International Discourse: More Attention to Women, or a Perpetuation of Patterns of Objectification and Sexualisation?

Another line of criticism of the dominant approach to women and conflict, especially in the international arena, focuses on a tendency towards an over-simplified narrative which equates men with perpetrators and women with victims, automatically relegated in the same category as children and presented as naturally and inevitably powerless, in need of protection, and lacking agency. As hegemonic masculinities and femininities have been identified, also a hegemonic model of victimhood has developed in the international discourse, which portrays the typical victim as a non-white, poor and uneducated woman, a civilian, maybe with children.[52] This rhetoric with regards to women and victims reinforces patriarchal perceptions of women as inherently vulnerable, while, in fact, what makes women primary targets of violence are exactly those unequal gender relations that foster inequality and discrimination.[53] In other words, women are not per sé weaker, nor more vulnerable; rather, they become predominant objects of violence because of this dominant understanding of women as passive, weak, at the mercy of men as protectors and defenders.[54]

Similarly, by reinforcing superficial understandings of women as passive subjects, this dominant narrative implicitly justifies women's absence in peace processes and denies the many roles women play during conflicts – as combatants, perpetrators, providers, activists and agents of change.[55] Women who do not fit into the category of victims are therefore ignored and sidelined. An example is that of women combatants, which just recently caught the public interest, especially in relation to contexts such as Colombia, where at least 25 per cent of combatants are believed to be women.[56] Addressing women combatants presents some specific challenges for transitional processes. Among others, these subjects often struggle to reintegrate into society: they have openly disregarded traditional gender norms and power relations, as well as social expectations with regards to what it means to be a woman; as a consequence, in the aftermath of conflicts they will often be marginalised by the local community, while also in the difficult process of finding and renegotiating their identity outside a context of hostility.[57]

Finally, merely conceiving of women as victims precludes recognising – and consequently addressing – the role that women themselves play in perpetuating unequal gender dynamics: women often internalise certain expectations concerning the "natural" role of the man as provider and protector, and in situations of conflicts they may sustain a hegemonic hyper-masculinity, for example by pushing men to commit violence[58] or exalting macho attitudes.[59] This is not in any way to suggest that women bear any responsibility for the abuses they suffer. On the contrary, revealing these dynamics shows how entrenched and internalised oppressive gender norms are, and helps configuring programmes and processes able to tackle the very root causes of violence in conflicts as well as post-conflict scenarios, aware that in order to move towards a more equal and respectful society it is necessary to act not only on women's experiences, but also on men's perceptions of women, and on women's perceptions of men.

Boys Don't Cry: The Complex Relationship between Masculinities and Conflict

If a well-rounded concern for women's issues during and in the aftermath of conflicts is still developing, men appear to be often ignored in the discourse around transitions and gender, with only a few exceptions,[60] to the point that "gender" is too often equated with "women".[61] This is, quite paradoxically, the effect of a dominant patriarchal ideology which is almost incapable of accommodating an understanding of man as victim, and which has imposed the "man" as the paradigmatic subject of any legal as well as socio-political discourse; in this way, the conversation has been focusing on specific groups (such as women, children, indigenous peoples), ignoring men as other than perpetrators.[62] Similarly, there is an assumption that in the aftermath of conflicts, to which men typically participate as combatants, men maintain their traditional positions of power – as the dominant gender – and thus there is no need for a specific focus on their experiences and needs.[63] However, by engaging or otherwise enduring conflict men suffer multiple negative consequences, often worsened because of pressures to conform to dominant ideas concerning manhood; thus, this lack of attention to the experiences of men from a gender perspective is extremely problematic, and not only for them. Indeed, failing to provide redress to men and to intervene on dominant gender dynamics can foster a never-ending cycle of violence against women, and potentially impair the success of transitional processes, whose very design could have the perverse effect of exacerbating frustrations and abuses.

***

Masculinity can be defined as a "set of traits or patterns of behaviour that in a given society are considered typical of men".[64] These patterns are not inherent or natural, although often deep-rooted in one's identity, but rather constructed, as informed by several factors related to the person (such as race, class, religion),[65] by his experiences, and by social expectations. Indeed, gender norms are contextual, in constant flux, and developing within patriarchy, a system of power which sees men as inherently superior to women, and which in turn pressures men to meet certain expectations of manhood.[66] Finally, masculinity is understood as something that is "done", and as such as something that must be achieved[67]: men are not automatically perceived as meeting the said expectations, rather, they need to prove their manhood to society (meaning, other men and women). External manifestations thus play a constitutive role, and as such masculinity incorporates a relational element: not only is it affected and informed by others' perceptions, but also it is formed and maintained in a dynamic relationship with other masculinities.[68] In her ground-breaking study, Raewyn Connell describes masculinities as inevitably plural, and distinguishes between different kinds of masculinities, also examining how they relate to and inform each other. In particular, the Australian sociologist identifies a "hegemonic masculinity", as the system of practices related to male identity that prevails in a certain society as ideal, which few men actually incarnate, but to which many aspire.[69] As aforementioned, the characteristics of this dominant masculinity are shaped by the local context and culture; however, in today's global village similar features can be identified that most men are called to meet, such as: economic independence and self-reliance, confidence, successful career, ability to provide for the family[70]; in sum, the hegemonic man is a man of power.[71]

Masculinities are therefore informed and shaped by continuous external and internal pressures and expectations, conscious and unconscious dynamics within families and societies – and as such gender roles play a pivotal role in determining individual choices: men (as well as females) undergo a constant testing of their meeting gender expectations.[72] Such perceptions and expectations therefore can also provide an at least partial explanation of why men engage in conflict and violence. In particular, when more traditional means for affirming one's manhood are precluded (because of the lack of educational or economic opportunities),[73] and/or where men have been exposed to violence since early ages, conflict becomes a "pathway to socially recognized manhood"[74]; additionally, gender relations play a role in processes of indoctrination and militarisation of men and boys, which often involve practices and rituals aimed at brutalising the person, through the internalisation of a militarised "hypermasculinity"[75] built around physical strength and toughness, easy resort to weapons and violence, repression of emotions, objectification of women.[76]

The relationship between manhood and violence is extremely complex and not entirely clear, and while it is now widely recognised that men are not intrinsically, biologically violent,[77] it also appears that violence (not rarely violence against women) often constitutes an aspect, sometimes a dominant one, of certain masculinities.[78] Once internalised as a learned response and a way to navigate power dynamics, violence therefore becomes the means to which a person resorts to prove his masculinity, absent alternatives. Similarly, violence often comes to represent a key tenet of hegemonic masculinities in conflicted societies, in which male identities are formed, since childhood, in opposition to that of members of other ethnic, political or religious groups.[79] Additionally, the widespread understanding of men as the paradigmatic perpetrators of violence, both in war[80] and in ordinary contexts often works as a sort of self-fulfilling prophecy:[81] the more men are seen and represented as violent, the more a certain masculinity will develop, of which violence forms a dominant part.

This described dominant perception of men as combatants and perpetrators has provoked a disregard for male experiences of victimhood, especially in the design of post-conflict interventions, together with the (understandable) concern that focusing on men might once again shift attention away from women's issues. However, because of the revealed relations between male experiences of victimhood and emasculation, and abuses towards women, a more substantial and informed focus on men would prove beneficial not only to men, but also to women, as well as to society as a whole.

Men suffer from a plethora of abuses and violations during conflicts, which can also be examined through the lenses of gender. Notably, they are the main victims of homicide, and the main subjects to be killed in combat[82]; when surviving, they carry the physical and psychological scars of war. Additionally, both combatants and civilian men and boys can be victims of sexual violence in contexts of war: the documentary film *Gender against Men* investigates the dreadful abuses committed against men during the conflicts of the Great Lakes Region, their longstanding effects, as well as the deaf ears men too often encounter in the aftermath of hostilities, when seeking help. These violations are also rooted in dominant gender and power dynamics, as they often encompass an element of feminisation of the victim, with the final purpose of humiliating and stigmatising the subject by denying his manhood.[83] For this same reason, sexual violence against men is still a taboo in most cultures (non-Western and Western alike), and in some societies it is equated with homosexuality, which is in turn prohibited and/or drastically stigmatised.[84] As a consequence, the phenomenon is grossly underreported, and mostly ignored in the design of social programmes and post-conflict initiatives: criminal trials do not address the issue, while medical help and psychological support are often lacking, also for a paucity of trained personnel able to look beyond the assumption that gender-based violence and sexual violence are a "woman's thing".[85]

Kidnappings, abductions and forced recruitment and enlistment also represent a form of gender-based violence, as they target men and boys because of their gender, and feed off assumptions concerning men and their assumed natural inclination to violence[86]; once apprehended, these same subjects often also undergo a process of militarisation which – as seen before – involves not only training and exposure to violence, but also, not uncommonly, drug use, violent rites and sometimes sexual abuses[87] – perversely with the scope of breaking natural familial and social bonds and brutalise the subject. In addition to the physical scars, these abuses provoke particularly harsh and lasting psychological traumas, these also linked to an extreme approach to masculinity, which marginalises victims as passive and feminised subjects.[88]

More in general, conflicts provoke radical changes in gender patterns, in a way that affect male experiences in their aftermath. Among the many consequences, in the post-conflict phase it often becomes even harder for men to prove their masculinity: not rarely, men are captured between public and domestic expectations on one side, and a social context that precludes them from even aspiring to meet these same expectations on the other side.[89] More specifically, men who served in the military or were part of armed groups typically adhered to that aforementioned militarised hyper-masculinity posited on the use of violence, objectification of women, repression of emotions,[90] and being a combatant often became the very core of their identity.[91] At the end of the conflict this tenet of identity gets lost, and replacing it with other indicators proves challenging. For example, men struggle to provide for their family (or to build one in the first place), because of the widespread unemployment typical of the fragile and dysfunctional post-conflict economy,[92] the destruction of traditional means of livelihood,[93] and maybe injuries suffered in conflict which have affected their ability to work[94] (the same frustration is often experienced by men who are refugees or internally displaced, who used to lead active and productive lives and suddenly find themselves in a precarious and passive situation); in addition, ex-combatants might struggle to find their place in the household as fathers and husbands, because of an inability to express emotions and relate with the family, and in some cases because of unaddressed psychological traumas;[95] in addition, these subjects might feel unable to fulfil their role as protectors, because of shifts in power and gender dynamics, in at least two ways. Firstly, conflicts, although tragic, also often provide women with spaces for empowerment and emancipation, opening them access to resources, roles and responsibilities traditionally reserved to men, both in private – as heads of the household – and in the public sphere, as activists, professionals and civil society leaders.[96] At the same time, the presence of the international community, which in its role of provider and protector "takes the place of the husbands",[97] can provoke further tensions: with the intervention of the international community a new male – an outsider, typically Western and white – enters the scene and alters traditional power relations, imposing himself as hegemonic and dominant, as in charge of protecting women and children and guiding the country towards peace.[98] In a context in which gender relations are perceived as antagonistic and hierarchic, and the man is pressured to dominate on the woman, unless a new, more positive model of masculinity is embraced[99] these new power dynamics can result unacceptable, and provoke extreme attempts to reaffirm one's manhood, through violence and abuse, often against women.[100]

Missing Links: When War Enters the Household

In particular, several authors reveal an increase in domestic violence in post-conflict societies, which in many cases has been at least partially explained with reference to this frustrated masculinity.[101] The end of the conflict therefore often does not coincide with an improvement in women's lives, this again problematising traditional compartmentalisations of conflict and post-conflict periods. In particular, in the experiences of women conflict often cannot be described as an exceptional and temporary drift away from an ordinary peaceful situation, with a clear-cut beginning and end; rather, it qualifies as a phase, often particularly brutal, in a continuum of violence: wars do not really "explode", rather, they are rooted in structural power dynamics which foster women oppression both in the private and in the public sphere; in the same way, the signing of ceasefire or peace agreements often does not coincide with the end of violence and struggles; indeed, in the aftermath of hostilities gender norms impose on women a series of expectations of care – towards traumatised children, husbands, members of the family and the community – in a tragically fragile context[102]; also, as outlined previously, frustrated and emasculated men see women's bodies as the locus where to reaffirm a lost masculinity. As a consequence, rather than ceasing, violence shifts from the public to the private sphere.

Highlighting this dynamic in post-conflict contexts is crucial, as it compels a necessary reflection on the objectives and definitional parameters of transitional justice: for example, can we be satisfied with a notion of justice and security evaluated according to a decrease in public violence, when in reality this same violence has in fact not ceased, but has rather mutated its shape and target?[103] Are victims worthy of attention on the part of post-conflict processes only when abused in the public sphere? Also, by revealing these links it becomes apparent how gender is not a "zero-sum game"[104]: in the same way as empowering women can be beneficial for society as a whole, so expanding the focus to masculinities does not mean denying hard-won battles for women's rights; on the contrary, understanding and addressing men's issues, by working on mutual perceptions and expectations, as well as through reforming existing structures and institutions (among which oppressive laws and customs)[105] will be of benefit for all.

A Hard-Won Place at the Table: How Victims' Participation and Grievances Shape Post-Conflict Initiatives

Victims not only should be part of the transitional enterprise, rather, they should be their primary and final constituent, and not only as addressees or ideal inspiration, but also as agents and shapers, and for several reasons. Most importantly, victims are the subjects who directly experienced the horrors of conflicts and atrocities, and who bear the physical and psychological scars; at the same time, they will live the everyday life of the country after the transition has concluded (if this can ever be said for a transition), as they form a relevant portion, when not the majority, of the population.[106] In other words, these individuals, because of their experiences and struggles, are more competent to shape and intervene in transitional initiatives. These justifications might sound simplistic or banal, but they are not, as demonstrated by the striking absence of victims characterising the first transitional experiments, if not in the role of witnesses, or as distant, symbolic beneficiaries of a justice informed and provided by others.

Placing victims at the core of the transitional enterprise is also instrumental in providing acknowledgement. Indeed, in this way victims are recognised by the society and the state in their truths, experiences, sufferings, and their acknowledgement also implies that of the past wrongs, hence ending periods of denial and suspect.[107] Inclusion and acknowledgement in turn foster empowerment: victims come to be recognised as active subjects, resisters and survivors, who can contribute meaningfully to the future of their country, thus transforming their suffering from a burden into an asset. In the words of Humphrey and Valverde,

> Victims use human rights as a discourse to constitute themselves as political subjects, to claim a moral relationship to power as victims of abuse and to demand recognition on the basis of their humanity and compassion, [..] to reclaim personhood and gain moral visibility.[108]

Consequently, the inclusion of victims in the transitional dialogue is pivotal in avoiding further marginalisation this condition often provokes. As aforementioned, victims are often silenced, lacking resources, discriminated by the enemy and sometimes by their own community. This can lead to a growing exclusion from social life: engagement in post-conflict initiatives can break this cycle of marginalisation (and in conflicted societies prevent potential radicalisation), empowerment builds antibodies against new oppressive attempts, and in this way a second victimisation is resisted. Furthermore, the engagement of victims potentially provides the post-conflict machinery and the new political landscape with greater legitimacy[109]; indeed, being shaped through victims' participation, and incorporating victims' perspectives, makes these instruments and politics more likely to be endorsed by all those who lived the same traumatic experiences.

As analysed more thoroughly in the following chapters,[110] the role of victims in post-conflict experiences has radically evolved over time. In particular, in the first phase (following World War II) victims were addressed as a symbol, the ideal beneficiaries of the justice provided, but absent in the flesh, if not as witnesses, as tools of defence and prosecution, insomuch as "paradoxically, the Nuremberg Trial echoed and replicated the anonymity of the victims of mass murder and genocide in the very procedure these were to be adjudicated".[111] The victims' presence was missing not only at the centre of the courtroom but also around it, as spectators; for this reason, some authors conclude that the trial was aimed not much at vindicating victims, but rather at the German *volk*, as a way of identifying and labelling few guilty for the horrors of the Holocaust and consequently provide the general population with a much-needed absolution.[112]

Over the years victims have gained more and more space, also thanks to the growing phenomenon of victims' associations and NGOs, and to a deeper sensitivity of international agents. This tendency intensified especially since the 1980s with the creation of more comprehensive instruments,[113] such as truth commissions, which define themselves as victim-centred – as opposed to the Nuremberg experience – in their focusing on the voices of those who suffered the most as a basis for (re-)constructing a peaceful state. This evolution also influenced the design of international and ad hoc tribunals, such as the ICTY and the International Criminal Court (ICC), whose structures encompass mechanisms aimed at enhancing victims' engagement and addressing their needs more satisfactorily.[114] However, as emerging in the next chapters, these experiences keep proving extremely limited for what concerns both their inclusivity and their outreach capacity,[115] insofar that they often appear more focused on the rehabilitation and legitimisation of national and supranational political institutions.[116] Despite these drawbacks, the relevance of victims in transitional contexts has constantly grown, insomuch that now their perspectives and needs constitute one of the key normative basis and ideological justifications for dealing with the past.[117] In other words, victims' satisfaction and redress are now the ideal objectives pursued by every transitional instrument, at least on paper. This follows from an implicit acknowledgement that justice serves someone, that it finds purpose and meaning in its being of benefit to a recipient, and that the most "legitimate" beneficiaries are indeed the victims.

However, a diametrical opposition in approach can be perceived between retributive and restorative mechanisms. In particular, the former focus on justice as punishment and just desert, and as such inevitably on the perpetrator, while victims only play an instrumental role, narrating their experiences in a cold environment, with several substantial and procedural limitations: criminal processes compel victims to translate their narrative into legal stories, where no space is left for perceptions and emotions, and where others decide what is admissible, desirable or irrelevant.[118] On the contrary, in the latter attention is shifted, at least ideally, to the victim as the fulcrum of the forum, whose private experience in its entirety (facts, feelings, needs) is converted into public knowledge[119]: in this way the victim is transformed from object to subject. However, also truth commissions are not free from criticism. For example, Humphrey and Valverde claim that these mechanisms, despite being created to enhance victims' participation, in fact have turned them into "objects for political management and therapeutic attention",[120] rather than subjects and bearers of rights. In particular, the involvement of victims has (in various degrees) been exploited as a way to legitimate and therefore facilitate the transition to the new political and economic order.

Another risk is the imposition by restorative instruments of a general narrative of the events, in which the voice of the individual gets lost – at least in the parts that do not fit into the selected dominant narrative.[121] As a result, victims might feel compelled to adhere to this official version and to an archetypal idea of victimhood, while the complex, multifaceted character of their experiences remains overlooked.[122] At the same time, the voices of those who do not fully accept, or fully conform, to the sponsored version, both of the events and of the post-conflict objectives, risk to be silenced and marginalised from the transitional project.[123] A typical example is that of the Argentinian Madres, who were harshly criticised when asking for justice in the form of prosecutions during the operations of the CONADEP – the Commission instituted in the South American country to investigate the horrors of the dictatorship – and accused to impinge the reconciliation and pacification process for egoistic purposes.[124]

While undeniably true that truth commissions' operations provoke, to a certain extent, an objectification of victims, this drawback also appears to be less pronounced in restorative projects than in trials, and related mostly to the fact that truth commissions are ultimately political instruments charged with the difficult task of laying the foundations for a peaceful and stable future. This criticism, however, is precious, as it highlights how a substantial involvement of victims is only realised through the design of a comprehensive, differentiated project, which involves victims in the definition of objectives, priorities and approaches.[125] Indeed, truth commissions alone – for how inclusive they can be – actively engage in their activities a very limited number of victims,[126] while the majority only play a passive role, as spectators or recipients of the reports, and many just remain totally unaffected by the commissions' work, because of their physical and cultural distance from these essentially top-down mechanisms.[127] Furthermore, trials and truth commissions are not sufficient in addressing the multiple needs of the victims, and a comprehensive project needs to envisage other initiatives, such as reparations. Indeed, these instruments can constitute a concrete acknowledgement of the victims' suffering, and demonstrate the shift in the state approach from oppression to attentiveness, hence showing that the law, which had been a weapon for discrimination and coercion, can and will, from that moment on, be an instrument of acknowledgement and empowerment.[128] Furthermore, through economic and material redress victims are provided with a basis on which to rebuild their lives, while failing to address their most urgent needs can negatively affect the efficacy of all the other transitional initiatives.[129] For the same reason, reparations should ideally be coupled with redistributive policies and development efforts, as systemic changes which go beyond the mere satisfaction of the individual and aim at reversing those socio-economical inequalities that constitute the deeper causes of many conflicts, and whose permanence would obstacle the successful transition to a peaceful democracy.[130]

Finally, a valuable effort that should be undertaken in the interest of the victims is the one for memorialisation. Memorials are perfect symbols of transitions, as they work as a bridge between past, present and future, capitalising upon the harsh experiences of past generations as a reminder, for the sake of today's visitors and spectators.[131] The most various instruments are adopted: from monuments to museums – maybe by transforming former sites of horrors, from national anniversaries and public ceremonies to community projects. These initiatives can be extremely important for the victims, because they stand as a public symbol of acknowledgement of their struggles and losses, which are thus dignified; also, by attracting visitors they often support the development of the local economy.[132] On the other side, the risks related to memorialisation are basically of two kinds. Firstly, these projects are inherently political, as they are adopted in order to commemorate political events, and usually as a result of political controversies[133]; this political character can lead to tensions and strives, which can in turn undermine the original purpose of the initiatives and obstacle the achievement of peace and reconciliation.[134] Secondly, inherent to memorialisation projects is the risk to simplify and thus limit the narrative regarding past events, in this way denying or overlooking the experience of victimhood of certain subjects. For example, Christiane Wilke, who studied several Berlin memorials celebrating the victims of the Holocaust, reveals how some categories of victims (like Jewish ones) appear to be more recurrent than others (like homosexuals, especially lesbians, or gipsies), and how the fact that every memorial focuses on a particular category of victims in fact prevents visitors from grasping with the complexity of individual experiences – for example of resisters and fighters, or of those subjects who identify within multiple victims' groups.[135] The purpose of this consideration is neither to deny the enormity and uniqueness of the Shoah, nor to devaluate the reality that Jewish people were the group most targeted by the Nazi rage, and for particularly gratuitous and heinous reasons. Rather, the aim is to illustrate how the narrative sanctioned by the state through initiatives such as memorials can foster (often unwittingly) an underestimation of the sufferings of certain individuals or groups. Similarly, memorials tend to perpetuate the myth of the "pure victims",[136] thus fostering in the popular imaginary the idea that the victim is a pure hero and martyr. While most of the times this corresponds to reality, some of the aforementioned issues with regards to victims' identities could emerge.

Perpetuating Silences: The Absence of Women in Post-Conflict Processes

With specific regards to gender, the aforementioned dominant perception of women as victims also affects their participation in the design and implementation of peace agreements and transitional mechanisms. Notably, law is a

> Masculinist practice, elevating rationality and objectivity over context and nuance, preferring process to substance, master-narrative to nuance, and being generally ill-suited to the kind of empathic listening that would transform the speaking self into a healing self.[137]

This gendered nature of law also affects transitional justice, as a primary legalistic exercise, and can be witnessed in delicate phases such as peace negotiations. Indeed, these processes are strongly dominated by military and political figures and by a technical and apparently neutral rhetoric, with traditionally limited involvement of civil society[138] and even more limited participation of women, in any form; additionally, even when admitted to the process, women's participation appears to be almost tokenistic, and/or mostly relegated to the discussion of issues commonly regarded as "soft",[139] while arguments such as security or disarmament are discussed at the "adults table", which is a table made of men. In addition, the international community (in terms of state officials and international organisations, both governmental and non-governmental) is itself a reflection of the dominant patriarchal ideology, constituted of (often white) males at the top, and carrying with it a certain hegemonic masculinity that is consequently effused in transitional programmes.[140]

In this way, gender dynamics are perpetuated,[141] and women's perspectives are ignored at a fundamental turning point. Indeed, in the past decades the content and reach of peace agreements have gradually expanded, and nowadays these instruments often not only address the cessation of hostilities, but also lay the basis for the transitional process, as well as for the post-conflict social and political order. As such, they constitute a sort of gatekeeper, a unique opportunity to cement positive changes emerging from the conflict and address abusive pre-conflict patterns; however, when women are excluded from the negotiations this potential to create a transitional process which can be effective in reconfiguring the society and remove structural inequalities and marginalisation is gravely impinged.

Therefore, substantial women's participation (together with the involvement of local communities as well as traditionally marginalised subjects, such as indigenous peoples) is fundamental in order to incorporate a more comprehensive and dynamic understanding of the conflict, and therefore for the determination of the instruments necessary in order to effectively address these issues, with an eye not only to retribution but also to prevent ulterior conflicts. For example, in the aftermath of conflicts women tend to prioritise socio-economic issues (in opposition to a limited understanding of justice as punishment for violations of physical integrity) such as housing, health care, access to land, and employment, in their interest and that of their families[142]; also, as women are more likely to perceive violence in a continuum, they often promote the expansion of the focus of post-conflict mechanisms to the domestic sphere. Additionally, women might advocate against an understanding of transitions as restoration. Indeed, if restoring means going back to the pre-war situation, then it might provoke recementing unequal and violent power relations that women might have overcome during the conflict.[143] As a consequence, women often promote a more farsighted understanding of transitions: not only backward-looking, as processes providing accountability, but also forward-looking, as opportunities to reshape power dynamics, by addressing long-standing unequal patterns and formalising positive changes women might have experienced during the conflict – as described in previous paragraphs – in terms of empowerment and greater responsibilities within and outside the household.[144]

More in general, women often have a more comprehensive, multi-dimensional understanding of security.[145] In most post-conflict scenarios, indeed, security is framed in a gendered way as militarised security in the public sphere[146]; as such, this goal is pursued mainly through Disarmament, Demobilisation and Reintegration (DDR) programmes focused on the first third of the triplet (disarmament and patrolling)[147] and shaped upon Western models, uncritically adopted as successful examples; in this way, local needs and peculiarities, as well as the biases inherent to these mechanisms, are rarely taken into consideration.[148] On the contrary, as seen, women perceive security as incorporating socio-economic aspects (such as access to land ownerships, inheritance and loans)[149] and extending to the private sphere; as a consequence, in the eyes of women the focus should be not merely on disarmament, but rather also on reintegration of combatants, in society as well as in the family; indeed, weapons are just enablers, facilitators, while the core problem resides in underlying power relations and in the emasculation men often experience in the aftermath of hostilities. Notably, in some cases the process of disarmament could actually worsen, rather than improve, the situation – when men believe that having a weapon in a fragile and conflicted society in which the state is unable to provide protection constitutes a fundamental, potentially the only, way to protect their families.[150]

Finally, women's participation in peace processes is not only instrumental to the design of a satisfactory transitional machinery, but can also form part of the reparation process[151]; in other words, recognising substantial spaces of participation to women is symbolically extremely significant, as well as highly therapeutic, for the participants as well as for the public.

Conclusions

In the previous paragraphs the evolution of the victims' role in the transitional justice tradition has been retraced, ranging from a substantial exclusion to a prioritisation and praise of victim-centredness.[152] As a result, transitional justice projects are nowadays inevitably about victims, which through these mechanisms are "constituted by what they have lacked, i.e the protection of law".[153] Victims have thus become the fundamental ratio of these programmes, in their being more tangible than other ideal justifications, while their past sufferings invest the whole process with an aura of almost non-criticability. This development is cause, while at the same time consequence, of a sort of revolution in the popular and political perspective, which has experienced a shift "from the cult of the hero to the cult of the victim, [as] suffering instead of heroism now attracts public and political consideration".[154]

However, some issues have been raised concerning the forms and purposes of victims' engagement in the transitional enterprise. For example, the victim category is an intricate one, as in post-atrocities contexts the line between innocence and guilt may prove blurred, and partly subjective: individuals and groups survived complex and unique experiences of oppression and resistance that are hardly classifiable. Also, a cultural dimension can be identified, regarding both the groups targeted by the acts of violence and potential phenomena of "hierarchies of victimhood"[155] that should be avoided in order to prevent further silencing of particular categories of victims.[156] Also to be avoided is the appropriation of victims' voices, as exploitation of the cathartic potential of suffering in order to justify mechanisms that are substantially externally imposed. For all these reasons, this focus on victims, which is surely to welcome, should be not merely apparent or superficial, but rather grounded on a real willingness to "put victims of injustice in charge and make room for diverse truths and diverse forms of truth telling",[157] without fear of tensions and contrasts.

Additionally, dissecting the issue of victims from a gender perspective shows how necessary it is to move beyond traditional limitations and compartmentalisations typical of the transitional justice discourse, and thus develop a more inclusive and comprehensive understanding of conflict and peace. For example, in order to build a more effective transitional project, war should be approached not as a limited, clearly situated and exceptional phase in the history of the country, but rather as part of a continuum – deterministically linked to long-standing unequal power dynamics (between classes, genders, ethnics) and whose effects outlast formal peace agreements.[158] As a consequence, a transitional machinery should be preoccupied not only with the most immediate and visible by-products of the conflict, but also with its underlying causes, as well as with the trails of violence and oppression endured far away from the public eyes, and especially within the household.[159]

Another dichotomy that is worth problematising is the "victim-versus-perpetrator" one. These categories are essential in providing a clear-cut version of the events as well as in legal arenas, where there is just no space for in-depth, multidisciplinary analyses of individual experiences; however, when stepping out of the sterile context of a criminal court, it becomes easier to see the lights and the shadows, the undertones, the uniqueness of people's existences, and this inevitably fosters more well-rounded, sensitive evaluations. For example, how is to be labelled, and consequently addressed, an ex-combatant with a family that, in the impossibility of finding a job and unable to redefine its identity in the absence of hostilities, joins a gang, and maybe resorts to violence? In these complex situations law provides the answer, but not the solution; for this reason, it is fundamental for transitional processes to include other perspectives and disciplines (such as anthropology and psychology), to identify – and to act on – existing structures and institutions (such as laws and customs) which reinforce unequal power dynamics, as well as to reflect on the dynamics inherent to the transitional process, for example those between the international community and the local population. These reflections are crucial in order to appreciate transitional justice more ambitiously as an opportunity, and as instrumental for conflict prevention, as it would be just unreasonable to pursue accountability and punishment while at the same time ignoring, or exacerbating, those same patterns which made conflicts possible in the first place.

Notes

1. Matt James, "A Carnival of Truth? Knowledge, Ignorance and the Canadian Truth and Reconciliation Commission", *The International Journal of Transitional Justice* 6 (2012): 128
2. Kieran McEvoy and Kirsten McConnachie, "Victimology in Transitional Justice: Victimhood, Innocence and Hierarchy", *European Journal of Criminology* 9 (2012): 528
3. Examples are provided by David Bloomfeld, Teresa Barnes and Luc Huyse, eds., "Reconciliation After Violent Conflict: A Handbook" (Stockholm: International Institute for Democracy and Electoral Assistance, 2003): 57
4. Jemima Garcia-Godos, "Victim Reparations in the Peruvian Truth Commission and the Challenge of Historical Interpretation", *The International Journal of Transitional Justice* 2 (2008): 63
5. See ibid., 63–82
6. Ruth Rubio-Marin and Pablo de Greiff, "Women and Reparations", *The International Journal of Transitional Justice* 1 (2007): 328
7. Ibid., 329
8. Kieran McEvoy and Kirsten McConnachie, "Victims and Transitional Justice: Voice, Agency and Blame", *Social & Legal Studies* 22 (2013): 493
9. Christiane Wilke, "Remembering Complexity? Memorials for Nazi Victims in Berlin", *The International Journal of Transitional Justice* 7 (2013): 144
10. Amy Propen and Mary Lay Schuster, "Degrees of Emotion: Judicial Responses to Victim Impact Statements", *Law, Culture and the Humanities* 6 (2010): 82
11. McEvoy and McConnachie, "Victims and Transitional Justice", 501
12. Susanne Karstedt, "From Absence to Presence, From Silence to Voice: Victims in International and Transitional Justice since the Nuremberg Trials", *International Review of Victimology* 17 (2010): 24
13. See McEvoy and McConnachie, "Victims and Transitional Justice", 489–513
14. Nevan T. Aiken, "Learning to Live Together: Transitional Justice and Intergroup Reconciliation in Northern Ireland", *The International Journal of Transitional Justice* 4 (2010): 181
15. Ibid.

16. Ibid.
17. James L. Gibson, "Overcoming Apartheid: Can Truth Reconcile a Divided Nation?", *Politikon* 31 (2004): 149. One example is that of Rwanda, where being the victims of genocide predominantly Tutsis, Hutus individuals struggled to be acknowledged in their experience of victimhood: among others, see Michael Humphrey, "From Victim to Victimhood: Truth Commissions and Trials as Rituals of Political Transition and Individual Healing", *The Australian Journal of Anthropology* 14(2) (2003): 183
18. Rebecca Saunders, "Questionable Associations: The Role of Forgiveness in Transitional Justice", *The International Journal of Transitional Justice* 5 (2011): 136. For example, the South African TRC, in order to foster inclusion and limit collective blaming of the Afrikaaners, decided to hear victims from all ethnical groups. However, the resulting proportion of white and black witnesses was criticised for offering a distort representation of the dimension of white and black victimhood.
19. McEvoy and Kirsten McConnachie, "Victimology in Transitional Justice", 531
20. Bloomfeld et al., "Reconciliation After Violent Conflict", 54
21. For example, some soldiers suffering from Post-Traumatic Stress Disorder identify and understand themselves as victims, consequently being unable to acknowledge their responsibilities for the atrocities committed. See Thorsten Bonacker, "Global Victimhood: On the Charisma of the Victim in Transitional Justice Processes", *World Political Science Review* 9(1) (2013): 122
22. Ari Edward Gandsman, "Retributive Justice, Public Intimacies and the Micropolitics of the Restitution of Kidnapped Children of the Disappeared in Argentina", *The International Journal of Transitional Justice* 6 (2012): 423–443
23. Bloomfeld et al., "Reconciliation After Violent Conflict", 60
24. Lia Kent, "Local Memory Practices in East Timor: Disrupting Transitional Justice Narratives", *The International Journal of Transitional Justice* 5 (2011): 451
25. McEvoy and McConnachie, "Victims and Transitional Justice", 495
26. Ibid., 499
27. Mahmood Mamdani, "Saviors and Survivors: Darfur, Politics and the War on Terror" (London: Verso, 2009), 66
28. See McEvoy and McConnachie, "Victims and Transitional Justice", 503. Talking about Jewish victims of the Holocaust, the authors quote Hannah Arendt, who poses the question whether "Jewish people's unprecedented historical suffering somehow transform them from victims to Victims, guaranteeing them, and by extension the State of Israel, an unconditional status of moral untouchability."

29. Bonacker, "Global Victimhood", 97–129
30. Ibid., 110
31. Ibid.
32. Mark Findlay, "Activating a Victim Constituency in International Criminal Justice", *The International Journal of Transitional Justice* 3 (2009): 194
33. Gibson, "Overcoming Apartheid", 147
34. Saferworld, "Masculinities, Conflict and Peacebuilding. Perspectives on Men Through a Gender Lens" (London: Saferworld, 2014), 5
35. As a way of example, Theo Hollander reconstructs the effects colonialism had on the formation of gender identities and perceptions in the Democratic Republic of the Congo (DRC). Theo Hollander, "Neglected Voices. Untold Stories of Gender, Conflict and Transitional Justice in the Great Lakes Region" (PhD diss., Utrecht University, 2014), 106
36. Saferworld, "Masculinities, Conflict and Peacebuilding", 4
37. Ibid., 10
38. Naomi R. Cahn and Fionnuala Ni Aolain, "Gender, Masculinities and Transition in Conflicted Societies", *New England Law Review* 1 (2010): 102
39. Shana Tabak, "False Dichotomies of Transitional Justice: Gender, Conflict and Combatants in Colombia", *International Law and Politics* 44 (2011): 119
40. Bloomfeld et al., "Reconciliation After Violent Conflict", 55
41. Alison Crosby and Brinton M. Lykes, "Mayan Women Survivors Speak: The Gendered Relations of Truth Telling in Postwar Guatemala", *The International Journal of Transitional Justice* 5 (2011), 472
42. For a reconstruction see Tabak, "False Dichotomies of Transitional Justice", 119–125
43. Christine Bell and Catherine O'Rourke, "Does Feminism Need a Theory of Transitional Justice? An Introductory Essay", *The International Journal of Transitional Justice* 1 (2007): 24
44. An in-depth analysis is offered by Rashida Manjoo and Calleigh McRaith, "Gender-Based Violence in Conflict and Post-Conflict Areas", *Cornell International Law Journal* 44 (2011): 11–31
45. Bell and O'Rourke, "Does Feminism Need a Theory of Transitional Justice?", 27
46. Hollander, "Neglected Voices", 41
47. Tabak, "False Dichotomies of Transitional Justice", 110
48. Fionnuala Ní Aolain, Catherine O'Rourke and Aisling Swaine, "Transforming Reparations for Conflict-Related Sexual Violence: Principles and Practice", *Harvard Human Rights Journal* 28 (2015): 107
49. Hollander, "Neglected Voices", 41
50. Tabak, "False Dichotomies of Transitional Justice", 122

51. Christine Chinkin, "Peace Agreements as a Means for Promoting Gender Equality and Ensuring Participation of Women" (United Nations Division for the Advancement of Women, 2003): 24
52. Among others see Makau Mutua, "Savages, Victims and Saviors: The Metaphor of Human Rights", *Harvard International Law Journal* 42(1) (2001): 203
53. Nadine Puechguirbal, "The Cost of Ignoring Gender in Conflict and Post-Conflict Situations: A Feminist Perspective", *Amsterdam Law Forum* 4(1): 8
54. Notably, several authors stress how international sources, such as NGOs and media outlets, often depict women as victims not only of conflicts, but more in general of their "barbaric" culture. Among others, see Mutua, "Savages, Victims and Saviors", 227–233
55. Puechguirbal, "The Cost of Ignoring Gender", 9
56. Tabak, "False Dichotomies of Transitional Justice", 105
57. Ibid., 139 and 151
58. Saferworld, "Masculinities, Conflict and Peacebuilding", 16
59. See Kimberly Theidon, "Reconstructing Masculinities: The Disarmament, Demobilization, and Reintegration of Former Combatants in Colombia", *Human Rights Quarterly* 31 (2009): 20
60. A partial bibliography is offered by Brandon Hamber, "Masculinity and Transitional Justice: An Exploratory Essay", *The International Journal of Transitional Justice* 1 (2007): 377
61. Theidon, "Reconstructing Masculinities", 4
62. Ibid., 4
63. Hollander, "Neglected Voices", 106
64. Mozammel Haque, "Hope for Gender Equality? A Pattern of Post-Conflict Transition in Masculinity", *Gender, Technology and Development* 17(1): 62
65. Theidon, "Reconstructing Masculinities", 5
66. Saferworld, "Masculinities, Conflict and Peacebuilding", 4
67. Haque, "Hope for Gender Equality?", 63
68. Hamber, "Masculinity and Transitional Justice", 379
69. Hollander, "Neglected Voices", 75
70. Ibid., 152
71. Naomi R. Cahn, Dina Francesca Haynes and Fionnuala Ní Aolain, "Masculinities and Child Soldiers in Post-Conflict Societies", in Frank Cooper and Ann McGinley (eds.), *Masculinities and Law: A Multidimensional Approach* (New York: NYU Press, 2011), 3
72. Antonia Porter, "'What is Constructed can be Transformed': Masculinities in Post-Conflict Societies in Africa", *International Peacekeeping* 20(4) (2013): 488
73. Saferworld, "Masculinities, Conflict and Peacebuilding", 11

74. Joseph Vess, Gary Barker, Sanam Naraghi-Anderlini and Alexa Hassink, "The Other Side of Gender: Men as Critical Agents of Change" (Washington: United States Institute of Peace, 2013): 4
75. Theidon, "Reconstructing Masculinities", 17
76. Cahn et al., "Masculinities and Child Soldiers in Post-Conflict Societies", 5
77. Vess et. Al, "The Other Side of Gender", 2
78. Cahn et al., "Masculinities and Child Soldiers in Post-Conflict Societies", 8
79. Ibid., 17
80. Vess et al., "The Other Side of Gender", 1
81. Saferworld, "Masculinities, Conflict and Peacebuilding", 1
82. Ibid.
83. Cahn et al., "Masculinities and Child Soldiers in Post-Conflict Societies", 12
84. Ibid., 12
85. Hollander, "Neglected Voices", 41
86. Saferworld, "Masculinities, Conflict and Peacebuilding", 12
87. Cahn and Ni Aolain, "Gender, Masculinities and Transition in Conflicted Societies", 121
88. Cahn et al., "Masculinities and Child Soldiers in Post-Conflict Societies", 12
89. Porter, "'What is Constructed can be Transformed", 489
90. Ibid., 492
91. Tabak, "False Dichotomies of Transitional Justice", 161
92. Cahn and Ní Aolain, "Gender, Masculinities and Transition in Conflicted Societies", 109
93. Saferworld, "Masculinities, Conflict and Peacebuilding", 6
94. Hollander, "Neglected Voices", 183–210
95. Theidon, "Reconstructing Masculinities", 31
96. Cahn and Ní Aolain, "Gender, Masculinities and Transition in Conflicted Societies", 103
97. Vess et al., "The Other Side of Gender", 6
98. Cahn et al., "Masculinities and Child Soldiers in Post-Conflict Societies", 7
99. Haque, "Hope for Gender Equality?" offers examples of men positively reconstructing their masculine identity in the aftermath of conflicts.
100. Hollander, "Neglected Voices", 164
101. Object of several studies is the case of South Africa. See Cahn and Ní Aolain, "Gender, Masculinities and Transition in Conflicted Societies", 119
102. Chinkin, "Peace Agreements as a Means for Promoting Gender Equality and Ensuring Participation of Women", 11
103. Fionnuala Ní Aolain, "Women, Security, and the Patriarchy of Internationalized Transitional Justice", *Human Rights Quarterly* 31 (2009): 1068
104. Hollander, "Neglected Voices", 162

105. Just as a way of example, customs which require a price to be paid for a bride, and thus in order to start a family – which is in turn one of the core factors indicating men's manhood – not only objectify the woman as property, but also place a strong burden on boys and men who cannot afford to pay such price, thus provoking frustration and humiliation. See Laura Woodbury, "Reconstructing Gender Identity for Child Combatants in Post-Conflict African Societies", *Journal of International Service* (2011), 23
106. Erin Daly, "Truth Skepticism: An Inquiry Into the Value of Truth in Times of Transition", *The International Journal of Transitional Justice* 2 (2008): 30
107. Janine Natalya Clark, "Reconciliation through Remembrance? War Memorials and the Victims of Vukovar", *The International Journal of Transitional Justice* 7 (2013): 130
108. Michael Humphrey and Estela Valverde, "Human Rights Politics and Injustice: Transitional Justice in Argentina and South Africa", *The International Journal of Transitional Justice* 2 (2008): 84
109. This evolution is not limited to the field of transitional justice, as it is retraceable also in the "ordinary dimension" of criminal justice. See McEvoy and McConnachie, "Victims and Transitional Justice", 492
110. See infra, chapters 6–10
111. Karstedt, "From Absence to Presence, From Silence to Voice", 13
112. Ibid.,14
113. Bonacker, "Global Victimhood", 98
114. For an in-depth analysis see David Taylor, "Victim Participation in Transitional Justice Mechanisms: Real Power or Empty Ritual?" (Discussion Paper, Impunity Watch, Utrecht, 2014)
115. See infra, Chapter 7 analysing ad-hoc tribunals
116. James, "A Carnival of Truth?", 187
117. Bonacker, "Global Victimhood", 99
118. Katherine M. Franke, "Gendered Subjects of Transitional Justice", *Columbia Journal of Gender and Law* 15(3) (2006): 818
119. Humphrey, "From Victim to Victimhood", 172
120. Humphrey and Valverde, "Human Rights Politics and Injustice", 91
121. Among others, see Humphrey, "From Victim to Victimhood", 179
122. Kirk Simpson, "Victims of Political Violence: A Habermasian Model of Truth Recovery", *Journal of Human Rights* 6/3 (2007): 330
123. Ibid.
124. Among others, see Louise Mallinder, "The Ongoing Quest for Truth and Justice: Enacting and Annulling Argentina's Amnesty Laws" (Working paper, Institute of Criminology and Criminal Justice, Queen's University Belfast, Belfast, 2009), 26 & 64

125. Bonacker, "Global Victimhood", 107
126. For example, the South African Commission heard about 21,000 witnesses: a huge number, but only a small fraction of the regime's direct and indirect victims.
127. Daly, "Truth Skepticism", 31
128. Simon Robins, "Towards Victim-Centred Transitional Justice: Understanding the Needs of Families of the Disappeared in Postconflict Nepal", *The International Journal of Transitional Justice* 5 (2011): 86
129. Ibid.
130. Roger Duthie, "Toward a Development-sensitive Approach to Transitional Justice", *The International Journal of Transitional Justice* 2 (2008): 292–309
131. Wilke, "Remembering Complexity?", 136
132. Duthie, "Toward a Development-sensitive Approach to Transitional Justice", 300
133. Clark, "Reconciliation Through Remembrance?", 116–135
134. Ibid.
135. Wilke, "Remembering Complexity?" In this regard, the example of Magnus Hirschfeld is provided: physicist and sexologist, persecuted as being Jewish gay, and communist.
136. Ibid.,144
137. Franke, "Gendered Subjects of Transitional Justice", 825
138. Ní Aolain, "Women, Security, and the Patriarchy of Internationalized Transitional Justice", 1074
139. Cahn and Ní Aolain, "Gender, Masculinities and Transition in Conflicted Societies", 110
140. Puechguirbal, "The Cost of Ignoring Gender", 16
141. Ibid., 5. At the same time, women participation is not per sé enough; on the contrary, it is crucial for different experiences to be included, by ensuring the participation of community leaders, women combatants, and so on.
142. Chinkin, "Peace Agreements as a Means for Promoting Gender Equality and Ensuring Participation of Women", 10
143. Tabak, "False Dichotomies of Transitional Justice", 115
144. Chinkin, "Peace Agreements as a Means for Promoting Gender Equality and Ensuring Participation of Women", 11
145. Laura Sjoberg, "Gendering Global Conflict: Toward a Feminist Theory of War" (New York: Columbia University Press, 2013), 132 for a reflection on security and gender
146. Bell and O'Rourke, "Does Feminism Need a Theory of Transitional Justice?", 30
147. Puechguirbal, "The Cost of Ignoring Gender", 11

148. Ní Aolain, "Women, Security, and the Patriarchy of Internationalized Transitional Justice", 1072
149. Chinkin, "Peace Agreements as a Means for Promoting Gender Equality and Ensuring Participation of Women", 25
150. Theidon, "Reconstructing Masculinities", 20
151. Ní Aolain, O'Rourke and Swaine, "Transforming Reparations for Conflict-Related Sexual Violence", 134
152. Robins, "Towards Victim-Centred Transitional Justice", 77
153. Michael Humphrey, "From Victim to Victimhood", 182
154. Bloomfeld et al., "Reconciliation After Violent Conflict", 63
155. Ibid., 64, recalls the expression "Olympics of genocide", coined in order to refer to the (extremely circumscribed) phenomenon of Jewish individuals or associations which tried to prevent other groups from claiming to be victims of genocide, on the basis that "the" only genocide was the one perpetrated by the Nazi forces.
156. McEvoy and McConnachie, "Victimology in Transitional Justice", 532
157. James, "A Carnival of Truth?", 188
158. Tabak, "False Dichotomies of Transitional Justice", 113
159. Ibid., 114

CHAPTER 3

Truth: Chasing an Illusion?

Introduction

One of the primary defining objectives of transitional processes is truth, often praised as a fundamental value, and a necessary foundation of a more peaceful and inclusive order, almost as a panacea for the wrongs experienced by victims and society. Investigating, discovering and acknowledging the truth surely represent a fundamental step in addressing the legacies of violence and bringing redress to those affected by it. However, this process also conceals some intrinsic perils and limitations, which are too often overlooked, and which are in part related to the complexity of the concept of truth itself.

This chapter aims at reflecting upon some of the key debates around the issue of truth. Therefore, it first outlines the concept of truth, briefly retracing some of the main philosophical approaches to it, with a specific focus on the Habermasian perspective and its application in the realm of transitional justice. Following, the development and scope of a legal human right to know the truth will be retraced, also pausing on its merits and inherent limitations. Finally, the potential benefits, and some of the shortcomings, that are normally attached to truth-recovery and truth-narration processes in post-conflict scenarios will be described; a critical reflection upon these issues will lead to the conclusion that truth, with its inevitably political and contested character, should mainly be approached

G. Girelli, *Understanding Transitional Justice*,
Philosophy, Public Policy, and Transnational Law,
DOI 10.1007/978-3-319-53606-4_3

and pursued as a dynamic, long-term process, embracing – rather than resisting – its limitations and tensions.

Is There a Truth, Beyond Perception?

Truth is one of the primary issues analysed and debated by philosophers and intellectuals of all times, and one that poses many challenges.[1] Indeed, after centuries of thought and study, several questions still await answer, about the nature of truth; the existence and verifiability of a single, objective reality; the relationship between truth and language; the best instruments to be adopted in the quest for truth, and so on. The scope of this paragraph is to outline, at an introductory level, some of the approaches to the meaning(s) of truth, and especially those with more resonance in post-conflict scenarios.

The history of philosophy is filled with theories concerning the nature and characteristics of truth, which range from more objectives to purely subjective ones. One of the most cited definitions describe truth as the "agreement of the mind with reality"[2]; such an approach is informed by one of the most well-known, classical theories of truth – the correspondence theory, developed by intellectuals such as Aristotle, whose main assumption is that the truth of a proposition is dependent on its being correspondent to the facts.[3] Similarly, according to the coherence theory, a proposition is true if it is consistent with a system of beliefs or propositions.[4] Therefore, these approaches imply the existence of an objective, verifiable, "true" dimension, whose characteristics can be discovered, claimed and corroborated by evidence. Unfortunately, these theories fall short of satisfyingly portraying the essence of truth, nor offer a viable process to adopt in order to conclusively reach the truth.

However, the most diverse theories can be found. For example, several authors have elaborated deflationary theories, postulated on the idea that truth is essentially a semantically redundant concept: truth is simple; it does not have any deeper meaning than what emerges from the everyday discourse.[5] A different approach is followed by existentialist philosophers (such as Jean Paul Sartre and Simone de Beauvoir), according to which truth starts with the individual, with his experiences, perceptions, upbringing, which shape his own understanding of the world to the point of providing meaning to his life; in a sense, truth is anything that makes the subject feel or live better.[6] This purely subjective reconstruction of the concept clashes with the more traditional understanding of truth as something external to the individual, with an objective and "shareable" dimension. Interestingly, these two contrasting understandings of truth also appear reconcilable, or, quite paradoxically, both "true": indeed, while truth appears as something with an objective dimension, we are also aware of how our perceptions, assumptions and prejudices affect our interpretation of the truth, to the point of defining it. This tension between contrasting, but at the same time coexisting understandings of truth is felt even stronger today, in the age of social media, that several authors are already defining as a "post-truth"[7] era, in which the result of unprecedented, constant and (only apparently) unfiltered availability of universal knowledge is more uncertainty and superficiality, in which facts and opinions merge to the point of being indistinguishable.

A relativistic approach to truth is therefore highly fascinating. However, embracing such an understanding with regards to social and historical truths, like the ones that transitional projects aim to reconstruct, is problematic, as it opens up excessive spaces for denying or downsizing mass violations of rights and the suffering of millions. In other words, in post-conflict scenarios – where the reconstruction of past events constitutes a key step in the determination of priorities, reparative measures, characteristics of the new political, economic and social order, with extremely real consequences on the lives of individuals as much as of countries – a concept of truth is needed which encompasses an objective foundation, an evidentiary basis (although at the same time able to accommodate different interpretations and experiences).[8]

Another fundamental contribution to the debate around truth is the one provided by Michel Foucault, who perceives truth as inextricably linked to power; for the French philosopher

> Truth isn't the reward of free spirits, the child of protracted solitude nor the privilege of those who have succeeded in liberating themselves. Truth is a thing of this world: it is produced by virtue of multiple forms of constraint. And it induces regular effects of power. Each society has its regime of truth.[9]

Meaning, its own rules for determining the truthfulness of a statement, the discourses accepted as true, the mechanisms used to sanction truth and so on.[10] Foucault's reflection is fundamental, as it reveals how truth – especially public truth – is never neutral, nor a purely technical matter; with regards to post-conflict scenarios, therefore, it is important to reflect and expose the interests and priorities of the different actors, in order to appreciate how these are influencing the narrative with regards to both past events and the future of the country.

Truth as a Process: The Habermasian Theory and Its Reverberations Post-Conflict

One of the most interesting approaches to the issue of truth, however, is offered by Jürgen Habermas, who values truth primarily as the result of a process; as a consequence, he focuses on the latter, and in particular, on how the process should be designed in order to achieve a shared understanding of reality at the social level (*truth*).[11] Habermas' theory has also been applied, in the field of transitional justice, by Kirk Simpson, who proposed, with specific reference to the highly conflicted scenario of Northern Ireland, a transitional mechanism inspired by Habermas' Ideal Speech Situation.[12] Habermas elaborated a consensual (or deliberative) theory of truth, whose core principle is that "competing truth claims can only be resolved through rational discussion aimed at the creation of a consensus".[13] Therefore, truth is a social project, and one which requires the participants to adopt a communicative approach, as opposed to a strategic one: while the latter comes into play when a subject identifies – individually – a goal, and interacts with others merely in order to reach such an objective (in fact treating the other as a means, towards an egoistic end), communicative action is fulfilled when

> Actors are prepared to harmonize their plans of action through internal means, committing themselves to pursuing their goals only in the condition of an agreement – one that already exists or one to be negotiated – about definitions of the situation and prospective outcomes.[14]

The aim of such action is therefore reaching an understanding, a shared truth, among the participants.[15] Habermas also distinguishes between several kinds of communicative actions, among which the moral, and particularly the political, use, stand out as specially relevant with regard to transitional phases; indeed, according to the German philosopher, the best way to solve together common problems, in such a way to develop a social order within which everybody is provided with the best chances for self-fulfilment, consists in adopting deliberative procedures, whose success is in turn dependent on procedural fairness, as well as on the authenticity of the participants, full openness and equal participation.[16] In other words, for a truth-recovery process to be legitimate and successful, everybody must be granted the opportunity to fully and equally participate.[17]

Furthermore, Habermas identifies three goals served by speech acts, as means for reaching a common understating of the events,[18] which, in turn, appear to reflect fundamental objectives of the transitional machinery per sé. In particular, such speech acts serve to:

a) (Re-)establish interpersonal relations.[19] Similarly, a fundamental goal of transitional processes is to recreate a democratic and inclusive order, in which citizens are free to participate, without fear of oppression and retaliation.
b) Represent states and events,[20] or – as usually framed in transitional scenarios – establish an authoritative record of the events, in order to counteract attempts of denial and disrupt alternative reconstructions of the past, as well as to acknowledge and dignify the experiences of the victims.
c) Manifest experiences.[21] Notably, and as described more thoroughly further on, truth-recovery procedures are potentially beneficial not only in the moment they reach their goal, but also as processes. As such, transitional mechanisms are also to be valued as supportive forums where victims can contribute to discovering the truth, by narrating their experiences and expressing their feelings.

Finally, transitional instruments themselves have dealt with the problem of defining truth, and now it is not uncommon for these bodies – especially truth commissions – to explicitly articulate, in their reports, their own understanding of truth.[22] In this context, particularly noteworthy is the approach adopted by the South African Truth and Reconciliation Commission (TRC), which – conscious of the complex and multilayered nature of truth – rather than endorsing a monolithic and artificial understanding of the concept, resolved to explicitly identify four different profiles of truth, all intertwined and relevant in a transitional phase.[23] The first is the factual truth, reached by "bringing to light factual, corroborated evidence, of obtaining accurate information through reliable (impartial, objective) procedures"[24]; this is therefore the objective version of truth. Also identified by the TRC is a personal or narrative truth, which emerges from listening to "people's perceptions, stories, myths and experiences"[25]; this more subjective truth is therefore mainly pursued through testimonies, which provide "unique insights into the pain of

(South Africa's) past",[26] while also carrying a strong healing potential. Further, a social, dialogical – Habermasian? – truth is described by the TRC, instrumental to "transcend the divisions of the past, to provide an environment in which all possible views could be considered and weighed",[27] and thus particularly instrumental for reconciliation. Finally, a healing and restorative truth was pursued by the South African body, "that places facts and what they mean within the context of human relationships – both amongst citizens and between the state and its citizens".[28] The Commission acknowledged the importance of all these shades of the notion of truth, as each of them helps to pursue different purposes of a transitional project, and it succeeded in "mixing" them together without privileging any of it, thus creating "a tapestry that was truer than any single type could have produced on its own".[29]

A Legal Right to Know

Although truth has always been a central theme in the discourse about transitions, only in the last decades national and international bodies started acknowledging a legal right to know the truth, participating in shaping the content and legal standing of this right, which is now by many considered more than a mere "concession of States".[30] At a closer look, however, the existence, contours and status of a right to truth remain controversial, with some authors affirming that the right "has achieved customary status",[31] while others consider it as little more than a "narrative device".[32]

Notably, this right is not explicitly stated in a general way in any source, with the closest exception being Article 24(2) of the Convention for the Protection of All Persons from Enforced Disappearances,[33] which recognises the right of each victim of this specific violation (defined by the same article as the person disappeared as well as anyone directly harmed by the enforced disappearance) to know the truth.[34] However, the right has been recognised and implemented by a plethora of actors, from national and regional courts, to the United Nations, in many cases with relation to specific contexts or violations. Unfortunately, a thorough and comprehensive description of all the relevant sources exceeds the space of this chapter; therefore, this paragraph will only provide a brief overview of some of the key mechanisms and sources which have played a role in shaping this entitlement, also reconstructing what the acknowledgement of such a right entails in the practice.

A first formulation of a right to know the truth can be found in the laws regulating armed conflicts,[35] and especially in Articles 32 and 33 of

Additional Protocol I of the Geneva Conventions of 1977,[36] which impose on the state parties to armed conflicts a duty to search for missing persons, as well as the "right of families to know the fate of their relatives".[37] Notably, although the scope of the provision was the source of controversies, it appears that the term *right* was not used accidentally, but rather was "adopted after careful reflection, and made in full consciousness".[38] Also, these obligations are now understood as customary duties of states, arising both in international and in non-international armed conflicts.[39]

Other fundamental actors in the development of a right to the truth are the Inter-American Commission (IACHR) and the Inter-American Court of Human Rights (IACtHR), which once again proved particularly proactive, in sanctioning this right and clarifying its content, initially with regards to the infamously widespread phenomenon of enforced disappearances.[40] Indeed, one of the elements that characterises this crime, and that makes it so heinous and nerve-racking, is precisely the condition of "not knowing", the suffocating uncertainty that both victims and their relatives (as well as society) experience as a result. For these reasons, from the *Velasquez-Rodriguez* case[41]onwards both bodies have found enforced disappearances to constitute a "multiple and continuous violation of many rights",[42] not only of the direct victims, but also of their relatives; in particular, the IACHR and IACtHR found the inter-American human rights system as imposing on the member states several positive obligations every time a violation of fundamental rights occurs, among which the duty to carry out prompt, genuine and effective investigations[43]; the duty to inform the families of the victims of the facts of the case, as well as the fate and (if applicable) the location of the remains of the victim[44]; the obligation to communicate the actions taken or planned in order to make justice.[45] Therefore, the right to know the truth came into being as a fairly limited entitlement – recognised with regard to a specific violation, and at the benefit of specific subjects (the families and relatives of the disappeared), mainly on the basis of Articles 8, 13 and 25 of the American Convention of Human Rights,[46] which sanction the rights to fair trial, judicial protection and information. However, through a growing body of jurisprudence, and also in line with the decisions of other human rights mechanisms, the IACHR and IACtHR gradually expanded the scope and reach of this right, recognising both an individual and a collective dimension, and its emerging in every case of grave violation of fundamental rights. Unlike other sources though, the American bodies mainly see this right as "a fundamental element of the rights to judicial guarantees and judicial protection",[47] and as such as a sort of enabling and instrumental right, rather than autonomous and self-standing.

The European Court of Human Rights (ECtHR) has also embraced the existence of a right to know the truth, although more implicitly than its American counterpart. In particular, mostly in cases of enforced disappearances and torture, the Court has clarified the positive obligations of states to investigate, prosecute and punish violations of human rights recognised by the European Convention on Human Rights (ECHR),[48] implicitly sanctioned by Articles 2 (right to life) and 3 (prohibition of torture) of the ECHR (especially when read in light of Articles 1 and 13)[49]; in many of these cases, therefore, the Court found a violation of these articles, in their procedural dimension, due to the states failure to carry out prompt and thorough investigations, as well as a violation of Article 3 in respect to the victims' families (the applicants in cases of forced disappearances), due to the mental suffering and distress the disappearance of a relative provokes.[50] Additionally, in 2012 the Court expanded its jurisprudence on the matter; in the judgment on the *El Masri* case,[51] whose applicant had been subject to extraordinary rendition with the participation of CIA operatives, the Grand Chamber of the ECtHR explicitly acknowledged the existence of a right to truth, and found that the inadequate investigations carried out by the Former Yugoslav Republic of Macedonia "deprived the applicant of being informed of what had happened, including of getting an accurate account of the suffering he had allegedly endured and the role of those responsible for his alleged ordeal",[52] thus violating Article 3 of the ECHR in its procedural limb, in respect to the victim himself.[53]

Analogous conclusions with regards to the existence and content of the right to truth have been reached by other regional and international bodies, such as the Human Rights Committee[54] and the African Commission on Human and People's Rights.[55]

The UN also played a fundamental role in promoting the establishment and recognition of a right to know the truth. Indeed, starting from the 1970s, bodies such as the General Assembly, the Security Council and the Human Rights Council (as well as the Human Rights Commission as its predecessor,)[56] adopted several resolutions, declarations as well as other initiatives focused on the right to truth,[57] and the General Assembly even dedicated to this right an "International Day".[58] Among the many initiatives and policies promoted, strategically relevant in supporting the existence of a legal right to know the truth are the so-called Principles to

Combat Impunity, adopted in 1997, and their updated version developed by Diane Orentlicher and published in 2005[59]. This document, which specifies the obligations of the states with regard to the right, the role of victims in post-conflict scenarios, and the ideal characteristics of a truth commissions, qualifies the right to know the truth as inalienable[60] and imprescriptible.[61] Similarly, a 2006 study on the right to truth,[62] which also aimed at clarifying origins, content and reach of the right, affirmed the inalienable, autonomous and non-derogable nature of this right,[63] thus offering arguably its most far-reaching interpretation.

Finally, in determining the existence (and for some, the customary status) of a right to know the truth, with both individual and collective underpinnings, several authors point to the establishment of dozens of truth commissions around the world, entrusted with investigating past violations and abusive patterns and developing an authoritative record of the events,[64] as well as to the incorporation of the right in several national legislations.[65]

In conclusion, although not explicitly recognised as a general right in multilateral treaties, and although its autonomous nature remains contested, a right to know the truth with regard to grave violations of human rights has been firmly acknowledged at the national, regional and international levels – according to some having customary status – as a crucial aspect of fundamental rights, such as: the right to access to justice, the right to information, the right to life and the prohibition of torture.[66]

***

As aforementioned, this right presents both an individual and a collective dimension. With regards to the former, it compels public authorities to "undertake a sustained and systematic effort to investigate and accumulate evidence"[67] with regard to potential violations of fundamental rights. As a consequence, the right to truth enables victims, as well as their families, to obtain all the possible information about: violations of their (relatives') rights, and the circumstances in which these violations happened; the subjects responsible for the abuses and the fate of the victims, as well as the location of the victims' remains; the status of the investigations, and in general the actions that the authorities have taken, or are planning to take, in order to investigate the crime and ensure that justice is done.[68] The state must therefore gather all the possible information, without exceptions, and irrespective of an official request from the part of the victims or their families.[69] Due to potential practical limitations of the investigations, this duty to uncover the truth is not one of results, but rather of means; however, several bodies have clarified how states' investigations must be prompt, thorough and effective,[70] and the IACtHR has stressed the need for a *judicial* investigation into the facts.[71] Additionally, in order to ensure that these obligations do not become a mere formality, states also need to put in place an adequate, accessible and effective judicial and administrative system, as well as an effective remedy for applicants to appeal potential decisions or initiatives which limit the enjoyment of the right to truth.[72]

However, victims and their families are not the exclusive holders of this right, which also has a collective dimension; in other words, society as a whole has the right to be informed of the truth with regard to violations of fundamental rights – especially in the aftermath of conflicts and oppressive regimes; the existence of systematic plans or structural patterns of violence, and potential involvement of state forces; the circumstances and factors that enabled the commission of the abuses.[73] Additionally, governments have a duty to communicate to society how they plan to hold perpetrators accountable, address root causes of the conflict, and bring redress to the victims, which also deserve to be acknowledged in their experiences and suffering.[74]

Additionally, in post-conflict scenarios states are required to set up policies and mechanisms with the specific objective of uncovering, acknowledging and preserving the truth with regard to past events,[75] also ensuring spaces for victims to narrate their stories and present their claims.[76] Consequently, descending from the right to truth is also an obligation of states to create records and preserve the information concerning mass violence and grave abuses of rights – for example by establishing and ensuring public access to archives[77]; as aforementioned, the adoption of instruments such as truth commissions, as well as tribunals, could also reveal fundamental in creating and preserving an authoritative body of knowledge, and in turn to achieve the goals of deterrence and non-repetition.[78]

In sum, the right to truth, which ultimately resides in the general obligation of states to respect, protect and ensure human rights, is best understood, especially in its collective dimension, as a procedural right, an enabler or "meta-right",[79] instrumental to the pursuit of other fundamental rights (both in ordinary and in transitional contexts) as well as to combat impunity and to prevent the resurgence of violence. The states' obligations arising from the right to truth therefore stand in a causal relationship with traditional goals of transitional processes, such as reparation and deterrence[80]: finding and publicly proclaiming the truth, as well as the very procedural commitment adopted by then new institutions to investigate past violations (in opposition to an oppressive state which actively sought to bury the truth) appear to be fundamental steps in building a more peaceful state.

Acknowledgement, Closure and Justice: Seeking Painful Truths

Truth and knowledge have always been a fundamental and imperishable desire of the human being, idealised by societies and pursued sometimes irrespective of the potential consequences. In post-conflict scenarios, this need is felt even stronger, insomuch that truth has become one of the key goals of any transitional enterprise, strongly advocated by human rights organisations, and vocally promised by governments. However, even accepting the possibility of establishing one, shareable truth, this process could also provoke some unexpected consequences.

There are many, valid reasons for undertaking truth-finding efforts in transitional contexts. For example, such a process fosters the development and establishment of an authoritative collective memory, a shared record of past events which can help societies decode their history and build a better future, while also providing the tools for resisting attempts to deny or downsize the traumatic events of the past.[81] Officially declaring the truth can thus prepare the ground for a new beginning, while the truth-finding process as such can foster participation and empowerment, thus reinforcing (or establishing ex novo) individual and collective commitments to the new social and political order.[82]

Furthermore, truth-finding exercises are believed to restrict spaces for impunity,[83] by promoting accountability and working as a deterrent of future abuses. Indeed, truth is by many valued as crucial in preventing further violations, as a sort of antibody society develops for itself.[84] Exposing the truth can also strengthen calls for accountability, and for bringing perpetrators to justice; and, also in those cases in which criminal prosecution is precluded, truth can itself constitute a form of punishment or retribution; indeed, truth gives everyone the possibility to issue a (moral) judgement, thus opposing false claims of innocence.[85]

However, in order to maximise this potential for ensuring non-repetition, the truth process needs to be as inclusive and comprehensive as possible. Not only should it involve as many parties as feasible, in such a way to allow for a more inclusive reconstruction of the events, of the bureaucracy of abuses, and of the underlying justifications for mass violations of rights; also, investigations into the events of the past should dig deep, analysing and reconstructing the root causes of conflicts and violence, as well as their enabling factors, which often can be identified in structural patterns of political-economic violence and inequality. In this way, truth also becomes instrumental in promoting institutional reforms.[86]

Moreover, establishing the truth ideally provides the victims with acknowledgement and a sense of closure.[87] Indeed, the truth-telling process can be a cathartic and empowering one, as through the narration of their truth victims are transformed from objects of violence into active political subjects, into survivors and resisters[88]; also, what victims knew in their hearts is invested with official recognition, thus turning suspect into certainty. Additionally, the reconstruction of the truth often kick-starts the reparation process, thus constituting a fundamental step in providing redress – both symbolic and material – to the victims,[89] while the very act of acknowledging the truth has itself been praised as reparatory.[90]

In the opinion of many, truth also leads to reconciliation: this "has to be built in the hearts and minds of all members of society through a process that recognizes every human beings worth and dignity"[91] – what in South Africa was referred to as *ubuntu*[92] – but in order to acknowledge humanity in the others and to forgive,[93] it is first necessary to know, to see who the other is, to abandon the suspects and know the facts,[94] through a process that is not forced or artificial, but rather inclusive, supported, open to critiques and disagreements.[95] In addition, acknowledging the full truth and entering a debate with the former enemy can promote the creation of a new, shared social identity, especially in traditionally divided societies; indeed, through this process individuals and communities are led to reconsider their initial positions and interpretations of the past, and to accommodate other perspectives and histories of suffering and loss[96]; ideally, this critical rethinking of one's partial truth allows for the overcoming of unrealistic Saint-versus-Evil discourses and for admitting mutual responsibilities, thus potentially fostering the formation of a new social identity.[97]

When Truth Hurts: Lessons from Pandora

As outlined in the previous paragraph, the quest for the truth, its discovery and narration, can ideally constitute fundamental, game-changing steps towards peace, justice and reconciliation. However, when considered more realistically, several potential shortcomings emerge of truth-finding processes, and an excessive focus on the truth – or too much truth, in the wrong context – could in fact impinge on the success of the whole transitional project.

Firstly, no narrator, for how expert or seemingly impartial, is ever completely neutral in front of the truth – which is also made of perceptions and assumptions. At the same time, no narrative "can explain in a convincing and satisfying way the mysteries of human nature, the banality of evil. The most important part of the story may very well remain untold"[98]; every reconstruction of the truth is therefore inevitably partial – and in most transitional scenarios developed and shaped by the victor.[99] In these contexts, therefore, a tension emerges, between a heightened need for truth and acknowledgement, on one side, and a heightened controversy with regards to the nature and content of truth, on the other; in other words, truth is the most contested precisely in those situations in which is needed the most, and while this tension, if adequately managed, can prove constructive, if unsatisfactorily addressed by transitional mechanisms it can lead to intensified conflict and frustration.

Similarly, the establishment of one, official truth, while important in providing acknowledgement, also risks essentialising individual experiences and supporting artificial dichotomies between victims and perpetrators, right and wrong, which deny complex individual experiences, in turn fostering further polarisation. In this way, truth-telling could therefore hinder, rather than promote, reconciliation, especially in deeply divided societies where history is strongly contested, and/or the institutions appointed for the inquiry and reconstruction of the official truth appear partial (as almost inevitable in conflicted contexts.)[100]

Similarly, a truth that only focuses on certain violations and abuses (e.g., those that qualify as international crimes), while failing to account for the deepest causes of conflicts, and for the responsibilities of bystanders or traditionally ignored actors (such as private companies) is an incomplete truth, which, as a basis for the post-conflict process, limits its potential to effectively guide the transition of the country, as development of a more equal and just society.

Uncritically imposing the truth-finding, and truth-narrating processes at the core of the transitional machinery could also contrast with local, traditional ways of dealing with trauma. As described more thoroughly in the chapter dedicated to truth commissions,[101] the assumption that speaking the truth, and knowing the truth, is always positive, and thus crucial in providing closure to the victims and society, is influenced by a specific understanding of healing, which is in turn informed by Western psychological and cultural traditions; on the contrary, other cultures might value silence and forgetting, at least in the public sphere.[102] Truth can therefore be destabilising, and even more so in those contexts in which its uncovering is not followed by reparatory measures, in the form of reconstruction, satisfaction or punishment of those identified as responsible. Indeed, in several cases truth just exceeds what transitional processes, as well as the newly established government, are able (or willing) to cope with. In other words, investigating and exposing the truth creates in the individuals, as well as in the society, a series of claims, demands and expectations, which in turn require investing considerable time and resources, which in fragile post-conflict scenarios might just not be available: in many contexts truth is a luxury, and the price for failing to follow up on the findings is further frustration and instability, especially if truth-finding efforts came at the expenses of satisfying more immediate needs of the population.[103]

Finally, some authors reveal potential downsides of recognising truth – with all the complexities this concept entails – as a right, a legal device. Indeed, by formalising a legal entitlement to the truth, courts are imposed an impossible goal: to find, declare and officialise something that is inevitably complex, contested and multifaceted, to shed light on a past that is forever gone, and lost in a myriad of fragmented memories; to make the controversial uncontested. Additionally, establishing a right is never a neutral act, but rather a "a way of inculcating certain values into a society, whether those values belong to Western liberalism, a broader humanist human rights liturgy, or even those of an empowered community of victims".[104] Therefore, the formalisation of the goal of truth into a right is expressive of official, national and international, priorities and understandings of justice,[105] which might be in contrast with the needs and desire of the local communities, and sometimes also of victims themselves.[106] Additionally, by framing truth as a right the risk is to have the narrative caged into legalistic and technical terms, distant from the deeply emotional experiences of the victims, in this way potentially alienating its primary beneficiaries.[107]

Conclusions

Because of its symbolical undertones, and its purported instrumentality for peace, justice and reconciliation, truth has become one of the key constitutive objectives of transitional justice, central to each process of shifting from a traumatic past to a peaceful and democratic future. Additionally, a legal right to truth has been identified, carrying an individual as well as a collective dimension, which states have the duty to fulfil with regards to any potential violation of fundamental rights.

However, truth is by nature a thorny concept, and one open to multiple interpretations, uses and abuses. Therefore, before uncritically electing truth as an inevitable and unproblematic objective of post-conflict projects, some reflections are worth considering, which emerge from the previous discussion. Firstly, truth is a powerful instrument, especially in the post-conflict period: the framing of the past, the root causes identified, the designated victims and perpetrators, all influence the choices made for the future, in such a way to potentially shape societal relations and the country's development for decades to come. However, notably, truth is also never neutral[108]; on the contrary, it is inevitably political, as shaped by our naturally biased assumptions about society and the world, as well as by politically charged decisions adopted both preceding and in response to the conflict. Among many examples, the process of framing human rights and international crimes – on whose blueprint past events are increasingly reconstructed – is a political one, informed by a specific understanding of violence and crime which penalises certain conducts while overlooking others[109]; at the same time, the post-conflict government, in charge of shaping the mandate and composition of transitional institutions, is a political body, and the same applies to the international community, that while often participating as a neutral and technical party, also has a peculiar understanding of violence, and value-based priorities with regard to the objectives of the transition. Additionally, truth means different things to different people,[110] and it also entails cultural elements, in its meaning and in its instrumentality; for example, while some subjects might be focused on the identification of perpetrators, some communities might stress the importance of knowing the whereabouts of the victims' bodies, being burial ceremonies a valued tenet of their culture, thus fundamental in fostering individual and social healing and closure.[111]

Because of these competing understandings and perceptions, too often the reconstruction of the truth emerging from transitional exercises results partial, as focusing on specific abuses, perpetrators and facts while ignoring others. For example, conflicts are often officially described as stories of physical violence committed in the public sphere, while overlooking the impact of structural factors that enabled or influenced the conflict in the first place; in turn, this influences the narrative with regard to the initiatives necessary in order to avoid the resurgence of the conflict. An effective and beneficial truth-finding effort, therefore, should aim at including as many different characters and perspectives as possible, in particular integrating the narrative of traditionally marginalised and silenced actors, such as indigenous peoples and women. Indeed – as outlined in the previous chapter[112] – these subjects often understand violence and conflict more holistically, as expanding to the private sphere and being ineluctably linked to histories of socio-economic marginalisation and inequality, and therefore contribute with a different perspective, thus ideally allowing for a more complete reconstruction of the truth, as well as for a more thoughtful definition of the objectives and priorities of the transitional enterprise.

More generally, truth-finding processes should abandon the illusion of truth as monolithic and definitive, and rather approach it primarily as a process (shaped around communication and inclusion), a long-term struggle, a never-ending project; in the words of Erin Daly:

> Perhaps transitional governments ought to approach truth not like an infatuation that satisfies an immediate need but rather like a long-term relationship that one nurtures over the course of many years.[113]

Indeed, the process of investigating, narrating and discovering the truth is often just as instrumental in reaching the objectives of reconciliation, reparation, and justice as the final findings, on many levels.[114] Firstly, this process is highly symbolic: the commitment of the state to actively investigate, admit responsibilities, dialogue with the civil society and with traditionally marginalised constituencies manifests a stark break with a past in which state forces were mostly preoccupied with burying and/or shaping a specific version of the truth. Also, allowing victims to narrate their stories and present their demands with their own voice, to reclaim their space in society as active subjects, represents a fundamental step in the reparation process, while, at the same time, listening to the narrative of those involved in oppressive regimes or the commission of crimes increases the chances of reconstructing a full, more comprehensive truth, with a stronger educational and deterrent potential. Opening the process clearly increases the possibility of inconsistencies, contrasts and tensions; however, as seen, truth is inevitably complex and multifaceted, and embracing those tensions and debates (when properly managed and capitalised upon) can result more fruitful than imposing a monolithic and inevitably biased version of the events.[115]

Finally, truth should be pursued not only per sé, as its own reward, but primarily as instrumental to *something*; indeed, as aforementioned, knowing the truth creates demands and expectations that, if not properly confronted, risk provoking more frustration and polarisation. Additionally, truth can be dangerous, as a potential source of intra-community tensions, resentment and marginalisation (e.g., in the case of victims of sexual violence): if not complemented by measures aimed at addressing these issues, therefore, it could end up being detrimental and destabilising. Therefore, truth-finding initiatives should always be clear, to its constituents and beneficiaries, with regard to what they mean by truth, which processes will be adopted to find the truth and confront its consequences, which are their objectives and limitations. Also, because of this necessary instrumentality of truth, it is crucial for the process to envisage ways to "get to" the victims; for example, attention should be devoted to ensuring that the transitional process reaches local communities where they are, also promoting the involvement of individuals whose resources are limited, and in a language that is understood. At the same time, however, subjects should be given the possibility to opt out from the truth, to not be exposed to it, if they willingly choose to.[116]

In conclusion, transitional processes have the complex task of sustaining a hard-to-find balance between official narrative and individual experiences, between monolithic legal truths and complex personal truths, and between multiple and seemingly irreconcilable moral truths.[117] As such, a successful truth-finding process is necessarily one that accepts its own limitations, that surrenders to the impossibility of its task. In admitting the tensions, a more comprehensive narrative can emerge, that is dynamic and inclusive, while also providing the factual knowledge that is necessary to combat the resurgence of violence, and shaping the foundations of a more inclusive, peaceful and open society.

Notes

1. For an introduction to the main philosophical approaches to truth see Richard L. Kirkham, *Theories of Truth: A Critical Introduction* (Cambridge: MIT Press, 1995)
2. Yasmin Naqvi, "The Right to the Truth in International Law: Fact or Fiction?", *International Review of the Red Cross* 88 (2006): 250
3. Kirkham, *Theories of Truth,* 131

4. Felipe Fernandez-Armesto, *Truth: A History and a Guide for the Perplexed* (New York: St. Martin's Press, 1997), 219
5. As a way of example, saying that "the sky is blue" is the same as saying that "it is true that the sky is blue". See Kirkham, *Theories of Truth,* 329
6. Fernandez-Armesto, *Truth: A History and a Guide for the Perplexed,* 177
7. Among others, see "Politics in a Post-truth Age", Harvard Gazette, accessed 30 September 2016, http://news.harvard.edu/gazette/story/2016/07/politics-in-a-post-truth-age/
8. Naqvi, "The Right to the Truth in International Law: Fact or Fiction?", 253
9. Michel Foucault, *Power/Knowledge: Selected Interviews and Other Writing, 1972–77,* ed. Colin Gordon (Brighton: Harvester, 1980), 131
10. Ibid.
11. See Jürgen Habermas, *The Theory of Communicative Action Vol.1: Reason and the Rationalization of Society* (Boston: Beacon Press, 1984)
12. Kirk Simpson, "Victims of Political Violence: A Habermasian Model of Truth Recovery", *Journal of Human Rights* 6(3) (2007): 325–343
13. Ibid., 331
14. Jürgen Habermas, *Moral Consciousness and Communicative Action* (Cambridge: Massachusetts Institute of Technology, 1990), 134
15. Habermas, *The Theory of Communicative Action,* 307
16. Armin von Bogdandy and Sergio Dellavalle, *Paradigmi dell'Ordine* (Torino: Trauben, 2010), 164
17. Simpson, "Victims of Political Violence", 332
18. Habermas, *The Theory of Communicative Action,* 308
19. Ibid.
20. Ibid.
21. Ibid.
22. See Audrey R. Chapman and Patrick Ball, "The Truth of Truth Commissions: Comparative Lessons from Haiti, South Africa, and Guatemala", *Human Rights Quarterly* 23(1) (2001): 9
23. Deborah Posel, "History as Confession: The Case of South African Truth and Reconciliation Commission, *Public Culture Winter* 20 (2008): 132
24. Truth and Reconciliation Commission, "Truth and Reconciliation Commission of South Africa Report" *(TRC Report)* (Cape Town: Juta and Co., 1998), Vol.1, Chapter 5, Par. 30
25. *TRC Report,* Vol.1, Chapter 5, Par. 37
26. Ibid., Par. 36
27. Ibid., Par. 41
28. Ibid., Par. 43
29. Erin Daly, "Truth Skepticism: An Inquiry Into the Value of Truth in Times of Transition", *The International Journal of Transitional Justice* 2 (2008): 25

30. Avril McDonald, "A Right to Truth, Justice and a Remedy for African Victims of Serious Violations of International Humanitarian Law", *Law, Democracy and Development* 2 (1999): 147
31. Dermot Groome, "The Right to Truth: The Evolution of a Right", available at *Social Science Research Network* (2015): 5
32. Naqvi, "The Right to the Truth in International Law: Fact or Fiction?", 273
33. Ibid., 255
34. Ibid., 255
35. For a complete list of sources, see Greisy Lorena Rodriguez Medina, "Transitional Justice and Enforced Disappearance: The Right to Truth and the Obligation to Search for Disappeared Persons. The Colombian Case" (Master diss., University of Oslo, 2013): 130
36. *Protocol Additional to the Geneva Conventions of 12 August 1949, and Relating to the Protection of Victims of International Armed Conflicts (Protocol I),* Geneva, 8 June 1977, 1125 UNTS 3
37. Ibid., Art. 33
38. International Committee of the Red Cross, "Protocol Additional to the Geneva Conventions of 12 August 1949, and relating to the protection of victims of international armed conflicts (Protocol I), Geneva, 8 June 1977. Commentary of 1987", Par. 1211
39. As interpreted in Jean-Marie Henckaerts and Louise Doswald-Beck, eds., *Customary International Humanitarian Law. Volume I: Rules.* (Cambridge: Cambridge University Press and International Committee of the Red Cross, 2009), Rule 117
40. For an in-depth analysis see Inter-American Commission on Human Rights (IACHR), "The Right to Truth in the Americas" (Washngton, DC: Organization of American States, 2014): 27–48
41. *Case of Velásquez Rodríguez v Honduras* (Judgment) Inter-American Court of Human Rights Series C no. 4 (29 July 1988)
42. Among others, see ibid., Par.154; *Case of Radilla-Pacheco v Mexico* (Preliminary Objections, Merits, Reparations and Costs) Inter-American Court of Human Rights Series C no 209 (23 November 2009), Par. 138
43. Among others, see *Case of the Pueblo Bello Massacre v Colombia* (Judgment) Inter-American Court of Human Rights Series C no 140, Par. 142–145
44. See IACHR, "The Right to Truth in the Americas", 9 for a comprehensive list of judgments clarifying the scope of the obligation
45. Dermot Groome, "The Right to Truth in the Fight Against Impunity", *Berkeley Journal of International Law* 29 (2012): 184
46. *American Convention on Human Rights,* San José, 21 November 1969, 1144 UNTS 123
47. IACHR, "The Right to Truth in the Americas", 36

48. *European Convention for the Protection of Human Rights and Fundamental Freedoms,* Rome, 04 November 1950, 213 UNTS 221
49. Naqvi, “The Right to the Truth in International Law: Fact or Fiction?”, 257. Among others, see *Case of Cyprus v Turkey* (Judgment) European Court of Human Rights, Application no. 25781/94 (10 May 2001), Par. 131; *Case of Bazorkina v Russia* (Judgment) European Court of Human Rights, Application no. 69481/01 (27 July 2006), Parr. 117–120
50. Among many, see *Case of Imakayeva v Russia* (Judgment) European Court of Human Rights, Application no.7615/02 (9 November 2006), Par. 164
51. *Case of El-Masri v The Former Yugoslav Republic of Macedonia* (Judgment) European Court of Human Rights, Application no.39630/09 (13 December 2012)
52. Ibid. Par. 192
53. Ibid., Parr. 191–194
54. Human Rights Committee, Communication no. 1469/2006 (*Sharma v. Nepal)*, Un Doc. CCPR/C/94/D/1469/2006 (6 November 2008), Par. 7.5
55. *Zimbabwe Human Rights NGO Forum v Zimbabwe,* African Commission on Human and Peoples’ Rights, Communication no. 245/02 (25 June 2002), Par. 115. See also Szoke-Burke, “Searching for the Right to Truth”, 540
56. Rodriguez Medina, “Transitional Justice and Enforced Disappearance”, 133
57. See Groome, “The Right to Truth”, 2
58. Linn Bergenfelz, “On Truth and Ideology in International Criminal Law” (Master diss., Lund University, 2012), 17
59. UNCHR, “Report of Diane Orentlicher, independent expert to update the Set of principles to combat impunity – Updated Set of Principles for the Protection and Promotion of Human Rights through Action to Combat Impunity” (2005) Un Doc E/CN.4/2005/102/Add.1.
60. Ibid., Principles 1 and 2
61. Ibid., Principle 4
62. UNCHR (Economic and Social Council), “Promotion and Protection of Human Rights: Study on the Right to Truth” (2006) Un Doc E/CN.4/ 2006/91
63. Ibid., Parr. 55–60
64. Groome, “The Right to Truth in the Fight against Impunity”, 182
65. Naqvi, “The Right to the Truth in International Law: Fact or Fiction?”, 263
66. Groome, “The Right to Truth in the Fight against Impunity”, 177
67. Juan E. Mendez and Francisco J. Bariffi, “Truth, Right to, International Protection” (Max Planck Encyclopedia of Public International Law, 2012), Par. 4

68. Szoke-Burke, "Searching for the Right to Truth", 533; UNCHR (Economic and Social Council), "Promotion and Protection of Human Rights: Study on the Right to Truth", Par. 38
69. Among others, see Human Rights Committee, Communication no. 59/1996 *(Blanco Abad v Spain)* UN Doc. CAT/T/C/20/D/59/1996 (14 May 1998), Par. 8.2
70. Szoke-Burke, "Searching for the Right to Truth", 534
71. Mendez and Bariffi, "Truth, Right to, International Protection", Par. 5 2
72. IACHR, "The Right to Truth in the Americas", 56
73. Naqvi, "The right to the truth in international law: fact or fiction?", 260
74. Ibid.
75. IACHR, "The Right to Truth in the Americas", 40
76. Szoke-Burke, "Searching for the Right to Truth", 534
77. Mendez and Bariffi, "Truth, Right to, International Protection", Par. 8
78. Groome, "The Right to Truth", 10
79. Ibid., 3
80. Bergenfelz, "On Truth and Ideology in International Criminal Law", 23
81. Bronwyn Anne Leebaw, "The Irreconcilable Goals of Transitional Justice", *Human Rights Quarterly* 95 (2008), 107
82. Ibid.
83. Naqvi, "The Right to the Truth in International Law: Fact or Fiction?", 247–248
84. IACHR, "The Right to Truth in the Americas", 59
85. Louise Mallinder and Kieran McEvoy, "Rethinking Amnesties: Atrocity, Accountability and Impunity in Post-Conflict Societies" in *Transitional Justice Institute Research Paper* 11(2): 30
86. Rodriguez Medina, "Transitional Justice and Enforced Disappearance", 22
87. See Nicola Henry, "Witness to Rape: The Limits and Potential of International War Crimes Trials for Victims of Wartime Sexual Violence", *The International Journal of Transitional Justice* 3 (2009): 114–134
88. Anita Isaacs, "At War with the past? The Politics of Truth Seeking in Guatemala", *The International Journal of Transitional Justice* 4 (2010): 268
89. Naqvi, "The Right to the Truth in International Law: Fact or Fiction?", 249
90. IACHR, "The Right to Truth in the Americas", 59
91. Juan E Mendez, "Accountability for Past Abuses" *Human Rights Quarterly* 19(2) (1997): 277
92. For an in-depth analysis of the concept and its significance in post-apartheid South Africa, see Drucilla Cornell and Nyoko Muvangua, *Ubuntu and the Law: African Ideals and Post Apartheid Jurisprudence* (New York: Fordham University Press, 2012), 103–122
93. Daly, "Truth Skepticism", 8
94. Posel, "History as Confession", 126

95. James L. Gibson, "Overcoming Apartheid: can Truth Reconcile a Divided Nation?", *Politikon* 31 (2004): 151
96. Ibid.
97. Cheryl Lawther, "Denial, Silence and the Politics of the Past: Unpicking the Opposition to Truth Recovery in Northern Ireland", *The International Journal of Transitional Justice* 7 (2013): 162
98. Daly, "Truth Skepticism", 27
99. Ibid., 26. Also, see infra chapters 6 and 7 on international tribunals and the accusations moved to these bodies being tools of the victors.
100. Androff, "Can Civil Society reclaim Truth?", 298
101. Infra, Chapter 9
102. Gearoid Millar, "Assessing Local Experiences of Truth-Telling in Sierra Leone: Getting to 'Why' through a Qualitative Case Study Analysis", *The International Journal of Transitional Justice* 4 (2010): 489
103. Daly, "Truth Skepticism", 32
104. Georgina Duffin, "Past Truths and Present Justice: The Right to Truth in Transition" (Master diss., School of Oriental and African Studies, 2010), 26
105. Ibid., 36
106. See Leora Bilsky, "Transitional Justice as a Modern Oedipus: The Emergence of a Right to Truth", *Critical Analysys of Law* 2(2) (2015): 447–466, on Argentinian legislation which, in the quest for truth, allows courts to request samples of DNA from "suspected" children of disappeared subjects (often upon request of the potential grandmothers).
107. Duffin, "Past Truths and Present Justice", 35
108. Ibid., 29
109. See Kamari Clarke, "Rethinking Africa through its Exclusions: The Politics of Naming Criminal Responsibility" *Anthropological Quarterly* 83(3) (2010): 625–651
110. Rodriguez Medina, "Transitional Justice and Enforced Disappearance", 20
111. A vast literature reveals the strong healing potential of exhumations and reburials. Among others, see Shari Eppel, "'Bones in the Forest' in Matabeleland, Zimbabwe: Exhumations as a Tool for Transformation", *The International Journal of Transitional Justice* 8(3) (2014): 404–425
112. Infra, Chapter 2
113. Daly, "Truth Skepticism", 39
114. Ibid., 32
115. Szoke-Burke, "Searching for the Right to Truth", 545
116. Bilsky, "Transitional Justice as a Modern Oedipus", 460
117. Daly, "Truth Skepticism", 25 & 38–41

CHAPTER 4

Reconciliation: A Journey "From Madness to Hope"

Introduction

Reconciliation is one of the most peculiar and typical goals of transitional justice exercises, increasingly praised – in parallel to the promotion of restorative justice initiatives[1] – as a fundamental ingredient for achieving peace, justice and stability in post-conflict countries. However, at the same time, reconciliation also appears as the most slippery concept of all: the term is now employed in the most diverse of circumstances and by a plethora of actors, but its precise meaning and significance, as well as the criteria for its evaluation in the practice, are at best elusive.

The next paragraphs will therefore attempt to define this concept, by considering several definitions and classifications found in literature, from which the complexity and heterogeneity of the term emerge. Following, some of the key factors and mechanisms will be considered, which are identified as instrumental in pursuing reconciliation among former enemies, while also outlining some of the obstacles and potential flipsides related to this complex process, as well as to its establishment as a central theme of post-conflict initiatives.

From Madness to Hope (De la Locura a La Esperanza) is the title of the report published by the Salvadoran Truth Commission. Available at http://www.derechos.org/nizkor/salvador/informes/truth.html

G. Girelli, *Understanding Transitional Justice*,
Philosophy, Public Policy, and Transnational Law,
DOI 10.1007/978-3-319-53606-4_4

A Process of Domesticating Tensions, Towards an Ambitious Objective

The concept of reconciliation is a highly recurrent one, in the post-conflict literature as well as in the practice, as it has rapidly emerged as a quintessential and inalienable objective of any well-rounded and effective transitional project – and one which strongly appeals to donors.[2] One of the reasons why this notion is so central in the discussion is its implying a transformative effort concerning relationships, perceptions, interpretations of the past, in a moment – the transitional one – which is the transformative moment par excellence.[3] However, as acknowledged by many among those who engaged with this subject,[4] a clear definition of the term is missing; or rather, in the words of James Gibson, "the problem with the concept may be that it has too many meanings, not too few".[5] Indeed, reconciliation is a bit like love (although Harvey Weinstein has actually compared it to pornography, in that "we know it when we see it")[6]: universally praised as a rare and precious award and a panacea for many ills, many strive towards it, with a feeling – a sense – of what it looks and feels like, but unable to precisely and conclusively define it. And indeed, the literature and the practice offer several definitions and classifications of this concept, which reveal its numerous different profiles. The following paragraphs will focus on some among these many distinctions and qualifications, outlining the different spatial and temporal levels, all intertwined, in which reconciliation – whatever this is – is expected to happen, hoping to provide some clarification and guidance in approaching this multifaceted concept.

One of the most recurring distinctions is the one between individual or personal reconciliation on one side, and societal or political reconciliation on the other. The former is defined as the "pacification" between individuals – most likely a victim (or his family) and a perpetrator,[7] but also family members, acquaintances, neighbours who stood on different political or ethnical sides[8]: individual reconciliation is therefore understood as a deeply intimate process,[9] a personal effort which necessarily requires interaction between formally estranged and opposed subjects, a coming into contact of sorts[10]; as a consequence, it is debated whether the state, and official mechanisms more in general, can and should promote it as an objective of the transitional project – with the risk of forcing an extremely delicate process – or whether the choice of if, when and how it will take place should be entirely left to the individuals, whose prejudices and suffering might however impede it indefinitely. Also, notably, this interpersonal level is the one in which the concept of reconciliation, together with its corollary vocabulary (among which the concepts of pain, trauma and healing) were firstly developed and employed,[11] and from which they were then borrowed, and applied to the relations between very different subjects – meaning communities, social groups and societies. Reconciliation is therefore one of the least legalistic terms employed in post-conflict scenarios, and this might help explaining, in a field dominated by legal narratives and professionals, its appeal and at the same time its enduring indeterminateness. On the other side, societal or political reconciliation[12] consists in a rapprochement, a renewed understanding among social groups – especially in societies traditionally divided along ethnic lines; it has also been defined as "accepting the rules of the democratic game",[13] through a mutual agreement to coexist and cooperate towards the (re)construction of a country where former enemies can fruitfully and safely debate and compromise on their ideological and institutional perspectives.[14] Societal reconciliation can therefore also be appreciated, paraphrasing Johan Galtung, as constructive (rather than destructive) redirection and management of the conflict inherent to society.[15] While these two dimensions of reconciliation often coexist and influence each other, they also typically follow different dynamics and unfold at different paces; in particular, several authors stress how interpersonal reconciliation, which is typically more ideologically and emotionally charged, and thus harder to pursue for the individual, should not be situated as a necessary and unavoidable element towards political reconciliation, which on its part is crucial in fostering stability and development.[16]

A similar distinction is also made between reconciliation at the local or micro level[17] – where the difference between personal and political is more blurred – and reconciliation at the macro level, as (re-)construction of harmony between enemy groups, between the society and the state, or even between nations,[18] necessarily requiring an element of publicity (such as public apologies or gestures of forgiveness).[19] This is not to be confused with the differentiation between reconciliation from the top-down and from the bottom-up, which rather depends on the mechanisms employed in order to pursue this objective: the former refers to national, state-driven reconciliation processes at any level (among which, but not limited to, truth commissions and constitutional reform), while the latter points to instruments, such as informal mechanisms and grassroots initiatives, instituted at the local level.[20] Notably, different mechanisms often coexist and complement each other, and both dimensions present positive peculiarities as well as limitations, which mirror those of formal and informal mechanisms more in general.[21] For example, national initiatives ideally have a wider reach and are better-suited to promote a harmonious and coherent narrative state-wide, but at the same time require a level of resources and state authority which is often absent in post-conflict scenarios; on the contrary, community-level mechanisms are more flexible, more malleable and require less resources, but also risk adopting an excessively limited focus, as well as marginalising precisely those subjects who have suffered and endured the most during the conflict, thus reinforcing unequal dynamics.[22]

Furthermore, reconciliation is also increasingly praised as both an objective and a long-term process[23] (a journey, as the TRC report defines it)[24]: it is both the reparation and reconfiguration of broken or still-born relationships and bonds of trust, and the process towards it.[25] At a closer (and more realistic) look, this second dimension of reconciliation as a process appears to actually be its dominant one. Indeed, in practice reconciliation appears as something that is always pursued but never definitely achieved, while the very term *reconciliation* implies a dynamism, a movement[26]; moreover, it is precisely through the constant process of being resisted, contested and defended that reconciliation is fostered. Reconciliation thus appears to be primarily a struggle – towards compromise, to make sense of apparently irreconcilable goals and narratives, towards managing and constructively incorporating tensions,[27] while its dimension as an end-goal results in being more idealistic, almost utopic, and according to some even potentially detrimental, as it risks creating unrealistic expectations in an already fragile environment.[28]

This dimension of reconciliation as a process also emerges from other typical classifications. For example, although a distinction is commonplace between thin (mere tolerance and coexistence) and thick (cooperation, sharing of values and social vision, mercy) reconciliation,[29] the two are best understood as phases of the same project, in an ideal movement from a more modest to a more ambitious cooperation. The same applies to the concept of coexistence, which is increasingly employed as a synonym to reconciliation for its being apparently more neutral and less value-charged.[30] However, rather than a synonym, this also can be best comprehended as a phase of a relationship-building process – which depending on the specific society which has embarked on it can either be a very initial or a very ambitious one.[31]

Finally, reconciliation is appreciated as both backward- and forward-looking,[32] as it entails both discussing about the past and committing to a peaceful and democratic future. This second dimension is particularly relevant in those societies where inequalities and prejudices are long-standing and deeply rooted, as in these cases transitional projects cannot strive towards re-establishing a past harmony (that has in fact never existed) but rather will primarily concentrate on building new and more equitable relationships.[33]

This brief overview of some of the main discourses and elaborations on the theme reveals the multifaceted character of reconciliation. For example, as seen, this notion carries a strong psychological dimension, as the reconciliatory process attempts to reconcile an angry heart – looking for vengeance and retribution – with what the mind knows to be necessary, meaning coexistence and peace. However, both at the interpersonal and at the societal level, reconciliation also has religious and cultural underpinnings. Concerning the former, authors such as Isabel Furtado de Mendonça have retraced the role and significance of reconciliation in the Christian tradition, where it stands in a close relation with the concept of forgiveness, although neither as precondition nor as consequence, but rather as the clarifying process thanks to which forgiveness happens.[34] Also, in this context reconciliation is understood not as an obligation, a compulsory behaviour, but rather as an ability – a quality – of the believer, inspired and supported by God's love.[35] Conceived in such a way, the rhetoric of reconciliation can be empowering of the victims, who by accepting to engage and reconcile with their oppressor consciously abandon past dynamics of vengeance and retribution and choose to play an active role within the newly reformed society.[36] These religious overtones, that enrich the transitional discourse with notions of penance, purification, restoration of the relationship with God and with the community, have however been criticised as attempting to the ideally neutral (as non-religious) character of post-conflict initiatives, especially in contexts in which religion – or religious authorities and identities – played a role in furthering the conflict or marginalising sectors of the society. However, they should not be rejected everywhere and a priori; rather, the determination of the exact meaning and reach of reconciliation should be left to those directly involved in the transitional process, most notably to the victims, whose religious beliefs will inevitably play a role in their understanding of harmony and of one's place in society.[37] For example, religion had an important influence on the transitional dynamics of countries such as South Africa (where Archbishop Tutu established reconciliation and forgiveness as leitmotifs of the transitional project, widely resonating with the numerous Christian community in the country)[38] and Argentina, where the concept's religious undertones were employed in order to convey reconciliation to ordinary citizens, as a politically relevant term.

With regard to the cultural dimension of the concept, as also illustrated in the following chapters[39] local traditions and understandings have a fundamental impact on the personal and social approach towards transitions in general, and towards reconciliation and forgiveness in particular, which are therefore valued differently in different contexts. Just as a way of example, restoring harmony within the social group is often regarded as crucial in many holistic cultures, in which the interests and needs of the community tend to prevail over those of the individuals, who could thus be more inclined to abandon – or suppress – desires of vengeance and retribution for the benefit of the community.[40] Additionally, the quest for reconciliation can provide this struggle for reconstruction and coexistence with a much needed moral authority and justification[41]: once again, this was probably represented best in the context of South Africa, where "the Christian connotations of reconciliation worked to extend its meaning *beyond* the idea of pragmatic settlement or agreement, with the effect of representing human actions 'as higher that they actually are', of elevating human conduct and experience".[42]

In conclusion, these many distinctions, stratifications and classifications point to two fundamental characteristics of reconciliation. Firstly, this notion is as appealing as it is obscure, to the point that its dissection leaves us back to the starting point, with no clearer idea of what this term means and entails. A useful working definition, however, could be Susan Dwyer's, who proposes to

> Think of human reconciliation quite generally in terms of *tensions* – tensions between two or more beliefs; tensions between two or more differing interpretations of events; tensions between two or more apparently incommensurable sets of values – and our responses to them.[43]

Indeed, this approach to reconciliation as a struggle towards coherence and incorporation of tensions into one (individual, group, or society)'s life narrative has the merit of accommodating the aforementioned different dimensions on the concept (its being a process as well as an end, its unfolding at the personal and political level and so on) while being sufficiently abstract to adequately describe different local and individual understandings and instruments.

Secondly, the inevitably contextual nature of reconciliation emerges, its being inextricably intertwined with moral determinations as well as personal and social attitudes. Indeed, one's approach towards reconciliation is strongly dependent on "a religious understanding of the world and humanity's place in it",[44] or at least on cultural understandings of desirable societal organisation. As a consequence, rather than concentrating on finding one, conclusive definition, it should be left to the local constituencies of each transitional scenario to define not only whether this objective is desirable, but also how it should be pursued, and what it entails: reconciliation, as a necessarily voluntary commitment, cannot be imposed.

Truth, Justice, and a Spoonful of Patience: Factors Contributing to Reconciliation

The factors identified by several actors as contributing to reconciliation are at least as many and diverse as its definitions and descriptions, and while some of them are largely agreed-upon, others meet more resistance and are more vehemently debated. As aforementioned, reconciliation (on any level) necessarily requires mutual acknowledgement of and interaction with "the other", who needs to be identified, known and engaged with.[45] As a consequence, one of the most crucial factors – and an only seemingly obvious one – is the substantial involvement of the intended beneficiaries in all the phases of the process, from the definition of reconciliation and the required mechanisms, to their implementation.[46] Additionally, reconciliation inevitably entails a process of questioning and renegotiating one (individual, group or nation)'s identity, that entails "engaging former enemies in redefining the antagonistic identities and belief systems that motivated past violence and (re)creating a more positive system of relations governing their interactions".[47] This process of renegotiation also implies calling into questions prejudices and preconceptions about oneself and the other, about social order and fundamental values,[48] as well as a reconsideration of one's narrative concerning the historical and moral world, and not only with regard to the conflict, but also concerning the past (e.g., the events which contributed to the formation of one's identity)[49] and the future (especially in terms of objectives and goals).[50] This often reveals particularly difficult, because conflicts – especially when fought along ethnic lines – tend to provoke an exacerbation, a fixation of individual and social identities, which as a result are more rigid and more fiercely defended; additionally, in the aftermath of a conflict one's sense of victimhood tends to become an integral, and often a primary, part of one's identity, which might be felt as threatened by a process of engagement with the (former) enemy.

These complex and demanding processes are referred to by Professor Arie Nadler and Nurit Shnabel as "instrumental" and "socio-emotional" reconciliation.[51] The former comprises all those initiatives whose purpose is to engage former enemies in interactions and discussions, with the final purpose of fostering processes of identity renegotiation and creation of an inclusive society, while the latter refers to "interventions designed to confront directly the emotional and perceptual legacies of past conflict by way of breaking down obstacles to reconciliation caused by existing feelings of victimization, guilt, distrust and fear between groups".[52] A fundamental step in this regard is providing accountability which, as analysed more in-depth further on, has the potential to acknowledge the victims' pain, reconstruct an official version of the events, and demonstrate the commitment of the government to a new, more democratic and respectful state. Also fundamental is security: as seen reconciliation processes require engagement, discussion and disagreement, coexistence between formerly opposed or estranged subjects, which – in turn – cannot occur outside a safe space, where the different parties can reasonably expect not to be in peril and have at least a minimum level of trust in each other, as well as in the overseeing institutions.[53]

As introduced, several instruments and objectives typical of post-conflict processes are identified as instrumental towards reconciliation. Firstly, reconciliation should be posited upon a comprehensive and effective justice process.[54] More specifically, authors such as Coleen Murphy envisage a role of criminal trials – especially when international in nature – in contributing to political reconciliation, by "fostering the social conditions required for law's efficacy"[55]: while in less recent times prosecutions were largely perceived as detrimental to peace and stability,[56] in Murphy's (and others') opinion post-conflict tribunals can in fact provide an alternative to the unlawful practices adopted in the past, and a different model regarding how to conduct fair criminal proceedings[57]; additionally, they are instrumental in the training of a new generation of domestic lawmakers and judges, and help restoring the faith of citizens in the law and its agents, as instruments of justice rather than discrimination, violence and oppression. Finally, trials also ideally promote reconciliation by individualising responsibility, which helps in destigmatising groups and correcting prejudices towards their members.[58]

Notwithstanding, as the practical examples in the following chapters will show, the relationship between trials and reconciliation is strongly debated and not conclusively assessed, and many stress the destabilising and inflammatory potential of criminal proceedings, especially when these are not part of a broader and nuanced set of measures.[59] Moreover, justice cannot be equated merely with criminal punishment, as one of the key reasons for incorporating reconciliation in transitional processes is precisely to cultivate an idea of justice that goes beyond mere retribution and deterrence; a justice which is participated and participatory, as well as definitional of a shared and inclusive society.[60] As a consequence, a justice process which commits to individual and societal reconciliation cannot shy away from addressing socio-economical inequalities and basic, fundamental needs, for at least two reasons.[61] On one side, in post-conflict scenarios a large portion of the population has urgent material necessities that, if ignored, obstacle their involvement in processes of justice and rebuilding; on the other side, a substantial and honest reconciliation cannot be pursued between subjects which are in a situation characterised by structural asymmetries of power[62]; therefore, systemic inequalities and discrimination – which are increasingly acknowledged as the very root causes of several contemporary conflicts – have to be redressed; in turn, this also requires intervening on those state structures and institutions which foster marginalisation and exclusion, reshaping them in such a way to make them instrumental to preventing – rather than fomenting – abuses and conflict, promote the respect of human rights and ensure to everybody guarantees for development.[63] As a way of example, Rosemary Nagy includes – with reference to the context of Canada – decolonisation and consequent redistribution of land among the necessary steps towards reconciliation,[64] as only by remedying the quality-of-life gap between former oppressed and oppressor and acknowledging the structural system of violence it is possible to move beyond the past and lay the foundations for a harmonic, inclusive state. Incidentally, although it would deserve a more in-depth consideration, which regrettably exceeds the space of this chapter, it is here also worth to mention Galtung's "triad": the sociologist understood the three problems of reconstructing, reconciling the conflict parties, and resolving root conflicts as inextricably linked, insomuch that achieving one is only possible through a comprehensive project which also promotes the other two, while failing one means failing all of them.[65]

A strong importance is also accorded to the truth-recovery process,[66] and in particular to officially establishing and acknowledging an agreed-upon version of the traumatic events[67]; indeed, it is virtually impossible to reconcile with someone without knowing who that person is, and what he is responsible for.[68] Importantly, reconciliation does not require the whole society to adhere to a single version of the events, but it rather presumes an acceptance of mutually compatible ("reconciled") versions, or at the very least a recognition of one's partial understanding of the facts.[69] This in turn allows for the reconstruction of key facts, and at the same time the acknowledgement and incorporation into a larger narrative of the multiple perspectives, emotions, interpretations that different subjects attach to them. A truth-finding process is also fundamental in that it fosters the adoption of a renewed perspective on the often essentialised experience of others: reconciliation can therefore be understood as finding oneself in the narrative of pain, suffering and loss of the other, in this way recognised not exclusively as an enemy, but as a survivor and a human being. [70] Additionally, truth-telling is often a prerequisite for other practical initiatives, such as reparations, which in turn can promote reconciliation by providing official acknowledgement,[71] promoting confidence and trust in the new state,[72] and empowering – both symbolically and materially – the victims.[73]

Truth-finding and acknowledgement in turn need to be supported by efforts focused on memorialisation and education, fundamental in preventing attempts of denial and manipulation of the past – which can foster new conflicts or detract attention from the most profound causes of the atrocities. Additionally, this kind of initiatives can help in shaping a constructive and unifying understanding of the country's history and values, thus fostering the development of a more inclusive collective memory,[74] while also teaching respect for human rights and the rule of law. Also, by preserving the memory of the past abuses, glimpsing the early warnings of new conflicts, and thus preventing them, becomes easier.[75]

Finally, a fundamental factor is time. Reconciliation is a long-term struggle that requires commitment to the new institutions and restoration of a trust that has been disrupted by tragic events, or which never really existed in the first place, and which also entails difficult and painful psychological processes of pacifying rationality with emotions: rushing it can prove counterproductive or even damaging.[76]

Contested Factors: The Role of Apologies and Forgiveness

Apologies and forgiveness are amongst the most strongly debated concepts in their relation to reconciliation: while some authors praise them as essential in leading towards it, others warn against an excessive reliance on these concepts, because of their intrinsic limitations or because of their being excessively ideologically charged. For what concerns apologies, in extreme synthesis (and with a level of simplification), these are sometimes resisted as "the easy way out", a hypocritical collection of empty words spent with the final objective of avoiding more meaningful and substantial initiatives,[77] while other times lauded as an important ritual: apologies can have a strong cathartic effect on both perpetrators and victims, hence fostering the (re-)approachment between former enemies, by providing acknowledgement and demonstrating a real commitment to change.[78] The impact of official apologies on reconciliation is thus far from being conclusively assessed, and many are the debates not only on their desirability, but also on issues such as the "amount" of contrition or resentment necessary to make a satisfactory apology, dissecting these measures sometimes to the excess. Nevertheless, what clearly emerges from many of these studies and debates is – once again – the crucial weight of the specific circumstances and the local culture, as well as of the larger transitional scheme; in particular, in order to play a potentially beneficial role, apologies need to be part and complement of – rather than substitute for – a comprehensive post-conflict project.[79] Also, while potentially effective in promoting societal reconciliation, official apologies appear to play a more limited role in influencing interpersonal relations.[80]

With regard to forgiveness, this concept has become recurrent in the transitional justice discourse, and it has been established by several instruments as a general goal of their activities.[81] Nevertheless, several authors question its use and utility in post-conflict scenarios, as well as its relation with reconciliation,[82] with much of the debate revolving around the morally charged character of this notion, which many perceive – also because of its paradigmatic employment in the context of South Africa – as excessively tied to religious beliefs. Indeed, although there is no final and univocal definition of the term, and its understanding partially changes depending on the specific context and culture, forgiveness implies an act of clemency, of pardon by the part of the victim towards its oppressor; accordingly, in most understandings of the notion the dimension of mutuality, of necessary engagement between the parties which characterises reconciliation is in this case absent. In other words, while the concept of reconciliation implies a commitment of both parts, a shared willingness to move towards each other in order to reach a common ground, forgiveness appears more as a one-way exercise, a burden – or an entitlement – exclusive of the victims; this might reveal problematic, especially in those situations in which the perpetrator asks for it, thus potentially catching the victim between two burdensome options: unwillingly forgive, in this way suppress ing feelings of anger, pain and resentment – or refuse, at the risk of being labelled as rancorous and obstructing the peace process.[83]

Indeed, one of the main issues with forgiveness concerns precisely the burden that this objective potentially places on the victims, who may also feel compelled to respond to moral and religious imperatives officialised by the transitional project without being ready to do so, and who often fear expressions of forgiveness will lead to impunity. This was one of the key criticisms moved to the transitional project in South Africa, charismatically guided by Archbishop Tutu, who capitalised upon the concept of forgiveness as borrowed from the Christian tradition (and thus strongly charged ideologically), presenting it as a constitutive phase in the process of reconciliation as reconstruction of a primordial and temporarily lost harmony between social groups.[84] This causal link between interpersonal forgiveness and social reconciliation placed a heavy burden on victims, many of whom were practising Christians, while its supposed spontaneity and voluntariness were corrupted by the interference of the amnesty process.[85] As a consequence, in the final stages its centrality in the transitional process was in part downplayed.[86]

However, this understanding of forgiveness as a sword of Damocles pending on victims' heads is not universally shared. For example, Ari Kohen advocates for a non-religious approach to the latter as the final empowering act for the victims, who by choosing to forgive refuse to be defined by the wrongs committed against them and reaffirm their control, their active place in society[87]; according to this perspective, therefore, forgiveness is – or at least can be – a definitional and narrative effort, whose effect is to empower who undergoes it.

Additionally, the very issue of the relationship between forgiveness, reconciliation and apologies is debated. For example, while some believe that forgiveness is only possible after the perpetrator acknowledges and takes responsibility for his actions, or at least after the two parties enter some kind of interaction,[88] others consider forgiveness as "belonging" exclusively and entirely to the victims, who can grant it if and how they feel and believe appropriate, irrespective and sometimes in spite of the actions of the wish-to-be forgiven. Similarly, while some authors link causally forgiveness and reconciliation, for others these should be maintained separate and independent, even though in many circumstances they happen to be addressed together.[89]

In conclusion, although widely debated the very significance of the term – in its meaning and instrumentality – is partially indeterminate, as strongly dependent on cultural and religious beliefs. As a consequence, it cannot be others but the victims who decide what forgiveness is, what it entails, and whether it is worth and right to grant it. At the same time – unlike reconciliation, which can also be understood as a collective exercise of coexistence and mutual acknowledgement, forgiveness appears to require a strictly personal and intimate process; as such, it should be approached and envisaged as a possibility, an entitlement of the victim,[90] but not as a general objective of the transitional process, or a necessary and inevitable step towards social peace, stability and reconciliation. Indeed,

> If we can detach forgiveness from reconciliation, we can begin to define a much more realistic process of reconciliation that does not depend on peace and love, or on forgiving: immediately, we remove some of victims' most serious objections to it. But we also move towards a more pragmatic description of reconciliation as rebuilding the minimal working relations [...] that will permit a divided society to take the first steps towards a shared sustainable future.[91]

Unrealistic Pursuit of Peace and Tranquillity?

In spite of the centrality reconciliation has gained in the transitional justice discourse and practice, the concept is also met with criticism and resistance, either in itself or in its uncritical implementation in fragile and divided contexts such as post-conflict ones.

One of the main issues concerns the possibility of ever achieving a substantial and meaningful reconciliation in deeply divided societies (such as Northern Ireland), where the understandings of truth and the individual and social identities of the different parties are so conflicting to appear just irreconcilable.[92] As a consequence, embarking on such a pursuit would risk not only revealing ineffectual, but also antagonising society against the transitional process as a whole. Similarly, several authors stress how in many post-conflict contexts there has just never been a situation of harmony that can be restored, as sometimes opposing groups never had meaningful interactions or relations[93]: in these cases, emphasis should be placed not on reconciling but on "conciling", on creating ex novo a peaceful society.[94] This points to a more general limitation of the concept per se; indeed, "reconciliation is a story told in a single word. It tells a tale of prior harmony, a rupture (a wrong perpetrated), and a subsequent reunion".[95] As such, the concept has a strong cathartic potential, which rests on its ability to narrate a peaceful past while at the same time depicting it as a utopic end-goal, by implying the idea of a return to it. However, the problem is that this harmonious past often just never was, and going back is precisely the contrary of what is needed – that might be a rupture of vicious cycles, a contestation, a revolution of long-standing patterns and dynamics between genders, classes, authorities.[96] As a consequence, if promoted uncritically the concepts of *re*conciling and *re*building risk promoting a further entrenchment, rather than the overcoming, of some of the most profound causes of conflicts and abuses.[97]

A different but related concern is expressed by James Gibson who, although being a strong advocate of reconciliation initiatives and restorative justice processes, admits that efforts towards reconciliation can have a harmful effect on the democratisation process, when the rhetoric of unification and harmonisation results in an excessive pressure towards consensus and standardisation, which suffocate contrasts and disagreements that, on the contrary, constitute the core of a healthy democracy.[98] In other words, the risk is that talks of reconciliation support an essentialising rhetoric which denies and impedes plurality, that imposes one and only path, one and only narrative with regards to the past, the present and the future,[99] and which in elevating peace and tranquillity above justice closes off spaces for debate.[100] Reconciliation should not be advanced with the aim of quashing critical voices, of fostering a forced pacification process: reconciliation cannot be the instrument through which revolutionary voices are silenced. For analogous reasons, the election of reconciliation as a central transitional theme is sometimes criticised for its potential to work as a smokescreen concealing the inability or unwillingness of the state to adopt more substantial initiatives, or as a substitute to, rather than a complement of, a comprehensive post-conflict process. For example, in the post-dictatorship Argentina victims and survivors largely resisted talks of reconciliation, which according to them were exploited in order to avoid providing accountability and criminal justice (and they were in turn harshly criticised as "spoilers" of peace): by being pushed to reconcile, victims and their families felt obliged to engage with an enemy who was asked to do nothing and managed to escape accountability, while their suffering was being once again denied.[101] This reveals one of the key problems with reconciliation as a buzzword,[102] as a steady and central element of the one-size-fits-all transitional project, and on the contrary how essential it is to entrust the victims with defining the notion and deciding whether or not to pursue it.[103] Indeed, as aforementioned, an excessive pressure towards reconciliation can make the victims feel compelled to create or re-establish a painful relationship; this in turn might lead to a suppression of painful memories, as well as of feelings of anger and resentment,[104] which are normal and whose repression can reveal to be extremely harmful in the long term, both at a psychological and at a social level.[105]

Finally, the temptation should be resisted not only of imposing reconciliation too early or too vigorously, but also of expecting too much from such a process. Indeed, placing an excessive emphasis on reconciliatory efforts can create unreasonable expectations, towards a goal that requires time and commitment, and which often cannot be achieved in a particular society, as well as towards mechanisms, such as the transitional ones, that are limited in scope, time and resources. For example, several authors were sceptical about the inclusion of the term "reconciliation" in the name of the South African Commission, as it led to a strong expectation among the population (and the international community) that a single organ, with many limitations, could in a short period address and solve the many, deep-rooted problems that both led to and were created by the Apartheid regime. The commission itself was aware of this risk,[106] insomuch that it soon started to recalibrate its approach towards reconciliation, by referring to it as something not to be achieved, but rather to be promoted, by laying the foundation on which, with time and commitment, the population could build a harmonious society, without the risk of new repression and violence.[107]

In sum, when incorporating reconciliation in the transitional discourse it is fundamental to grant victims the flexibility to define it, and if necessary to refuse it: sometimes, reconciliation is just not feasible. At the same time, it is important to ensure that the promotion of reconciliation in post-conflict contexts is not just a play of smoke and mirrors, but rather one of many elements of a comprehensive programme.

Conclusions

The theme of reconciliation is complex and forcefully discussed, and one at the intersection of several fields, from law to psychology and sociology; therefore, the previous paragraphs are to be approached as an introduction to some key arguments and debates on the notion, rather than as a comprehensive analysis.

As outlined, one of the core issues with regard to reconciliation lies in its being perceived as much as fundamental as it is indeterminate. Indeed, reconciliation appears as an essential and inevitable component of transitional processes: it fosters peace and stability, which are instinctively preferable to violence and turmoil,[108] especially in post-conflict scenarios in which overburdened and underfunded authorities have to confront a multitude of problems and emergencies; it works as a bridge between the past and the future, capitalising upon a painful history in order to prevent its repetition[109]; it provides the whole process with an incisive moral narrative; and, ideally, it can be highly empowering of the victims who choose to participate in this project. However, at the same time, reconciliation is never completely and conclusively defined, and this can generate tensions between competing understandings, unduly pressure on the victims, as well as difficulties in designing programmes and evaluating their efficacy. Some help comes from authors such as Susan Dwyer, who highlights how the term does not only refer to a renewed relationship among people, but more in general to a process of reconciling tensions – among individuals and groups, among different conceptions of state and society, among contrasting narratives of the past events.[110] A fundamental step towards reconciliation – however defined – therefore consists in harmonising "incommensurable world views so the inevitable and continuing conflicts and differences stand at least within a single universe of comprehensibility".[111] This does not require that tensions are eliminated, as conflict is an irrevocable part of a mature democracy, but rather that they are constructively managed, their energy redirected towards peace and development.

Additionally, at a closer look, indeterminacy – for how frustrating to the legal mind – is not necessarily negative[112]; on the contrary, it could be the key to crafting a transitional project which is respectful and responsive of the local culture and needs. In other words, rather than being corrected or suppressed, this flexibility in understanding should be capitalised upon in order to ensure that reconciliation is of the kind and degree that the local population wants and needs at any particular stage of the post-conflict process. Therefore, while the international community can participate by sharing best practices and lessons learned,[113] reconciliation should be defined, pursued and then assessed primarily from the bottom up. From this also follows that reconciliation should not be imposed as obligatory, especially at the individual level, and that it should be – at least initially – envisaged as one of many elements of a broad and comprehensive set of measures,[114] rather than the cornerstone on which the whole transitional process rests, and one from which individual victims should be able to opt out.[115] Indeed, such a process cannot but entail conflict, strife, discussion, facing one's fear and willingness to reach compromises; as a consequence, it needs to be open and inclusive, especially of the victims and of traditionally marginalised constituencies, which are more likely to advance a progressive understanding of reconciliation as structural reconfiguration of relationships, rather than a "reactionary" one as merely going back to a past harmony, which in many cases never really was.[116]

Notes

1. Ari Kohen, "The Personal and the Political: Forgiveness and Reconciliation in Restorative Justice", *Critical Review of International Social and Political Philosophy* 12(3) (2009): 399
2. David Bloomfield, *On Good Terms: Clarifying Reconciliation* (Berlin: Berghof Research Center for Constructive Conflict Management, 2006): 4
3. Nevan T. Aiken, "Learning to Live Together: Transitional Justice and Intergroup Reconciliation in Northern Ireland", *The International Journal of Transitional Justice* 4 (2010): 168
4. Bloomfield, *On Good Terms: Clarifying Reconciliation*, 4
5. James L. Gibson, "Overcoming Apartheid: can Truth Reconcile a Divided Nation?", *Politikon* 31 (2004): 132
6. Harvey M. Weinstein, "Editorial Note: The Myth of Closure, the Illusion of Reconciliation: Final Thoughts on Five Years as Co-Editor-In-Chief", *The International Journal for Transitional Justice* 5 (2011): 3
7. Elin Skaar, "Reconciliation in a Transitional Justice Perspective", *Transitional Justice Review* 1 (2012): 64
8. Gibson, "Overcoming Apartheid", 132
9. Ibid., 155
10. Kohen, "The Personal and the Political", 408

11. Bloomfield, *On Good Terms: Clarifying Reconciliation*, 10
12. Ari Kohen, Michael Zanchelli and Levi Drake, "Personal and Political Reconciliation in Post-Genocide Rwanda", *Social Justice Research* 1 (2011): 3
13. Priscilla B. Hayner, *Unspeakable Truths: Confronting State Terror and Atrocity* (New York: Routledge, 2001), 159
14. Kohen, "The Personal and the Political", 416
15. Johan Galtung, *After Violence: 3R, Reconstruction, Reconciliation, Resolution: Coping with the Invisible Effects of War and Violence* (Transcend, 1998), 3
16. Weinstein, "The Myth of Closure, the Illusion of Reconciliation", 7
17. Skaar, "Reconciliation in a Transitional Justice Perspective", 66
18. Susan Dwyer, "Reconciliation for Realists", *Ethics & International Affairs* 13(1) (1999): 83
19. Hayner, *Unspeakable Truths*, 155
20. Bloomfield, *On Good Terms: Clarifying Reconciliation*, 25
21. Andrew Rigby, "Reflections on Reconciliation", *Committee for Conflict Transformation Support Review* 29 (2005–2006): 3
22. Bloomfield, *On Good Terms: Clarifying Reconciliation*, 25
23. For an overview of the several sources see Bloomfield, *On Good Terms: Clarifying Reconciliation*, 6
24. Truth and Reconciliation Commission, *Truth and Reconciliation Commission of South Africa Report* (Cape Town: Juta and Co., 1998): Vol.1, Chapter 5, Par. 11
25. Rigby, "Reflections on Reconciliation", 2
26. Camilla Riesenfeld, *Instruments of Reconciliation?: Potentials and Risks of Reparation Measures in post-Conflict Guatemala* (Uppsala: Department of Peace and Conflict Research, Uppsala University, 2008): 8
27. Dwyer, "Reconciliation for Realists", 84
28. Bloomfield, *On Good Terms: Clarifying Reconciliation*, 6
29. Skaar, "Reconciliation in a Transitional Justice Perspective", 65
30. For more on the notion of coexistence see Bloomfield, *On Good Terms: Clarifying Reconciliation*, 13
31. Ibid., 20
32. Dwyer, "Reconciliation for Realists", 83
33. Bloomfield, *On Good Terms: Clarifying Reconciliation*, 16
34. Isabel Furtado de Mendonça, "Searching for Reconciliation in a Post Complex Political Emergency Scenario", *Naçao e Defesa* 105(2) (2003): 132
35. Furtado de Mendonça, "Searching for Reconciliation in a Post Complex Political Emergency Scenario", 132
36. Kohen, "The Personal and the Political", 401
37. Dwyer, "Reconciliation for Realists", 82

38. Kohen, "The Personal and the Political", 412
39. See infra chapters 6, 8 and 10 on the Tokyo Tribunal, the hybrid tribunals and bottom-up experiences
40. Kohen, "The Personal and the Political", 416
41. Dwyer, "Reconciliation for Realists", 82
42. Claire Moon, "Prelapsarian State: Forgiveness and Reconciliation in Transitional Justice", *International Journal for the Semiotics of Law* 17(2) (2004): 195
43. Dwyer, "Reconciliation for Realists", 82
44. Kohen, "The Personal and the Political", 410
45. Bloomfield, *On Good Terms: Clarifying Reconciliation*, 28
46. Beatrix Austin, Martina Fischer and Hans J. Giessmann, eds., *Advancing Conflict Transformation. The Berghof Handbook II* (Opladen/Framington Hills: Barbara Budrich Publishers, 2011): 421
47. Aiken, "Learning to Live Together", 169
48. Riesenfeld, *Instruments of Reconciliation?*, 13
49. Austin et al., *Advancing Conflict Transformation*, 418
50. Riesenfeld, *Instruments of Reconciliation?*, 12
51. Arie Nadler and Nurit Shnabel, "Instrumental and Socio-Emotional Paths to Intergroup Reconciliation and the Need-Based Model of Socio-Emotional Reconciliation", in Arie Nadler, Thomas Malloy and Jeffrey D. Fisher, eds., *Social Psychology of Intergroup Reconciliation* (New York: Oxford University Press, 2008), 7
52. Aiken, "Learning to Live Together", 170
53. Austin et al., *Advancing Conflict Transformation*, 417
54. Bloomfield, *On Good Terms: Clarifying Reconciliation*, 12
55. Colleen Murphy, "Political Reconciliation and International Criminal Trials", in Larry May and Zachary Hoskins, eds., *International Criminal Law and Philosophy* (Cambridge: Cambridge University Press, 2010), 225
56. Skaar, "Reconciliation in a Transitional Justice Perspective", 68
57. Murphy, "Political Reconciliation and International Criminal Trials", 238
58. Skaar, "Reconciliation in a Transitional Justice Perspective", 72
59. Ibid., 69
60. Bloomfield, *On Good Terms: Clarifying Reconciliation*, 19
61. Hayner, *Unspeakable Truths*, 164
62. Austin et al., *Advancing Conflict Transformation*, 417
63. Riesenfeld, *Instruments of Reconciliation?*, 11
64. Rosemary Nagy, "The Scope and Bound of Transitional Justice and the Canadian Truth and Reconciliation Commission", *The International Journal of Transitional Justice* 7 (2013): 60s. The theme of decolonisation as part to the transitional process is discussed more in depth infra, chapters 10 and 11

65. Galtung, *After Violence*, 7
66. Truth and Reconciliation Commission, *Truth and Reconciliation Commission of South Africa Report*, Vol.1, Chapter 1, Par. 70
67. Hayner, *Unspeakable Truths*, 163
68. Juan E. Mendez, "Accountability for Past Abuses", *Human Rights Quarterly* 19(2) (1997): 274
69. Austin et al., *Advancing Conflict Transformation*, 417
70. Bloomfeld et al., "*Reconciliation After Violent Conflict*", 21
71. Riesenfeld, *Instruments of Reconciliation?*, 21
72. Bloomfeld et al., *Reconciliation After Violent Conflict*, 20
73. Riesenfeld, *Instruments of Reconciliation?*, 16
74. Rigby, "Reflections on Reconciliation", 3
75. Bloomfeld et al.,*Reconciliation After Violent Conflict*, 30
76. Ibid., 32
77. Ibid., 31
78. Danielle Celermajer, "Mere Ritual? Displacing the Myth of Sincerity in Transitional Rituals", *The International Journal of Transitional Justice* 7 (2013): 288
79. Riesenfeld, *Instruments of Reconciliation?*, 28
80. Ibid., 36
81. Rebecca Saunders, "Questionable Associations: The Role of Forgiveness in Transitional Justice", *The International Journal of Transitional Justice* 5 (2011): 121
82. Saunders, "Questionable Associations", 123
83. Ibid., 138
84. Moon, "Prelapsarian State", 186
85. Moon, "Prelapsarian State", 191
86. Bloomfield, *On Good Terms: Clarifying Reconciliation*, 23
87. Kohen, "The Personal and the Political", 403
88. Moon, "Prelapsarian State", 188
89. Dwyer, "Reconciliation for Realists", 90
90. Moon, "Prelapsarian State", 188
91. Bloomfield, *On Good Terms: Clarifying Reconciliation*, 25
92. Erin Daly, "Truth Skepticism: An Inquiry into the Value of Truth in Times of Transition", *The International Journal of Transitional Justice* 2 (2008): 37
93. Kohen, "The Personal and the Political", 407
94. Daly, "Truth Skepticism", 37
95. Moon, "Prelapsarian State", 194
96. Ibid., 187
97. Austin et al., *Advancing Conflict Transformation*, 421
98. Gibson, "Overcoming Apartheid", 150

99. Moon, "Prelapsarian State", 195
100. Rigby, "Reflections on Reconciliation", 1
101. Hayner, *Unspeakable Truths*, 60
102. Weinstein, "The Myth of Closure, the Illusion of Reconciliation", 3
103. Ibid., 9
104. Dwyer, "Reconciliation for Realists", 82
105. Saunders, "Questionable Associations", 119
106. Truth and Reconciliation Commission, *Truth and Reconciliation Commission of South Africa Report*, Vol.1, Chapter 5, Par. 20
107. Hayner, *Unspeakable Truths*, 156
108. Riesenfeld, *Instruments of Reconciliation?*, 11
109. Bloomfeld et al., *Reconciliation After Violent Conflict,* 19
110. Dwyer, "Reconciliation for Realists", 87
111. Hayner, *Unspeakable Truths*, 162
112. Bloomfield, *On Good Terms: Clarifying Reconciliation*, 5
113. Weinstein, "The Myth of Closure, the Illusion of Reconciliation", 8
114. Skaar, "Reconciliation in a Transitional Justice Perspective", 95
115. Truth and Reconciliation Commission, *Truth and Reconciliation Commission of South Africa Report*, Vol.1, Chapter 5, Par. 48
116. Kora Andrieu, "Civilizing Peacebuilding: Transitional Justice, Civil Society and the Liberal Paradigm", *Security Dialogue* 41 (2010): 547

CHAPTER 5

Amnesties: Juggling Tensions within the Transitional Justice Discourse

Introduction

The issue of amnesties is extremely complex and at the same time fascinating, as it stands at the crossroads between some of the main recurrent themes of the transitional justice discourse, such as reconciliation, retribution, memory and truth. In particular, amnesties are often approached as the embodiment of the peace-versus-justice (perceived) dichotomy, as – according to several voices – through the concession of an amnesty the state trades and renounces the latter, in hope to achieve the former.[1] Also, these instruments represent an umpteenth expression of the contrast between a typically Western approach to justice, individualistic and legalistic, and as such prioritising retribution and punishment, and a non-Western, holistic perspective, which focuses on restoration of peace and social order, hence being more prone to incorporate measures (such as, indeed, amnesties) which may leave individual needs unsatisfied, but carry a potential to foster the reparation of broken relationships. Furthermore, this phenomenon is extremely differentiated in its practical expressions, and the term "amnesty" is widely, and sometimes inaccurately, employed to refer to mechanisms which share somehow similar legal effects, but have different (and not rarely antipodal) origins and justifications, characteristics, as well as outcomes.

For these reasons, in addressing the theme of amnesties many of the tensions underlying the transitional justice debate are brought to the

G. Girelli, *Understanding Transitional Justice*,
Philosophy, Public Policy, and Transnational Law,
DOI 10.1007/978-3-319-53606-4_5

forefront, proving how the several objectives this discipline is called to accomplish (as well as the subjects involved) are often in contrast with each other, and that difficult and painful choices between "irreconcilable goals"[2] are inevitable.

In order to address this topic, both in its theoretical dimension and in its practical manifestations, the following paragraphs will provide a working definition of the mechanism, while also briefly reconstructing its evolution throughout the centuries, as well as its typical legal effects. Further on, the main advantages and disadvantages will be outlined, typically attached to the adoption of these instruments in the aftermath of conflicts and grave violations of rights; in this context, particular attention will be reserved to the issue of the compatibility of amnesties with international law. The phenomenon will then be considered in the practice, by differentiating between different kinds of amnesties and focusing on the Argentinian and the South African experiences, as examples of how diverse the design and implementation of this instrument can be, depending on the peculiarities of each scenario. The discussion will lead to the conclusion that by adopting a broader, restorative understanding of justice the "peace-versus-justice" dichotomy loses its criticality and can thus be overcome: the two objectives can be reconciled and achieved – or at least pursued – together, and amnesties can work as precious allies.

Ancient Measures, Modern Conflicts, within a New International Order

The term "amnesty" derives from the Greek word *amnestia,* which means oblivion, or forgetfulness.[3] Thus, this expression efficiently conveys how these instruments were originally understood as means for burying the past for the sake of the future, for forgetting and forgiving.[4]

Amnesties have been widely employed throughout the centuries in virtually every corner of the globe[5]: by Greeks and Romans,[6] especially towards traitors or war enemies, often as part of religious celebrations[7]; but also by Chinese emperors, as envisaged by their "Mandate of Heaven",[8] and in France, during the restoration of monarchy.[9] In these contexts, they had both symbolical and pragmatic undertones, in that they were employed not only with the aim of restoring social and political peace – by promoting a "fresh start with former enemies",[10] but also, at the same time, as a way to show the strength and the mercy of the state.[11] Authors such as Robert Parker emphasise how the virtues of mercy and forgiveness are lauded and promoted by the main religious traditions around the world,[12] thus also informing attitudes of governors and kings, who often resorted to amnesties with the final purpose of asserting and manifesting the reach of their powers, precisely by self-restraining them.

Amnesties – in their broadest understanding – are still widely employed today, and cover the most disparate offences, from mass murder to tax evasion[13]; however, because of the topic of this book, the following paragraphs will primarily focus on amnesties adopted in transitional scenarios, typically covering crimes and violations of fundamental rights committed during a non-international armed conflict. Interestingly, the general approach to amnesties in post-conflict phases has undergone an evolution, and nowadays these mechanisms are increasingly discussed not as political instruments, but rather also (and primarily) as legal ones.[14] This is due to several factors.

Firstly, the evolution, and expansion in reach, of international criminal law, human rights and humanitarian law has encouraged – while at the same time manifesting – a growing preoccupation of the international community with accountability, which has now arguably become one of the linchpins of the current system of international relations. In particular, it is now widely accepted that all human beings as such – in virtue of their common humanity and dignity[15] – have some inalienable rights, which must be respected in times of peace as well as in periods of conflict, and whose violation triggers both state and individual accountability.[16] As a consequence, states have progressively lost their traditional absolute power on the fate of their citizens, and individuals can now be held responsible for the commission of certain (particularly heinous) crimes, and not only by national courts, but also in international tribunals, as well as in third-countries courts, through the mechanism of universal jurisdiction.[17] In such a context, amnesties are increasingly perceived as a tool for sabotaging concerted efforts against impunity. Notably, according to some authors the recently recorded escalation in the adoption of amnesties should be interpreted as a manifestation not of a weakening, but rather of a strengthening, of this international system of justice: amnesties are increasingly needed precisely because of the extended reach of international law to individuals (such as state officials) and acts (such as acts of state) which were traditionally considered under the exclusive sovereignty of the nation-state.[18]

Secondly, in an increasingly interconnected world, in which news moves fast and transnational human rights and advocacy movements have emerged, the "truth-versus-peace-versus-justice" dilemma has acquired global resonance, and seemingly local events undergo close and widespread scrutiny.[19] In the past decades, the world has witnessed – often in live television – the abuses and atrocities committed in otherwise "peripheral" countries such as Rwanda and Cambodia; followed the quest of the Argentinian Mothers for acknowledgement and truth; grasped with the cathartic potential of truth commissions in South Africa; but also, observed and reacted to subjects such as Omar Al Bashir and Efráin Rios Montt repeatedly escaping the reach of justice. In this scenario, legal arguments are increasingly employed – alongside, and sometimes in substitution of – political and moral ones in the debate of issues such as amnesties, accountability and conflict resolution, on both sides of the fence.

Third, this aforementioned expansion of the human rights movement and of the field of transitional justice, coupled with this "legalisation" of the system of international relations, resulted in a growing expectation that states "do something" to address the legacies of conflicts and authoritarian regimes, that instruments are adopted in order to investigate and shed light on the events of the past, as well as to grant redress to the victims and to prevent the resurgence of violent confrontation.[20] Interestingly, in designing post-conflict processes, amnesties have been increasingly employed not only as tools towards impunity and forgetfulness, but also, almost paradoxically, as instruments aimed at providing accountability, often in circumstances where more traditionally punitive approaches were considered ineffective or not feasible[21]: their dual and flexible nature has emerged, as obstacles while also potential facilitators in the quest for justice.

Finally, it is worth to highlight how all these transformations are symptoms of the substantial crumbling of the Westphalian model of international relationships, resulting in a compression of the absolute powers and independence of national governments on their respective citizens and territories, in favour of the international community. This shift towards a post-Westphalian system of international relations affects the predominant approach to amnesties at its core. Indeed, because of this development, what was arguably the most typical power of the state – the power to prosecute and punish – in the past conceived as absolute and purely "internal", has now acquired an international relevance, thus being "affected" by external forces: the international community has framed and defined new crimes, established new instruments and progressively limited the admissibility of traditional immunities. As a consequence, amnesties, which used to be an exclusive and typical prerogative of the state, and one of the primary tools through which governments manifested their sovereignty, are now being held under increasingly close scrutiny at the international level, with a crescent concern for their potential to obstruct the rise of accountability as a sacred value of the global community.[22]

Defining Amnesties

As analysed in the following paragraphs, measures nowadays generically defined as "amnesties" are in fact created with different purposes, present different features and produce different outcomes.[23] As a consequence, attempting to sketch an inclusive and satisfactory definition appears to be an almost redundant exercise. One relatively unproblematic working definition of the phenomenon is offered by Mark Freeman, who describes these mechanisms as

> An extraordinary legal measure whose primary function is to remove the prospects and consequences of criminal liability for designated individuals or classes of persons in respect of designated types irrespective of whether the persons concerned have been tried for such offenses in a court of law.[24]

This definition appears to be sufficiently neutral – as free from moral connotations – and adequate to describe the different practical cases, without being too restrictive,[25] thus also conveying how ample and differentiated the category is. Some typical features emerge from this description, which most amnesties share. Firstly, being a legal measure, amnesties are aimed at producing specific legal effects. In particular, they serve to

(a) Prospectively barring criminal prosecution and, in some cases, civil actions against certain individuals or categories of individuals in respect of specified criminal conduct committed before the amnesty's adoption; or
(b) Retroactively nullifying legal liability previously established.[26]

As such, they have to be distinguished from other similar instruments, which however produce different legal consequences, such as pardons and official immunities[27] – although these terms are sometimes used interchangeably, both in the literature and in governmental and institutional documents.

Additionally, amnesties are exceptional instruments, in the sense of constituting an exception to a rule (criminal and/or civil prosecution). As such, they are often adopted as a "one-time measure", and they are mainly preoccupied with events of the past: through amnesties, a class of individuals is shielded from prosecution for specific acts which have already been committed, within a limited time-frame and/or in the context of a specific event, this also defined by the relevant amnesty law.[28] In this extra-ordinary dimension, amnesties thus maintain their traditional character as manifestations of the very core of the state's sovereignty, of instruments through which the state reaffirms its power on its citizens; power that is however simultaneously challenged and limited by the current international order.

Amnesties are therefore sites of tensions, the result of difficult and unpleasant choices: their adoption in any post-conflict scenario manifests the contrasts between local and global, between national sensitivities and international imperatives; they embody the tensions – which always linger underneath the transitional justice discourse, but rarely emerge – not only between peace and justice, but also between justice (and truth) and survival, between yesterday's and tomorrow's victims,[29] between ideals and reality.

This inevitably problematic nature of amnesties is what makes the issue so fascinating and at the same time seemingly impossible to untangle, as manifested by the many different positions towards these instruments, outlined in the next paragraph.

One Problem, Countless Perspectives

As introduced, amnesties stand at the crossroads between several typical goals of transitional justice, thus revealing the inherent tensions among them. For this reason, they are extensively debated among scholars and practitioners, producing innumerable different approaches; notably, what strikes about the discussions around amnesties is that, depending on the perspective adopted, the same mechanism is judged as either hindering or promoting the same goals. This is also due to the variety of practical examples and their effects, which are inevitably dependent on the context, on the particular characteristics of every specific amnesty, and on whether and how they coexist with other post-conflict initiatives.

Following is a brief reconstruction of some of the key arguments in favour and against the employment of amnesties in post-conflict scenarios; the aim is neither to provide a definitive answer nor to endorse any specific position, but rather to outline – and enable to assess critically – the main recurring approaches to these measures.

Resisting Amnesties: Betrayals of Justice and Victims

Amnesties are generally resisted on several grounds; beyond the "ideological" hostility maintained by philosophers such as Cesare Beccaria or Immanuel Kant,[30] these mechanisms draw several criticisms related to their practical effects, often rooted in the fear that granting amnesties would foster a "culture of impunity, [that] can arguably erode and trivialize notions of truth and justice, allowing them to become merely rhetorical concepts that are eventually drained of all meaning".[31] According to this perspective, amnesties violate the right to justice of victims, as well as of society as a whole,[32] while also weakening the reach of and respect for national and international norms protecting fundamental human rights[33]; consequently, they would hinder the embedding, in a fragile society, of the rule of law.

The arguments against amnesties can be broadly divided into two categories: amnesties as denials of justice, and amnesties as violations of victims' rights.

With regards to the first category, amnesties are by many parts criticised as an – apparently insurmountable – obstacle to the realisation of all those objectives that states typically pursue through criminal prosecutions.[34] For example, their adoption would prevent the achievement of retribution, as they allow perpetrators to escape responsibility for their misdeeds, also violating the fundamental principle that for every crime there should be a proportionate, "just" punishment[35]; therefore, through the adoption of an amnesty, the state fails one of its primary duties, nowadays enshrined not only in national but also – for the most serious abuses – in international law,[36] meaning to ensure that offenders face justice and accountability.[37] Also, amnesties would impede the rehabilitation of the subjects who commit crimes or violate fundamental rights, and their reintegration as productive and law-abiding members of society. Additionally, by failing to hold them accountable for the consequences of abusive actions, the state would essentially sanction the commission of crimes as an effective way to achieve results.[38] For this same reason, these instruments also appear unfit to achieve special as well as general deterrence, as they send a perverse message to potential perpetrators of mass crimes, namely that if they endure long enough in their struggle, or if they manage to build a sufficiently relevant political movement, they will eventually avoid accountability for their wrongdoings.[39]

Concerning the second class of criticisms, amnesties are often decried for being a cause of amnesia: they deny the victims and their families acknowledgement of their suffering, while also preventing the unveiling of the full truth about the past, and induce a widespread forgetfulness about a painful period in the history of the country. This lack of retribution and acknowledgement violates victims' rights to justice and to effective remedies,[40] while also fostering a further victimisation: perpetrators are allowed to "walk free" and "reboot" their existences, while victims' lives have been irreparably destroyed, in the interest of a state that has for long oppressed them. Additionally, in the long term amnesties can provoke the resurgence of conflicts and violence: the wounds created by past confrontations are not properly healed, and – by choosing impunity – the post-conflict state shows its vulnerabilities and weaknesses as guardian of the post-conflict order[41]; amnesties would thus obstacle the achievement of a positive peace, understood not as mere absence of armed confrontation, but rather as fruitful coexistence between reconciled former enemies.[42]

A More Realistic and Sensitive Approach to Accountability?

Alongside these and other fierce criticisms, several voices can also be found – both in the literature and in the practice – favourable to the employment of amnesties, or at least cautioning against the temptation to discard amnesties as such, and rather calling for a more contextual evaluation of this instrument.

The main argument in favour of amnesty provisions is usually a pragmatic one. Amnesties are often perceived as a painful and undesirable choice, which is however necessary – in a specific context – in order to cease the hostilities and lay the foundation for the resolution of the conflict, and consequently to prevent further deaths.[43] Amnesties are therefore described as a necessary evil, instrumental in responding to a widespread societal desire for peace and security, which in the midst of war often prevails on the call for (uncertain and limited) criminal justice: "the lesser-evil argument is more than mere philosophy. One can measure it in real lives and in pain."[44] Such an argument in favour of amnesties as mechanisms for conflict resolution is adopted especially with regards to conflicts and abuses which have been prolonged in time, where no clear victor emerged from the confrontations, and/or when the representatives of the old regime maintain their socio-political power and influential positions (as in South Africa and Argentina).[45] In these contexts, amnesties often appear as crucial peace negotiations devices, as powerful enemies would not agree to lay down arms at the risk of criminal prosecutions,[46] and/or the number of potential responsibles for crimes is just too high, while resources are scarce: an element of compromise is thus needed, while acting too early and too firmly with generalised prosecutions could reveal to be dangerous and unproductive, while also potentially impinging on the pacification process. The intervention of the International Criminal Court with regards to Darfur[47] and Uganda are only two examples of how indictments of political leaders in sensitive phases of the conflict, although justified by a desire for justice and accountability, can in practice obstruct negotiations and influence the continuation of the conflict.[48]

Furthermore, several sources stress how criminal punishment does not constitute the only possible instrument for promoting accountability and justice. In particular, when a broader – and more context-sensitive – approach to justice is embraced (especially one that incorporates restorative elements), amnesties appear much more "acceptable" and not in contrast, but rather potentially instrumental, to the pursuit of those objectives typically attached to prosecutions, such as retribution, rehabilitation and deterrence. As aforementioned, this potential of amnesties to promote peace and justice in a transitional society is strictly dependent on their characteristics, as well as on their interplay with a broader set of measures which can complement their effects, such as truth commissions' investigations and reports, reparations, vetting, even targeted prosecutions. In other words, amnesties can reveal to be instrumental in providing retribution, while by insisting on trials as the only tool for accountability, the risk is to end up with few costly and ineffective judgments of an irrelevant number of individuals who become scapegoats, many "false innocents" living alongside their victims, and a very limited amount of truth.[49] On the contrary, by conceding amnesties (even only to a limited group of perpetrators) the available resources can be invested in non-criminal mechanisms, reparations, and social reconstruction, which have often proved more satisfying and more effective in providing redress to the victims.[50]

More specifically, as mentioned adopting an amnesty could in fact work in the interest of deterrence, especially when its concession is subordinated to specific conditions, such as non-recidivism.[51] Also to be considered with regard to this point is that the potential of (national and international) criminal law and prosecutions to deter perpetrators of mass violence and violations of fundamental rights is strongly debated, on several grounds.[52] In particular, the whole concept of deterrence is based on the presumption that the potential criminal is a rational actor, whose choice to commit a crime depends on the estimated trade-off between the benefit of the crime and the risk of being "caught" and punished for it. However, it is strongly questionable whether perpetrators of mass crimes follow this same logic: these subjects are often motivated by compelling ideological, political or religious beliefs, which are of utmost importance to them, the core of their very identity, and they are ready to face virtually any consequence for their actions, including being tortured or killed in combat; in some cases, actually, the very act of dying in martyrdom for the cause is perceived as a privilege, rather than a risk.[53] Therefore, these subjects will not be easily detracted by a mere chance of prosecution and imprisonment in a somewhat comfortable cell.[54] Additionally, because of the very limited reach of prosecutions in post-conflict scenarios, their influence on criminal behaviour is largely questioned, and very hard to prove empirically.[55]

With regard to victims' rights, amnesties have proved, in the right circumstances, as valuable leverage in the process of discovering and acknowledging the full truth with regard to past events, such as when employed as bargaining tools in exchange for disclosure and confession. In a post-conflict society, the subjects who can reveal the most information are typically perpetrators or members of the old regime, and they are much more inclined to share this knowledge if reassured that this will not lead to their criminal prosecution and punishment.[56] As analysed more in-depth in the following paragraphs, this "amnesty-for-truth" exchange stood at the core of the transitional enterprise in South Africa, where perpetrators obtained to be shielded from both criminal and civil responsibility, but only if and when fully disclosing information with regard to crimes they committed during the Apartheid-era with political purposes.[57]

More generally, the interests of the victims cannot be determined by anyone but the victims themselves. And in several scenarios, the local population has stressed their paramount need for security,[58] consequently backing approaches to justice and retribution not centred around criminal prosecutions,[59] which can also be more easily reconciled with local instruments of conflict resolution.[60]

***

In sum, amnesties go against our "societal instincts": as law, and the threat of punishment following breach of law, are perceived as the cornerstone of societal order, a conscious decision not to apply the law feels like a betrayal of the very core of the social contract.[61] However, a more context-sensitive, less ideological appreciation of amnesties reveals their potential to further, rather than hindering, peace and security,[62] as they could reveal to be necessary for the cessation of the hostilities, and in laying the basis for inclusive and effective peace negotiations, while (maybe counterintuitively) prosecutions – or the threat thereof – could be what stands in the way of conflict resolution. As such, amnesties could reveal precisely *the* instrument required in order to establish a transitional process, and thus – ideally – to further justice and respect for human rights.[63] Similarly, present the right conditions, amnesties can play a relevant role in promoting reconciliation: not only can they facilitate the acknowledgement of the victims' narrative and foster their empowerment; also, these instruments can – at least ideally – more substantively include in the transitional process the "losers", the "others"[64] – especially the small fries – rather than witch-hunting them through inevitably selective prosecutions. This inclusive approach will potentially make these subjects feel pardoned, rather than emarginated, and soothe feelings of anger and resentment. Amnesties can therefore also facilitate the rehabilitation of the wrongdoers,[65] as well as the encounter and pacification between former enemies, thus furthering the commitment of these subject to the reconstruction of a more peaceful and inclusive society.

In conclusion, amnesties are primarily an instrument, a means to an end. As such, their effects on the pursuit of peace and justice will inevitably depend on the context, their objective and their features. As such, amnesties can be potentially destructive instruments, furthering impunity and violations, and denying peace and justice. However, when designed carefully and as part of a broader set of measures these instruments can provide accountability, foster security and have a deterrent effect.[66] Also, they could promote rehabilitation, as instead of making the person responsible for wrongdoings the passive recipient of a judicial decision, they empower him, by giving him a choice (e.g., between telling the truth and taking responsibility for his misdeeds or face prosecution).[67]

However, before considering the different cases in which amnesty provisions are adopted, and their effects on the ground, one question must be answered, that could make the whole discussion redundant: in a legal and political international order built around accountability, are amnesties as such even admissible?

On the Legality of Amnesties Under International Law

The issue of the legitimacy of amnesties under international law – especially following the post-World War II "justice cascade"[68] – is debated both in the academia and by key actors such as international organisations and tribunals, essentially revolving around two questions: first, is there a general prohibition of amnesties established at the international level? And if not, are there any other state obligations which in practice prevent a government from lawfully adopting an amnesty? The following paragraphs thus provide a brief reconstruction of the current status of international law, as emerging from international treaties, customary law, as well as secondary sources.[69]

International Treaties: Have State Agreed to Surrender Amnesties?

Notwithstanding the intensity and persistence of the amnesty debate, no international treaty explicitly prohibits the adoption of amnesty laws, nor imposes the state parties a general and absolute duty to prosecute.[70] Rather, some treaties – which because of their very nature as voluntary agreements only bind the signatory parties – outline some obligations to prosecute and/or punish specific crimes or human rights violations.[71] Particularly significant examples are the four Geneva Conventions of 1949, which constitute the main source of international humanitarian law.[72] These treaties, which have now been ratified by most countries around the world, and whose main provisions have acquired status of international customary law,[73] require member states to prosecute – by determining "effective penal sanctions"[74] – persons committing, or ordering to be committed, grave breaches of the laws of war[75]. This obligation is considered to be absolute (as not subject to exceptions, such as amnesties);[76] however, importantly, the four treaties only refer to breaches perpetrated in the context of international armed conflicts, this inevitably limiting the reach and relevance of their provisions to contemporary transitional scenarios, which primarily address conflicts erupted within the borders of a state. Non-international armed conflicts are instead the subject of common Article 3 of the Conventions, which focuses on the protection of individuals who do not take active part in the hostilities, such as the civilian population or hors de combat; as such, it is widely believed that this article does not itself impose a specific obligation to prosecute violations committed in domestic contexts,[77] and being generally considered as a sort of autonomous convention within the convention, its interpretation and implementation are not "affected" by the aforementioned Article 146.[78]

Non-international conflicts are also the subject of Additional Protocol II to the Geneva Conventions,[79] adopted in 1977, which is particularly significant in the debate around amnesties. Indeed, Article 6(5) of this charter contains the only provision of an international treaty explicitly referring to these mechanisms, and – surprisingly to some – it is an encouraging one.[80] More specifically, this article advises authorities, at the end of a non-international armed confrontation, to "grant the broadest amnesty possible" to persons who took part in the hostilities, or who had been deprived of liberty in the context of the conflict.[81] This norm is aimed at providing state parties with some discretion on how to handle the country's reconstruction in the aftermath of an internal conflict, with an eye to reconciliation between warring parties who (unlike after international hostilities) are destined to share a nation.[82] Because of its uniqueness, this article is highly significant in concluding for the absence of a general prohibition of amnesties in international law.[83] However, also relevant is the evolution its interpretation has gradually undergone. Indeed, while this article has been used by some national courts as a reference to uphold domestic amnesty laws,[84] several sources and bodies – such as, most notably, the International Committee of the Red Cross – have read the provision in such a way to circumscribe its scope; for example, it has been asserted that this norm only permits amnesties for crimes consistent with international humanitarian law (thus excluding war crimes),[85] or that it only refers to amnesties aimed at correcting wrongs, for example those pardoning subjects incriminated by oppressive regimes essentially on political grounds.[86] As a consequence, and also following a gradual expansion of international humanitarian law to situations of domestic conflict,[87] there is growing acceptance that all war crimes – and not only those committed within international hostilities – raise states' obligation to investigate, prosecute and punish.[88] As analysed further on, however, the practice is much less unanimous and amnesties are still commonplace in many post-conflict scenarios.[89]

Another treaty imposing similar obligations on state parties is the Genocide Convention of 1948,[90] in which Article 1 qualifies genocide as a "crime under international law which [the Contracting Parties] undertake to prevent and punish"[91]; in the same vein, Articles 4 and 6 require state parties to prosecute and punish perpetrators in a national or international tribunal.[92] Therefore, this charter states a clear duty to prosecute and punish, but only limited to the crime object of the treaty – which is given a narrow and specific definition, in particular requiring specific intent by the part of the defendant "to destroy, in whole or in part, a national, ethnical, racial or religious group, as such".[93] As a consequence, the contexts in which the Convention is actually relevant are quite debated, and in practice fairly limited.[94]

Other sources follow the same approach of the Genocide Convention, in imposing a clear duty to prosecute and punish, but only with regard to specific offences. In particular, the Convention against Torture and Other Cruel, Inhuman or Degrading Treatment or Punishment[95] of 1987 requires state parties to criminalise and prosecute acts of torture as defined by the Convention itself,[96] according to the "aut dedere aut iudicare" principle,[97] and essentially the same formula is contained in the Convention on Enforced Disappearances.[98]

Also noteworthy are international agreements which require state parties to punish certain conducts, but without explicitly imposing a general or absolute obligation to prosecute,[99] thus – at least apparently – granting states more leeway in determining how to provide accountability and pursue justice. Examples are the International Convention on the Elimination of all forms of Racial Discrimination[100] and the International Convention on the Suppression and Punishment of the Crime of Apartheid.[101]

Finally, several international agreements explicitly recognise a right of victims of international crimes and human rights violations to effective remedies, that states must respect and fulfil by carrying out serious and thorough investigations, followed by prosecutions and punishment. Among others, noteworthy are the International Covenant on Civil and Political right, at Article 2.3(a), as well as the key regional human rights conventions. Monitoring bodies have further explored and clarified resulting states' obligations, for example specifying how in the case of grave violations of human rights, merely administrative remedies do not qualify as "effective remedies",[102] and finding that amnesties that prevent victims from pursuing civil remedies violate their fundamental rights.[103] However, although the term "remedy" expresses the need for accountability and redress, it is not to be equated with "prosecutions": as a consequence, this obligation of states to provide an effective remedy should not be read as strictly preventing states from adopting amnesty provisions, when these are part of a broader set of measures promoting accountability, or constructed in such a way to further – rather than hinder – the interests of justice.[104]

In conclusion, although international treaties impose some obligations to address the commission of crimes relevant under international law, they outline neither an absolute duty to prosecute, nor a general prohibition of amnesty laws. Further, the obligations outlined in these sources are inherently limited under many profiles, such as the type of crime and the subjects with regards to whom the obligations arise, the type of relevant conflict, the countries bound to respect them.[105] Absent decisive treaty provisions, we turn now to customary law, investigating whether an unwritten but observed rule exists in the international realm prohibiting the adoption of amnesties.

International Customary Law

International customs are a particularly compelling source of obligation, as – unlike treaties – they bind all states irrespective of their having formally consented to them; at the same time, however, they are by nature indeterminate, and – with the exception of few fundamental principles – establishing the customary status of a certain provision is a complex and controversial exercise. The determination of the existence of a custom relies on two elements: consistent state practice, and opinio juris (the belief in the binding nature of the rule).[106]

With regard to the former, three considerations are central when assessing the legality of amnesties under international law. Firstly, the very fact that no international agreement between states actually prohibits amnesties (and rather, the only explicit norm favours them as instrumental to peace processes) speaks volumes about states' attitudes towards these measures. Secondly, amnesty laws are, in practice, widely employed by governments around the world, sometimes covering grave crimes and violations, although with very different features and goals, and sometimes in disguise[107]: the Amnesty Law Database created by

Louise Mallinder identifies more than 500 amnesty laws adopted in five continents between 1945 and 2010.[108] Thirdly, nation-states – as well as the international community as such – have consistently encouraged or supported, openly or implicitly, the adoption of amnesties as instrumental to end complex and brutal conflicts, as witnessed in Guatemala and Sierra Leone.[109] Consequently (although the issue could be further eviscerated) these three circumstances alone allow to safely conclude that the international community does not conceive of amnesties as prohibited – in fact, quite the contrary. This conclusion is further reinforced looking at the Rome Statute establishing the International Criminal Court.[110] Several authors have examined in-depth the drafting process,[111] and stressed the absence of any explicit mention of amnesties in the final agreement, which could be explained by an inability of state parties to the negotiations to reach any consensus on this issue.[112] A certain deliberate ambiguity in the approach of negotiating powers would also be confirmed by the content of the Statute[113]: provisions such as Article 17 and Article 53, in particular, provide the prosecutor with some discretion in the choice of the situations to focus on, for example allowing her not to initiate an investigation if she believes that "would not serve the interests of justice".[114] This and other provisions thus manifest an underlying understanding of justice and accountability as encompassing more than mere criminal prosecutions, thus also potentially leaving some space for amnesties to be lawfully adopted, when necessary for the resolution of conflicts.[115]

Once acknowledged the absence of a customary prohibition of amnesties, more debated is whether states' discretion in resorting to these instruments is in practice limited by other customary obligations. In particular, a small but significant group of crimes and violations of fundamental rights has been gradually identified, whose prohibition is now widely recognised as enshrined in customary law; further, this prohibition has been interpreted as also implying positive obligations of states, namely to prevent, investigate, prosecute and punish these same offences,[116] among which figure genocide, crimes against humanity,[117] grave breaches of the Geneva Conventions, and grave violations of human rights such as torture[118] and enforced disappearances.[119] These state obligations are understood by several sources as implying the inadmissibility of amnesties for these same crimes, as obstacles to a positive state duty, and the very fact that recent amnesties are increasingly complex in imposing conditions and limitations is sometimes interpreted as a confirmation of the existence of such duty.[120] This positive obligation of states is now widely recognised, by treaties, national[121] and international jurisprudence, and in the literature.[122] However, its actual effects on the admissibility of amnesties are debatable, in particular in relation to measures that are conditional, or complemented by other mechanisms aimed at providing truth and accountability. A key factor to keep into consideration is that this positive obligation of states entails not only punishment but, as seen, also prevention of these crimes; this raises the issue of how to assess the admissibility of an amnesty which shields potential perpetrators of heinous crimes from prosecution, but at the same time is considered necessary in order to cease the hostilities, and thus prevent further violations.[123]

A Trend towards Accountability: Jurisprudence and United Nations Practice

Finally, relevant indicators of the position of the international community, and of the predominant interpretation of the aforementioned principles, are subordinate sources of international law, such as the jurisprudence of regional, international and ad hoc tribunals, as well as UN practice. This paragraph will thus briefly introduce some of the main judicial decisions and UN policies with regard to amnesties, which are indicative of a trend towards accountability as prosecution, and against amnesties.

International and regional tribunals are probably the bodies that have shown more resistance towards the admissibility of amnesties, due to their natural focus on prosecutions and punishment, and the most active in stressing the states' positive obligations to investigate and provide effective remedies for violations of human rights. The most proactive body in this regard is surely the Inter-American Court of Human Rights (IACtHR), which adjudicated on the compatibility of several national amnesties with the American human rights system.[124] The court has always proven innovative in its approach, and strongly focused on accountability, as confirmed by the landmark case *Velásquez Rodríguez v Honduras*,[125] its first merits judgment[126]; here, the court stressed the responsibility of member states to put in place a legal and governmental structure adequate to ensure the enjoyment of human rights (organisational duty) and to "prevent, investigate and punish"[127] any violation of rights enshrined in the Convention (enforcement duty).[128] However, the most significant decision with regard to amnesty provisions was arguably adopted in the *Barrios Altos (Chumbipuma Aguirre et al. v*

Peru) case,[129] in which the court pronounced itself on two self-amnesty laws passed by the Peruvian Congress in 1995, shielding from prosecution members of the army and police forces who had committed grave violations of human rights between 1980 and 1995.[130] Here, the IACtHR affirmed the incompatibility of amnesty measures covering serious violations of rights and crimes under international law with the duty of the state to investigate and punish perpetrators, as well as with the rights of the victims to justice, truth and reparation[131]; additionally, the court stressed how amnesties go against the very spirit of the Convention, as they "lead to the defenceless of victims and perpetuate impunity",[132] and thus declared the Peruvian amnesties as void. These findings, later reiterated in other judgments,[133] shaped the IACtHR approach towards domestic post-conflict processes[134] and triggered a new phase of accountability in the region: criminal proceedings were reopened in Peru, and the judgment was used by the Argentinian Supreme Court in 2005 as a key reference in declaring the unconstitutionality of national amnesty laws.[135]

Also telling is the jurisprudence of ad hoc tribunals, such as the ICTY and the Special Court for Sierra Leone (SCSL), both established in the aftermath of violent internal conflicts. The former, in the judgment on the *Furundzija* case,[136] declared (in an obiter dictum) the incompatibility with international law of amnesty provisions covering the crime of torture, on the basis of the jus cogens nature of the prohibition of torture, together with the principle of universal jurisdiction.[137] Similarly, the Appeals Chamber of the SCSL repeatedly relied on universal jurisdiction and on states' obligation to prosecute or extradite perpetrators of grave violations, to conclude against the legality of amnesties for serious crimes and human rights violations under international law[138]; in particular, in *Prosecutor v Augustine Gbao*,[139] the hybrid tribunal went as far as to declare the existence of a "crystallized international norm"[140] against amnesties for serious international crimes.[141]

These judgments, which are cited by several sources as clear indicators of a trend in international law against the use of amnesties, are however at the same time criticised by many voices in the solidity of the legal arguments employed.[142] Also, more open to the possibility of amnesties was the Trial Chamber of the Extraordinary Chambers of the Courts of Cambodia (ECCC), which in the *Ieng Sary* case[143] acknowledged the potential of conditional amnesties to provide some form of accountability and further reconciliation in transitional scenarios.[144]

In conclusion, international and ad hoc courts are generally strongly resistant to amnesties, in part because of their very nature. However, interestingly, several authors note how these bodies have to this date only addressed so-called blanket or self-amnesties shielding perpetrators of grave violations of human rights and clearly adopted in order to obstruct the pursuit of justice; it is thus debatable whether the same tribunals would reach a different conclusion if addressing conditional amnesties, maybe adopted in parallel with the creation of truth commissions.[145]

Finally, it is worth to briefly mention the UN practices and position on amnesties, as expressed in countless official documents and widely analysed by the literature,[146] from which an evolution in the UN approach emerges. More precisely, in the past the UN has encouraged (in the context of peace negotiations) or endorsed the adoption of amnesty provisions around the world, such as in South Africa, Haiti or Guatemala,[147] in particular when considered necessary for achieving peace.[148] Especially significant are the Secretary General remarks on potential dynamics between the South African truth commission (whose mand ate allowed granting of amnesties for – among others – gross violations of human rights) and the International Criminal Court, reported by Mark Freeman, stating that "it is inconceivable that, in such a case, the [ICC] would seek to substitute its judgment for that of a whole nation which is seeking the best way to put a traumatic past behind it and build a better future."[149] However, since the late 1990s the UN position has undergone a shift towards a stricter version of accountability and towards a preference for judicial remedies, as witnessed in the current UN official policy, which is strictly against amnesties "that prevent prosecution of those responsible for serious crimes under international law, such as war crimes, genocide and crimes against humanity, or gross violations of human rights".[150]

Looking for the Devil in the Details

In conclusion, despite a trend – informed and supported by actors such as courts, international organisations and the UN – unfavourable to amnesties, perceived as instruments which further impunity, the international law system, rooted in treaties and customary law, does not contain any express and general prohibition. Rather, each country is subject to a specific set of obligations – some of which shared with fellow states, others peculiar and dependent on the ratification of treaties – which also need to be balanced with each other, absent a rigid and clear hierarchy[151]; in particular with regard to amnesties, a tension can be perceived between states' duty to prevent (and to ensure the security of its citizens) on one side, and the duty to prosecute and punish to the other.

This absence of a general prohibition to adopt amnesties, however, does not imply an absolute freedom and discretion of states in the design of these measures. In particular, what appears to be crystallised in international law is a customary obligation of the states to investigate, prosecute and punish international crimes, as well as gross violations of human rights.[152] As a consequence, the admissibility and legality of amnesties adopted by national governments will have to be considered case-by-case in light of their specific obligations, and in particular against their duties to prevent, investigate, prosecute and punish international crimes and gross violations of human rights; victims' rights to remedy; as well as victims' and society's right to know the truth with regard to past violations.[153] As such, a blanket amnesty that grants absolute impunity to persons responsible for gross violation of human rights will probably be widely criticised, while a carefully tailored mechanism, which subordinates the granting of the pardon to specific conditions, and which is coupled with instruments providing accountability (such as truth commissions or vetting) is more likely to be accepted.[154] Also, a pragmatic approach cannot prescind from considering the effects that an amnesty – or resistance to such a measure – would have on the lives of the local population.

Amnesties in Practice: "Same Cover, Different Book"

Amnesties, like conflicts, are all unique. As reiterated throughout this chapter, amnesty provisions are adopted in order to address profoundly different contexts, with often discordant intentions, and diverse features: the result is a variegated assortment of legal mechanisms, with sometimes very little in common. As a consequence, virtually every author and body examining the issue of amnesties provides some classification of these instruments, according to different kinds of parameters.

This paragraph builds upon the reconstruction offered by Ronald Slye, who groups amnesties into different categories on the basis of three elements: content (acts covered and eligible subjects, eventual procedural requirements and forms of relief envisaged for victims), creation and implementation process, and purpose (reconstruct the truth, end hostilities or others) of the amnesty.[155] After an introduction to the four categories of amnesties identified by the author, more attention will be reserved to the experiences of South Africa and Argentina, which are now as paradigmatic, as they are antipodal.

The first category of amnesties identified by Slye are so-called amnesic amnesties, often approved by subjects involved in the acts of violence, or in oppressive regimes, maybe in the form of self-amnesties. These mechanisms are primarily aimed at granting anonymity and suppressing the truth with regard to past events, and consequently tend to be quite broad in their reach, for what concerns both the beneficiaries and the covered crimes, while also normally not imposing specific procedural requirements, nor envisaging forms of redress for the victims.[156] As a consequence, their adoption is often justified to the population with a purported need to bury and forget the past, encouraging a sort of collective amnesia in the interest of social and political peace.[157] Amnesties with these characteristics – qualified by most sources as "blanket amnesties"[158] – represent the first and, at least until the 1980s, the most common category of amnesties. Also, they are the variety detractors of the instrument typically refer to, when denouncing the instrumentality of amnesties to grant impunity and deny justice. This kind of mechanisms has been widely employed in Latin American countries, substantially as a form of indiscriminate pardon,[159] and the Argentinian experience will be analysed more thoroughly in the following section.

Slye also identifies two intermediate types of amnesties, defined as "compromise" and "corrective" amnesties. Regarding the former, compromise amnesties are mechanisms which aim at providing some degree of acknowledgement, but usually just at the institutional level, not at the individual one; these instruments are also characterised by a series of limitations, such as with regard to the potential beneficiaries, the crimes covered, the relief provided to the victims, and they are often created together with other post-conflict mechanisms. Therefore, they may be implemented with the honest purpose of facilitating the transition of the country, but much of their legitimacy and popular acceptance will in fact depend on the combined efficacy of these measures with other, parallel initiatives adopted.[160]

Concerning the latter, corrective amnesties are quite sui generis amnesties, whose features and objectives do not fit within the traditional, prevailing preconception of these mechanisms, not least in that they are adopted with the final objective of remedying a wrong. To be identified as corrective are, for example, amnesties adopted in order to prevent the enforcement of a formally legitimate but at the same time disused law, normally in the aftermath of radical socio-political changes; or also, amnesties approved with the intention of correcting injustices which occurred during a conflict or an authoritarian period – by reversing or invalidating politically motivated judgements.[161] One example is the so-called "Amnistia Togliatti"[162] adopted in Italy in 1946, which – among other things – invalidated political decisions adopted during the fascist regime against members of the resistance movement (however, this law was later harshly criticised for its ambiguity and its extremely broad application, which eventually benefitted the members and supporters of the regime more than the *partigiani*).[163]

Finally, Slye's analysis focuses on "accountable amnesties", considered by the author as the only legitimate kind of amnesties, as the only potentially suited to provide a satisfactory degree of accountability and relief to the victims. In particular, the author identifies six characteristics that amnesties should meet, in order to be qualified as accountable.[164] First of all, the provision needs to be democratically created (e.g., allowing the population to participate in the drafting process) or otherwise approved, ideally through democratic vote. Secondly, it cannot benefit subjects suspected to be responsible for the most heinous crimes, such as those relevant under international law. Also, the measure "must impose some form of public procedure or accountability on its recipients",[165] for example by subordinating its concession to disclosure, public apologies or public hearings. Furthermore, an opportunity should be provided to the victims to challenge one's request for amnesty, in order to allow them to be included in the process, not only in the approval stage – as members of the social community – but also in the implementation phase, and in their individual capacity. Always in the interest of the victims, accountable amnesties should envisage some concrete benefits to them, ideally in the form of reparations. Finally, these mechanisms should be designed in such a way to potentially foster the transition to a democratic regime; in particular, they should promote the respect of fundamental rights of the individuals and/or be part of a comprehensive project aimed at achieving reconciliation, while successfully addressing the root causes of the acts of violence.[166]

In order to meet all these requirements, these mechanisms will inevitably result in being quite narrow, with regard to the crimes covered and/or the subjects that can benefit from it. Nevertheless, these conditions are considered as crucial in order to guarantee that amnesties are being implemented not to foster impunity or obstruct the reconstruction of the truth about a controversial and painful phase of the country's history, but rather as an alternative and potentially effective means of accountability.[167] This also explains the attention reserved by Slye to the role of the victims: as the subjects who have suffered the consequences of crimes and abuses, and who will potentially be the most affected – both at a legal and at a psychological level – by the adoption of an amnesty, it is crucial that they are included in all stages of the process, and that they can benefit from it.

The only amnesty satisfying these elements, in Slye's opinion, is the South African one, which will therefore be described more in-depth below, as it has come to represent the paradigmatic model of a "good transitional amnesty".

Amnesic Amnesties and Justice Delayed in Argentina

One paradigmatic example of amnesic amnesties can be found in Argentina, where not one, but three amnesty laws, as well as several pardons, were passed in the years following the collapse of the *junta* regime. Although only one of these mechanisms is, strictly speaking, an amnesic amnesty, the whole set of measures adopted deserves some attention, as they appear to all share the same underlying ratio of obstructing prosecutions, ostensibly to "heal old wounds".[168] Firstly, in September 1983, just before stepping aside, the military government adopted the "Ley de Pacificación Nacional",[169] substantially a self-amnesty which – under the pretext of "leaving behind of confrontation [and] forgiving of mutual harm"[170] – shielded members of the military (and, in a much more limited part, guerrillas) from civil and criminal liability for the commission of broadly defined political crimes.[171] The law was repealed few months later by the newly elected president Raul Alfonsín, following increasing popular resistance and legal challenges, in parallel with the establishment of a national truth commission.[172] However, after a few years of fruitful investigations against the regime,[173] in 1986 and 1987 the president surrendered to pressures coming from the military, and adopted two new laws, namely the "Full Stop Law"[174] and the "Due Obedience Law"[175] – which are not >strictly amnesty laws, but rather introduce a series of substantial limitations to prosecutions of members of the armed forces. More in detail, the "Ley de Punto Final" establishes a (extremely short) 60-day limit for bringing new cases against military officials for crimes committed during the Dirty War.[176] The law, passed just before the Christmas holidays, aimed at impeding the launch of new investigations. However, several courts throughout the country responded with incredible activism, suspending the holidays and working tirelessly to process hundreds of applications for gruesome crimes before the "expiry date".[177] Confronted with growing military unrest, the government passed, in 1987, a new law, this time introducing a presumption that during the regime low- and middle-level officials acted "under duress, in subordination to a superior authority and following orders",[178] and therefore could not be deemed criminally liable for their wrongdoings.[179] This time, the law was much more successful in discouraging prosecutions, thus essentially granting impunity to perpetrators[180] – although the exclusion of crimes related to kidnapping of children was later creatively capitalised upon by courts and activists.[181]

Therefore, although not explicitly defined as amnesties, the combined effect of the laws – reinforced by a series of pardon decrees adopted by President Carlos Menem between 1989 and 1990[182] – was to essentially remove those responsible for crimes against humanity and gruesome violations of fundamental rights from the grasp of national courts, in this way also endangering the transitional process. Indeed, these amnesties encountered stark resistance on the part of human rights groups and civil society, which had always been very vocal in advocating for prosecutions, while also limiting the cooperation with the CONADEP (and later on with courts carrying out truth trials) of inside witnesses, fundamental in proving the existence of systematic criminal plans, thus making the discovery of the full truth extremely difficult.[183] Further, in a fragile and critical context such as the transitional one, the passing of such measures eroded people's confidence in the government and the political process, and according to some it fostered a radicalisation of rights organisations and civil society, which further antagonised the political discourse.[184] These dynamics changed in the late 1990s, when the activism of human rights organisations started to bear fruit: loopholes in the amnesty laws – and in particular the exclusion of crimes related to the kidnapping of children of the disappeared – were creatively exploited to conduct so-called truth trials,[185] and in 2001 Federal Judge Cavallo declared for the first time the unconstitutionality of the Full Stop and Due Obedience Laws, followed by more and more federal courts.[186] This influenced, in 2003, the legislative annulment of the same laws, followed by the Supreme Court declaration of unconstitutionality of 2005.[187]

The Amnesty Process in South Africa

The South African mechanism represents the best-known example of an amnesty implemented as an integral, constitutive, and instrumental element of the truth and reconciliation process.[188]

In the post-Apartheid era, adopting an amnesty appeared as a necessary compromise: members as well as supporters of the old regime had preserved a good deal of political, economic and military power, and they would not have allowed for a peaceful transition – nor shared the wealth of information they had on the abusive practices of the regime – at the risk of criminal prosecutions[189]: amnesties were thus on the table (and well at the centre) since the inception of the negotiations between the two parties[190]; perpetrators – on both sides – were too numerous, while resources were critically scarce[191]: in a sense, there was very little to lose, and much more to gain, at least ideally, by renouncing already slim chances of prosecutions; also, in many situations the line between guilt and innocence was extremely blurred. Thus, the decision to make use of amnesties was relatively clear-cut. On the contrary, extremely complex was the determination of which characteristics this mechanism should have, so as to make it politically and morally acceptable in the eyes of the population.[192] The way this issue was addressed constitutes arguably the most typical – and most innovative – feature of the whole South African transitional process: the concession of the pardon was made dependent on the applicants' full and honest disclosure of the truth about their crimes, in a public hearing in which the victims had the right to participate and intervene[193]; the offences to be potentially covered were only those committed between March 1960 and May 1994, with a political objective, and proportionate to said goal.[194]

This process presents several positive features. Firstly, its granting was neither automatic nor generalised, but rather individualised and conditioned on the submission of an application,[195] followed by an evaluation conducted by a competent body, which had to verify the existence of a series of requirements, with limited discretionary powers.[196] An active commitment from the part of the perpetrator was thus required, who needed to file the request, show up in front of the Committee and confess his or her crimes, also accepting the possibility of a harsh confrontation with the victims: by taking the initiative and surrendering to the process, the applicant manifested his choice in favour of the new democratic order, his willingness to admit responsibilities and to be readmitted to the community.[197] Similarly laudable is the fact that the amnesty was supported by democratic approval[198]: the process for the institution of the Truth and Reconciliation Commission (TRC) was incredibly inclusive, and the National Unity and Reconciliation Act establishing the TRC was adopted by the first democratically elected government in decades.[199] Furthermore, the whole process aimed at ensuring substantial participation of victims. As aforementioned, the victims had to be notified about the hearing, and had the right not only to assist, but also to actively participate, for example by confronting the applicant or expressing their opinions with regard to the granting of the amnesty (and the victim's support of the application in several occasions played a decisive role in the final determination)[200]; additionally, victims had the possibility to challenge the decision of the Amnesty Committee in a court of law (although the judicial process has been accused of being too slow and costly).[201] Notably, the discovery of truth ideally resulting from the hearing had several beneficial effects on the victims – arguably greater than the satisfaction coming from the punishment of a few individuals. For example, the acknowledgement of a fact is believed to be more comforting when coming not from a judicial organ, in a cold and legalistic setting, but rather from the same subject who participated in the violations,[202] who also stands as a representative of a regime based on the denial of those same facts (or at least of their abusive nature), thus symbolising its decadence. Finally, a good degree of accountability came from the fact that the subjects granted amnesty were named in the final TRC report, their responsibilities for the listed crimes acknowledged.

Finally, particularly striking in the context of the debate around amnesties is Andrea Lollini's interpretation of the phenomenon. According to this author, thanks to the particular design of the amnesty provision, truth became in the South African context the compensation, the exchange ("controprestazione") for the state's renounce to exercise its power to prosecute and punish,[203] while those who refused this redemptive offer remained subject, at least potentially, to criminal accountability. Amnesties thus played a foundational role, as through their adoption "the constituent pact [was] based on the exchange of confession for the state's temporary waiving of exercising one of its most important public powers"[204]: Through this process the state renounced the vengeful, adversarial approach typical of the apartheid-era, and demonstrated, in this way reinforcing, its strength and legitimacy through mercy. As such, the amnesty process in South Africa – although far from perfect[205] – also played a fundamental role in reshaping global perspectives and approaches to these measures, increasingly appreciated not only and always as means for oblivion, but as potential tools for justice and accountability.

Conclusions

The previous paragraphs have stressed how variegated the world of amnesties is. In the evocative words of Ronald Slye, amnesties

> Have been used to express public grace and forgiveness, and to further government corruption and oppression. They have been used to bring law into compliance with an accepted reality, and to exempt a contested reality from public scrutiny and moral and legal accountability. They have been granted at times of great social stability and at times of great social unrest; at the start of and during wars for the purpose of recruiting troops, and at the end of wars to foster peace and reconciliation.[206]

This calls for particular sensitivity and caution in reaching and expressing generalised conclusions on the argument. However, some points can be safely made.

Firstly, an historical evolution in the understanding of this instrument can be retraced. As seen, amnesties have ancient roots, and were traditionally primarily used by rulers to show mercy and foster forgetfulness, to turn to a new page in the history of the country. However, over the last decades they have been affected by several changes in the international political and legal landscape. For example, accountability has gradually been elevated as one of the foundational values of the international community, this inevitably limiting states' discretion in deciding whether and how to confront past abuses and crimes. At the same time, the nature of conflicts has changed, these exploding more and more within – rather than between – nation-states; as a consequence, national governments, even when in good faith, find themselves caught, in the aftermath of hostilities, between contrasting claims and needs, pushed to creatively and effectively address the brutal effects of conflicts, in a way that allows former enemies to coexist in the same territory. As a result, amnesties are increasingly resisted, perceived as almost anachronistic, while simultaneously seemingly inevitable.

One of the main sources of criticism relates to an asserted incompatibility of amnesties with the current system of international law, which recognises fundamental rights of every human being, whose violation triggers not only state responsibility, but also individual criminal accountability, both nationally and internationally. However, an analysis – although brief – of the main sources of international law (which is essentially dependent on state willingness, manifested either through practice or through signing of agreement) shows the absence of any general and absolute prohibition with regard to the adoption of these measures. Nevertheless, states' leeway is restricted by some fundamental principles, which inevitably affect the design and implementation of transitional processes, and limit state discretion with regard to amnesties. In particular, states have a customary obligation to investigate, prosecute and punish international crimes, as well as gross violations of human rights (in parallel to additional, specific obligations assumed under treaties); similarly, victims have been recognised some fundamental and inalienable rights to truth and remedy. As a consequence, the legality of an amnesty will in fact depend on the context and its inevitability in that context, its features, as well as its practical application, while legal arguments could virtually sustain both positions.

Law, however, does not end the debate. Indeed, amnesties are as much a political (and moral) issue as they are a legal one. Under this profile, they are broadly criticised for their furthering impunity, and for constituting per sé, in their very nature, a denial of justice and of the foundational tenets of our social order. However, such an approach is ultimately informed by a retributive understanding of accountability, that equates justice with prosecution and punishment. Although understandable and in part instinctively embraceable, this approach is in fact quite partial, and informed by a specific legal and political tradition. On the contrary, a more sensitive understanding of justice as more contextual (in other words, more receptive of the victims' own understanding of justice), and open to incorporating restorative elements, allows for rethinking the justice-versus-peace perceived dichotomy in such a way that it loses its criticality: amnesties, in the right circumstances, could promote both. A more sensitive approach to this instrument however requires rethinking them, in at least two ways.

First of all, amnesties should be thought of not through an antagonistic rhetoric, but rather as issues of choices, often difficult and undesirable, many times constrained, always strictly contextual: between states' duty to prevent and states' obligation to prosecute and punish; between today's and tomorrow's victims; between security and punishment. Also, they should be appreciated, less ideologically, as primarily an instrument, a tool. In this sense, they can work as much as obstacles, as they can be enablers (of peace, security, justice).[207] Reframing the discourse around amnesties through the lenses of their instrumentality allows to grasp, more clearly, with the importance of not dismissing them a priori, in the name of principles and values (although the noblest ones), as this would deprive actors on the ground of a potentially crucial tool, with very real consequences on peoples' chances of survival.

Consequently, the "peace-versus-justice" debate should be rebooted as an "accountability-versus-impunity" one, approached in restorative perspective, and amnesties should be evaluated accordingly, always considering the context they emerge from. Just as a way of example, the Argentinian amnesties of 1986 and 1987 appear more justifiable than the self-amnesty adopted in 1983, not only because of their content, but also in guise of their ratio: the former were prompted by a fear for the peace and security of the country, following increasing unrest by the part of the military and a perceived risk to plunge in a new civil war, while the latter appears as a shameless attempt to escape justice. Other strong indicators of amnesties' acceptability is their being part of a broader set of measures, their being a complement – rather than a substitute – to other transitional instruments, such as truth commissions, reparations and vetting, which ensure closer supervision as well as popular satisfaction. Notably, amnesties and criminal prosecutions are not mutually exclusive.[208] On the contrary, some of the most lauded examples of amnesties worked in parallel to national or international criminal tribunals, which in this way managed to focus on a more limited number of crimes and perpetrators, such as the leaders of repressive movements or those most responsible for the acts of violence. In particular, in the South African case the choice was left to the subject himself, to either accept the redemptive offer of the state, and provide in exchange a full confession, or face a criminal judgment.

In conclusion, amnesties are far from ideal mechanisms, and their very existence reminds us of the limitations of international criminal law and human rights to make order in a chaotic world. However, realistically, they constitute a necessary tool, and not only for the resolution of conflicts, but also for their prevention. The challenge lies in designing them in a way that pursues the collective interest, rather than the egoistic purposes of those in charge of designing and implementing them.

Notes

1. Charles P. Trumbull IV, "Giving Amnesties a Second Chance", *Berkeley Journal of International Law* 25(2) (2007): 320
2. Bronwyn Anne Leebaw, "The Irreconcilable Goals of Transitional Justice", *Human Rights Quarterly* 95 (2008): 95–118
3. Shawn Fields, "Private Crimes and Public Forgiveness: Towards a Refined Restorative Justice Amnesty Regime", *International Journal of Civil Society Law* 5(2): 9
4. Rebecca Saunders, "Questionable Associations: The Role of Forgiveness in Transitional Justice", *The International Journal of Transitional Justice* 5 (2011): 124
5. Ronald C. Slye, "The Legitimacy of Amnesties Under International Law and General Principles of Anglo-American Law: Is a Legitimate Amnesty Possible?", *Virginia Journal of International Law* 43(2002): 174
6. Saunders, "Questionable Associations", 125
7. Jon Elster, *Closing the Books: Transitional Justice in Historical Perspective* (Cambridge: Cambridge University Press, 2004), 10
8. Robert Parker, "Fighting the Sirens' Song: The Problem of Amnesty in Historical and Contemporary Perspective", *Acta Juridica Hungarica* 42 (2001): 78
9. Elster, *Closing the Books,* 26
10. Mark Freeman, *Necessary Evils. Amnesties and the Search for Justice* (Cambridge: Cambridge University Press, 2009), 5
11. Fields, "Private Crimes and Public Forgiveness", 10
12. Parker, "Fighting the Sirens' Song", 74–76
13. Slye, "The Legitimacy of Amnesties Under International Law", 174
14. Freeman, *Necessary Evils,* 2
15. For an in-depth analysis and assessment of the evolution of the concept and field of human rights, see Jack Donnelly, *Universal Human Rights in Theory and in Practice* (Ithaca and London: Cornell University Press, 2003)
16. Trumbull, "Giving Amnesties a Second Chance", 285
17. Slye, "The Legitimacy of Amnesties Under International Law", 179
18. Ibid., 175
19. Freeman, *Necessary Evils,* 1
20. Ibid.,18
21. See the example of South Africa, infra Chapter 9

22. See the reconstruction provided in Diane Orentlicher, "Settling Accounts: The Duty to Prosecute Human Rights Violations of a Prior Regime", *Yale Law Journal* 100(8) (1991): 2537–2615
23. Freeman, *Necessary Evils*, 12
24. Ibid., 13
25. Ibid.
26. Office of the United Nations High Commissioner for Human Rights (OHCHR), *Rule-of-Law Tools for Post-Conflict States: Amnesties* (New York and Geneva: United Nations, 2009): 5
27. OHCHR, *Amnesties*, 6
28. Ibid.
29. Freeman, *Necessary Evils*, 8
30. For a more complete analysis see Parker, "Fighting the Sirens' Song", 81
31. Kirk Simpson, "Victims of Political Violence: A Habermasian Model of Truth Recovery", *Journal of Human Rights* 6(3) (2007): 337
32. Slye, "The Legitimacy of Amnesties Under International Law", 192
33. Milena Sterio, "Rethinking Amnesty", *Denver Journal of International Law & Policy* 34(3) (2006): 379
34. Freeman, *Necessary Evils*, 20–23
35. Ibid., 20
36. Parker, "Fighting the Sirens' Song", 82
37. Max Pensky, "Amnesty on Trial: Impunity, Accountability, and the Norms of International Law", *Ethics & Global Politics* 1(1) (2008): 21
38. Peter A. Schey, Dinah L. Shelton and Naomi Roht-Arriaza, "Addressing Human Rights Abuses: Truth Commissions and the Value of Amnesty", *Whittier Law Review* 19 (1997): 332
39. Slye, "The Legitimacy of Amnesties Under International Law", 197
40. Ibid., 192
41. Saunders, "Questionable Associations", 66
42. Dustin N. Sharp, "Addressing Economic Violence in Times of Transition: Toward a Positive-Peace Paradigm for Transitional Justice", *Fordham international Law Journal* 35(3) (2012): 804
43. Elizabeth B. Ludwin King, "Amnesties in a Time of Transition", *The George Washington International Law Review* 41 (2010): 610
44. Freeman, *Necessary Evils*, 23
45. Tricia D. Olsen, Leigh A. Payne and Andrew G. Reiter, "The Justice Balance: When Transitional Justice Improves Human Rights and Democracy", *Human Rights Quarterly* 32 (2010): 985
46. Trumbull, "Giving Amnesties a Second Chance", 316
47. Several authors have supported the opinion that the decision of the ICC Prosecutor to indict Omar Al Bashir played a role in prolonging and exacerbating the conflict in Darfur. Among others, see Kamari Clarke,

"Rethinking Africa through its Exclusions: The Politics of Naming Criminal Responsibility", *Anthropological Quarterly* 83(3) (2010): 632

48. Louise Mallinder, "Amnesties and International Criminal Law", in *The Handbook of International Criminal Law,* ed. William A. Schabas and Nadia Bérnaz (London: Routledge, 2010), 2
49. King, "Amnesties in a Time of Transition", 612
50. Olsen, Payne and Reiter, "The Justice Balance", 987
51. Freeman, *Necessary Evils,* 20
52. For more on the potential deterrent effect of international criminal law, see Chris Jenks and Guido Acquaviva, "Debate: The Role of International Criminal Justice in Fostering Compliance with International Humanitarian Law", *International Review of the Red Cross* 96 (2014): 775–794
53. Trumbull, "Giving Amnesties a Second Chance", 309
54. Ibid., 310
55. Ibid., 309
56. Jeremy Sarkin, *Carrots and Sticks: The TRC and the South African Amnesty Process* (Antwerp and London: Intersentia, 2004), 355
57. Slye, "The Legitimacy of Amnesties Under International Law", 194
58. Freeman, *Necessary Evils,* 8
59. Trumbull, "Giving Amnesties a Second Chance", 312
60. See Victor Igreja, "Amnesty Law, Political Struggles for Legitimacy and Violence in Mozambique", *The International Journal for Transitional Justice* 9(2) (2015): 239–258
61. Parker, "Fighting the Sirens' Song", 70
62. Trumbull, "Giving Amnesties a Second Chance", 318
63. Freeman, *Necessary Evils,* 19
64. Olsen, Payne and Reiter, "The Justice Balance", 986
65. Freeman, *Necessary Evils,* 21
66. Ibid., 20
67. Ibid., 22
68. Francesca Lessa and Leigh A. Payne, eds., *Amnesty in the Age of Human Rights Accountability: Comparative and International Perspectives* (Cambridge: Cambridge University Press, 2012), 8
69. *Statute of the International Court of Justice,* San Francisco, 24 October 1945, *United States Treaty Series* 993, art. 38(1)
70. Mallinder, "Amnesties and International Criminal Law", 4
71. Trumbull, "Giving Amnesties a Second Chance", 288
72. OHCHR, *Amnesties,* 14
73. Trumbull, "Giving Amnesties a Second Chance", 288
74. *Geneva Convention Relative to the Protection of Civilian Persons in Time of War (Fourth Geneva Convention)*, Geneva, 12 August 1949, 75 UNTS 287, Art. 146

75. Ibid., Art. 147
76. Mallinder, "Amnesties and International Criminal Law", 4
77. Ibid.
78. Karen Gallagher, "No Justice, No Peace: The Legalities and Realities of Amnesty in Sierra Leone", *Thomas Jefferson Law Review* 23 (2000): 176
79. *Protocol Additional to the Geneva Conventions of 12 August 1949 and Relating to the Protection of Victims of Non-International Armed Conflicts (Protocol II)*, Geneva, 8 June 1977, 1125 UNTS 609
80. Freeman, *Necessary Evils*, 33
81. *Protocol II Additional to the Geneva Conventions*, Art. 6(5)
82. Mallinder, "Amnesties and International Criminal Law", 5
83. Freeman, *Necessary Evils*, 33
84. Ibid., 34
85. Jean-Marie Henckaerts and Louise Doswald-Beck, eds., *Customary International Humanitarian Law. Volume I: Rules* (Cambridge: Cambridge University Press and International Committee of the Red Cross, 2009), Rule 159
86. Slye, "The Legitimacy of Amnesties Under International Law", 178
87. Ilias Bantekas and Lutz Oette, *International Human Rights Law and Practice* (Cambridge: Cambridge University Press, 2012), 572
88. OHCHR, *Amnesties*, 15
89. Freeman, *Necessary Evils*, 36
90. *Convention on the Prevention and Punishment of the Crime of Genocide*, Paris, 12 September 1948, 78 UNTS 277 (*Genocide Convention*)
91. *Genocide Convention*, Art. 1
92. Ibid., Art. 6
93. Ibid., Art. 2
94. Ludwin King, "Amnesties in a Time of Transition", 599
95. *Convention against Torture and Other Cruel, Inhuman or Degrading Treatment or Punishment*, New York, 10 December 1984, 1465 UNTS 85
96. *Ibid.*, Art. 4
97. Ibid., Art. 7
98. *International Convention for the Protection of all Persons from Enforced Disappearance*, New York, 20 December 2016, A/RES/61/177, Artt. 3–7
99. Freeman, *Necessary Evils*, 39
100. *International Convention on the Elimination of All Forms of Racial Discrimination*, New York, 07 March 1966, 660 UNTS 195
101. *International Convention on the Suppression and Punishment of the Crime of Apartheid*, New York, 30 November 1973, 1015 UNTS 243
102. OHCHR, *Amnesties*, 22
103. Ibid., 21
104. Ludwin King, "Amnesties in a Time of Transition", 597

105. Freeman, *Necessary Evils*, 70
106. Bantekas and Oette, *International Human Rights Law and Practice,* 59
107. Trumbull, "Giving Amnesties a Second Chance", 295
108. "The Amnesty Law Database", last modified July 26, 2011
109. Trumbull, "Giving Amnesties a Second Chance", 298
110. *Rome Statute of the International Criminal Court*, Rome, 17 July 1998, 2187 UNTS 90
111. Among others, see Mallinder, "Amnesties and International Criminal Law", 8; Darryl Robinson, "Serving the Interests of Justice: Amnesties, Truth Commissions and the International Criminal Court", *European Journal of International Law* 14 (2003): 481–505
112. Mallinder, "Amnesties and International Criminal Law", 8
113. Freeman, *Necessary Evils*, 75
114. *Rome Statute of the International Criminal Court*, Art. 53
115. Mallinder, "Amnesties and International Criminal Law", 10
116. For a reconstruction see OHCHR, *Amnesties,* 29
117. Among others, Human Rights Committee, General Comment No.31: The Nature of the General Legal Obligation Imposed on States Parties to the Covenant, para.18, UN Doc. CCPR/C/21/Rev.1/Add. 13 (26 May 2004)
118. *Prosecutor v Anto Furundzija* (Judgment) ICTY-95-27/1-T (10 December 1998), para. 151
119. OHCHR, *Amnesties,* 12–20
120. Ibid., 7
121. See, for example, Louise Mallinder, "The Ongoing Quest for Truth and Justice: Enacting and Annulling Argentina's Amnesty Laws" (Working paper, Institute of Criminology and Criminal Justice, Queen's University Belfast, Belfast, 2001), 112 on the jurisprudence of Argentinian courts
122. Oette, *International Human Rights Law and Practice,* 321 & 335
123. Freeman, *Necessary Evils*, 58–64
124. Oette, *International Human Rights Law and Practice,* 143–154
125. *Case of Velásquez Rodríguez v Honduras* (Judgment) Inter-American Court of Human Rights Series C no. 4 (29 July 1988)
126. Due Process of Law Foundation, Victims Unsilenced: The Inter-American Human Rights System and Transitional Justice in Latin America (Washington, DC: Due Process of Law Foundation, 2012), 153
127. *Velásquez Rodríguez v Honduras,* para. 164
128. Due Process of Law Foundation, *Victims Unsilenced*, 153
129. *Case of Barrios Altos v Peru* (Judgment) Inter-American Court of Human Rights Series C no. 75 (14 May 2001)
130. *Case of Barrios Altos v Peru,* para. 2
131. Ibid., para. 41–44
132. Ibid., para. 43

133. For example, *Case of Almonacid-Arellano et al v Chile* (Judgment) Inter-American Court of Human Rights Series C no. 154 (26 September 2006), addressing the self-amnesty passed by Pinochet government in 1978
134. Freeman, *Necessary Evils*, 49
135. Douglas Jacobson, "A Break with the Past or Justice in Pieces: Divergent Paths on the Question of Amnesty in Argentina and Colombia", *Georgia Journal of International and Comparative Law* 175 (2006): 194
136. *Prosecutor v Anto Furundzija* (Judgment) ICTY-95-27/1-T (10 December 1998)
137. On this also see Mallinder, "Amnesties and International Criminal Law", 16
138. OHCHR, *Amnesties,* 30
139. *Prosecutor v Augustine Gbao* (Decision on Preliminary Motion on the Invalidity of the Agreement between the United Nations and the Government of Sierra Leone on the Establishment of the Special Court) SCSL-04-15-PT-141 (25 May 2004), 13
140. *Prosecutor v Augustine Gbao,* para. 9
141. Mallinder, "Amnesties and International Criminal Law", 20
142. See, for example, William Schabas, *The UN International Criminal Tribunals* (Cambridge: Cambridge University Press), 338
143. *Ieng Sary case* (Provisional Detention Order) ECCC Criminal Case File No. 002/14-08-2006 (14 November 2007), 13
144. Mallinder, "Amnesties and International Criminal Law", 20
145. OHCHR, *Amnesties,* 33
146. A more detailed analysis is provided by Freeman, *Necessary Evils*, 43
147. Trumbull, "Giving Amnesties a Second Chance", 293ss
148. Ibid., 294
149. Charles Villa-Vicencio and Erik Doxtader, eds., *Pieces of the Puzzle: Keywords on Reconciliation and Transitional Justice* (Cape Town: Institute for Justice and Reconciliation, 2004), 91 as cited in Freeman, *Necessary Evils*, 88
150. OHCHR, *Amnesties,* 27
151. Freeman, *Necessary Evils*, 59–63
152. Trumbull, "Giving Amnesties a Second Chance", 302
153. OHCHR, *Amnesties,* 11
154. William W. Burke-White, "Protecting the Minority: A Place for Impunity? An illustrated Survey of Amnesty Legislation, Its Conformity with International Legal Obligations, and Its Potential as a Tool for Minority-Majority Reconciliation", *Journal of Ethnopolitics and Minority Issues in Europe* 1 (2000): 42
155. Slye, "The Legitimacy of Amnesties Under International Law", 240
156. Ibid., 241
157. Burke-White, "Protecting the Minority: A Place for Impunity?", 7
158. Ibid., 4

159. Naomi Roht-Arriaza, "After Amnesties are Gone: Latin American National Courts and the New Contours of the Fight Against Impunity", *Human Rights Quarterly* 37(2) (2015): 350. This source analyses in depth the recent wave of overcoming of many amnesties, pardons and other obstacles to prosecution that had been passed in Latin America in the past decades.
160. Slye, "The Legitimacy of Amnesties Under International Law", 241
161. Ibid., 243
162. *Amnistia e Indulto per Reati Comuni, Politici e Militari* (Amnesty and Pardon for Common, Political and Military Crimes): Decreto Presidenziale 22 Giugno 1946 No. 4, G.U. 137 (23 June 1946)
163. Mimmo Franzinelli, *L'amnistia Togliatti*, (Milano: Mondadori, 2006)
164. Slye, "The Legitimacy of Amnesties Under International Law", 239
165. Ibid., 245
166. Ibid., 245–246
167. Ibid., 246
168. See Mallinder, "The Ongoing Quest for Truth and Justice", for a description of the rhetoric employed by Argentina's post-conflict governments when adopting amnesties, pardons and statues of limitations
169. *Ley de Pacificación Nacional* (Law of National Pacification): Ley No. 22.924, A.L.J.A., 1983-B-1681
170. Ibid., Preamble
171. Mallinder, "The Ongoing Quest for Truth and Justice", 17
172. Ludwin King, "Amnesties in a Time of Transition", 584
173. Sang Wook Daniel Han, "Transitional Justice: When Justice Strikes Back – Case Studies of Delayed Justice in Argentina and South Korea", *Houston Journal of International Law* 30(3) (2008): 657
174. *Ley de Punto Final* (Full Stop Law): Ley no. 23.492, A.D.L.A XLVII-A, 192
175. *Ley de Obediencia Debida* (Due Obedience Law): Ley no. 23.521, A.D.L.A XLVII-B, 1548
176. Jose Sebastian Elias, "Constitutional Changes, Transitional Justice, and Legitimacy: The Life and Death of Argentina's 'Amnesty' Laws", *Yale Student Scholarship Papers* 57 (2007): 33
177. Ibid., 34
178. Ley de Obedencia Debida ("Due Obedience" Law), Law No. 23.521 (4 June 1987), Art. 1
179. Han, "Transitional Justice", 660
180. Elias, "Constitutional Changes, Transitional Justice, and Legitimacy", 35
181. Mallinder, "The Ongoing Quest for Truth and Justice", 67 & 86
182. Ibid., 76–80
183. Elena Maculan, "Prosecuting International Crimes at National Level: Lessons from the Argentine 'Truth-Finding Trials' ", *Utrecht Law Review* 8 (2012): 115
184. Mallinder, "The Ongoing Quest for Truth and Justice", 70

185. Maculan, "Prosecuting International Crimes at National Level", 113
186. Han, "Transitional Justice", 662
187. Jacobson, "A Break with the Past or Justice in Pieces", 193
188. Gibson, "The Contributions of Truth to Reconciliation", 425
189. Jeremy Sarkin, "An Evaluation of the South African Amnesty Process", in *Truth and Reconciliation in South Africa: Did the TRC Deliver?*, ed. Audrey E. Chapman, Hugo van der Merwe (Philadelphia: University of Pennsylvania Press, 2008), 21
190. Max Pensky, "Transition, Amnesty, and Social Trust: Lessons from South Africa", in *Trust and Transitions: Social Capital in a Changing World*, ed. Joseph D. Lewandowski and Milan Znoj (Newcastle: Cambridge Scholars Publishing, 2008), 94
191. Emily H. McCarthy, "South Africa's Amnesty Process: a Viable Route Toward Truth and Reconciliation?", *Michigan Journal of Race and Law* 3 (1997): 187
192. Priscilla B. Hayner, *Unspeakable Truths: Confronting State Terror and Atrocity* (New York: Routledge, 2001), 99
193. Pensky, "Transition, Amnesty, and Social Trust", 102
194. McCarthy, "South Africa's Amnesty Process", 210
195. Pensky, "Transition, Amnesty, and Social Trust", 98
196. Truth and Reconciliation Commission, *Truth and Reconciliation Commission of South Africa Report (TRC Report)* (Cape Town: Juta and Co., 1998), Vol.1, Chapter 5, Par. 60
197. Fields, "Private Crimes and Public Forgiveness", 11
198. Among others, see Louise Mallinder, "Can Amnesties and International Justice be Reconciled?", *The International Journal of Transitional Justice* 1 (2007): 226
199. Sam Garkawe, "The South African Truth and Reconciliation Commission: A Suitable Model to Enhance the Role and Rights of the Victims of Gross Violations of Human Rights", *Melbourne University Law Review* 27 (2003): 348
200. Sarkin, "An Evaluation of the South African Amnesty Process", 16
201. Garkawe, "The South African Truth and Reconciliation Commission", 353
202. Slye, "The Legitimacy of Amnesties Under International Law", 246
203. Andrea Lollini, *Constitutionalism and Transitional Justice in South Africa* (Oxford: Bergham Books, 2011), 120
204. Ibid., 121
205. Ibid., 120–122
206. Slye, "The Legitimacy of Amnesties Under International Law", 174
207. Freeman, *Necessary Evils*, 19
208. Olsen, Payne and Reiter, "The Justice Balance", 1005

CHAPTER 6

The Origins of International Criminal Accountability: The Nuremberg and Tokyo Tribunals

Introduction

On the morning of November 20, 1945,[1] curtains rose on one of the most innovative and awaited legal events in modern history: the International Military Tribunal (IMT) set up in the German city of Nuremberg to pronounce on the responsibilities of some among the most renowned figures of the fallen Nazi regime – the first tribunal successfully created to deal, supranationally, with mass atrocities.[2] A few months later, the operations began of the International Military Tribunal for the Far East (IMTFE), better known as the Tokyo Tribunal, responsible for judging representatives of the Japanese military and political élite for the events that unfolded during World War II.[3] One will become the archetype of international criminal justice, while the other sunk into oblivion, as little more than a façade installed by the Americans to sanctify their victories in the region while shifting the conversation away from the horrors of Hiroshima and Nagasaki.[4]

The two bodies will be discussed here jointly, as together they constitute a first phase in the development of the model of individual criminal accountability at the supranational level, for acts that will be identified as the worst menaces and insults to a shared humanity. After a brief reconstruction of the negotiation processes that led to the creation of the two bodies, and an overview of the key features of the statutes of the courts, attention will be devoted to some dilemmas emerging in many debates

G. Girelli, *Understanding Transitional Justice*,
Philosophy, Public Policy, and Transnational Law,
DOI 10.1007/978-3-319-53606-4_6

around these institutions (and more generally relevant to international criminal justice – and transitional justice – per sé), such as: whether they manifest a new consciousness and sensitivity at the international level, or rather constitute a mere form of victors' justice; whether they shaped and developed international law, or rather violated, in their prosecuting newly established crimes, fundamental principles of law; whether they succeeded in educating consciences and societies, or were only little more than a political spectacle. Finally, the results of the courts' operations will be outlined, pausing – in the conclusions – on their legacies, highlighting lessons as well as missteps.

The Negotiations: Confronting Different Understandings of Justice

Although the Allied powers began discussing the post-conflict scenario while the war was still raging,[5] the decision to confront the atrocities experienced in Europe through the adoption of a one-of-a-kind judicial mechanism was "far from inevitable",[6] as different solutions were being proposed with regards to the fate of the German leadership. In particular, Stalin advocated for a political show-trial to officially and formally proclaim the group "obvious" responsibilities, followed by execution[7]; while Churchill supported the possibility of summary capital punishment, firmly opposing the establishment of a tribunal, by raising precisely some of the objections that will haunt the courts' legacies for long after the judgments. Among others, concerns were expressed that criminal trials would have been exploited for Nazi propaganda, or remembered as mere shows leading to a predetermined decision; also, any failure in convicting the masterminds of the Holocaust would have had catastrophic consequences on the public morale, as well as on the political legacy of their promoters.[8]

Only Roosevelt, who at first had agreed with the idea of summary executions,[9] eventually resolved to advocate for the institution of a criminal tribunal, which in the opinion of the US government would have allowed for the development of a reliable and authoritative historical record, while at the same time serving as an example of civilisation and democracy that would have informed the international relationships for years to come.[10] Also decisive in determining the USA's shift in perspective was the fear that publicly executed leaders could be idealised by the local population as martyrs, in this way fostering a partial and polarising reconstruction of past events.[11]

One of the first, decisive steps towards the creation of the tribunal was the Declaration of Saint James's Palace of 1941,[12] in which the governments of nine countries occupied by the Axis Powers, together with some of the most influential representatives of the "free world",[13] agreed to cooperate against German and Italian oppression and towards a long-lasting peace, as well as to hold the individuals responsible for the Nazi crimes accountable[14]; this commitment was reiterated in one of the four Moscow Declarations[15] signed on November 1, 1943, through solemn words:

> Let those who have hitherto not imbrued their hands with innocent blood beware lest they join the ranks of the guilty, for most assuredly the three Allied powers will pursue them to the uttermost ends of the earth and will deliver them to their accusers in order that justice may be done.[16]

Accordingly, the signatory powers agreed that German criminals would be brought to trial in the countries where they had committed crimes, where a territorial nexus could be found, or "by joint decision of the government of the Allies",[17] if the crimes lacked a particular geographical localisation. That same year the USA, Great Britain and China signed the Cairo Declaration,[18] in which for the first time the will was officially stated to "punish the aggression of Japan",[19] although without specifying how and to what extent[20]; therefore, through this accord the project of individual criminal accountability was extended to the Far East, as confirmed, in more precise terms, through the Potsdam Declaration of 1945,[21] agreed among the same powers, and to which Russia itself would later adhere.[22]

The Nuremberg Tribunal (IMT) was finally instituted through the Charter of the International Military Tribunal (more commonly known as London Charter),[23] signed by the USA, France, UK and the Union of Soviet Socialist Republics. This treaty gave the tribunal jurisdiction to try "persons who, acting in the interests of the European Axis countries, whether as individuals or as members of organizations",[24] committed crimes against peace, crimes against humanity or war crimes.[25] Also, the traditionally acceptable "acts of state" and "due obedience" defences were declared inadmissible (the latter could only be invoked as mitigating factor),[26] and the so-called conspiracy theory was formalised, on the basis of which a conspirator for the commission of one of the listed crimes could be held individually responsible for acts performed by anybody in the execution of the same plan.[27] Additionally, the Charter authorised the tribunal to declare the criminal nature of groups and organisations[28] – also allowing national authorities of the signatory powers to try individuals for their mere membership in such groups.[29]

With regards to the Tokyo Tribunal, a fundamental step towards its creation was the Japanese Instrument of Surrender of September 2, 1945,[30] through which the Japanese Government agreed to the terms of the Potsdam Declaration, and subjected itself to the authority of the Supreme Commander for the Allied Powers (SCAP) – Douglas MacArthur.[31] This US General will play a defining role in the functioning of the tribunal, starting from its constitution, which indeed occurred through a MacArthur Special Declaration of January 19, 1946 also containing the Charter of the court,[32] which was crafted along the same lines as the London Charter. In particular, the Tokyo Tribunal was also given jurisdiction for crimes against humanity, crimes against peace and war crimes,[33] while the main divergences were probably the absence of any authorisation to adjudicate upon the criminal liability of organisations,[34] and the subordination of the other charges to the indictment for crimes against peace.[35]

An American Tale?

As emerging from the previous paragraph, the USA played a critical role in the establishment of the courts, as well as in the definition of their jurisdiction and powers, to the point that several commentators consider these bodies essentially as American creatures. For example, Elizabeth Borgwardt refers to the IMT as a "show produced and directed almost entirely by Americans",[36] while James Owen portrays it as a redemptive tool created for the promotion of the US ideals of justice, freedom and democracy, presented as in diametrical opposition with the typical features of an evil dictatorship, in this way also shaping a global narrative that would later inform the Western rhetoric against Russia's plans for supremacy.[37] Such an allegation appears even more well-founded with regards to the Tokyo Tribunal, which was shaped and dominated by General MacArthur[38]: although formally acting as an "agent of the Allied Powers",[39] the Supreme Commander was in in fact the hands (and the brains) of the US Government in Post-War Japan.[40] This clearly emerges looking at the mechanics of the court; for example, while the IMT had four prosecutors – each representing one Allied Power – the IMTFE only had one chief prosecutor, American, aided by associated prosecutors coming from other countries.[41]

Similarly, the USA played a primary role, in both scenarios, in the incredibly sensitive process of selecting the defendants, who inevitably only represented a very limited portion of those involved in the commission of atrocities and crimes.[42] As the USA considered Nuremberg primarily as the opportunity for judging the Regime's structure and underlying ideology, the accused were identified not merely because of their individual contributions or positions in the state hierarchy, but rather as symbols of the values and institutions they represented, as actors on a stage (although in many cases the two went hand in hand).[43] However, even more striking than the choices were the omissions, and in particular the absence, in the dock, of Emperor Hirohito, well alive but shielded from prosecution by the Tokyo Tribunal following US decision – and against the will of other Powers, as well as of part of the domestic and international public opinion.[44] Although this decision was presumably reached on the basis of political arguments, and also in the interest of internal peace and security (the Americans feared that treating a Head of State with divine features as a criminal would have incited hatred and insurrection among his people),[45] it nevertheless had extremely negative effects on the credibility, per sé already weak, of the tribunal.[46]

Such an American imprint would also lend support to many of the criticisms the courts were subjected to, some of which will be examined in more depth in the following paragraphs.

Innovation or Violation? Situating the Tribunals within the International Legal System

These international tribunals were ambitious and for many aspects fortunate experiments, which had a formative influence on the development of international criminal law and human rights standards. However, partly because of their innovative character, and their navigating a largely undefined field, they also underwent stark criticisms; the following paragraphs aim at offering a brief overview of some of the tribunals' key objectives and characteristics, and of their relative flipsides.

Models of Just Retribution or Mere Victors' Justice?

Through the London Agreement and the institution of the two tribunals, the Allied powers sought the punishment of (some of) the individuals most responsible for one of the darkest periods in recent history, and – at least ideally – the prevention of future atrocities[47]; remarkably, through the IMT and the IMTFE these objectives were pursued, for the first time, not through purely political means, but rather by empowering a legal, supranational instrument.

However, despite attempts to depict these bodies as merely judicial, neutral and technical, the courts had an inevitable political character: they were instituted by political entities with very specific agendas, were called to adjudicate upon a brutal political experiment, and their judgments could have had a primary influence on the development of national and international relations, within an already complex and fragile geopolitical scenario. As a consequence, they were by many parts criticised as mere tools of the victorious powers, lacking neutrality and impartiality.[48]As aforementioned, one of the most debatable issue was the selectivity in the choice of the defendants. In particular, Article 6 of the London Charter only allowed the Germany-based court to try subjects suspected of having perpetrated crimes in the interest of the Axis Powers, thus preventing the prosecution of members of the Allied forces guilty of those same atrocities. Additionally, the courts rejected the "tu-quoque argument" strategy initially pursued by the defence teams, which attempted to submit evidence of war crimes, crimes against peace and crimes against humanity arguably committed by Allied forces[49]: the courts declared such evidence inadmissible, mainly referring to the limited scope of the tribunals, and stressing how the potential commission of crimes by one part does not free the other from criminal liability.[50] Nevertheless, such an overly technical approach fostered further criticisms and accuses of impartiality; the most problematic position was probably the one faced by Russia, which, among others, cooperated with Germany to attack Poland in 1939, and invaded Finland less than one year later.[51] However, as the American-driven apocalypse at Hiroshima and Nagasaki shows, none of the victors could be considered blameless.

The Austrian philosopher Hans Kelsen defines this biased system a "privilegium odiosum",[52] which undermines the legitimacy of the London Charter and its Japanese counterpart, as well as of the courts' judgments, in this way also weakening their authority as precedents for the future development of international law (and in particular for strengthening the principle of individual criminal accountability).[53] On his part, Robert Jackson – the US-appointed prosecutor in Nuremberg and one of the tribunal's most influential figures – offered a different interpretation of the Charter. In particular,

Jackson acknowledged and addressed the issue of selectivity in his opening statement, where he admitted that "the nature of the crimes is such that both prosecution and judgment must be by victor nations over vanquished foes"[54]; however, he also firmly rejected any representation of the trial as a mere exercise of power by the Allies over a defeated country, stressing that "they [German defendants] are here not because they lost the war, but because they started it."[55] Similarly, in his *Legacies of Nuremberg*, David Luban asserts that "only victors' justice is possible",[56] at least in a world of nation-states in which the principle of national sovereignty, although weakened under many profiles, still plays a defining role of the dynamics at the international level.[57]

Nevertheless, some lines can be drawn. In particular, while it is undeniable that, realistically, a power would never submit its actions to the judgement of the enemy (and not even to an impartial, although politically charged, forum such as the International Criminal Court – as the ongoing, successful resistance of Omar Al Bashir reminds us), it is also true that a justice mechanism can, and must, be constructed in such a way to ensure as much impartiality and fairness as possible: justice must be fair, and must be seen to be fair.[58] In the case of the Tokyo and Nuremberg tribunals, multiple factors manifested their political character. For example, several commentators point to the absence, among the judges and the prosecutors in Nuremberg, of personalities from Germany, or even from neutral countries (in representation of that humanity, whose dignity the tribunals claimed to be protecting and defending).[59] Moreover, Professor Luban himself provides a convincing example of an American citizen that could have been easily tried at Nuremberg, in this way potentially enhancing the credibility of the tribunal[60]: from a realistic point of view, this could have been decried as an exercise in hypocrisy, a show in the show set up by the victors in order to shift the focus away from the undemocratic and imperialistic nature of the trial; nevertheless, it would have demonstrated to the public opinion and the international community that nobody, notwithstanding one's nationality, was immune from judgement.

Foundation of a New International Law or Violation of Its Most Fundamental Principles?

In order to achieve the goals of punishment and deterrence, the London Charter, as well as the IMT itself, introduced in international law several new principles, that would heavily influence its evolution, contributing to – maybe even provoking – the crisis and the partial overthrowing of the Westphalian model of international relations.[61] Most notably, the

Charter acknowledged, for the first time, the existence of the individual within a system of international law which traditionally only recognised one subject: the state.[62] This is one of the most fundamental merits of the Nuremberg experience, as it

> Made it clear that the society of nations was also a society of men and that international law would reach beyond the artificial borders of the state to punish those who breach the most basic precepts of that society of men and who endanger the peace of the world.[63]

In order to allow the court to adjudicate on individual accountability, the London Charter also sanctioned (in Articles 7 and 8) the inadmissibility of the traditional "due obedience" and "acts of State" defences that, combined, would have shielded almost every defendant from criminal liability.[64] Such a departure from well-established principles of international law was justified with the argument that "it is possible to refuse evil orders, and thus culpable to comply".[65] While not undisputed (as analysed in the following paragraph), as well as not completely novel – some national codes already stated that manifestly illegal orders should not be complied with[66] – this apparently procedural provision manifested a new understanding of justice and accountability, as well as a new approach to the international order itself; in particular, it marked a shift from a system that only recognised states as active subjects, to one that acknowledges individuals, and not only as objects of protection, but also as responsible and accountable for their own decisions, even when adopted in an official position. As such, the Charter is sending a message: from that moment on, acting in the name of the state will carry not only political, but also legal, criminal, individual consequences.

Equally innovative was the formalisation of new charges. Indeed, the Charter criminalised aggressive war, although without defining it,[67] while also introducing new "crimes against humanity".[68] This new category is particularly significant, in that it manifests a growing commitment by the part of the international community (or at least some of its most powerful components) to regulate and restrain the power of governments on their own citizens, which was traditionally considered as absolute and purely discretionary (at the very least in the sense that other states could not interfere with these domestic businesses). By introducing this new charge, the society of states acknowledged the existence of certain thresholds that, in the interest of a shared human dignity, could not be exceeded – thus setting a new standard of civilisation (although that common human dignity was conveniently denied in the territories colonised by the European powers, as well as with reference to the ethnic minorities discriminated and abused in the USA). This represented a landmark step in the evolution of international humanitarian law and human rights law, but it was only a partial one. Indeed, although the Charter gave the IMT jurisdiction to try crimes against humanity committed "before or during the war",[69] in this way allowing the Prosecution to reach back to the events unfolded between 1933 and 1939, and prosecute purely domestic acts perpetrated against civilians in times of peace,[70] the court decided to only include in its enquiry violations committed during the war, in this way limiting its innovative potential.[71] This position of the court was probably influenced by an awareness of the already strong, potentially destabilising consequences of this new charge on states' sovereignty,[72] as also manifested by Goering's defence that "that was our right! We were a sovereign state and that [the extermination of their own citizens] was strictly our business".[73]

In conclusion, the institution of innovative bodies such as international criminal tribunals, with jurisdiction on individuals and for crimes never adjudicated before, provoked the weakening of a fundamental concept of international law – the principle of state sovereignty (and relative immunities). In particular, although this principle was not discarded (the charge of aggressive war was essentially aimed at protecting such sovereignty)[74] the institution of the tribunals sensibly affected the discretionary powers of states: both at the internal level, where some fundamental rights of the citizens had to be respected,[75] and in the international realm, where the recourse to war, and in general the use of force, was sensibly restrained. Additionally, it demonstrated how breaches of international principles could activate legal and individualised consequences (rather than merely political ones),[76] and that criminal prosecution was not only a domestic concern anymore.[77]

However, all these innovations were not introduced without resistance. In particular, the Charters and the Tribunals were accused of violating foundational principles of law, such as the prohibition of retroactive legislation, which is considered even more absolute with regard to criminal law: as the acts the courts had jurisdiction upon were not crimes at the time they were committed, they just could not be prosecuted, irrespective of their gravity. Underlying was a more general contrast between two diametrical understandings of the relationship between law and justice – meaning the positivist and the natural-law one – which in transitional contexts acquires new relevance and complexity; such opposition has been at its best articulated, with reference to Post-War Germany, in the debate between two of the most egregious legal philosophers of their time, Herbert L. A. Hart and Lon Fuller, precisely on the issue of prosecuting Nazi collaborators.[78] In particular, Hart claimed, following his positivistic approach, that respect for the Rule of Law required accepting the norms formally in force as still valid, although passed by the fallen regime. Indeed, this continuity was believed to be necessary in order to restore the society's faith and belief in the "procedural regularity"[79] of the law, which is warranty of fairness and consequently of justice.[80] On the contrary, Fuller advocated in favour of breaking with the Nazi regime and its legislation, as the immorality of that political system impinged on the validity of its laws, to the point of neutralising it. Indeed, according to his natural-law perspective, the validity of law is not inevitable and intrinsic; rather, it is to be based on a moral ground that precedes law itself.[81]

The courts, which by nature tended to embrace a positivist philosophy, but also grasped with the exceptionality of the context, eventually attempted to justify this unprecedented establishment of individual, criminal responsibility at the international level through formalistic arguments (in this way appeasing positivistic spirits)[82]; more specifically, the Nuremberg Tribunal recalled supposed precedents in international agreements and customs, such as the 1907 Hague Convention, the 1928 Kellogg-Briand Pact and some non-aggression pacts of which Germany was a party.[83] This line of justification, however, was extremely weak, as the cited instruments "forbade only resort to war, and not planning, perpetration, initiation of war or conspiracy [nor] stipulated individual criminal liability"[84]; some of them were not even in force anymore at the time of the war, while others could only be infringed by acts of state; additionally, these only envisaged a political, collective liability, surely not a juridical and personal one.[85] In short, rather than fully acknowledging and capitalising upon the exceptionality of the context, the court questionably derived an individual criminal liability from sources of international law directed exclusively to states.

Such an approach is even more debatable when considering that, with regard to other issues, the court embraced a much more "naturalistic" approach; as aforementioned, the IMT concluded that the defendants could be prosecuted and convicted on the basis of charges introduced after the commission of the crimes – in apparent violation of the principle of non-retroactivity – because what they had done was so horrible, they just had to know that their actions were immoral, and deserving punishment.[86] As stated in the judgment, "in such circumstances the attacker must know that he is doing wrong, and so far from it being unjust to punish him, it would be unjust if his wrong would be allowed to go unpunished".[87] This schizophrenic approach of the court was for many reasons problematic, and it affected the overall credibility and legitimacy of this mechanism. Among others, it was used as an example to lend support to the aforementioned accuses moved to both courts, of being political tools of the Allied Powers. Particularly vocal in this sense was Judge Radhabinod Pal of the Tokyo Tribunal, who in his well-known dissenting opinion depicted the Tokyo trial as a partial instrument instituted by the Allies with the final purpose of taking revenge for the losses suffered in the Far East[88]; such an instrument would have only been legitimate, as an international legal mechanism, if founded on an international treaty defining both the crimes and the sanctions, and signed by the vanquished state itself.[89] On the contrary,

> To say that the victor can define a crime at his will and then punish for that crime would be to revert back to those days when he was allowed to devastate the occupied country with fire and sword.[90]

However, the court's reasoning was endorsed by other personalities, such as Hans Kelsen who, despite being vigorously critical about the introduction of individual criminal accountability at the international level, and especially only against representatives of defeated powers,[91] was in fact much more supportive with regard to the formalisation of brand-new charges, on several bases. Firstly, he stressed how the prohibition of ex post facto law is only a domestic – not also an international – principle (although probably because at the time there was just no international criminal law as nowadays understood), and one subject to many exceptions.[92] Secondly, he highlighted how the prosecuted crimes were "morally the most objectionable",[93] therefore justifying extreme answers. Kelsen's approach has the merit of exposing how pressing needs of justice, when strongly felt and shared, could justify exceptions to strict legality, and how the two do not always converge.[94] Nevertheless, grounding legal mechanisms and responses in moral arguments (even the most appealing ones) is strongly problematic, as it opens excessive spaces for instrumentalisation and abuse (especially when judging regimes, such as Hitler's, which are firmly grounded on perverse while normalised ethical and moral principles).[95]

A more nuanced approach justifies the exceptionality of these mechanisms with the exceptionality of the circumstances that brought to their institution,[96] such as: the macabre, bureaucratic organisation set up to further the criminal plan and its surprising efficacy; the targeting of the civilian population; the racial and genocidal nature of the crimes. As a consequence, the idea is that these crimes could not have been codified or otherwise formalised before, simply because they had never been experienced in such magnitude (at least by Europeans and their American descendants, who were shaping international law).[97] This "realistic" approach, although similarly open to instrumentalisation, however also appears to be less hypocritical and more intellectually responsible than the formalistic one followed by the courts, "because it eludes the difficult contortions involved in finding individual criminal liability for aggression and crimes against humanity before 1945",[98] while at the same time avoiding the philosophical diatribes linked to the natural-law justifications adopted by the two tribunals on other key issues.[99] Notably, this tension between strict legalism and more nuanced and context-sensitive approaches is still relevant today, as manifested by countless discussions concerning the legality and admissibility of informal mechanisms of conflict resolutions, which appear to be better responsive to the local populations' worldviews and priorities, while being opposed and criticised for their failing to meet established standards of due process, in this way also violating fundamental human rights (as shaped and defined according to Western standards).[100]

Educational Forum or Theatrical Show?

Another primary goal of the trials was the establishment of an official, impartial and authoritative historical record.[101] By reconstructing, narrating and officialising the truth, the trials would also have served "an expressive and educative function",[102] in at least two directions. On one side, the emerging narrative would have ideally prevented future generations from committing (and enduring) similar horrors, while also providing an authoritative tool against attempts of revisionism of what the Nazi regime as well as the crimes of the Japanese army had caused and signified.[103] On the other side, the proceedings were meant to teach the defeated people (as well as the global community) about the consequences of illiberal and despotic systems, and to re-educate them in the Rule of Law.[104] In order to increase their potential of realising these objectives, the tribunals were structured in such a way to strike people's imagination: notably, Judge Roeling describes the Tokyo Tribunal as a "huge-scale theatrical production [with] more Hollywoodesque things around that there should have been".[105]

These symbolic features and connotations, and their being created in order to fulfil non-strictly-legal objectives, were at the core of one of the most enduring criticisms moved to the tribunals, and in general to international criminal justice: meaning, the accusation of being a show, a stage from where to further non-judicial goals, in this way violating fundamental principles of criminal law, such as the primary focus on the defendants and their legal responsibilities. In other words, because of their multiple objectives and expectations towards them, the trials would inevitably fail to focus on the defendants in their subjectivity, and would instead treat them as means (objects, towards an external goal), thus betraying their core principles.

This issue of the nature and goals of ad hoc trials has been extensively discussed in the literature concerning transitional justice,[106] precisely because of the extraordinary circumstances these mechanisms emerge from, and for. In particular, their being established as synonyms of justice in a war-torn territory, the high number of suspected subjects, the moving testimonies, the wide media coverage and public scrutiny, all make these bodies particularly exposed to the accusation of being adopted not with the purpose of analysing evidence and punishing perpetrators, but rather to further ulterior goals, such as to legitimise the new political order, by offering to the population a foundational show of civilised revenge, a sort of arena where a cathartic performance happens, on which to ground a new chapter in the history of the nation.

However, this cathartic potential of criminal trials (which also characterises these bodies in ordinary situations, although to a more limited degree) is not necessarily a negative feature. In particular, by witnessing justice "happening" after a phase of uncertainty, denial and abuse, society as a whole, as well as its individual members, might find peace and closure, and eventually reconcile with one another.[107] Indeed, this expressive dimension of criminal trials can play an instrumental role in bringing the population closer together, by reconstructing a public truth, and identifying clear, individual responsibles for past violence, in this way also reaffirming moral and legal values. Therefore, this expressive and educational function, although potentially problematic (as resting on an instrumentalisation of the defendants) should always be acknowledged, capitalised upon at the benefit of the transitional process, but not abused; as such, it should be envisaged as a further, almost incidental, effect of a tribunal's activity (as exemplified by the ICTY official approach, analysed in the upcoming chapter)[108]: its primary, direct purpose should be "to render justice, and nothing else"[109]; its main focus, the person who stands accused, the evaluation of his innocence or guilt. Any diversion from it in the interest of a further objective, even the noblest one, would betray fundamental principles of law.

The Judgments, and Their Aftermath

The Nuremberg Tribunal concluded its activities with the reading of the judgment, on October 1, 1946: 19 defendants were convicted, 12 of which to death (among these Hermann Goering, one of the protagonists of the Nuremberg spectacle, who succeeded in committing suicide just hours before the execution, thus denying the public one of the most awaited closing acts of the show).[110] While this represented a milestone in the post-conflict process, equally significant were the acquittals of three of the accused, namely Hans Fritzsche, Franz von Papen and Hjalmar Schacht[111]: these absolutions have often been employed as arguments against the accusations made to the trial of being a mere show, as they would prove that nothing was predetermined, that the process was fair and respectful of fundamental standards of law – such as the presumption of innocence of the defendants, which in some cases the Prosecution failed to override.

The IMT proceedings did not exhaust the process of criminal adjudicating the faults of the Axis Powers, as it was followed by several domestic trials confronting the Nazi atrocities, such as those based on Control Council Law n.10,[112] separately held by the Allies in the parts of Germany each of them supervised.[113] Particularly interesting were the 12 trials the US forces held against representatives of specific professional categories, or other entities (such as private companies) that had colluded with the dictatorship; one of the most renowned is the "Doctors' trial", which ascertained the responsibilities of medical professionals accused of having participated in the perverse scientific experiments of the Regime.[114] The resulting judgment constitutes the ideological foundation on which the Nuremberg Code was developed, which formalises fundamental principles and standards for experimentation on human subjects.[115] This achievement demonstrates how a judicial instrument set up in transitional contexts to deal with the horrors of the past can inform the future of societies well beyond criminal deterrence.

On the contrary, the Tokyo Military Tribunal saw no acquittals, and seven of the defendants were sentenced to execution.[116] Unlike Nuremberg, both sides tried to forget about the trial, if not to actively undermine its memory and legacy: the judgment was never officially published,[117] and by the end of the 1950s almost all convicted prisoners were released.[118]

With regard to the reconstruction and narration of the truth, although the narrative developed by the Nuremberg Tribunal is in few respects debated[119] this trial substantially succeeded in shaping a complete and authoritative tale of the events, highly endorsed and able to weaken attempts of revisionism or denial. The same cannot be said of the Tokyo experience, which leaves a "confused view of history, [as] the judgments taken as a whole are of course totally irreconcilable, either demonizing (the majority) or eulogizing (Judge Pal) Japanese intentions".[120] Indeed, one of the main causes for such failure were the many dissenting judgments expressed at the end of the Tokyo trial, at least in part caused by biases of prosecutors and judges, who held strong and divergent political opinions[121] and were quite ill-equipped to adequately assess the Japanese case in its specificity.[122] In their dissenting opinions judges exposed concerns and criticisms – about the institution of the court, the law applied, the truth-telling process – endowed with a particular authoritative force, as coming from within the tribunal itself, and this in turn undermined the overall credibility of the judgment, and of the narrative of the events it presented.[123]

Furthermore, judges and prosecutors in Tokyo failed to satisfactorily address the accuses of partiality, which were being moved to the court by a significant portion of Japan's public opinion. Indeed, many Japanese considered the Western powers just as responsible and despicable as those actually awaiting judgment (if not more than them), and such perceptions supported the characterisation, by the part of the defence team, of their clients as victims of the imperialistic politics of the West, thus critically impinging on the credibility and authority of the reconstruction of the events developed by the court.[124] Notably, this ghost of imperialism was also raised in other ways. For example, the American prosecutor stressed the instrumentality of the trial to setting and defending a certain "standard of civilization",[125] thus reaffirming what was already expressed within the Nuremberg trial. However, while this assumption was essentially uncontested in Germany – where the Allied Powers were considered as "culturally analogous" liberators from the despotism of a barbaric power, more resistance was expressed in Japan, where at least part of the population felt to be victims of Western racial discrimination,[126] and did not perceive its leaders as tyrants or brutes.[127] The Allies were therefore accused of violating those same principles they were pretending to defend, and this furthered the de-legitimisation of the court, and of the whole USA-led post-conflict exercise.[128]

Conclusions

This chapter aimed at providing a brief overview of the Nuremberg and Tokyo trials, by reconstructing the negotiation processes – which manifest a tension between new sensitivities and traditional approaches to justice post-war, the operations of the courts, as well as some of the mostly debated issues around these experiences. Notably, the dilemmas investigated are not typical or exclusive of these experiments; on the contrary, they have informed, and still inform (as emerging from the following chapters) many reflections around transitional justice, in particular with regard to the employment of tribunals and other strictly legal instruments for confronting legacies of violence and assessing the responsibilities of individuals for complex and often long-standing abuses.

The Nuremberg and Tokyo Tribunals have quite different legacies. In particular, the IMTFE is primarily remembered as a political trial led by the USA with the final purposes of justifying their actions in the Pacific while avenging their many losses, shaping and disseminating a biased version of the events unfolded in Asia during World War II, and at the same time expanding their influence in the Far East, thus setting the chessboard for the Cold War, which was already warming up.[129] As a consequence, the Japanese trial is mostly regarded as a lost opportunity to capitalise upon the achievements of Nuremberg, and evolve in the practice of international legal retribution. A primary factor for such failure was the spectre of colonialism and imperialism, which (for good reasons) weighted on the Allies in a way that in the German context was just not imaginable. As a consequence, this experiment will be abandoned for almost 50 years, only to be resumed with the International Criminal Tribunal for former Yugoslavia, which will refer to the Tokyo experience mainly as an example of what had to be avoided, in order to protect the legitimacy of the tribunal.[130]

On the contrary, the Nuremberg International Military Tribunal is considered as an ambitious and innovative experiment, and for these very reasons an imperfect one. Some authors are ferociously critical of this organism: Makau Mutua, for example, judges it as nothing more than "a patchwork of political convenience, the arrogance of military victory over defeat, and the ascendancy of American, Anglo-Saxon hegemony over the globe".[131] Indeed, one of the most debated issues concerns the political character of these bodies, which although being often denied or minimised, appears as unavoidable, and particularly difficult to manage constructively and in a context-sensitive way.

Despite the many – often well-founded – criticisms, however, this mechanism is valued as a turning point in the evolution of international criminal law,[132] humanitarian law[133] and also laws of war: it played a "constitutive role in contemporary international human rights"[134] and in the progressive overcoming of the classic Westphalian system, while its judgment is now considered as a seminal legal basis for fundamental international treaties such as the Genocide Convention of 1948 and the Geneva Conventions of 1949.[135] Also pivotal in crystallising its influence was the adoption, in 1950, of the Nuremberg Principles,[136] a set of guidelines developed by the International Law Commission with the aim of clarifying the constitutive elements of war crimes.

With specific regards to the history of transitional justice, the IMT is often considered as the starting point in the evolution of the discipline, the archetype of the retributive-justice model, whose inevitable deficiencies would be, at least ideally, adjusted in successive experiments, such as the ICTY and the ICTR. Additionally, the experience of Nuremberg shows the fundamental importance that the context has when shaping a post-conflict process.[137] For example, a legal, criminal proceeding was perceived as an appropriate way to assess and confront the atrocities committed by the Axis Powers, because these were largely understood as "the result of the machinations of a small, evil cabal",[138] an élite composed by few identified – or at least easily identifiable – individuals, who could thus be prosecuted in their individual capacity.[139] Additionally, the German regime had been destroyed, their few representatives left powerless, and a good portion of the population, which had somehow tolerated its excesses, felt a pressing need for absolution. On the contrary, the institution of a criminal tribunal would have met more resistance in a context in which a large portion of the population was regarded as responsible for the commission of the crimes (as in the case of South Africa or Rwanda). Furthermore, the events that unfolded in Europe during World War II were broadly perceived as absolutely exceptional: the sheer scale of the atrocities, as well as the perverse justifications that moved the regime, were unlike anything that Europe had experienced in recent history, to the point of being almost unconceivable – and this justified extraordinary responses.

Another factor that limited critical voices was a sort of "dirty conscience" of the Western powers, conscious that the German authoritarian regime and World War II had been provoked, at least in part, by the unfair political and economic measures adopted as a "punishment" for the misdeeds of the defeated powers during World War I.[140] Notably, this sense of guilt – although often blatantly denied – is not unique of this situation; on the contrary, it appears to be a recurring feature in the approach of the international community to several transitional contexts, from former Yugoslavia and Rwanda to Iraq. Moreover, the tribunal was in some ways legitimated by the unsatisfactory nature of the alternatives;[141] for example, Jens David Ohlin examined the main potential alternatives – let the Nazi leaders free or execute them – and concluded that none of them would have been accepted neither by the victims nor by other countries, as they could not satisfy the need for justice, atonement and truth-telling.[142]

In sum, in the particular context in which the tribunal operated, the exceptions introduced to fundamental principles of law, although problematic, appeared justified and supported by the victims and the population, and this provided the tribunal with a strong authority and legitimation; on the contrary, in Japan, where the court was widely perceived as a culturally insensitive experiment set up by a partial foreign power to further self-serving interests, the trial lacked support and credibility, and therefore authority.

In conclusion, this chapter has tried to portray how the ambitious "achievements at which the trial was aiming were compromised, rendered equivocal, by the trial itself; but its very failure has much to teach us"[143]: Nuremberg, with all its contradictions, has been a milestone in the evolution of transitional justice, a landmark experiment still debated, constructively criticised and replicated today; as such, one of its most significant merits is precisely its having started an on-going discussion on the banality of evil, and on how to confront unspeakable atrocities with an eye to rebuilding a traumatised society, also exposing the inevitable tensions and blind-spots inherent to this project.

Notes

1. John Q. Barrett, "Opening the Nuremberg Trial: The Moment of November 20, 1945", *St. John Legal Studies Research Paper December* 1 (2015): 1
2. M. Cherif Bassiouni, "The Nuremberg Legacy", in *Perspectives on The Nuremberg Trial,* ed. Guénaël Mettraux (Oxford: Oxford University Press, 2008), 584

3. Madoka Futamura, *War Crimes Tribunals and Transitional Justice. The Tokyo Trial and the Nuremberg Legacy* (New York: Routledge, 2008): 52–67
4. Nicola Henry, "Memory of an Injustice: The 'Comfort Women' and the Legacy of the Tokyo Trial", *Asian Studies Review* 37(3): 367
5. Susanna Sgroi, "Il principio di retroattività e il processo di Norimberga", *Diritto & questioni pubbliche* 3 (2003): 316
6. Richard Falk, "Telford Taylor and the Legacy of Nuremberg", *Columbia Journal of Transnational Law* 37 (1998–1999): 704
7. Aaron Fichtelberg, "Fair Trials and International Courts: A Critical Evaluation of The Nuremberg Legacy", *Criminal Justice Ethics* 28(1) (2009): 6
8. Matthew Lippman, "Nuremberg: Forty-Five Years Later" in *Perspectives on The Nuremberg Trial,* ed. Guénaël Mettraux (Oxford: Oxford University Press, 2008), 508
9. The USA affirmed this intention in several circumstances. See Tara Helfman, "Francis Biddle and the Nuremberg Legacy: Waking the Human Conscience", *The Journal Jurisprudence* 15 (2012): 357
10. James Owen, *Nuremberg: Evil on Trial* (London: Headline Review, 2006), 3
11. Helfman, "Francis Biddle and the Nuremberg Legacy", 358
12. *Declaration of Solidarity of the United Nations,* London, 12 June 1941. In Royal Institute of International Affairs, *United Nations Documents 1941–1945* (London and New York: Oxford University Press, 1946)
13. Belgium, Czechoslovakia, Greece, Luxembourg, The Netherlands, Norway, Poland, Yugoslavia, France – together with Great Britain, Canada, Australia, New Zealand and the Union of South Africa
14. Sgroi, "Il principio di retroattività e il processo di Norimberga", 316
15. *Declaration on Atrocities,* Moscow, 19–30 October 1943. In Royal Institute of International Affairs, *United Nations Documents 1941–1945* (London and New York: Oxford University Press, 1946)
16. Ibid.
17. Ibid.
18. *Cairo Communique 1,* Cairo, 1 December 1943. In Royal Institute of International Affairs, *United Nations Documents 1941–1945* (London and New York: Oxford University Press, 1946)
19. Ibid.
20. Neil Boister and Robert Cryer, *The Tokyo International Military Tribunal – A Reappraisal* (Oxford: Oxford University Press, 2008), 19
21. *Proclamation defining Terms for Japanese Surrender,* Postdam, 26 July 1945
22. Boister and Cryer, *The Tokyo International Military Tribunal,* 20
23. *Charter of the International Military Tribunal – Annex to the Agreement for the Prosecution and Punishment of the Major War Criminals of the European Axis Powers,* London 08 August 1945, 82 UNTS 27

24. *Charter of the International Military Tribunal*, Art. 6
25. Ibid., Art. 6
26. Ibid., Artt. 7 and 8
27. Ibid., Art. 6
28. Ibid., Art. 9
29. Lippman, "Nuremberg: Forty-Five Years Later", 513
30. *Japanese Instrument of Surrender,* Tokyo, 02 September 1945
31. Madoka Futamura, "Revisiting the Nuremberg Legacy: Societal Transformation and the Strategic Success of International War Crimes Tribunals – Lessons from the Tokyo Trial and Japanese Experience" (PhD Diss., king's College London, 2008), 116
32. *International Military Tribunal for the Far East Charter*, Tokyo, 19 January 1946
33. Ibid., Art. 5
34. Boister and Cryer, *The Tokyo International Military Tribunal,* 53
35. *International Military Tribunal for the Far East Charter*, Art. 5
36. Elizabeth Borgwardt, "Re-examining Nuremberg as a New Deal Institution: Politics, Culture and the Limits of Law in Generating Human Rights Norms", *Berkeley Journal of International Law* 23(2) (2005): 445
37. See Owen, *Nuremberg: Evil on Trial*, 3
38. David Luban, Julie O'Sullivan and David P. Stewart, *International and Transnational Criminal Law* (New York: Aspen Publishers, 2010), 144
39. Boister and Cryer, *The Tokyo International Military Tribunal,* 36
40. Futamura, "Revisiting the Nuremberg Legacy", 140
41. Bernard Victor Aloysius Roeling and Antonio Cassese, *The Tokyo Trial and Beyond* (Cambridge: Polity Press, 1993), 3
42. The choice of the defendants – as well as the choice of the crimes worth prosecuting – has a defining influence on the narrative of the events developed by tribunals
43. Among others, see Eric A. Posner, "Political trials in Domestic and International Law", *Duke Law Journal* 55 (2005): 138
44. Boister and Cryer, *The Tokyo International Military Tribunal,* 65
45. Futamura, "Revisiting the Nuremberg Legacy", 141
46. Boister and Cryer, *The Tokyo International Military Tribunal,* 67
47. See, for example, the opening statement of the lead Tokyo Prosecutor, Joseph B. Keenan, as quoted in Futamura, "Revisiting the Nuremberg Legacy", 123
48. Among others, see Futamura, "Revisiting the Nuremberg Legacy", 135
49. Reinhard Merkel, "The Law of the Nuremberg Trial", in *Perspectives on The Nuremberg Trial,* ed. (Oxford: Oxford University Press, 2008), 571
50. Ibid.
51. Falk, "Telford Taylor and the Legacy of Nuremberg", 700

52. Hans Kelsen, "Will the Judgment in the Nuremberg Trial Constitute a Precedent in International Law?", *The International Law Quarterly,* 1(2) (1947): 170
53. Ibid.
54. *The Trial of German Major War Criminals,* Volume 2, 98
55. Ibid., 102
56. David Luban, "The Legacies of Nuremberg", *Social Research* 54(4) (1987): 809
57. Ibid.
58. Paraphrasing the famous aphorism: "*Not only must Justice be done; it must also be seen to be done*"
59. Kelsen, "Will the Judgment in the Nuremberg Trial Constitute a Precedent in International Law?", 170
60. Luban, "The Legacies of Nuremberg", 811
61. Ibid., 786
62. Otto Kranzbuhler, "Nuremberg Eighteen Years Afterwards", in *Perspectives on The Nuremberg Trial,* ed. Guénaël Mettraux (Oxford: Oxford University Press, 2008), 437
63. Guénaël Mettraux, "Judicial Inheritance: The Value and Significance of the Nuremberg Trial to Contemporary War Crimes Trials" in *Perspectives on The Nuremberg Trial,* ed. Guénaël Mettraux (Oxford: Oxford University Press, 2008), 602
64. Borgwardt, "Re-examining Nuremberg as a New Deal Institution", 444
65. Luban, "The Legacies of Nuremberg", 817
66. Sgroi, "Il principio di retroattività e il processo di Norimberga", 327. As specified in this article, one of those codes was the German Military Code itself
67. Helfman, "Francis Biddle and the Nuremberg Legacy", 12
68. For an analysis of the development of this new crime see Martti Koskenniemi, "Hersch Lauterpacht and the Development of International Criminal Law", *Journal of International Criminal Justice* 2(3) (2004): 810–825
69. *Charter of the International Military Tribunal,* Art. 6
70. Lippman, "Nuremberg: Forty-Five Years Later", 511
71. Ruti Teitel, "Transitional Justice: Postwar Legacies", *Cardozo Law Review* 27 (2006): 1629
72. Ibid.
73. Gustave Gilbert, *Nuremberg Diary* (New York: First da Capo Press, 1961), 39 as quoted in Helfman, "Francis Biddle and the Nuremberg Legacy", 13
74. Luban, in "The Legacies of Nuremberg", 781 exposes this "bipolarity" in the approach of the Court towards sovereignty, that through its institution and judgment is at the same time undermined and protected

75. Roeling and Cassese, *The Tokyo Trial and Beyond,* 56
76. Kranzbuhler, "Nuremberg Eighteen Years Afterwards", 438
77. *The Trial of German Major War Criminals,* Volume 2, 98–102
78. The debate is described and analysed in Ruti Teitel, "Transitional Jurisprudence: The Role of Law in Political Transformation", *The Yale Law Journal* 106(7) (1997): 2019–22
79. Ibid., 2020
80. Hart expresses his position in H.L.A. Hart, "Positivism and the Separation of Law and Morals", *Harvard Law Review* 71(4) (1958): 593–629
81. See Lon L. Fuller, "Positivism and Fidelity to Law – A Reply to professor Hart", *Harvard Law Review* 71(4) (1958): 630 – 672. In his article Fuller also recognises his (and Hart's) position of advantage and safety, which inevitably affects their understanding of the law; and even from this perspective, it is clear that "if we felt that the law itself was our safest refuge, would it not be because even in the most perverted regimes there is a certain hesitancy about writing cruelties, intolerances and inhumanities into law? And is it not cleat that his hesitancy derives, not from a separation of law and morals, but precisely from an identification of law with those elements of morality that are most urgent and the most obviously justifiable [. . .] ?"
82. Luban, "The Legacies of Nuremberg", 797
83. *The Trial of German Major War Criminals,* Volume 22 (Judgment), 445–448
84. Kelsen, "Will the Judgment in the Nuremberg Trial Constitute a Precedent in International Law?", 155
85. Ibid., 156
86. Borgwardt, "Re-examining Nuremberg as a New Deal Institution", 436
87. *The Trial of German Major War Criminals. Proceedings of the International Military Tribunal sitting at Nuremberg, Germany,* Volume 22 (judgment), (Published at Nuremberg, Germany, 1949), 445
88. International Military Tribunal for the Far East, *Dissenting Judgment of Justice Pal* (Tokyo: Kokusho-Kankonai, 1999)
89. Ibid., 22
90. Ibid., 23
91. Kelsen, "Will the Judgment in the Nuremberg Trial Constitute a Precedent in International Law?", 160
92. Ibid.,164
93. Ibid., 165
94. Merkel, "The Law of the Nuremberg Trial", 568
95. "Nazi Germany, communist regimes, or nationalist Serbia under Milosevic all heavily relied on a certain concept of the good. Each of those regimes used to present itself as the embodiment of the binding ultimate truth. The necessary feature of those ideologies was an arbitrary choice of the enemy group, the group presented in the same perverted ethical terms, as the

embodiment of the bad. In such ideologies, the circle is closed by inferring that destruction of the enemy group is both necessary and good". Nenad Dimitrijevic, "Justice Beyond Blame. Moral Justification of (the idea of) a Truth Commission", *Journal of Conflict Resolution* 50 (2006): 371

96. Among others, see Jens David Ohlin, "On the Very Idea of Transitional Justice," *The Whitehead Journal of Diplomacy and International Relations* 8 (2007): 59
97. Ibid., 60
98. Ibid.
99. Sgroi, "Il principio di retroattività e il processo di Norimberga", 319
100. See Infra, Chapter 10
101. Boister and Cryer, *The Tokyo International Military Tribunal,* 311
102. Luban, "The Legacies of Nuremberg", 791
103. Helfman, "Francis Biddle and the Nuremberg Legacy", 359
104. Martti Koskenniemi, "Between Impunity and Show Trials", *Max Planck Yearbook of United Nations Law* 6 (2002): 19
105. Roeling and Cassese, *The Tokyo Trial and Beyond,* 20
106. Among others, see Awol K. Allo, "The 'Show' in the 'Show Trial': Contextualizing the Politicization of the Courtroom", *Barry Law Review* 15 (2010): 41–72; Koskenniemi, "Between Impunity and Show Trials", 1–35
107. Maria Elander, "The Victim's Address: Expressivism and the Victim at the Extraordinary Chambers in the Courts of Cambodia", *The International Journal of Transitional Justice* 7 (2013): 99
108. See infra, Chapter 7
109. Hannah Arendt, *Eichmann in Jerusalem: a Report on the Banality of Evil* (New York: The Viking Press, 1963), 254
110. Zachary Kaufman, "The Nuremberg Tribunal V. The Tokyo Tribunal: Designs, Staffs, and Operations", *The John Marshall Law Review* 43 (2009–2010): 762
111. Ibid., 763
112. *Control Council Law No. 10: Punishment of Persons Guilty of War Crimes, Crimes Against Peace and Against Humanity,* 3 Official Gazette Control Council for Germany 50–55, 1946 (December 20, 1945)
113. Luban et al., *International and Transnational Criminal Law*, 142
114. For an in-depth analysis of the trial and its consequences on medicine see Sheldon Rubenfeld, *Medicine after the Holocaust* (Berlin: Springer, 2010), 94–105
115. Luban et al., *International and Transnational Criminal Law*, 143
116. Kaufman, "The Nuremberg Tribunal V. The Tokyo Tribunal", 763
117. Roeling and Cassese, *The Tokyo Trial and Beyond,* 81
118. Futamura, "Revisiting the Nuremberg Legacy", 123

119. For example, strongly criticised was the choice of the Prosecution to focus on the charge of aggressive war, thus determining "an interpretation of the Nazi regime as predominantly one of aggressive militarists that put its racist and genocide character in a secondary and at times almost invisible role". Koskenniemi, "Between Impunity and Show Trials", 20
120. Boister and Cryer, *The Tokyo International Military Tribunal,* 312
121. Ibid., 94
122. Roeling and Cassese, *The Tokyo Trial and Beyond,* 36
123. Ibid., 322
124. Posner, "Political trials in Domestic and International Law", 141
125. Among others, see Boister and Cryer, *The Tokyo International Military Tribunal,* 276
126. Roeling and Cassese, *The Tokyo Trial and Beyond,* 24
127. Posner, "Political trials in Domestic and International Law", 149
128. Boister and Cryer, *The Tokyo International Military Tribunal,* 276
129. Roeling and Cassese, *The Tokyo Trial and Beyond,* 78
130. Boister and Cryer, *The Tokyo International Military Tribunal,* 310
131. Makau Mutua, "Never Again: Questioning the Yugoslav and Rwanda Tribunals", *Temple International and Comparative Law Journal* 11 (1997): 170
132. Fichtelberg, "Fair Trials and International Courts", 5
133. Teitel, "Transitional Justice: Postwar Legacies", 1631
134. Ibid.
135. Bassiouni, "The Nuremberg Legacy", 590
136. International Law Commission, "Principles of International Law Recognized in the Charter of the Nuremberg Tribunal and in the Judgment of the Tribunal, 1950" (Report of the International Law Commission covering its Second Session, Document A/1316, 29 July 1950)
137. Borgwardt, "Re-examining Nuremberg as a New Deal Institution", 411
138. Lippman, "Nuremberg: Forty-Five Years Later", 525
139. Ibid. See also Borgwardt, "A New Deal for the Nuremberg Trial", 688
140. Among others, Falk, "Telford Taylor and the Legacy of Nuremberg", 711
141. As an example, see Borgwardt, "Re-examining Nuremberg as a New Deal Institution", 460
142. Ohlin, "On the very Idea of Transitional Justice", 59
143. Luban, "The Legacies of Nuremberg", 779

CHAPTER 7

International Criminal Justice Revisited: The Ad Hoc Tribunals for the Former Yugoslavia and Rwanda

Introduction

This chapter continues on the path of introducing some of the mechanisms that played a pivotal role in the evolution of the field of transitional justice, by providing an overview of the natural successors of the Nuremberg tribunal: the ad hoc international courts for Rwanda and former Yugoslavia, established by the United Nations Security Council (UNSC) with the tasks of investigating the truth and providing justice regarding two among the most cruel and bitter conflicts witnessed after World War II.

These tribunals bear testament to the strong faith of the international community in international criminal law as a key instrument to address and redress the legacies of conflicts, and to bring truth, justice and ultimately peace in war-torn territories; as such, their establishment – together with that of the International Criminal Court, on which they will have an important influence – marks the golden age of criminal accountability at the international level, the era of "firsts": first judicial instrument set up by the Security Council under the powers of Chapter 7 of the UN Charter; first prosecution and judgment of a Head of Government; first conviction for rape as an international crime.[1] However, at the same time, these courts are potentially the most scrutinised and criticised instruments ever instituted in post-conflict scenarios, insomuch that awareness of their many limitations

G. Girelli, *Understanding Transitional Justice*,
Philosophy, Public Policy, and Transnational Law,
DOI 10.1007/978-3-319-53606-4_7

will foster the development of alternative, restorative and hybrid means for conflict resolution and adjudication.

After retracing the events in former Yugoslavia and Rwanda, and the steps that led to the institution of the two courts, this chapter considers the main features of the statutes of the ICTY and ICTR, especially pausing on the (explicit, as well as assumed) objectives these bodies were entrusted with; following, attention will be devoted to some among the key criticisms moved to these bodies as the fulcrum of transitional initiatives, and more in general to the experiment of international criminal justice, also addressing the perceived dichotomy between law and politics.

Old Atrocities, in a New System of International Relationships

With the conclusion of the Nuremberg and Tokyo trials, the experiment of international criminal justice was abandoned for almost 50 years, and although much was written and discussed in abstract terms, no further attempts were initiated to establish international tribunals with jurisdiction on massive atrocities and heinous crimes. While some countries, such as Argentina, crafted and implemented new ways to deal internally with dictatorial regimes and repression, at the international level the Cold War nearly froze the official relationships between the two spheres of the world, while everything happened in the off-stage of international politics. In such a complex and fragile environment, the establishment, by the part of one or more countries, of an institution competent to adjudicate upon violations of an unclear and evolving body of law allegedly committed by other countries – all of them inevitably sided – was just unthinkable.

The situation drastically changed with the crumbling of the Eastern Bloc and the (at least apparent) cessation of this continuous struggle for supremacy between the two factions, and such reformation of the international dynamics was clearly manifested by the institution, in 1993, of the ICTY; the establishment of this body, which was given mandate to adjudicate upon some among the most heinous atrocities recorded on European soil since World War II, also speaks volumes about the failure of its German and Japanese predecessors to deter potential war criminals. In extreme synthesis, the Balkan Wars were spurred by the dissolution of the Socialist Federative Republic of Yugoslavia (SFRY), originally divided – mostly along ethnic lines – in six Republics, and consequent struggles for independence and control.[2] While Marshal Tito, with all his contradictions, had substantially managed to keep the territories united, on the onset of the 1990s economic problems and a growing nationalism determined Slovenia and Croatia to declare their independence.[3] This led to an attempt of Yugoslavia, guided by Serbia – in turn led by Slobodan Milosevic and his xenophobe ideology – to retrieve the lost regions, through violent actions that will soon degenerate in ethnic conflicts, also because of the resurfacing of latent but almost structural tensions between communities that shared a central government but were divided along ethnic and religious lines.[4] The scenario was extremely complex, with the conflict having, at the same time, features of a civil-ethnic war, an international hostility, and a struggle for (and against) self-determination,[5] and characterised by heinous episodes of persecution and ethnic cleansing which brought back, right on the doorsteps of the civilised (and civiliser) Europe, the horrors of the Nazi Holocaust.

The conflict generated "more than three million refugees, 200–250,000 persons killed, 50,000 victims of torture, 20,000 cases of rape and a large-scale destruction of public and private property".[6] In May 1993, while this bloodshed was still ongoing, the UNSC – after the failure of incremental measures regarding the Balkan situation and notwithstanding the objections of the SFRY – adopted Resolution 827, through which the institution of an international tribunal was formalised.[7] Unprecedented, while not uncontested, this resolution was based on Chapter 7 of the UN Charter[8]: as events of the gravity and the magnitude of those recorded in the territories of the former Yugoslavia were perceived as a threat to international stability – and to a shared humanity[9] – the ad hoc tribunal was created with the final purpose of achieving and protecting international peace and security.[10]

Similar features can be observed in the chain of events that led to the institution of the ICTR, whose organisation, strengths and frailties are in many profiles similar to those of the ICTY, and will therefore be discussed together. Despite all the similarities, one of the key historical and legal differences concerns the dimension of the conflict, which in the case of Rwanda was purely internal (although external powers firstly played – and then failed to play – a fundamental role): the shooting down of the plane carrying the Hutu President Juvenal Habyarimana on April 6, 1994 triggered one of the crudest genocides in recent history.[11] The two main Rwandan ethnic groups, Hutus and Tutsis, "spoke the same language, followed the same religion, intermarried, and lived intermingled, without territorial distinctions, on the same hills, sharing the same social and political culture",[12] insomuch that they are not unanimously considered as two different ethnic groups; however, they had a troubled relationship, whose gravity intensified in colonial times, when these originally fluid ethnic identities were officialised and "frozen into law"[13] by the colonial powers, and exploited for the administration of the territory by exacerbating oppositions and tensions. In time, this divide-et-impera strategy created a nation of victims, where both groups perceived themselves as discriminated and abused by the other, and this provoked cyclical strives and overturning of power.[14]

The responsibilities for the killing of Habyarimana are still an object of debate, but what followed was a surgically organised and swift genocide of the Tutsi minority, coupled with the elimination of whoever stood in the way: in roughly hundred days between 500,000 and one million people – one-tenth of the country's population – were slaughtered,[15] and in the following months almost two million people, both Hutus and Tutsis, fled to the neighbouring states (mostly Zaire – now DRC – and Burundi), causing a grave humanitarian emergency, while thousands died of cholera epidemics.[16] Once again, after standing idle and failing to intervene to stop the killings,[17] the international community eventually decided, through a Security Council Resolution, to exploit the powers conferred by Chapter 7 of the Charter to set up an international tribunal

> For the sole purpose of prosecuting persons responsible for genocide and other serious violations of international humanitarian law committed in the territory of Rwanda and Rwandan citizens responsible for genocide and other such violations committed in the territory of neighbouring States, between 1 January 1994 and 31 December 1994.[18]

The Twin Statutes: Organisation, Jurisdiction, Limitations

The statutes of the two courts share many key prescriptions relating to the organisation and the scope of the tribunals, as the foundational charter of the ICTY was used as a blueprint, a guide in the drafting of the ICTR statute, while their peculiarities are mostly justified by variances in the factual and political circumstances concerning the events the courts were called to adjudicate upon.

With regards to their structure, both courts are composed of three trial chambers and an appeals chamber, constituted of international judges elected by the UN General Assembly from a list of professionals and distinguished figures assembled by the Security Council,[19] which also appoints an independent Prosecutor for each court (although until 2003 one Prosecutor acted for both tribunals)[20]; the administrative issues are handled by a Registry. Moreover, both courts are situated outside, and far from, their territory of reference: the first sits in The Hague – principally because of political issues (such as the will and necessity to show impartiality), while the latter is located in Arusha, Tanzania, mostly because of security concerns; notably, although the decision of holding the trials outside the countries where the atrocities unfolded is supported by legitimate concerns of fairness and neutrality,[21] such distance from the local communities will have – as analysed further on – a detrimental impact on the courts' activities and legacies.

For what concerns their jurisdiction, the two bodies are ad hoc tribunals, meaning their reach is limited in space and time: while the mandate of the ICTR is really specific, as – not without criticisms – it only covers one year of the tormented history of the country,[22] the ICTY statute provides an initial date – January 1, 1991 – but not a final one, subordinating the jurisdiction of the court to the restoration of peace in the territory[23]: this open mandate was justified by the fact that the conflict was still ongoing when the tribunal was established (whereas the Rwandan genocide – seemingly the only domestic event the international community was concerned about – was over at the time of the constitution of the ICTR),[24] and it was fundamental in empowering the court to investigate the atrocities committed in Kosovo between 1996 and 1999.[25]

Additionally, diverting – on this specific element – from the example of Nuremberg, the two bodies were only given competence to try individuals (and not to adjudicate on the criminal character of entire organisations, although the collective dimension typical of these crimes was then given relevance, in a different form, by the ICTY through the contested doctrine of the Joint Criminal Enterprise),[26] and for a limited but significant cluster of crimes: while only the ICTY statute explicitly attributes competence for violations of the laws or customs of war -due to the international nature of the conflict,[27] both tribunals are recognised jurisdiction for grave breaches of the Geneva Conventions,[28] genocide[29] and crimes against humanity.[30] The latter crime, however, is formulated differently in the two statutes; in particular, while the ICTY Charter requires the war nexus – meaning that the crime be committed "in armed conflict, whether international or internal in character"[31] – the ICTR statute does not demand this nexus anymore, and in its place introduces a new requirement of the crime to be committed as part of a "widespread or systematic attack against any civilian population".[32] This change, which was largely determined by the peculiarity of the Rwandan events, that occurred entirely within the borders of one country and were not pacifically categorised as a "war",[33] revealed to be a crucial step in the evolution of international criminal law, insomuch that now the widespread or systematic character of the acts forms part of the constitutive elements of this crime. Additionally, by removing the war nexus and establishing this element, the ICTR definitively accomplished what Nuremberg had failed to, and the ICTY had just introduced: the jurisdiction of an extra-national body over acts committed against civilians by citizens or forces of the same country, and exclusively within that country's territorial borders, irrespective of the occurrence of an armed conflict as traditionally understood. This provoked a further corrosion of the traditional sovereignty of the nation-state, which held exclusive and final power over purely internal events, and of the Westphalian system with it.[34]

"Mere" Judicial Processes, or Comprehensive Transitional Mechanisms?

> Trials establish individual responsibility over collective assignation of guilt; *justice dissipates the call for revenge*, because when the Court metes out the perpetrator his just deserts, then the victims calls for retribution are met; [thus] victims are prepared to be *reconciled* with their erstwhile tormentors, because they know that the latter now paid for his crimes; a fully reliable *record* is established of atrocities so that future generations can remember.[35]

These words of Antonio Cassese, the first President of the ICTY, convey how multifaceted the mandates of post-conflict tribunals are, to include objectives well beyond those typical of a judicial body – although the courts were not created as part of a defined and comprehensive transitional programme. In particular, while punishment and deterrence of future war crimes were fundamental goals of these bodies, because of the exceptionality of the context, and also considering that the courts were founded by Chapter 7 of the UN Charter, these objectives were not contemplated as their exclusive or final ones; rather, the courts were also invested with contributing to achieving and maintaining peace and security in war-torn territories, and as a consequence at the international level.[36] Particularly audacious was UNSC Resolution 955/1994[37] establishing the ICTR, which explicitly envisaged a court which would "contribute to the process of national reconciliation",[38] in this way for the first time explicitly conferring such a typically extrajudicial goal to a criminal tribunal.[39]

All this created extremely high expectations towards the activities and the impact of quite limited and experimental judicial bodies, acting in precarious and complex circumstances.[40] At the same time, this marked an apex in the faith of the international community in the developing system of international criminal accountability (interestingly, in parallel with the promotion of truth commissions precisely as alternatives to a criminal justice increasingly perceived as limited), the apparent realisation of every legal professional's dream: to tame politics through law – especially in the aftermath of conflicts which the same international community, as a political community, had shamefully failed to prevent.[41] In this way, "international law is, in essence, presented as a dynamic emancipation project whereby international law has been reborn and the role of law, and implicitly western civilization, redeemed from the horrors of its past".[42]

However, how the courts were supposed to fulfil such delicate goals was far from evident; underlying was the idea that by hearing witnesses and putting heinous criminals behind bars they would automatically and inevitably foster justice, truth and reconciliation domestically. Notably, a dose of realism was retained by the courts themselves. In particular, one trial chamber of the ICTY clarified that "it does not seek to identify causal factors, nor through history explain why the conflict with which we are concerned occurred. It would indeed do no justice to the victims".[43] In this way, the court made the limits of its reach clear, as a judicial body whose exclusive task is to determine the guilt or innocence of a defendant according to the relevant body of law; with this purpose, it considers historical events and facts, but it is not its function to reconstruct, explain and account for the deepest causes of conflicts. More generally, international tribunals can in fact contribute to the process of ending violence and reconstructing a peaceful and reconciled society, but only through the implementation of their original and typical functions and activities. In other words, and as already introduced in previous chapters, criminal prosecutions can play an important role within well-thought transitional projects by resisting cultures of impunity, neutralising and physically removing subjects responsible for the atrocities, proving certain facts beyond reasonable doubt and deterring future criminals[44]; however, they should not be ascribed further autonomous goals – such as truth-telling or reconciliation – because in pursuing them they would risk betraying their fundamental mission, which is necessarily limited to judging the criminal responsibilities of individual subjects regarding specific crimes. Moreover, due to this delicate function, they encounter substantial and procedural limitations that make them ill-suited to pursue more general objectives.

New Achievements, New Challenges

One of the key lessons learned from Nuremberg and Tokyo was that, for the tribunals to be able to potentially contribute to the transition of Japan and Germany (as well as of Europe) to a peaceful future, it was critical that the population – and not only the international community, or the victors – would perceive them as legitimate and fair, and as pursuing their best interest. As a consequence, the founders of the ICTY and ICTR were committed to avoiding the limitations and shortcomings of their predecessors; for example, the importance was stressed of only applying rules and principles that were universally recognised and accepted as part of the body of international law, in such a way shielding the tribunals from accusations of violating the principle of non-retroactivity.[45] Nevertheless, peculiarities in their structure and the complexity of the contexts they were called to investigate determined for the courts new challenges that they were not always able to face appropriately, due to a lack of means and/or sensitivity.

Firstly, courts are by nature limited instruments, which in the aftermath of conflicts tackle extremely complex issues with a circumscribed focus on legally relevant events and subjects; inevitably, this strict judicial focus generates an essentialisation of the reconstructed narrative of the events, of the problem (violations of international criminal and humanitarian law through the perpetration of physical violence) and consequently of the solution offered (criminal punishment), which can prove unsatisfactory for the victims while also distortive of complex experiences of colonisation, abuse and marginalisation. At the same time, as the following chapters will highlight – by privileging a legal narrative of the events, their causes and consequences – criminal trials operate a selection of the relevant stories and experiences, which result in an inclusion of certain subjects and facts, but at the same time an exclusion of others.[46]

Additionally, the courts found themselves bound by numerous practical constraints, determined by the novelty and complexity of their activities – which were possibly underestimated in the design phase – and, at least for what concerns ICTY, by a likely unwillingness of the founding organs to create an effective institution. Indeed, the tribunal had initially been conceived, at least by some, as an "empty theatre of justice",[47] that should have served the political purposes of the powers involved through its mere existence, but without actually operating.[48] As a consequence, the two tribunals faced several financial, organisational and structural limitations,[49] such as limited funding and personnel, insomuch that, because of the discrepancy between the gargantuan task it was assigned and the paucity of resources and support it received, Antonio Cassese defined "his" ICTY as "a giant who has no arms and no legs".[50] For example, the court's budget – which for the 2012–2013 period reached $250,814,000[51] – in 1993 was limited to $276,000,[52] and it took more than one year to appoint the first Prosecutor.[53]

Also, the tribunals were not provided with adequate devices for promoting enforcement and compliance, and they are thus bound to rely on the cooperation of governments, which have often revealed unwilling to support them[54]; for example, the Rwandan RPF government voted against the constitution of the tribunal,[55] while Serb authorities have been actively obstructing the work of the ICTY for long.[56]

Additionally, even when a criminal court is well-founded and well-equipped, its judicial nature, imposing several procedural requirements and limitations, causes its being an inevitably selective institution: unlike other more inclusive mechanisms, such as truth commissions, a tribunal – especially when considering crimes of such complexity – can only prosecute a limited number of subjects.[57] This posed the problem, already faced by the IMT in Nuremberg, of selecting the defendants, which the two institutions tackled quite differently. In particular, the first ICTY Prosecutor decided to focus the earliest investigations on low- and middle-level perpetrators, principally because of a lack of information and sources directly implicating high-level officials.[58] This decision would lead to a grave waste of already scarce resources, paucity of results and strong criticisms from both the victims, who passively witnessed some among those most responsible for the crimes run free, and the global civil society, thus heavily affecting the efficacy and legitimacy of the court. Therefore, the ICTR wisely resolved to focus its activities on those suspected of bearing the gravest responsibilities for the genocide, delegating the investigation and prosecution of the "small-fries" to local tribunals and *Gacaca* courts.

However, one of the most criticised limitations of these bodies (beyond the ones concerning the costs) regards their outreach efforts. In particular, several authors denounce a lack of involvement of the courts with the local population, which appears as a particularly grave issue in the case of the ICTY, being the tribunal concerned with an extremely complex situation involving three different ethnic groups, with a long history of more or less forced coexistence and deep-rooted prejudices. Due to the tribunals' physical distance from the territories, which precludes the majority of the population from attending the trials in person, the courts proceedings and activities are mainly known on the ground through targeted outreach initiatives and the media. However, the latter are not rarely biased or influenced by local leaders and political dynamics,[59] while the courts, also because of their scarce budget, initially neglected this aspect[60]; for example, a study by the Open Society Institute revealed how the Hague-based tribunal failed, until 1999, to provide translations of its judgments in local languages, and only issued press releases in Serbia from 2000.[61] As a result, the population, and especially the victims, were "often neglected and left to be influenced by a hostile propaganda coming from different regimes".[62] In particular, several polls have registered a complete lack of awareness of the existence of the courts by the part of the local communities, indifference and – in too many cases – denial of their legitimacy and thus rejection of their decisions, together with the truth they report.[63] Concurrently, the communication gaps are more efficiently filled by the detractors of the courts, who exploit actual or claimed weaknesses to delegitimise their work, together with the international community these bodies represent, while at the same time strengthening nationalist or ethnically biased politics.[64] For example, 15 years after the creation of the ICTY, a relevant segment of the Serb population – heavily influenced by its leaders – still considered the court as a mechanism set up by the enemy and the international community with the purpose of blaming and subjugating their homeland.[65] The limitations and short-sightedness of the courts in getting closer to the locals, both in terms of striving towards a better understanding of culture and context and in spreading reliable information around their activities, gravely impinged on their efficacy, as an institution cannot hope to educate, serve as example or deter if it is not known and respected by the subjects it should be primarily addressing. The ICTY painfully learnt this lesson in July 1995 when – two years after its constitution and when the Prosecutor had already handed down indictments for 14 individuals[66] – Serbian troops committed in Srebrenica "the worst [crime] on European soil since the Second World War",[67] under the passive eyes of UN peacekeepers.

Still, the ICTY only established an Outreach programme in 1999 (after the umpteenth intensification of violence, this time in Kosovo),[68] entirely funded through voluntary contributions[69] and tasked with organising activities in local communities, broadcasting court sessions in local languages, trainings local professionals, among others.[70] Thanks to the committed work of the Outreach department (although in a condition of chronical scarcity of resources),[71] developments in the political scenarios of the most restive states, Serbia and Croatia,[72] and a more open attitude of the local media,[73] there are now signs of a deeper acceptance of the ICTY's work on the ground.[74] However, also because of this delay in involving and directly addressing the communities in former Yugoslavia,[75] a certain degree of hostility endures, especially due to deep-rooted individual beliefs about the court, which prevent many of its supposed beneficiaries from accepting its findings about the responsibilities of their fellow compatriots and the outcome of the conflict,[76] and make them feel collectively condemned.[77]

An interconnected issue is that of the involvement of the victims, who – as introduced in the previous chapter – in Nuremberg and Tokyo played a mostly passive role. Because of the judicial nature of ad hoc tribunals, also in these contexts the victims mainly participated as witnesses (notwithstanding the dangers and practical difficulties this implied).[78] Testimonies were fundamental both for the prosecution, as pivotal contributions in reconstructing the factual background and the criminal responsibilities of the defendants, and for the victims themselves, who by narrating their memories in an official forum would see them acknowledged and addressed[79]; indeed, ideally courts work as a platform in which victims can express their truths and have them validated, recorded and officialised, thus tearing down walls of silence, suspects and doubts. However, the importance of this acknowledgment was played down by limitations of the courts themselves – such as the constraints that the judicial nature of the forum imposes on the victims' narrative, the aforementioned inadequate resonance, in the countries, of the activities of the tribunals, and a lack of other, more substantial instruments of acknowledgment and support, such as reparations. Indeed – as stated throughout the book – in a war-torn society where hundreds of thousands of people have been brutally killed, injured or displaced, the survivors have more immediate needs to fulfil than merely retribution, and cannot imagine a "justice" that does not encompass forms of material help.[80] In addition, many of the courts' judgments have been considered by part of the population as too lenient, while some cannot accept the use – by both courts – of the practice of plea-bargaining, which allows perpetrators to obtain lighter sentences in exchange for admitting their responsibilities[81]: in practice, victims and survivors "want to see their own conception of justice at work, and we can only offer them our interpretation of the law".[82] The problem is, in other words, that "international judicial decision-making is rooted in law, precedent, and custom, which are typically intellectually and emotionally inaccessible to the affected communities".[83] As a consequence, tribunals employed during transitions appear as facing an impossible dilemma: either they intervene on some of their key features, in this way betraying their strictly judicial nature and what it entails, or they stick to their fundamental characteristics and objectives, thus almost inevitably failing to satisfy the many and complex needs of victims and survivors.

Law vs. Politics

Another crucial issue, which is frequently debated with reference to the ICTY and ICTR, concerns the reasons leading to their institution; in particular, several sources assert that the courts were primarily established not as judicial bodies aspiring to shed light on and promote justice for complex and violent events, but rather as political tools of international powers – in this way also echoing the accuse directed to the Nuremberg and Tokyo trials of being a (American) show. More precisely, according to this "realistic" argument, the two courts were established by the international community in order to avoid a more direct, politically charged and expensive intervention,[84] and/or to remedy for its inability (or unwillingness) to prevent and stop the massacres.[85] The latter allegation seems particularly well-founded with regards to the ICTR, which appeared, and still appears, to many as a quite flawed attempt of the international community to clear its conscience and save its reputation after the passivity and substantial indifference shown, in front of the whole world, towards the genocide.[86]

As a result, once again international courts faced a well substantiated criticism of being politicised bodies, exploited by international powers for extra-judicial purposes, and of being excessively influenced by political contingencies and dynamics to be able to act impartially. Notably, Thierry Cruvellier describes the ICTR as a case of "Losers Justice", a "court of remorse"[87] born out of the shame and discredit the international community faced for its failure to avoid the massacre,[88] while the

Rwandan Patriotic Front (RPF) was the only force that could claim credit for ending the genocide, and consequently, substantially define itself as the victor; this position of strength gave the Rwandan government several advantages with regards to the ICTR (irrespective of its strong aversion to the court itself, clearly manifested by its vote against UNSC Resolution 955),[89] as emerging both from its statute, which essentially restricts the jurisdiction of the court to the genocide, leaving out both prior events and its violent aftermath, and from the practice: none of the ICTR Prosecutors has sought indictments against members of the RPF,[90] essentially delegating this delicate task to feebly motivated national courts, in this way reinforcing accusations of unduly political interferences and lack of neutrality.[91]

More generally, the two courts have to constantly strike an extremely delicate balance. On one side, they are inevitably engaged with politics: they were founded by a political body and they are essentially dependent on states cooperation for funding and operational support (in particular, making arrests and supporting investigations)[92]; on the other side, in their judicial functions they are expected to be – and to appear – apolitical, free from influences and instrumentalisation by external powers. The ICTY Prosecutors proved in a particularly delicate position, and while they attracted praise from several sources (among others, for indicting Slobodan Milosevic),[93] their choices were also harshly criticised.[94] Particularly upsetting to many was the absence of any kind of investigations concerning potential responsibilities of Western forces, among others with regards to the UN peacekeepers complicit passivity in Srebrenica[95] and the NATO "humanitarian bombings" of 1999: despite Prosecutor Louise Arbour's determination to get to the bottom of those events, political forces were highly persuasive in convincing the court "not to bite the hand that feeds you",[96] and her successor Carla del Ponte eventually concluded that basis for such investigations were lacking.[97] Notwithstanding its legal justifications, this decision raised, once again, the spectre of victors' justice, thus reinforcing doubts concerning the legitimacy and impartiality of the court, further antagonising local communities, and offering precious arguments to its detractors.

In conclusion, the experiences of the ICTY and ICTR manifest the artificiality of the law vs. politics dichotomy, posited on a short-sighted understanding of the latter as the evil realm of particular interests and abuses, and of the former as the technical, professional and mature alternative and response to it. Also, it showed how intertwined with politics these bodies inevitably are – and how this is not necessarily something negative: they are founded by and rely on the cooperation of political bodies, which can potentially guarantee a fundamental support; they operate in conjunction with other political realities (such as the European Union, in the case of the ICTY, and the Security Council)[98]; they provide political bodies – in primis national governments – with vocabularies and narratives that are then employed in the domestic political arena.[99] As a consequence, in the practice, law and politics are best understood not as opposed and contrasting, but rather as elements of the same reality that influence and shape each other in a dynamic relationship: revealing, acknowledging and capitalising upon this relation, while intervening on its toxic effects is thus more useful than reasoning through unrealistic binomials.

Conclusions

The ICTR and ICTY were created as largely experimental bodies and entrusted with the impossible task of providing truth and justice in the aftermath of complex, violent and deeply rooted conflicts. Following the steps of Nuremberg, the courts are primarily admired for their impact on the evolution of international law, and especially for their focus on gender-based violence. Among others, the ICTR was the first international court to adjudicate on – and therefore interpret – the crime of genocide,[100] and in the *Akayesu* case it broadly defined and clearly identified rape as an international crime[101]; the ICTY, on its part, held the first international trial for crimes of sexual violence against men, and developed seminal jurisprudence on rape as torture and on its instrumentality to genocide and ethnic cleansing.[102] The innovations introduced by the two tribunals were then incorporated in the statute of the International Criminal Court, which for the first time explicitly recognises sexual and gender-based violence as crimes against humanity and war crimes (while the ICTY and ICTR statutes only envisaged rape as a crime against humanity).

Additionally, these ad hoc tribunals played a role in the post-conflict processes of the two countries by incapacitating, through fair procedures, some dangerous individuals and removing them from the political, military and administrative spheres,[103] promoting accountability,[104] and helping to reconstruct a mostly irrefutable narrative of the events,[105] in this way fostering the hope that "a tribunal created as an alibi can progressively escape from its creator to generate new initiatives".[106] In this way, the courts also succeeded in normalising a mechanism born out of exceptional circumstances,[107] thus paving the way for the institution of the International Criminal Court and of a brand new system of supranational justice[108]; key in this sense were a sensitivity of the founders in avoiding many of the obstacles and criticisms faced by the Tokyo and Nuremberg trials, as well as awareness by the part of the courts of their role and position on the international chessboard: both judges and Prosecutors have always been conscious of the importance of good diplomatic relationships with states and international organisations, and laudable efforts went into establishing and clarifying principles of international law. As aforementioned, through this contribution the courts furthered the process of corrosion of the Westphalian system of international relations, extending the reach of international law to domestic situations and replacing a "State-sovereignty-oriented approach [with a] human-being-oriented approach".[109] Also, they showed that anybody – also Head of States like Milosevic – could face international prosecution (politics permitting).[110]

These achievements are laudable, but they also pose a problem of priorities; indeed, the question arises if such mechanisms should privilege their functions within the international system or instead focus on their role in the local transitional process and on their meaning for the victims. What Mutua, and several other authors, conclude is that "while that effect [deterrence and evolution of international law] is salutary, it does little to respond to the real and graphic abuses and sufferings of the victims in Rwanda and the former Yugoslavia".[111] Despite being legal instruments, these courts are borne out of political circumstances, they are deeply involved in politics at the international level and privilege a legalistic narrative which inevitably diverts attention away from the experiences and needs of the local population; as a consequence, the latter feels alienated from an institution that is not seen, heard, understood on the ground. In other words, one of the key limitations of the tribunals is their being (or at least appearing to be) more concerned with the international community they were created by and represent than with the actual, local communities they are supposed to ultimately serve.[112] Indeed, despite their successes in the legal realm, the courts achievements in supporting the transitions in Rwanda and former Yugoslavia are much more limited[113]: they did not directly contribute to reforming the domestic judicial systems,[114] thus preventing the locals from pursuing a goal – bringing justice in the affected countries – to which international trials can only give a limited contribution. Also, they were not able to (as not designed to) address the deepest causes of the conflicts, that linger in well-rooted prejudices among ethnic groups, coupled with economic and material inequalities.[115] These go beyond the single episodes judged by the courts and cannot be solved without an inclusive and multifaceted intervention, that a judicial court cannot deliver alone. Moreover, efforts in providing a forum for the victims, where their experiences could be acknowledged and honoured, were taunted by poor outreach efforts, and the deficit of legitimacy and credibility the courts suffered among the local population. Finally, the courts failed to deter future crimes and promote peace and reconciliation: protracted conflicts in the area of former Yugoslavia endured until 1999, and in Rwanda thousands of people were brutally killed in a sort of revenge feud that for long time seemed impossible to stop.[116]

These limitations of extremely expensive and burdensome institutions also show how justice is always political, and consequently how superficial opposing law and politics is. In light of these limitations, probably the main merit of the two courts consists in their having started and supported a discourse, breaking the infamous wall of silence and providing some irrefutable evidence. In particular, the courts imposed a dialogue at the social and interpersonal levels, by making it just impossible to deny certain claims,[117] and as a consequence discussing and reflecting upon the conflict.[118] Additionally, they contributed to a dialogue at the "official level"; for example, Patrice McMahon and David Forsythe revealed how the presence of the ICTY contributed to putting Serbia, and the territories of the former Yugoslavia, on the "diplomatic map", attracting the attention of official bodies as well as NGOs, while at the same time international actors, such as the European Union and the USA, supported the court by subordinating aids and support to Serbia for its cooperation with the tribunal.[119]

In sum, the fundamental lesson learned by the ICTY and ICTR experience is that

> The ugliness of war, the political reality of various hatreds – racial, religious, and gender – cannot be isolated into an international courtroom for resolution. Such a court would only make sense if it was part of a comprehensive domestic and international process of punishment, reconstruction and reconciliation.[120]

These mechanisms undertook an appreciable course, but something is still to be adjusted, in order to enhance the efficacy of judicial bodies in transitional contexts; most of all, more engagement is required with the local population and territories, and this in turn compels shifting away from a "one-size-fits-all" to a more specific, comprehensive and context-sensitive approach. As more thoroughly analysed in the next chapter, this challenge will be taken up by hybrid courts, in which those international features that better guarantee fairness and competence will be mixed, integrated with elements of the domestic judicial system.

Notes

1. Eric Møse, "Main Achievements of the ICTR", *Journal of International Criminal Justice* 3 (2005): 934
2. Rachel Kerr, *The International Criminal Tribunal for the Former Yugoslavia: An Exercise in Law, Politics and Diplomacy* (New York: Oxford University Press, 2004), 27
3. Makau Mutua, "Never Again. Questioning the Yugoslav and Rwanda Tribunals", *Temple International and Comparative Law Journal* 11 (1997): 173
4. David Luban; Julie O'Sullivan, and David P. Stewart, *International and Transnational Criminal Law* (New York: Aspen Publishers, 2010), 145
5. Lilian A. Barria and Steven D. Roper, "How Effective are International Criminal Tribunals? An Analysis of the ICTY and ICTR", *The International Journal of Human Rights* 9 (2005): 351
6. Sanja Kutnjak Ivkovich and John Hagan, *Reclaiming Justice: The International Tribunal for the Former Yugoslavia and Local Courts* (New York: Oxford University Press, 2011), 1
7. UN Security Council Res 827 (1993), Un. Doc. S/RES/827
8. Kerr, *The International Criminal Tribunal for the Former Yugoslavia*, 39
9. Robert D. Sloane, "The Expressive Capacity of International Punishment: The Limits of the National Law Analogy and the Potential of International Criminal Law", *Stanford Journal of International Law* 43 (2007): 54
10. Mohamed Shahabuddeen, *International Criminal Justice at the Yugoslav Tribunal: A Judge's Recollection* (Oxford: Oxford University Press, 2012), 7
11. Barria and Roper, "How Effective are International Criminal Tribunals?", 352
12. Philip Gourevitch, *We Wish to Inform You That Tomorrow We Will Be Killed with Our Families* (London: Picador, 1999), 47
13. Mahmood Mamdani, *When Does a Settler Become a Native? Reflections of the Colonial Roots of Citizenship in Equatorial and South Africa* (University of Cape Town, Centre for African Studies, Inaugural Lecture, 13 May 1998): 5
14. Ibid., 6

15. Luban et al., *International and Transnational Criminal Law*, 162
16. Gourevitch, *We Wish to Inform You That Tomorrow We Will Be Killed with Our Families*, 164
17. See Gourevitch, *We Wish to Inform You That Tomorrow We Will Be Killed with Our Families*, for an extensive reconstruction of the international dynamics prior and during the genocide
18. UN Security Council, *Statute of the International Criminal Tribunal for Rwanda* (*ICTR Statute*), U.N. Doc. S/RES/955 (1994)
19. For a critical assessment of this aspect, see Michael G. Karnavas, "The ICTY Legacy: A Defense Counsel's Perspective", *Gottingen Journal of International Law* 3 (2011): 1059
20. Shahabuddeen, *International Criminal Justice at the Yugoslav Tribunal*, 11
21. David Tolbert, "The International Criminal Tribunal for the Former Yugoslavia: Unforeseen Successees and Foreseeable Shortcomings", *The Fletcher Forum of World Affairs* 7 (2002): 9
22. *ICTR Statute*
23. UN Security Council, *Updated Statute of the International Criminal Tribunal for the Former Yugoslavia* (last amended 7 July 2009) (*ICTY Statute*), 25 May 1993, UN Doc. S/RES/827
24. Barria and Roper, "How Effective Are International Criminal Tribunals?", 355
25. Kerr, *The International Criminal Tribunal for the Former Yugoslavia*, 67
26. For an overview of some key issues concerning this doctrine, see Karnavas, "The ICTY Legacy", 1066
27. *ICTY Statute*, Art. 3
28. *ICTY Statute*, Art. 2; *ICTR Statute*, Art. 3 (the latter only envisages jurisdiction for violations of Common Article 3, due to the purely internal dimension of the conflict)
29. *ICTY Statute*, Art. 4; *ICTR Statute*, Art. 2
30. *ICTY Statute*, Art. 5; *ICTR Statute*, Art. 3
31. *ICTY Statute*, Art. 5
32. *ICTR Statute*, Art. 3
33. Payam Akhavan, "The International Criminal Tribunal for Rwanda: The Politics and Pragmatics of Punishment", *The American Journal of International Law* 90 (1996): 503
34. Kerr, *The International Criminal Tribunal for the Former Yugoslavia*, 63
35. Antonio Cassese, "Reflections on International Criminal Justice", *Journal of International Criminal Justice* 9(1) (2011): 272 [emphasis added]
36. Shahabuddeen, *International Criminal Justice at the Yugoslav Tribunal*, 114
37. *ICTR Statute*
38. Ibid.

39. Barria and Roper, "How Effective Are International Criminal Tribunals?", 357
40. Møse, "Main Achievements of the ICTR", 938
41. Sloane, "The Expressive Capacity of International Punishment", 47
42. John D. Haskell, "The Complicity and Limits of International Law in Armed Conflict Rape", *Boston College Third World Law Journal* 29 (2009): 37
43. *Prosecutor v Zenjil Delalić et al* (Judgment) ICTY-96-21-T (16 November 1998), Par. 89
44. Philip Clark and Zachary Kaufman, eds., *After Genocide: Transitional Justice, Post-Conflict Reconstruction, and Reconciliation in Rwanda and Beyond* (New York: Columbia University Press, 2009), 263
45. Kerr, *The International Criminal Tribunal for the Former Yugoslavia,* 61
46. Haskell, "The Complicity and Limits of International Law in Armed Conflict Rape", 35–84 elaborates on this assertion with a specific focus on victims of rape in conflict
47. Pierre Hazan, *Justice in a Time of War: the True Story behind the International Criminal Tribunal for Former Yugoslavia* (College Station: Texas A&M University Press, 2004), 45
48. Ibid., 192
49. Among others see Mutua, "Never Again", 184
50. Kerr, *The International Criminal Tribunal for the Former Yugoslavia,* 115–146
51. "The Cost of Justice", last updated December 5, 2016, http://www.icty.org/sid/325
52. Barria and Roper, "How Effective Are International Criminal Tribunals?", 354
53. Kerr, *The International Criminal Tribunal for the Former Yugoslavia,* 51
54. Ioannis Armakolas and Eleni Vissou, "Transitional Justice in Practice: the International Criminal Tribunal for the Former Yugoslavia and Beyond" (Unisci Discussion Paper 18, 2008): 35
55. Akhavan, "The International Criminal Tribunal for Rwanda", 505
56. Among others, Armakolas and Vissou, "Transitional Justice in Practice", 39
57. Miriam J. Aukerman, "Extraordinary Evil, Ordinary Crime: A Framework for Undestanding Transitional Justice", *Harvard Human Rights Journal* 15 (2002): 51
58. Minna Schrag, "Lessons Learned from ICTY Experience", *Journal of International Criminal Justice* 2 (2004): 429
59. Bert Swart; Alexander Zahar, and Goran Sluiter, eds., *The Legacy of the International Criminal Tribunal of the Former Yugoslavia* (New York: Oxford University Press, 2011), 29

60. Frédéric Mégret, "The Legacy of the ICTY as Seen Through Some of Its Actors and Observers", *Goettingen Journal of International Law* 3 (2011): 1045
61. Diane F. Orentlicher, "Shrinking the Space for Denial: The Impact of the ICTY in Serbia" (New York: Open Society Institute, 2008): 27
62. Mégret, "The Legacy of the ICTY as Seen Through Some of Its Actors and Observers", 1039
63. Among otherse, see Michael P. Scharf and Ahran Kang, "Errors and Missteps: Key Lessons the Iraqi Special Tribunal Can Learn from the ICTY, ICTR and SCSL", *Cornell International Law Journal* 38 (2005): 911–947 and, more recently, Jaya Ramji-Nogales, "Designing Bespoke Transitional Justice: A Pluralist Process Approach", *Michigan Journal of International Law,* 32 (2010): 25
64. Ramji-Nogales, "Designing Bespoke Transitional Justice", 25
65. Swart et al, *The Legacy of the International Criminal Tribunal of the Former Yugoslavia,* 67
66. Orentlicher, "Shrinking the Space for Denial", 17
67. "'May we all Learn and Act on the Lessons of Srebrenica', says Secretary-General, in Message to Anniversary Ceremony", last updated July 11, 2005, http://www.un.org/News/Press/docs/2005/sgsm9993.doc.htm
68. Orentlicher, "Shrinking the Space for Denial", 17
69. Tolbert, "The International Criminal Tribunal for the Former Yugoslavia: Unforeseen Successees and Foreseeable Shortcomings", 13
70. Ivkovich and Hagan, *Reclaiming Justice,* 5
71. Orentlicher, "Shrinking the Space for Denial", 97
72. An analysis of the evolution of these countries' internal situation and their approaches to international justice can be found in Jelena Subotìc, "The Paradox of International Justice Compliance", *The International Journal of Transitional Justice* 3 (2009): 362–383
73. See McMahon and Forsythe, "The ICTY's Impact on Serbia", 424; Orentlicher, "Shrinking the Space for Denial", 103
74. Ivkovich and Hagan, *Reclaiming Justice,* 30
75. Orentlicher, "Shrinking the Space for Denial", 96
76. Ibid., 49
77. Armakolas and Vissou, *Transitional Justice in Practice,* 45
78. Mégret, "The Legacy of the ICTY as Seen Through Some of Its Actors and Observers", 1034
79. Hazan, *Justice in a Time of War,* 177
80. Armakolas and Vissou, *Transitional Justice in Practice,* 44
81. Luban et al., *International and Transnational Criminal Law,* 154
82. Hazan, *Justice in a Time of War,* 183

83. Swart et al., *The Legacy of the International Criminal Tribunal of the Former Yugoslavia,* 13
84. Barria and Roper, "How Effective Are International Criminal Tribunals?", 354
85. Armakolas and Vissou, *Transitional Justice in Practice,* 33
86. Among many others, Akhavan, "The International Criminal Tribunal for Rwanda", 501
87. Thierry Cruvellier, *Court of Remorse. Inside the International Criminal Tribunal for Rwanda* (Madison: University of Wisconsin Press, 2010), 167
88. Sloane, "The Expressive Capacity of International Punishment", 46
89. Lars Waldorf, "'A Mere Pretense of Justice': Complementarity, Sham Trials, and Victor's Justice at the Rwanda Tribunal", *Fordham International Law Journal* 33(4) (2011): 1272
90. Cruvellier, *Court of Remorse,* 164
91. Waldorf, "A Mere Pretense of Justice", 1271
92. McMahon and Forsythe, "The ICTY's Impact on Serbia", 428
93. Hazan, *Justice in a Time of War,* 112
94. For example, see Karnavas, "The ICTY Legacy", 1088 on the Imbalance in the "representation" of Ethnic Groups Among Defendants at the ICTY
95. Mégret, "The Legacy of the ICTY as Seen Through Some of Its Actors and Observers", 1048
96. Hazan, *Justice in a Time of War,* 132
97. Ibid.
98. McMahon and Forsythe, "The ICTY's Impact on Serbia", 414
99. Sarah M.H. Nouwen and Wouter G. Werner, "Doing Justice to the Political: The International Criminal Court in Uganda and Sudan", *The European Journal of International Law* 21(4) (2011): 962
100. Møse, "Main Achievements of the ICTR", 934
101. Ibid., 935
102. For a more in-depth analysis of the ICTY and ICTR jurisprudence on sexual and gender-based violence, see Khadija Ali, "Sexual and Gender Based Crimes in International Criminal Law: Moving Forwards or Backwards?", *International Journal of Law and Political Sciences* 2(10) (2015): 197–201
103. Møse, "Main Achievements of the ICTR", 932
104. Mégret, "The Legacy of the ICTY as Seen Through Some of Its Actors and Observers", 1030
105. Ibid., 1050
106. Hazan, *Justice in a Time of War,* 199
107. Fausto Pocar, "The Proliferation of International Criminal Courts and Tribunals", *Journal of International Criminal Justice* 2 (2004): 305
108. Shahabuddeen, *International Criminal Justice at the Yugoslav Tribunal: A Judge's Recollection,* 202
109. Ibid., 204

110. Among others, Barria and Roper, "How Effective Are International Criminal Tribunals?", 360
111. Mutua, "Never Again", 179
112. Sloane, "The Expressive Capacity of International Punishment", 49
113. Mégret, "The Legacy of the ICTY as Seen Through Some of Its Actors and Observers", 1029
114. Tolbert, "The International Criminal Tribunal for the Former Yugoslavia: Unforeseen Successees and Foreseeable Shortcomings", 12
115. Armakolas and Vissou, *Transitional Justice in Practice,* 41
116. Barria and Roper, "How Effective Are International Criminal Tribunals?", 358
117. Møse, "Main Achievements of the ICTR", 942
118. Orentlicher, "Shrinking the Space for Denial", 22
119. McMahon and Forsythe, "The ICTY's Impact on Serbia", 424
120. Mutua, "Never Again", 170

CHAPTER 8

The Hybrid Experiment: Assessing the Special Court for Sierra Leone

Introduction

"Hybrid" or "mixed" courts are an alternative type of tribunal emerged in post-conflict scenarios, typically when the local justice system is too weak, damaged and/or corrupted to deal efficiently with mass atrocities and complex crimes,[1] while pure international instruments are considered equally inappropriate, because of their distance from the local culture and their exclusionary character.[2] Hybrid courts therefore rest on a simple idea: mix the best of the two worlds, in this way promoting local ownership while at the same time ensuring impartiality, independence and high standards of justice. In turn, such a cooperation is meant to foster the reconstruction process, as by working hand in hand with international staff, local professionals are meant to "learn how to fish, instead of just be given fish"[3] (evoking a classical humanitarian maxim), and will therefore be empowered to rebuild the legal and administrative structures of the country.

Hybrid courts are one manifestation of a more general process of hybridisation and localisation of post-conflict programming, which developed in response to growing dissatisfaction towards more traditional approaches, such as ad hoc international tribunals, which, as emerged from the previous chapters, are increasingly perceived as inadequate to effectively pursue justice and further peace in war-torn territories. In turn, this hybridisation of transitional justice can be situated within a larger movement towards hybridity advocated in post-colonial studies as part

G. Girelli, *Understanding Transitional Justice*,
Philosophy, Public Policy, and Transnational Law,
DOI 10.1007/978-3-319-53606-4_8

of a critique of traditional neoliberal interventions, arguably responsible for the top-down imposition of partial but universalised understandings of progress and development.[4]

Several hybrid courts have been established to address conflicts and crimes in different parts of the world, such as the Special Panels for Serious Crimes in East Timor, the Special Tribunal for Lebanon and the Extraordinary Chambers in the Courts of Cambodia – created to adjudicate upon the atrocities of the Khmer Rouge regime roughly 20 years after its downfall.[5] Although these mechanisms share several characteristics, they also present many peculiarities, which make them all different from each other, to the point that some authors question the very existence of a separate model of hybrid courts. These issues will be herein addressed through the analysis of one of the archetypal examples of hybrid tribunals, the Special Court for Sierra Leone (SCSL)[6]: this chapter will briefly reconstruct the civil war in the African country and the establishment of the court, also outlining its most significant characteristics, merits and limitations, which largely reflect those of all hybrid courts. This reflection will also allow to pause on the concept of hybridity, with its many shades, and to consider potential problems related to its uncritical adoption as an objective of transitional justice processes.

Conflict and Post-Conflict in Sierra Leone: A Country Too Lush for Peace

Since Europeans discovered, in the fifteenth century, the African territory now known as Sierra Leone, the country has endured long periods of instability and violence,[7] and both the colonial and the postcolonial powers, attracted by the abundance of natural resources, fuelled a climate of partiality and injustice.[8]

The civil war that would paralyse the country for more than ten years began in 1991, when the Revolutionary United Front (RUF), a rebel force led by Foday Sankoh, invaded Sierra Leone from neighbouring Liberia, with the political and economic support of the president of the country, Charles Taylor.[9] Indeed, the attack was conceived as part of a larger project, involving Taylor, Gambian rebels and Libyan leader Mu'ammar Gaddafi, who offered training, resources and support to the rebels, and whose final aim was the overcoming of the existing relations of economic and political power in the area, with the further purpose of exploiting the resources (in particular diamonds and oil) of these countries to their personal advantage.[10] While the RUF claimed its final objective to be the establishment of a democratic system in the interest of the population, its struggle was in fact conducted not as an attack against the corrupt elites of the country or enemy (governmental) forces, but rather more as a campaign of terror targeting the peasants and the fishermen it was professing to protect and fight for.[11] The RUF rapidly gained control over a large portion of the territory, and in particular of several diamond mines, which revealed fundamental for funding its campaign. The following years saw a number of coups, as well as the intensification of an internal war which involved several actors, such as the RUF, the Civil Defence Forces (CDF) – initially formed to defend villages from the attacks of the rebels, and the Armed Forces Revolutionary Council (AFRC), a group of ex-soldiers colluding with the RUF.[12] The peak of the brutalities was presumably reached in 1998, when the RUF launched "Operation No Living Thing", assaulting the capital and killing over 7000 people.[13]

Unlike many contemporary conflicts, this war was not characterised by strong ethnic or racial tensions, nor particularly solid ideological components[14]; rather, it appeared to be motivated, in different measures, by a mix of greed and socio-economic grievances (specifically against corruption and unequal economic development),[15] and fuelled by a loose collection of figures with different objectives and charismas, who also played on a larger, regional chessboard. This conflict, which sometimes "resemble[d] a riot that had taken on a life of its own",[16] was characterised by exceptional cruelty and violence carried out by all parties in the conflict. The main targets of such brutality were civilians (in a small country of roughly four million inhabitants, virtually every single citizen was affected by it), especially those most vulnerable: rape was used as a weapon of war; children were abducted, drugged and brainwashed, and in this way transformed into devoted soldiers; mutilation was employed broadly, in order to prevent people from voting or just as a strategy of terror.[17]

In 1999, the RUF and the Government signed the Lomé Peace Accord,[18] which officialised the end of the conflict, and which envisaged the institution of a truth and reconciliation commission, and the concession of an essentially blanket amnesty to all rebel forces.[19] Unfortunately, the RUF proved to have no interest in respecting the terms of the agreement, and rebel forces persevered in destabilising the country.[20] However, the conflict was only thrust into the international spotlight at the end of 1999, when, in an attempt to oversee and promote the implementation of the Peace Agreement and support the delivery of humanitarian assistance,[21] the United Nations (UN) created UNAMSIL, one of the largest peacekeeping operations ever established.[22] Its presence (although brutally opposed by the RUF), coupled with the efforts of British forces on the territory, and the embargo on diamonds exports, prompted the final defeat of the RUF, and the beginning of a new pacification process.[23]

Shaping a New Form of Accountability

At the end of the conflict, the longing for accountability was deeply felt, and so was the struggle to find an appropriate instrument to pursue justice and foster the rebuilding of a peaceful society. In 2002, as disposed by the Lomé Peace Accord, a truth commission was established, which travelled the country collecting thousands of testimonies.[24] Although the participation was quite intense, the commission was also widely met with indifference and sometimes resentment: many engaged with this mechanism hoping to receive much-needed material help and support, while the talking-for-healing paradigm embraced and furthered by the commission appeared distant from the Sierra Leoneans' typical approach to justice and redress.[25] More specifically, several authors report how healing is broadly appreciated by the local population – for cultural and linguistic reasons – as primarily linked to the physical dimension of the individual and/or to his material needs, and how forgiving and forgetting is often preferred to publicly exposing one's story of suffering and abuse.[26] As such, this truth commission represents an example of top-down hybridisation, pursued through the contamination of local processes and rites with foreign concepts, values and priorities, thus making this mechanism at least partially ill-suited to efficiently address the most pressing needs of the population (interestingly, as analysed, further-on, the SCSL will meet similar criticisms.)

Additionally, the domestic judicial system – already fragile – had been practically dismantled, and most of its human resources had either fled the country or were killed during the conflict.[27] Concurrently, President Kabbah refused to take entire and exclusive responsibility for the prosecution of the rebels, which were supported by part of the population, while at the same time opposing a purely international solution.[28] Therefore, already in 2000 the UN (at this point even more deeply involved in the conflict, as the RUF had taken around 500 peacekeepers hostage)[29] had been requested to assist the Sierra Leonean government with the institution of a mixed court competent to try those identified as the most responsible for the atrocities witnessed during the conflict, and thus bring the latest phase of impunity in the country to an end.[30] The UN agreed, through Security Council Resolution 1315, to the establishment of

> A credible system of justice and accountability for the very serious crimes committed in Sierra Leone [that] would end impunity and would contribute to the process of national reconciliation and to the restoration and maintenance of peace.[31]

The outcome of the negotiations between the government and the UN was a court that incorporated some of the (perceived) best characteristics of national and international experiences. In particular, the tribunal maintains several features of the ICTR and ICTY, but with some innovations and adaptations inspired by local mechanisms, incorporated in its final structure with the purpose of overcoming the main limitations traditionally experienced by ad hoc tribunals – especially those related to the excessive costs, the lack of legitimacy and the difficulties in reaching and involving the victims and the population. Indeed, one of the key lessons learned from the experience of international tribunals is that subjecting local personalities, for how controversial, to the judgment of a foreign mechanism, which operates afar from the epicentres of conflict, risks exacerbating those very tensions that these processes are meant to address.

The first sign of a deeper involvement of the locals was the establishment of the tribunal not via UN Resolution (as in the case of the ICTY and ICTR), but rather through an agreement between the Government of Sierra Leone and the UN, signed in Freetown on January 16, 2002.[32] As a consequence, the court is neither part of the UN structure nor of the domestic judicial system, in this way being, at least formally, independent from both the internal government and the UN.[33] Moreover, the tribunal was located not in a foreign country, but rather in Freetown, within the territory affected by the war, in this way being more visible and approachable, while also facilitating the participation of the locals as staff, witnesses, audience.[34] Additionally, the agreement envisaged the construction of a state-of-the-art infrastructure to host the tribunal, which would then remain to Sierra Leone.[35]

However, the key feature that qualifies this court as a hybrid is the coexistence of national and international staff and laws. Concerning the former, the agreement provided for the majority of the judges, the Registrar and the Prosecutor to be appointed by the UN, while the remaining staff were to be identified by the domestic government, which, however, was not bound to nominate Sierra Leoneans.[36] This would have allowed for greater involvement of local professionals into the functioning of the tribunal, thus ensuring local ownership and at the same time increasing the potential for capacity building; however, in practice, the court – especially in its key roles – was principally composed of international personalities (unlike other experiences, such as the Cambodian one),[37] and the local government proved all but intentioned to select its own citizens for these roles.[38]

With regards to the latter, the Appeals Chamber itself recognised that the court's hybrid character is primarily due to "the nature of the law it is empowered to apply".[39] Indeed, the Statute of the court (annexed to the 2002 Agreement)[40] grants the SCSL jurisdiction for classical international crimes – meaning crimes against humanity,[41] violations of Common Article 3 of the Geneva Conventions (war crimes committed in the context of a non-international armed conflict)[42] and other serious violations of international humanitarian law[43] – but with special consideration for the peculiar characteristics of the conflict. For example, the court is explicitly conferred jurisdiction to prosecute conducts which were tragically widespread during the civil war, such as "conscripting or enlisting children under the age of 15 years into armed forces or groups or using them to participate actively in hostilities".[44] Furthermore, Article 5 of the Statute extends the jurisdiction of the court to certain domestic crimes, by incorporating national laws against child abuse and wanton destruction of properties.[45] Such a provision constitutes an innovative solution, aimed at ensuring a justice more tailored to the needs of the individuals and the communities most directly affected by the war, while also weakening potential accuses moved to the tribunal of representing a form of victors' justice, or an imperialistic project of the West[46]: thanks to these provisions not only international but also domestic crimes, already prohibited by law at the time of their commission, could be prosecuted. However, notably, the prosecution never charged any of these domestic crimes, in this way eluding potential issues related to domestic precedents and to the influence of the Lomé Accord amnesty,[47] but at the same time also missing a precious opportunity to overcome artificial distinctions between the national and the international realm, and to better connect with the local population.

The efficacy of this new experiment is debated and all but unchallenged, and while some authors stress its positive characteristics and effects, others reveal problems and shortcomings, some specific to the SCSL, while others apparently inherent to the retributive justice model (as shared by virtually every ad hoc tribunal).

A System Improved: Outreach, Capacity Building, Proximity to the Victims

The court has been praised for its many qualities and achievements, most of which linked to its being – or at least striving to be – much more involving, and involved with, the domestic constituencies than its ad hoc predecessors. Indeed, the court was built in such a way that it "could leave a strong legacy in Sierra Leone, including improved infrastructure, respect for the rule of law and trust in public institution, and improved professional standards".[48]

As aforementioned, the final purpose was to shape and implement a system of justice that would be accepted and endorsed by the population, and that could have a real and positive impact on the lives of victims and society; for these reasons, it was critical for the court not only to understand but also to incorporate in its structure and activities cultural elements as well as local understandings and priorities. This objective was first pursued by mixing national and international staff, relying on the fact that they would constructively influence each other[49]: the presence of national professionals would ensure a deeper knowledge and understanding of Sierra Leonean history, customs and social organisation – fundamental in reconstructing the root causes of the acts of violence and decipher usages and rituals that played a pivotal role in the conflict.[50] At the same time, the international staff was entrusted with ensuring neutrality and objectivity, as well as a high level of competence and experience in legally dealing with complex, widespread and brutal crimes.[51] Additionally, foreign professionals would have provided training to the locals, thus contributing to the development of a pool of competent Sierra Leonean lawyers, prosecutors and judges that would lead the reconstruction of the domestic judicial system.[52] This objective was ideally pursued not only by having local and international individuals working side by side but also through specific initiatives, such as courses and training to law students, legal professionals, prison guards and media.[53] As reported – notwithstanding some limitations, which will be explored in the next paragraph – the SCSL appears to have in part fulfilled its capacity building mandate, especially with regards to police officers and prison personnel.[54]

Furthermore, hybrid courts are engineered in such a way to be more accessible, both physically and linguistically, to the population, making it easier both to participate as witnesses and to be informed about the activities of the tribunal, also ensuring a wider, and more reliable, media coverage of the process.[55] Notably, the SCSL is the first ad hoc tribunal provided with an autonomous Outreach department, organised in regional offices and mostly constituted of Sierra Leoneans,[56] whose primary aim is "making the trials meaningful to the population on whose behalf justice is being done".[57] In order to achieve this purpose, the department organises local meetings to introduce the population to the court's activities and discuss with the civil society about potential obstacles, shortcomings and additional goals; it broadcasts radio and video programmes; it distributes informative material, while also developing educational programmes.[58] These and other initiatives strongly contributed to an overall positive reception by the part of the locals of the court's presence and activity, in turn fostering its legitimacy and authority.[59]

Additionally, the Sierra Leonean court is praised for its fundamental role in shaping and advancing international criminal law, and especially for its gender-sensitive focus on the conflict. Among others, the court handed down the first international convictions for sexual slavery (which had been only recently explicitly recognised as an international crime)[60] and forced marriage as crimes against humanity; also, as the latter offence was not expressly recognised by the court's Statute (it was formally prosecuted under "other inhumane acts"), the SCSL was the first body to formalise it as an autonomous and self-standing crime under international law, with specific characteristics as well as physical and psychological consequences.[61]

Finally, the SCSL appeared to have a positive effect in supporting and complementing the peace process, as it deterred potential perpetrators while at the same time isolating some of the main masterminds behind bars, in this way making it impossible for them to continue their campaign of terror.[62]

To conclude, this hybrid court aimed at overcoming the traditional obstacles of ad hoc tribunals by devoting primary attention to outreach and capacity building efforts, aware that its authority and effectiveness are inevitably dependent on its reception by the part of population; thanks to these and other characteristics, the victims and the citizens of the country have developed a sense of ownership towards the court, which is perceived as committed not only to political actors (the international community, in particular) but also to the people directly harmed by the conflict, while maintaining a standard of performance that the local justice system could not aspire to. However, the court has also experienced a number of drawbacks and limitations that gravely hampered its success, weakening its potential to further justice and peace in Sierra Leone; as analogous issues are experienced by other hybrid experiences, they call into question the overall ability of hybrid tribunals to overcome the classical limitations of courts in transition.

Flipsides: Design Faults and Practical Limitations

One of the main deficiencies of the tribunal is the lack of resources. The costs related to the functioning of the ICTY and ICTR are clearly excessive (at the peak of its activity the former was spending an average of 26 million dollars per accused),[63] especially considering the many necessities of a war-torn country; to avoid facing the same issue, and against the opinion of the UN Secretary General, the final agreement provided for the Sierra Leonean court to be financed exclusively through voluntary contributions.[64] This apparently technical provision has heavily influenced the design and functioning of the court, as it essentially denied this body the resources it needed to perform its tasks with stability.[65] Additionally, scarcity of funds means that those available are sub-optimally spent: excessive resources were invested in fundraising activities and ad hoc, short-term hiring, while this insecurity likely detracted skilled individuals from applying for positions within the court.[66]

More generally, the constant lack of resources, or at least insecurity about their availability – registered by all the hybrids mechanisms up to now, and particularly dramatic for the mixed Court of Bosnia and Herzegovina[67] – impeded any long-term planning, while also impacting on fundamental strategic choices. For example, it strongly influenced the decision of providing the tribunal with a very limited mandate, especially in terms of temporal and personal (limited to the subjects suspected to bear the greatest responsibility for the violence) jurisdiction,[68] as well as of a very limited time to complete its mission. The operations of the defence team were also obstacled,[69] while the Prosecutor was induced – partly because of this lack of resources – to further restrict the number of persons charged; in turn, this negatively affected the body's perceived legitimacy, as the population witnessed many well-known perpetrators run free, while victims struggled to satisfy basic needs (this is even more problematic if considering that the funding of the court had inevitably subtracted money from the truth commission and from other, more traditionally restorative projects, as well as from addressing other fundamental needs). As a result, "many Sierra Leoneans consider the overall cost of the SCSL too high a price to pay for what they received in return".[70]

In addition to financial problems, the decision to establish the court with an agreement between the State and the UN, rather than on a Security Council Resolution, provoked the lack of the typical enforcement powers the ICTY and the ICTR enjoy, their Statutes being based on Chapter 7 of the UN Charter.[71] As a consequence, other states have no obligation to cooperate with the court (e.g., by extraditing suspects), which is a grave deficiency, considering that the fighting factions, and the RUF in particular, had very close ties with other African countries, such as Liberia and Libya, and that many alleged perpetrators fled Sierra Leone and found shelter in neighbouring states.[72]

Moreover, the very same characteristics that are often mentioned as positive features of hybrid courts are at the same time criticised by others as either negative per sé or poorly implemented. For example, the court appears to have at least partly failed its capacity building purposes, as only few and sporadic trainings were offered, and often limited to certain individuals (such as the court's staff) or categories.[73] This was, to some extent, due to a lack of funding, strategic planning and coordination with other initiatives, and partly due to reported tensions between the court and domestic legal professionals, who felt alienated and not rarely snubbed by the court (because of reasons such as the predominantly international composition of the tribunal and its broad reliance on non-domestic standards).[74] Additionally, successful capacity building produced unexpected negative consequences: skilled human resources were drawn away from other sectors which also critically needed rebuilding,[75] while several of these well-trained experts eventually left the country to pursue international, and less precarious, careers.[76] This confirms how, in the words of Ethel Higonnet, "throwing international staff together with locals into a building will not provide a magic panacea to the problem of capacity building".[77] Rather, such an objective needs to be carefully planned and implemented, also in cooperation with other post-conflict mechanisms, in order to guarantee a long-term positive impact in the country undergoing the transition; as such, it cannot just be presumed to be accomplished by putting people together – especially within an organ structurally underfunded and overloaded, which works in a complex and fragile context.

Similarly, revealing a lack of strategic planning was the very decision to build a new structure to host the tribunal: while seemingly unproblematic, because of the extremely high maintenance costs of this modern infrastructure, which the country struggles to afford, the building risks remaining unused, or overburdening the state, thus becoming a memento, a symbol of a well-meaning but sometimes short-sighted process.[78]

Furthermore, the actual commitment and success of the court (as well as of its hybrid counterparts) is questioned in reaching and involving the victims. Indeed, a relevant share of Sierra Leoneans appears disconnected from the tribunal,[79] which is by some perceived as an unfamiliar, internationally imposed instrument applying a foreign law, as well as unsatisfied with its practical results; as a consequence, several sources refer to a "spaceship phenomenon", to describe a court which is alien to the territory and its priorities, resources and understandings.[80]

In considering these limitations and shortcomings, the question remains whether these are the result of flaws in this specific court's organisation and practice, or whether deeper, structural justifications should be acknowledged. For example, Padraig McAuliffe reports how the local civil societies of both Sierra Leone and East Timor were similarly unsatisfied with the domestic hybrid courts' policies concerning the selection of the defendants, although the former focused on the masterminds and the latter on lower-level perpetrators.[81] While the reason for such dissatisfaction could lie in issues related to the courts' approaches and decisions, they could also be linked to other, more structural factors, such as the tendency of most hybrid tribunals to be dominated by international figures, and to adopt concepts and approaches that are foreign to the local culture.[82] In particular, these seemingly irremediable flaws of hybrid courts lend support to the argument that the retributive justice approach per sé is of inevitably limited use in transitional contexts, or anyways presents some weaknesses that cannot be overcome. Proof of it is the fact that hybrid tribunals cannot elude the classical objections raised against international courts, such as those concerning the violation of fundamental principles of legality, or those related to the political character of these mechanisms. For example, the SCSL has itself been accused of being a political tool led by the USA, which are the main financial contributors of the tribunal, and are widely represented within the court's staff[83]; among them, the most controversial figure is surely that of the first Chief Prosecutor, David Crane, who played a strong political role within the court, by setting priorities (e.g., the strong focus on gender-based violence) and shaping the political strategy pursued to indict and apprehend Charles Taylor.[84] Not by chance, Taylor's defence in The Hague will revolve – as one of its key points – around this perceived political character of the court, which was the first to eventually convict a sitting Head of State for his responsibilities in supporting the commission of international crimes: while the prosecution essentially accused Taylor of being a greedy terrorist (an offence which is not central in the human rights and international criminal law discourses, but which is characteristic of the USA rhetoric at the international level),[85] Taylor's defence depicted the trial as the latest phase in a long history of colonisation and imperialism of the West on Africa.[86] Unwittingly, this accusation – which no ad hoc tribunal seems able to escape – was in this case somehow reinforced by the court itself, and in particular by the Trial Chamber, which in its reasoning made ample reference to the jurisprudence of the ICTY and of the Supreme Court of Canada, while making barely any use of the equally relevant jurisprudence of the ICTR or of other African courts and scholars.[87]

Similarly to the other tribunals analysed in previous chapters, the Sierra Leonean body was also harshly criticised for the selection of the defendants: as aforementioned, the formula "those who bear the greatest responsibility",[88] more limited than the one included in the ICTY and ICTR Statutes, appeared to many as too restrictive and arbitrary, and determined not by reasons of justice, but rather by the financial and temporal constraints of the tribunal. The prosecution ended up indicting 13 individuals, and the population was largely critical of both the inclusions and the exclusions: while respected local authorities were indicted, other well-known perpetrators walked free and unpunished (the local judiciary was practically dismantled and the unclear relationship between the SCSL and TRC prevented many from admitting their responsibilities in front of the Commission),[89] and – as already in the ICTY and ICTR – potential responsibilities of the international community were just ignored.[90] Particularly troublesome in the eyes of the population was the absence – from the list of the accused – of "Belgian, Dutch, Italian, Israeli, Lebanese, and other foreign businessmen and profiteers who allegedly played an equally critical role by financing the war from a distance and amassing the loot".[91] Notwithstanding the enormous obstacles a court would face in attempting to hold these subjects accountable, these omissions fostered the perception, among the population, of the court as a partial, political body, whose foundational charter allowed the indictment of former children whose lives had been irreparably destroyed by adults' greed, but overlooked the physical and legal persons who gained the most from the conflict.

Another critical issue was that of the impartiality of the court. The tribunal – especially the prosecution – was extremely cautious and willing to prove these perceptions wrong by being as neutral as possible; for this reason, the choice was made to try members of all the factions involved in the conflict.[92] Unfortunately, such a strategy led to even more criticisms, together with a lack of impartiality shown by the judges in the sentencing phase, who adopted a more lenient approach towards members of the CDF[93]: a large portion of the population could not accept the decision to charge subjects such as the leader of the CDF Sam Hinga Norman, a tribal chief considered by many as a local hero, while other, more obscure figures, such as President Kabbah himself and dozens of middle-level perpetrators, escaped any kind of accountability.[94] This "legally correct but politically blind insistence on carrying out equal prosecutions [. . .] without regard to their consequences in healing, or worsening, the raw wounds of ethnically, emotionally, and politically divided nation"[95] raises questions not only on the achievements of this specific court, or of the hybrid model, but rather on the potential of retributive justice as such.

Clashing Perspectives

Another significant criticism is moved by authors such as Tim Kelsall[96] and Graeme Young,[97] who reveal how, notwithstanding its attempts to be closer to the local culture and population than its predecessors, the SCSL integrated in its activities typically Western concepts, attitudes and understandings, which made it ill-suited to deal with a context, and a conflict, in which a fundamental role was played by customs and cultural beliefs.

For example, the very concept of justice underlying the court's activities appears to have little resonance on the ground, for several reasons. Firstly, the court (as already in the case of Japan and Rwanda) applied substantial and procedural rules which were quite distant from the domestic ones, and aiming at retribution and punishment while being largely insensitive to the longing for rehabilitation and reconciliation which was manifested on the ground.[98] Additionally, while the court focused on retribution, a relevant part of the local population was surviving in extremely precarious conditions, and thus prioritised demands for socio-economic justice and material support.[99] Indeed, justice is and must be, for many locals, something that "touches" the person directly[100]: in a territory crippled by inequality and poverty, where victims are forced by the circumstances of life to live right next to perpetrators, justice is reserved little expressive and symbolic value. However, the court, and the post-conflict project more in general (similar criticisms were expressed towards the truth commission), operate taking their values, functions and potentials for granted, as self-manifesting, consequently failing to explain and justify themselves to the population and thus again manifesting a certain insensitivity to the context. On the contrary, "truth telling *about* the court is as important in this case as truth telling *in* court".[101]

Similarly, the transitional process appeared as excessively focused on the state level, while ignoring the legal pluralism which characterises Sierra Leone (similarly to the majority of developing countries); therefore, other sources of law and order – such as local conflict resolution mechanisms – which often constitute the main providers of justice on the ground, were mostly excluded from advocacy, outreach and capacity building initiatives, and more in general from the transitional discourse.[102]

The court also adopted Western interpretations of fundamental substantial concepts, such as those of healing, childhood and marriage, which proved dissonant from local understandings, in a way that influenced its general reconstruction of the conflict.

More specifically, in considering the phenomenon of child soldiers, the SCSL employed an understanding of the child as an innocent, blameless and passive subject which was assumed as universal and natural, while in fact being constructed (as all understandings of childhood)[103] and very different from the one prevalent in Sierra Leone.[104] Indeed, in the local culture children are largely perceived as beings who maintain a connection with the spirits' world, which they only lose when transitioning into adulthood, through specific rituals; as such, children are conceived of as ambiguous beings, with hidden powers and energies.[105]

This same dynamic was repeated when dealing with the issue of forced marriage. Mariane Ferme analyses and reconstructs the peculiar understanding of woman and wife in Sierra Leone, where both concepts are expressed through the term *nyaha*, used in opposition to that of "girl": *nyaha* is the female subject who has transitioned away from that liminal state of childhood, in this way becoming adult (responsible, measured and mature). The fact that this term indicates both wives and women in general allows for some flexibility and ambiguity in describing complex marriage situations, thus making the term "bush wife" (which was central to the court jurisprudence) with all its underpinnings just not effectively translatable in the local language.[106]

Additionally, with regards to this issue, the court also did not adequately consider the structure of the local society and the traditional function of marriage, commonly perceived in Sierra Leone as a social event in which the wife's family, rather than the woman herself, expresses and performs the relevant will.[107]

Finally, the court failed to take into adequate account a system of spiritual and magical beliefs, which played a pivotal role in influencing the attitudes and choices of combatants during the conflict (some of them underwent rites which were deemed to make them invincible and resistant to bullets.)[108]

In light of all these issues, it appears well-founded the claim that when not adequately implemented,

> Incorporating local actors, processes and tradition into transitional justice mechanisms can be understood as a means of legitimization and disavowal; only those that adhere to the discursive parameters defined by international norms are engaged with, thereby promoting local ownership while minimizing the discursive space available for dissent.[109]

Once again, therefore, a criminal proceeding revealed to be, in a transitional context, out of focus. In particular, the court attempted to adjust to the exceptionality of the circumstances by adopting a wider scope, while remaining largely insensitive to the context. On the contrary, what appeared to be needed in this situation was a strict commitment to the traditional functions of a trial – in such a way to reaffirm and foster respect for and trust in the Rule of Law – together with a more profound and substantial sensitivity towards the local culture, the uniqueness of the past events, the needs of the victims.

New Model, or Manipulation of Local Values?

As outlined in the previous paragraphs, hybrid courts are a fairly recent experiment, emerging in response to growing dissatisfaction towards purely international initiatives, and from attempts to shape context-sensitive while efficient justice mechanisms. Because these bodies are still quite limited in number, and they all display different characteristics (e.g., in terms of jurisdiction and composition) and results, some authors actually reject the notion of a hybrid category of tribunals as representing a definite, autonomous model. In particular Sarah Nouwen, in her article

"Hybrid Courts. The Hybrid Category of a New Type of International Crimes Courts"[110] concludes, after examining the main features of the principal examples of hybrid courts, that the differences amongst them (concerning the historical and cultural backgrounds, the founding instruments, the applicable laws) are so significant, and the commonalities (such as their being physically present within the affected territory and the ad hoc nature) so limited and incidental, that speaking of a separate model is in fact inappropriate.[111]

Nouwen's theory is fascinating and well-articulated, and the author pinpoints many of the deficiencies of the practical experiences of hybrids tribunals so far. However, what her reconstruction appears to underestimate is how all these experiments, although different and on many levels flawed, also share the same rationale. In particular, each and every hybrid mechanism is established with the final purpose of overcoming the traditional limitations of purely international, ad hoc tribunals, by preserving their best features and adding what is missing, and can ideally be found in local systems, in this way promoting proximity to the victims and engagement with the population, flexibility, as well as better receptivity of the local culture and needs. In other words, these courts are "united" by their being all created as instruments able to combine the respect for international procedural and substantial standards of justice with local sensitivities,[112] in such a way to stimulate long-lasting effects not only in terms of accountability, but also towards peace, reconciliation and rebuilding. Therefore, flexibility and adaptability to the specific context – which make the category so difficult to define – are at the same time (the) fundamental characteristics of the model, which should be acknowledged and valued, while aware of the differences between a theoretical model and its practical manifestations.

That said, it is also noteworthy how hybridity is sometimes employed in the international discourse as the solution to any issue or limitation characterising more classical, international instruments. Nevertheless, it is important to stress how in the same way in which "international" and "domestic" are not always and necessarily something negative, so "hybrid" is not inevitably positive.[113] Indeed, hybrid mechanisms exist on a spectrum, they present extremely different characteristics and reaches, and they have very different results. Also, as the Sierra Leonean example shows, too often processes of hybridisation are generically and uncritically implemented (more or less unconsciously) as a vehicle for imposing and legitimising international attitudes, management and intervention in the domestic sphere – to maintain and reaffirm distances rather than removing them.[114] In other words,

> In implying joint creation and ownership, hybridity extends to all the right, perhaps even the responsibility, to intervene in conflict or to assist in peace-building. It is within this context that the hybrid label [. . .] has allowed both (a) recognition of the geographical distances between those who plan and those who experience conflict or post-conflict interventions and (b) a defense of continued theorizing, planning, and administration "for them" "over there".[115]

In order to maximise the potential of these processes in post-conflict scenarios, therefore, hybridity should not be approached as a goal, an objective to be pursued a priori and in itself, nor as a parameter of evaluation of the merits of a program. Rather, hybridity is to be appreciated as an instrument, a possibility, to be adopted only when and how required in that specific context. Indeed, in its former dimension hybridity risks becoming a legitimising tool, a "celebration of syncretism and hybridity per se, if not articulated in conjunction with questions of hegemony and neo-colonial power relations",[116] especially in scenarios and in interventions engineered in the global South.

Additionally, as Gearoid Millar rightly highlights, hybridity is not only relative to the post-conflict process; rather, it is also, often, a pre-existing characteristic of many countries, especially those that underwent experiences of colonisation.[117] This hybrid character is particularly apparent in the administration of justice, whose mechanisms are often informed by multiple experiences – such as informal processes, formal mechanisms developed during the colonial era, religious courts – which all influence each other and are in constant development.[118] As a consequence, identifying hybridity in local institutions and concepts might help to better decipher the local culture, and to design programmes that have better potential of responding to the needs and understandings of the population, while respecting fundamental values.

Conclusions

The hybrid model of ad hoc criminal justice presents several positive features, and represents a good improvement on the first- and second-generation tribunals, as – when adequately implemented – it allows to overcome some of their most criticised flaws, such as the physical and attitudinal distance from the people and the territories they are meant to address. Moreover, hybrid tribunals have proved to be more flexible and adaptable to the specific situation, and able to overcome the artificial distinction between national and international affairs, national and international law, in dealing with conflicts that inevitably involve both realms. For all these reasons, they can ideally be praised as the best version of criminal courts to be adopted in transitions, where an element of hybridity – at least in the interpretation of key concepts – appears necessary.

However, beyond the theory, an assessment of practical hybrid experiences casts some doubts on their feasibility and efficacy. As described, hybrid courts present many weaknesses, some of which are common to the vast majority of tribunals created post-conflict, while others (such as lack of strategic planning and sub-optimal funding and coordination with other transitional instruments) appear typical of hybrid experiments. The concept of hybridity also results open to abuse; in particular, when uncritically adopted as a goal in the design of transitional processes it might perpetrate neo-colonial, imperialistic dynamics (North–South, Center-Peripheries), in turn fostering structural inequalities characterising the international arena, while also antagonising the supposed beneficiaries. Further, the adoption of this concept also risks essentialising the discourse, by furthering an overly simplified approach to international and local spheres, which ignores complex intra-level dynamics; for example, hybridisation understood as combining international and domestic elements often focuses on formal structures, in this way overlooking informal or customary mechanisms, which often constitute the primary providers of justice. Therefore, hybridity should be primarily appreciated in its instrumentality, and it should always be built bottom-up, starting from the local attitudes and dynamics. Indeed, while the mere mixing-and-stirring of concepts, rules and staff proved unsuccessful, fundamental are cross-fertilisation and context-sensitivity, in such a way to ensure that the final result speaks the local language and respects local priorities.

For what specifically concerns the SCSL, this body – similarly to other ad hoc tribunals – appears to have succeeded in some among the most classical purposes of a judicial court, such as incapacitation and to a certain degree deterrence, at least in the short-term.[119] This confirms how a tribunal established, with international support, on the site where the acts of violence occurred, can potentially have a stronger influence on old and new perpetrators than a distant, unknown mechanism. However, such a deterrent effect will quickly vanish if the court will be perceived as weak, ineffective or politically biased. Similarly, the SCSL contributed to the evolution of international law, by adopting landmark decisions concerning the recruitment and enlistment of children as soldiers, the validity of amnesties regarding crimes for which universal jurisdiction has been recognised and the newly acknowledged crime of forced marriage.[120]

However, some limitations of this experiment have also been identified, such as the fairly limited impact on the population, which appears to be quite indifferent towards the court; indeed, the body is by many perceived as an out-of-place, top-down mechanism, parading its hybridity while in substance adopting Western concepts and understandings, and ignoring locals' priorities and approaches to conflict, justice and healing.[121] The Sierra Leonean experience thus demonstrates how hybridity must be carefully thought of, strategically planned, and – if deemed necessary – implemented on the ground[122]; on the contrary, if uncritically adopted as a panacea it risks becoming a façade for imperialistic interventions, and thus a source of further instability and tensions, rather than instrumental to furthering peace and justice. And in the practice, most hybrid tribunals appear to arise from the latter approach to hybridity: although they laudably incorporate local elements, most of these bodies can be considered yet another example of the top-down, backward-looking retributive model, which repeatedly proved inherently limited in dealing with transitional contexts. Indeed, these courts, although for some aspects innovative, still have (too) much in common with their purely international counterparts; as a consequence, the inclusion of local elements is perceived by many not as based on a genuine will to adopt and incorporate the victims' point of view, but rather as a way to foster their legitimacy in the eyes of the population, the international community and the donors, almost as a "marketing strategy".

Similarly, this brief analysis of hybrid experiments reconfirms how in post-conflict scenarios a court – of any kind – is never "just a court", as it is inevitably entrusted and charged with ulterior goals and multiple expectations, its activities constantly and ruthlessly dissected by a plethora of actors with differing perspectives and interests. As such, these instruments are, in a sense, created in order to fail: the impossibility of their tasks makes it seemingly impossible to satisfy competing but coexisting needs and priorities.

In light of these criticisms, the following chapter will focus on truth commissions, assessing whether restorative justice instruments have been able to more effectively respond to the demands of the victims, and to better manage the tensions typically encountered in post-conflict scenarios.

Notes

1. Ethel Higonnet, "Restructuring Hybrid Courts. Local Empowerment and National Criminal Justice Reform", *Yale Law School Legal Scholarship Repository (*2005): 5
2. Sarah M.H. Nouwen, "Hybrid Courts. The Hybrid Category of a New Type of International Crimes Court", *Utrecht Law Review* 2 (2006): 191
3. Higonnet, "Restructuring Hybrid Courts", 8
4. Jenny H. Peterson, "A Conceptual Unpacking of Hybridity: Accounting for Notions of Power, Politics and Progress in Analyses of Aid-Driven Interfaces", *Journal of Peacebuilding & Development* 7(2): 12
5. David Luban; Julie O'Sullivan, and David P. Stewart, *International and Transnational Criminal Law* (New York: Aspen Publishers, 2010), 171
6. For an overview of some of the most significant hybrid courts, see David Cohen, "Hybrid Justice in East Timor, Sierra Leone and Cambodia: 'Lessons Learned' and Prospects for the Future", *Stanford Journal of International Law* 43 (2007): 2–38
7. Tim Kelsall, *Culture Under Cross-Examination* (Cambridge: Cambridge University Press, 2009), 25
8. Stephen J. Rapp, "The Compact Model in International Criminal Justice: The Special Court for Sierra Leone", *Drake Law Review* 57 (2008): 12
9. Ibid., 14
10. Ibid., 13
11. Elizabeth M. Evenson, "Truth and Justice in Sierra Leone: Coordination between Commission and Court", *Columbia Law Review* 104 (2004): 734
12. Shahram Dana, "The Sentencing Legacy of the Special Court of Sierra Leone", *Georgia Journal of International Comparative Law* 42(3): 621
13. Beth K. Dougherty, "Right-Sizing International Criminal Justice: The Hybrid Experiment at the Special Court for Sierra Leone", *International Affairs* 80(2) (2004): 315
14. Friederike Mieth, "Bringing Justice and Enforcing Peace? An Ethnographic Perspective on the Impact of the Special Court for Sierra Leone", *International Journal of Conflict and Violence* 7(1): 3
15. Dana, "The Sentencing Legacy of the Special Court of Sierra Leone, 620
16. Mieth, "Bringing Justice and Enforcing Peace?", 3
17. Ibid., 4
18. *Peace Agreement between the Government of Sierra Leone and the Revolutionary United Front of Sierra Leone* (Lomé Peace Accord), Lomé, 7 July 1999
19. Lomé Peace Accord, Art. 9(3)
20. Evenson, "Truth and Justice in Sierra Leone", 735

21. UNAMSIL was created through UN Security Council Res 1270 (1999), Un. Doc. S/RES/1270
22. Elizabeth Nielsen, "Hybrid International Criminal Tribunals: Political Interference and Judicial Independence", *Ucla Journal of International Law and Foreign Affairs* 289 (2010): 317
23. Kelsall, *Culture Under Cross-Examination,* 28
24. Evenson, "Truth and Justice in Sierra Leone", 739
25. Rosalind Shaw, "Memory Frictions: Localizing the Truth and Reconciliation Commission in Sierra Leone", *The International Journal of Transitional Justice* 1 (2007): 184
26. Gearoid Millar, "Assessing Local Experiences of Truth-Telling in Sierra Leone: Getting to 'Why' through a Qualitative Case Study Analysis", *The International Journal of Transitional Justice* 4 (2010), 490
27. Higonnet, "Restructuring Hybrid Courts", 7
28. Laura A. Dickinson, "The Promise of Hybrid Courts", *The American Journal of International Law* 97(2) (2003): 299
29. Charles Chernor Jalloh, "Special Court for Sierra Leone: Achieving Justice?", *Michigan Journal of International Law* 32 (2011): 398
30. Dickinson, "The Promise of Hybrid Courts", 299
31. UN Security Council Res 1315 (2000), Un. Doc. S/RES/1315 (2000): 1
32. *Agreement between the United Nations and the Government of Sierra Leone on the Establishment of a Special Court for Sierra Leone,* 16 January 2002, 2178 UNTS 138
33. Jalloh, "Special Court for Sierra Leone: Achieving Justice?", 402
34. Ezequiel Jimenez, "Hybrid Tribunals as Capacity Building: Narrowing the Impunity Gap" (Master diss., University of Gothenburg, 2015): 22
35. Rapp, "The Compact Model in International Criminal Justice", 21
36. *Agreement between the United Nations and the Government of Sierra Leone on the Establishment of a Special Court for Sierra Leone,* Art. 2–4
37. Nouwen, "Hybrid Courts", 204
38. Padraig McAuliffe, "Hybrid Tribunal at Ten: How International Criminal Justice Golden Child Became an Orphan", *Journal of International Law and International Relations* 1 (2011): 35
39. Neha Jain, "Conceptualising Internationalisation in Hybrid Criminal Courts", *Singapore Year Book of International Law and Contributors* 12 (2008): 83
40. *Statute of the Special Court for Sierra Leone,* Lomé, 7 July 1999, 2178 UNTS 138
41. Ibid., Art. 2
42. Ibid., Art. 3
43. Ibid., Art. 4
44. Ibid.

45. Ibid., Art. 5
46. Jimenez, "Hybrid Tribunals as Capacity Building", 23
47. Jalloh, "Special Court for Sierra Leone: Achieving Justice?", 403
48. Higonnet, "Restructuring Hybrid Courts", 10
49. Ibid., 12
50. For example, the RUF often performed traditional rituals that were believed to make the soldiers invisible or bullet-proof, and that heavily influenced the behaviour of the combatants. See Kelsall, *Culture Under Cross-Examination,* 109
51. McAuliffe, "Hybrid Tribunal at Ten", 12
52. Ibid., 14
53. Jimenez, "Hybrid Tribunals as Capacity Building", 29
54. Ibid., 30
55. Jalloh, "Special Court for Sierra Leone: Achieving Justice?", 454
56. Cohen, "Hybrid Justice in East Timor, Sierra Leone and Cambodia", 22
57. Ibid., 5
58. Donna E. Arzt, "Views on the Ground: The Local Perception of International Criminal Tribunals in the Former Yugoslavia and Sierra Leone", *Annals of the American Academy of Political and Social Science* 603 (2006): 230
59. Ibid.
60. Valerie Oosterveld, "The Gender Jurisprudence of the Special Court for Sierra Leone: Progress in the Revolutionary United Front Judgments", *Cornell International Law Journal* 44 (2011): 60
61. Ibid., 65
62. Mieth, "Bringing Justice and Enforcing Peace", 10
63. Jalloh, "Special Court for Sierra Leone: Achieving Justice?", 429
64. *Agreement between the United Nations and the Government of Sierra Leone on the Establishment of a Special Court for Sierra Leone,* Art. 6
65. Dougherty, "Right-Sizing International Criminal Justice", 325
66. Antonio Cassese (Independent Expert), "Report on the Special Court for Sierra Leone" (12 December 2006): 54
67. Jalloh, "Special Court for Sierra Leone: Achieving Justice?", 429
68. *Statute of the Special Court for Sierra Leone,* Art. 1
69. Jalloh, "Special Court for Sierra Leone: Achieving Justice?", 437
70. Ibid., 450
71. Chandra Lekha Sriram, "Wrong-sizing International Justice? The Hybrid Tribunal in Sierra Leone", *Fordam International Law Journal* 29 (2005): 481
72. Ibid.
73. Jimenez, "Hybrid Tribunals as Capacity Building", 30
74. Ibid., 31

75. Sriram, "Wrong-sizing International Justice?", 499
76. Ibid., 503
77. Higonnet, "Restructuring Hybrid Courts", 13
78. Jimenez, "Hybrid Tribunals as Capacity Building", 32
79. Mieth, "Bringing Justice and Enforcing Peace?", 5
80. Among others, see McAuliffe, "Hybrid Tribunal at Ten", 36
81. Ibid., 41
82. Ibid., 42
83. Arzt, "Views on the Ground", 243
84. Luban et al., *International and Transnational Criminal Law*, 178
85. Glasius and Meijers, "Constructions of Legitimacy", 249
86. Ibid., 247
87. Dana, "The Sentencing Legacy of the Special Court of Sierra Leone", 676
88. *Statute of the Special Court for Sierra Leone,* Art. 1
89. Evenson, "Truth and Justice in Sierra Leone", 763
90. Jalloh, "Special Court for Sierra Leone: Achieving Justice?", 428
91. Ibid., 424
92. McAuliffe, "Hybrid Tribunal at Ten", 54
93. Dana, "The Sentencing Legacy of the Special Court of Sierra Leone", 655
94. Jalloh, "Special Court for Sierra Leone: Achieving Justice?", 418
95. Ibid., 459
96. Kelsall, *Culture Under Cross-Examination*
97. Graeme Young, "Transitional Justice in Sierra Leone: A Critical Analysis", *United Nations Peace and Progress* 1 (1): 3–17
98. Kelsall, *Culture Under Cross-Examination,* 12
99. Mieth, "Bringing Justice and Enforcing Peace?", 5
100. Ibid., 6
101. Sativa January, "*Tribunal Verite*: Documenting Transitional Justice in Sierra Leone", *The International Journal of Transitional Justice* 3(2009): 211
102. Mieth, "Bringing Justice and Enforcing Peace?", 7
103. For more on childhood and its perception in different cultures and environments, see Allison James and Alan Prout, eds., *Constructing and Reconstructing Childhood: Contemporary Issues in the Sociological Study of Childhood* (London and New York: Routledge, 1997)
104. Kelsall, *Culture Under Cross-Examination.*, 151
105. Gearoid Millar, "Disaggregating Hybridity: Why Hybrid Institutions Do Not Produce Predictable Experiences of Peace", *Journal of Peace Research* 51(4) (2014): 507
106. Mariane C. Ferme, "Archetypes of Humanitarian Discourse: Child Soldiers, Forced Marriage, and the Framing of Communities in Post-Conflict Sierra Leone", *Humanity* 4(1) (2013): 63
107. Kelsall, *Culture Under Cross-Examination.*, 248

108. Ibid., 106
109. Young, "Transitional Justice in Sierra Leone: A Critical Analysis", 8
110. Nouwen, "Hybrid Courts", 190–214
111. Ibid.
112. Jain, "Conceptualising Internationalisation in Hybrid Criminal Courts", 88
113. Millar, "Disaggregating Hybridity", 503
114. Ibid., 502
115. Ibid.
116. Ella Shohat, "Notes on the 'Post-Colonial'", *Social Text* 10(2–3) (1992) as quoted in Peterson, "A Conceptual Unpacking of Hybridity", 14
117. Millar, "Disaggregating Hybridity", 507
118. For a description of the justice system in Sierra Leone in historical perspective (with specific emphasis on the influence of the British rule), see Steven Archibald and Paul Richards, "Converts to Human Rights? Popular Debate about War and Justice in Rural Central Sierra Leone", *Africa* 72(3) (2002): 343
119. Jalloh, "Special Court for Sierra Leone: Achieving Justice?", 453
120. Luban et al., *International and Transnational Criminal Law*, 170
121. Millar, "Disaggregating Hybridity", 510
122. Jimenez, "Hybrid Tribunals as Capacity Building", 47

CHAPTER 9

Healing a Wounded Nation: The Reconciliatory Paradigm of Truth Commissions

Introduction

A truth commission can be described as an official, temporary body – normally created by a new government during a transition – whose task is to investigate, gather evidence and reconstruct the truth about a violent and abusive past, usually focusing on a single country or territory, and on a limited timeframe[1]; truth commissions are typically non-judicial institutions, lacking coercive and prosecuting powers and highly relying on the cooperation of the civil society.[2] Thus, different from tribunals – which are ordinary instruments adapted, when employed post-conflict, to extraordinary situations – truth commissions are extraordinary bodies, crafted for and within transitional contexts as extraordinary phases in the history of a society.

With the adoption of the "model" of truth commissions, the focus, and the pursuit of justice, is shifted from punishment to truth; not by chance, its first mature experiments unfolded in South America, in the aftermath of regimes characterised by silence and denial.[3] Also, the attention of truth commissions is not limited exclusively to the past (and to establishing guilt) but rather expands to the future, to the (re-)construction of a peaceful and inclusive society: for this and other reasons, they are considered as expressions of the restorative justice model. Thus far, more than 30 commissions have been established around the world,[4] each one with peculiarities, but at the same time all characterised by similar structures and goals. This chapter will primarily focus on the South African Truth

G. Girelli, *Understanding Transitional Justice*,
Philosophy, Public Policy, and Transnational Law,
DOI 10.1007/978-3-319-53606-4_9

and Reconciliation Commission (TRC), for several reasons. First, because this body is appreciated by many as the most successful example of truth commissions, and it is consequently being adopted as a model, a reference, in the design of new experiments around the world.[5] Secondly, for the inclusivity and pervasiveness of such instrument; indeed, as discussed later in this chapter, the TRC proved to be broadly engaging, both in its design and in the operational phase. Furthermore, the South African experiment marks the evolution of these bodies to their "mature" phase – as through this experience they move from focusing merely on the development of a plausible authoritative record, to incorporate a psychological, almost religious dimension, in this way acquiring a constitutive function of the new legal and social orders.[6] Moreover, the TRC presents some unique features, such as the power to grant amnesties to perpetrators in exchange for full disclosure, that are worth analysing, as they raise some thorny questions regarding the legitimacy and efficacy of these instruments.

The following paragraphs briefly reconstruct the characteristics of Apartheid in South Africa, retracing its development and identifying some of its deepest causes, before moving on to describe the institution and the structure of the TRC. This mechanism will then be employed as an example in the evaluation of truth commissions as manifestations of the restorative justice model post-conflict, whose merits and limitations will be considered in some detail.

Fighting from the Wrong Side of the Law: The Era of Apartheid in South Africa

The term *Apartheid* – literally apartness, separation[7] – is employed to refer to the pervasive system of social and geographical organisation that shaped the life of South Africa from 1948, when the National Party rose to power through elections, until the 1990s – although its ideology and organisational model are ultimately rooted in discriminatory strategies of the British Empire.[8] Indeed, Apartheid was not imposed overnight over a passive population; rather, it was built upon segregationist policies crafted and implemented in the country since the onset of the twentieth century, based on racist assumptions concerning the features of the different ethnic groups, and on a radicalised while at the same time romanticised conception of separate development of races (purportedly to each other's benefit).[9] Additionally, as highlighted by authors such as Harold Wolpe, segregation also had specific economic justifications; indeed, by confining black families to the countryside, white capitalists were able to maintain access to a black – and mostly male – under-skilled and underpaid workforce, whose costs were in this way predominantly borne by their families (rather than the employers) through subsistence agriculture.[10] In sum, Apartheid can be understood as the latest attempt by the part of the white minority to maintain political hegemony and economic control, by ideologically charging and building upon segregationist policies which had been introduced gradually in the previous 40 years. At its core was the belief that different racial groups should be treated differently, according to their different abilities and possibilities, and live and exist in separate spheres.[11] Accordingly, White-Afrikaners were strongly fav oured, while other ethnic groups, especially natives, were marginalised and constrained in the countryside, divided into tribes, controlled through passes and curfew systems and denied education, opportunities and equality,[12] gradually stripped of their rights and freedoms and prevented from striking or forming unions.[13] Moreover, they were denied their very right to citizenship, as formally they were not members of South Africa, but rather of the *bantustans* (or homelands), the tribes they were assigned to as temporary residents and confined in, through forced relocations and the pass system.[14]

This oppressed majority could either surrender to the system or resist, at the risk of being arrested, tortured, disappeared and murdered. Despite that, countless episodes of resistance were witnessed on a daily basis, often inspired by several social movements that actively fought to free the country from repression: from lawyers committed to public interest litigation to the United Democratic Front, a coalition of hundreds of organisations (such as churches, trade unions, students and women's groups), founded in 1983 and committed to non-violent resistance.[15] However, the most representative organisation was probably the African National Congress (ANC), a "nationalist liberation movement with a mass base that represented an alliance of African nationalists, communists, workers, intellectuals and civil activists"[16] established in 1912 to contrast the growth of the National Party, which represented the Afrikaner political ideology and, once in power, implemented and defended the Apartheid regime.[17] One of the leading figures of the ANC, which since the 1960s largely operated underground, was the black lawyer Nelson Mandela, who also co-founded the MK – the "armed branch" of the ANC[18] – and spent almost three decades in prison, becoming a worldwide-known symbol of the struggle of South Africa, and of peoples everywhere, for liberation and equality.

The Apartheid system has many features in common with the one developed in Germany under Nazism (as well as the one now in place in Palestine), in its being perversely legalistic and incredibly pervasive.[19] Indeed, for most of the Apartheid era, the government was extremely attentive in ensuring an aura of legality to its discriminatory efforts,[20] with the law being employed to protect the state rather than the citizens, also complicit many blindly positivistic courts and judges (although with some notable exceptions).[21] As such, Apartheid was ultimately a legalising effort, pursued through a gradual but constant contraction, through legislation and policies, of rights, freedoms and spaces for the black population, with the final objective of confining it, both physically and socially.[22] Accordingly, every single aspect of a person's life was influenced by discriminatory laws and policies, determining one's civil and political rights, educational and economic opportunities, address even romantic and sexual life.[23] As such, Apartheid was not the project of some lunatic dictator, but rather a surgically organised system of social segregation that relied on the (passive or active) cooperation of broad sectors of the population and insinuated into every layer of the social fabric[24]; it was a "monolithic system […] diabolical in its detail, inescapable in its reach, and overwhelming in its power",[25] characterised by violent repression and a daily routine based on discriminations and denial.

The first major changes occurred in the 1980s, thanks to the tireless struggle of the resistance movements, coupled with international pressure at the political and economic level; South Africa had become a pariah state, a stain on the map of the new decolonised world, and eventually political pressure, embargos and the fierce commitment of both the domestic and the international civil society eventually made the system untenable.[26] This urged the new President, F.W. de Klerk, to relax the rules of Apartheid.[27] One of his first moves towards this more liberal direction was granting amnesty to various ANC leaders, such as Nelson Mandela, with whom he had started an intense round of negotiations regarding the transition and the future of the country.[28] This dialogue led, in 1993, to the approval of an Interim Constitution and to the first non-racial elections in the history of South Africa, that saw the (largely expected) victory of the ANC and the consequent appointment of Mandela as first President of the new South Africa, the Rainbow Nation.[29]

The Institution of the TRC and Its Structure

The South African transition is regarded by many as "miraculous",[30] for the shift from such a pervasive and antagonising system of abuses to a democratic government was, surprisingly, relatively peaceful. This was in large part determined by peculiarities of the context (e.g., the substantial dependence of the white minority on black workforce),[31] and by the process itself, which encompassed intense and inclusive negotiations between the several forces involved. Indeed, the dismantling of the Apartheid system required a deep, utter reform of virtually every single institution in the country – in the political, economic, administrative and educational spheres; however, at the same time, the absence of a clear "winner" and the permanence in strategic positions of influence of representatives and supporters of the old regime made an ANC-only reform impossible. As a consequence, the only path towards a peaceful but meaningful transition was through inclusive negotiations.[32] Awareness of the specific circumstances, in terms of political, economic and historical contingencies, within which the transitional project unfolded and developed is fundamental, in order to fully appreciate several of its key features and their underlying justifications – such as the amnesty provision included in the Postamble of the Constitution and the exclusion of Nuremberg-style prosecutions, in favour of a more participative process of justice declined in restorative terms.[33]

The TRC, which is described by many as a compromise,[34] was finally established in 1995 with the Promotion of National Unity and Reconciliation Act,[35] as a result of a comprehensive public debate,[36] comprising two international conferences, hearings of victims and civil society organisations, as well as a public process for the selection of the Commissioners.[37] The Commission was given a specific, limited mandate: its enquiries would cover the period between the Sharpeville Massacre of 1960 and the establishment of the transitional government in December 1993.[38] Also, this body was to be primarily focused on gross violations of human rights, in terms of

> (a) The killing, abduction, torture or severe ill-treatment of any person; or (b) any attempt, conspiracy, incitement, instigation, command or procurement to commit an act referred to in paragraph (a), which emanated from conflicts of the past and which committed during the period 1 March 1960 to the cut-off date within or outside the Republic, and the commission of

> which was advised, planned, directed, commanded or ordered, by any person acting *with a political motive.*[39]

The Commission was invested with several complex objectives – both by its formal mandate and by social expectations – all intertwined but at the same time potentially clashing with one another, which now figure firmly among the principal, typical goals of most truth commissions around the world. First, the Commission was expected to promote national unity and reconciliation,[40] working as a bridge between a violent past and a future of peace and unity. Also, the TRC was meant to establish "as complete a picture as possible of the causes, nature and extent of the gross violations of human rights".[41] Indeed, as apparent from their title, one of the main tasks of truth commissions is to inquire, investigate, reconstruct and disseminate the truth about deeply divisive and typically contested events and their consequences as well as, although too often overlooked, their deepest causes. Such an endeavour ideally manifests a rupture with the culture of silence, denial and impunity typical of authoritarian regimes and periods of conflict, and it is therefore crucial both to provide accountability, and in order to promote the reconstruction of a peaceful and respectful society. For this reason, commissions normally conclude their activities with the drafting, and often publishing (with an educational purpose) of a report, in which its findings and the relative evidence are presented to the public, most of the times in legal terms (the events investigated are reconstructed as either historical background or violations of rights and freedoms recognised at the international level), and usually followed by recommendations for future governments.[42] Indeed, an additional goal of truth commissions – which the TRC itself pursued – consists in advising, through recommendations, the new political forces with regards to measures considered to be necessary, or at least desirable, at the judicial, legislative or political level, with the aim of redressing past injustices and preventing further abuses, and with a specific eye to reparations for the victims. This allows truth commissions to contribute to the restoration of the human and civil dignity of victims,[43] granting them redress and acknowledgment, while at the same time representing the forward-looking character of such institutions, and contributing to strengthening the legitimacy to the new regime.[44]

In order to fulfil its complex mandate, the South African Commission was structured into three Committees. The Committee on Human Rights Violations (HRVC), chaired by Archbishop Desmond Tutu, was competent for the inquiry of human rights violations that occurred during the Apartheid era, gathering information and evidence in order to reconstruct single episodes as well as wider patterns of abuse[45]; at the same time, it constituted a forum where the victims and their families could narrate their stories and have them acknowledged, "in a culturally appropriate and supportive atmosphere, without the threat of cross-examination".[46] Indeed, the former goal was mainly pursued by collecting statements in public (except rare cases) hearings, organised throughout the country and broadcasted, which were subsequently verified by an Investigative Unit and whose data were then gathered in a dedicated database.[47] The Reparation and Reconciliation Committee (RRC), on its part, was charged with multiple assignments, such as: evaluating the effects of the abuses on the victims and their families, also through engagement with the local communities; providing support to the witnesses before, during and after the TRC hearings; making recommendations about reparations and other measures that could help the victims reaching closure and moving on with their lives (although it lacked the power to directly grant economical help).[48] "Presumed" victims did not have direct access to the Committee, which rather worked on lists provided by the HRVC[49] in order to establish who qualified as a victim of the regime and was consequently entitled to benefits and support.[50] Finally, the mandate of the Amnesty Committee (AC) was to evaluate the applications for amnesty submitted to the TRC and decide whether or not to concede it, following a predetermined procedure that could include a public hearing.[51] As this power to grant amnesties is a peculiar and unparalleled feature of this Commission, raising several doubts about the balance between truth and justice, the activity of the AC will be addressed in more detail in the penultimate paragraph of this chapter.

Truth and Justice, with an Eye to the Future: The Merits of Truth Commissions

Supporters of the restorative justice approach embraced by truth commissions emphasise the several positive features and results of these experiments, especially when compared to the performance of criminal trials in similar contexts. Incidentally, it is important to keep in mind that, by discussing truth commissions, dozens of bodies are referred to, which are created in different circumstances, with different features, powers and effects.[52] However, at the same time, this very flexibility which characterises truth commissions as a model – a category – ideally allows for these mechanisms to be shaped according to the specific context while preserving some crucial characteristics, some of which outlined here.

First, truth commissions are considered by many as more suitable than criminal trials to reconstruct the full truth about the past, thus granting an impartial, well-documented, largely undisputable version of the events.[53] Indeed, despite the lack of enforcement powers typically enjoyed by strictly judicial instruments, well-designed commissions have less formal and procedural constraints and they are ideally more inclusive not only of the victims but also of the perpetrators, which are normally the subjects who retain more information and resources regarding past criminal activities. Also, while criminal trials focus exclusively on a limited number of events and subjects, and present their conclusions in criminal judgments – written in technical, legalistic terms and often restricted to the courtroom, the report that truth commissions usually conclude their endeavour with is written in a simpler, more popular language, and it is distributed to the general public.

The emerging truth, which is instrumental to, at the very least, subverting the old regime's narrative and contrasting attempts of denial or manipulation of the events,[54] can prove crucial to the formation of the country's collective memory regarding the traumatic past, while also constituting a starting point from which to craft a new, more respectful and inclusive society. Also, by acknowledging and disseminating the truth, these bodies symbolise a rupture with the past, especially in those societies that have experimented years of denial and secrecy, such as the Argentinian one, in which thousands of people just disappeared, and whose families were denied information, evidence, truth and therefore closure. Furthermore, during critical times people often renounce their moral autonomy and, fighting for their survival, they

> Abide the institutionalized lie [. . .]. After the change, the society remains deeply divided as a result of the recent crime, of its perception, and of the political abuse of its effect, the line between truth and lies about the past remains unclear, and lies are thus easily translated into a manipulative political discourse. [. . .] This all could mean that even if we refuse to deal with the past, the past would be still dealing with us. Hence, it is both morally right and politically necessary to explore its lessons.[55]

What Nenad Dimitrijević is stressing is how, in the aftermath of conflicts or oppressive regimes, the line between right and wrong, just and unjust, tends to be blurred, because of a prolonged culture of denial and ideological manipulation. This compels a concerted effort, by the part of society as a whole, to confront the past and interrogate itself on the reality of the events as well as on its deepest causes which – ideally – truth commissions are more suitable to investigate than trials; as already mentioned, while prosecutions need to limit their focus to specific aspects of specific events, these mechanisms can focus on the larger picture, on patterns of abuses and underlying dynamics and threads.

This research for an official truth was one of the primary goals of the TRC, which concluded its operations by drafting a five-volume report that tries to shed some light on contested subjects, such as the features and mechanics of the regime, the persons responsible for single atrocities and for the repression machinery, and the level of involvement of different sectors of the society.[56] In acknowledging the (unavoidable) limits of its work, the Commission stated that "it is not the Commission's task to write the history of this country. Rather, it is the Commission's function to expose the violations of all parties in an attempt to lay the basis for a culture in which human rights are respected and not violated".[57] In other words, reconstructing the truth was approached not only as an end, a final purpose, but rather, if not principally, as a means through which paving the way for reconciliation, accountability, deterrence and reform. Truth thus results necessary and instrumental for reaching any other objective of a transitional instrument, as "to understand the source of evils is not to condone it, it is only by recognising the potential for evil in each one of us that we can take full responsibility for ensuring that such evil will never be repeated".[58]

Secondly, truth commissions are often praised for their instrumentality to providing accountability, although not always in a strictly traditional, legal sense. Indeed, on one part they can support criminal prosecutions, thanks to the load of information gathered (the most famous example is the Argentinian one, where the information and evidence discovered by the local truth commission, the Comisión Nacional sobre la Desaparición de Personas, was subsequently employed in the trials which followed the repeal of key amnesty provisions).[59] Additionally, in many transitional scenarios where justice systems are too weak, corrupted or tied to the fallen regime to successfully fulfil their goals, or amnesty laws exclude legal prosecutions, truth commissions often constitute the only alternative to impunity[60]: by reconstructing and "proving" the commission of crimes and abuses they ensure at least a moral accountability, providing the victims with a sense of acknowledgment and justice.[61] With this purpose, several commissions adopted the decision to include in their reports the names of persons whose responsibilities had been proven by their investigations to a "sufficient degree", in this way sharing them with the general population, whose suspects were in many cases confirmed.[62] While not uncontested, the resulting stigmatisation was deemed by many as a satisfactory – although not "complete" – form of accountability, and not rarely it proved crucial in impelling persons involved with the old regime, or responsible for crimes, to relinquish positions of power or influence they had managed to maintain.[63]

The South African transition is a good example: despite a weakening of the Apartheid regime, several of its leading figures were still in key strategic positions during the first period of the De Klerk Government, and although pressured on several fronts they would have never allowed for a peaceful transition without concessions and guarantees, such as the amnesty provision included in the Postamble of the Interim Constitution.[64] Perpetrators and accomplices were just too many and too powerful to accept the risk of criminal trials, thus the choice was made to sacrifice a certain amount of legal justice – present certain conditions – in order to promote peace, deferring part of the onus of determining individual and collective responsibilities to the TRC. The constituents were then able to capitalise upon the flexibility provided by the Postamble, imposing full disclosure as a fundamental criterion to be met in order to be granted amnesty, thus pursuing accountability through confession and truth-telling.

Furthermore, as already mentioned, truth commissions can be appreciated as a more complete instrument than criminal trials, in that they not only focus on the past but also contribute to the future of the nation, through suggestions and recommendations. This is an extremely important task, as usually countries facing a transition bear the burden of years, if not decades, of authoritarianism and/or conflict, with ingrained discrimination and marginalisation reproduced in key institutions as well as interpersonal and intergroup relations; in such a context, a body which not only reflects upon ways to make justice but also identifies these deeper structures and considers how to refashion the state and society can make the difference. The members of a truth commission ideally have a dialogic relationship with the local society and a thorough knowledge of the conflict or the regime they are called to investigate upon, often coming from different professions and experiences; therefore, they are regarded as strongly qualified to profile ways in which to treat the scars left by the past while at the same time preventing the insurgence of new oppressive authorities.[65] This is one of the commission's most delicate and controversial tasks, considering that they operate in environments that need much and have nothing: resources are scarce, trained personnel have either died or fled, and everything is an emergency. Therefore, a commission charged with the task of proposing reforms faces the delicate issue of determining what to prioritise, and how to distribute time and resources, while at the same time having to defend its very existence.[66]

The TRC proved quite sensitive about this aspect, and – as aforementioned – one of its three committees, the RRC, was specifically charged with suggesting reforms and reparation schemes. However, many consider this organ the weakest component of the Commission, especially due to its lack of direct implementation powers.[67] Nevertheless, the RRC was at least partially successful, in that it ensured that several daily issues that survivors confronted were addressed, that can easily be overlooked in a complex post-conflict context, such as the issuing of death warrants and other official certificates, and the provision of headstones; these were small gestures, but they manifested to the victims the commitment of a formerly repressive state to include them and acknowledge their suffering and loss.[68]

Finally, reconciliation – a slippery concept and a difficult objective,[69] but one that, at least for those who believe it to be a valuable and achievable goal – is more efficiently pursued by truth commissions rather than criminal trials. Indeed, the process towards reconciliation requires inclusion and understanding, more than blaming; it admits assigning responsibilities but it also entails reaching compromises, embracing the concept of Ubuntu, find the strength to put oneself on the same footing as one's former enemy and enter a dialogue.[70] Criminal trials rest upon a logic of exclusion and disparity, with the accused (and the social, political, ethnic group this represents) in a position of inferiority, and a clear distinction between good – the judging side – and evil – the judged subject. On the contrary, truth commissions are, at least ideally, structured in such a way to allow different constituencies to enter a dialogue, aimed at mutual understanding,[71] through which acknowledging each other's responsibilities as well as humanity.[72]

Because of the complexity of this concept and the different approaches to it, truth commissions varied in its prioritisation[73]: while some have placed it at the core of their mission, others – like the Argentinian CONADEP – focused more closely on gathering information and designing reforms, leaving the issue of making peace with one's enemies to the individuals, or to other social institutions, such as the religious ones.[74] The South African TRC certainly forms part of the former group,[75] as it valued reconciliation as one, if not *the*, primary goal of its activities. This was the result of several concurring factors, such as the Christian approach promoted by figures such as Archbishop Tutu, the characteristics of the Apartheid regime, and the final purpose of creating a united and peaceful society in which different ethnic groups could coexist peacefully, despite a tragic history and mutual prejudices. In particular, Apartheid was a particularly long-lasting and pervasive system, which affected the lives of virtually everyone in the country, strongly influencing interpersonal and social relationships that now had to be reformed, for the country to move on; additionally, all the factions were responsible for acts of violence and crimes (although in very different measures),[76] while the government and public institutions took great care in creating, exacerbating and exploiting divisions not only between but also within ethnic groups, communities and families.[77] Also, this strong focus on reconciliation was justified by the predominantly holistic character of the South African culture, which recognises a primary importance to the community, with the consequence that renouncing some degree of personal satisfaction (such as the one provided by retributive justice mechanisms) for the good of the society as a whole results more acceptable than in more individualistic settings, where criminal punishment is often perceived as a civilised revenge.[78]

Placing Victims at the Centre

In addition to these relevant features, the main peculiarity, and possibly one of the main virtues of this institution, consists in its being focused on the victims, both as protagonists and as primary beneficiaries of the work of the commission. As outlined, truth commissions provide a forum in which victims can come forward and speak about years, if not decades, of repression, loss and trauma, surrounded by persons who went through analogous experiences and in front of an official body, which offers acknowledgment. This ritual is meant to provide strength and closure while furthering social unity, helping to overcome dynamics of isolation and denial typical of periods of conflict and oppression.[79]

The TRC was shaped in such a way to be centred on the victims' needs: two out of three Committees were designed specifically in order to address the victims' past – by reconstructing the abusive history of the Apartheid regime – and future, by proposing reparative measures (although, in the end, both activities were also meant to have beneficial effects on the society in general)[80]; moreover, one of the fundamental goals of the commission was the restoration of victims' dignity, by allowing them to narrate their story in a supportive environment, always ensuring respect and compassion.[81] Gearoid Millar values the focus of the TRC on the victims as particularly significant for the truth commission model as a whole, identifying the South African Commission as a cornerstone in the evolution of truth commissions as victim-centred mechanisms. Indeed,

> Since South Africa, commissions have become intricately involved not only in developing authoritarian records of the past but also in supposedly catalysing collective psychological, or "socio-emotional" reconciliation through the public performance of witnesses', victims' and perpetrators' stories of their experiences.[82]

In other words, the TRC had the merit of placing alongside the more traditional goal of truth-seeking – for which victims' testimonies were mainly a means for the reconstruction of the past – the dimension of truth-telling, in whose light the narration becomes an end per se', a cathartic moment with an intrinsic value, irrespective of its instrumentality in reconstructing an "official" history.

As introduced in the first chapter of this volume, such a victim-centred approach is praised for its supposed positive consequences, all intertwined. One of them is acknowledgment, a process that can be defined as the "translation of a private into a public truth",[83] the recognition that someone's suffering is real, worthy of attention and respect.[84] Commissions can be instrumental to pursuing this objective, in that they constitute a forum where victims can narrate their experiences and be listened to, thus feeling acknowledged in their individuality and identity, both as survivors and as citizens. Notably, in several cases the truth shared via a commission is not new to the population (on the contrary, it often confirms previous suspects and doubts); therefore, its value lies primarily not in its being discovered, but rather, or also, in its being stated officially and publicly, recognised by the state.[85] This subversion of the rhetoric of the previous regime carries further positive consequences – such as closure, and, on a more practical level, award of reparations and other benefits.[86] Indeed, acknowledgment is provided not only through the symbolic act of listening and upholding the victims' narrative but also through more substantial initiatives such as compensations, building memorials, issuing certificates, providing a proper burial to one's relatives. Even when limited in their practical effects, these are tangible signs of the willingness of the state to admit its faults and help its citizens reaching closure.

Another assumed merit of victim-centred initiatives is their potential to provide empowerment. Criminal trials can indirectly work as instruments empowering the victim of a crime, as the truth they establish reshapes, in his favour, his relation both with his oppressor and with the society. However, within a criminal trial the victim remains mainly an instrument, a talking evidence against the perpetrator, who stands as the main focus of the procedure. On the contrary, within a truth commission hearing victims have their space reclaimed at the centre of the transitional process. This shift in perspective is supposed to induce a remodelling of traditional power dynamics between the victim on one side and the perpetrator, the society and the state on the other, through the "elevation of victims' voices over those of perpetrators in the memory-making project".[87]

Also, by playing an active part in the transitional project, individuals and groups affected by conflicts manage to define themselves as more than mere victims, passive addressees of an act of violence, and instead claim a new identity, as survivors, resisters, citizens. In other words, "as they discover their voices, they also grasp their capacity to intervene politically and sense their potential influence"[88]; they impose their presence as active subjects on the political scene, reclaiming their spaces as necessary constituents of the new, democratic state that is being built.

Healing, intended – in its wider meaning – as coping with emotional, mental, even physical consequences of traumatic experiences is another goal that is prioritised by victim-centred, restorative projects.[89] And while acknowledgment might also be achieved through criminal prosecutions, as tribunals officially state a truth for long denied (or at least a portion of it), the healing power of truth-telling is something that is typically attached to truth commissions. Indeed, testimonies in the context of criminal trials are typically restrained by procedural rules, witnesses are imposed a cold, neutral, legalistic language and are often prevented from expressing their feelings and emotions. Also, cross-examination – which is a fundamental guarantee for the accused – essentially aims at weakening the witnesses' reconstruction of the events, and can thus have negative psychological consequences on the victims, who might feel re-traumatised.[90] On the contrary, several truth commissions have stressed their intention to provide healing to the victims, often using (such as in Argentina[91] and South Africa[92]) the metaphor of an open wound, that must be treated and closed in order to heal: cleansing is surely harmful, but an unhealed scar can affect the nation's health for long time, impeding a meaningful transition.[93] Truth commissions are believed to serve a healing purpose on different levels. On one side, the participatory, inclusive approach typical of a truth commission can bolster the process of psychological healing of the subjects who testify, both as victims and as perpetrators. The underlying idea – which stands at the core of the modern psychoanalytical disciplines – is that "speaking about traumatic experiences alleviates the psychological burden of silence and repression",[94] and in fact several studies conclude that the act of speaking, of expressing one's feelings and memories has a therapeutic value, while repressing memories and pain can negatively affect the emotional and sometimes even the physical life of the individual.[95] As introduced, this is true not only for the victims but also for perpetrators, insomuch that several authors praise the healing and cathartic potential of the act of confessing. Notably, such an approach to confession is not rarely influenced, more or less explicitly, by Christianity, in which confessing (as acknowledgment of one's misdeeds, implying an element of repentance) precedes the readmission of the subject into the religious community, granting him forgiveness and peace. As Andrea Lollini stresses, the act of confession in different cultures is believed to develop a dialogic and symbolic relation between the subject and the community, and therefore it is often the instrument through which such relationship is healed, and recovered.[96] Incidentally, it is also worth to mention that, aware of the fact that the healing process is a long and painful one, and in part dependent on the individuals' willingness and commitment,[97] the TRC also tried to provide the witnesses and their families (together with those who collected and processed the testimonies) with psychological support before, during and after the hearings.[98]

On the other side, this process of truth-telling is believed to have a cathartic effect on society as a whole, transforming not only those who speak but also those who listen; indeed, hearing a victim detailing the abuses suffered can have a strong impact on one's beliefs, while getting to know with certainty what happened to friends and relatives allows for grieving and eventually provides a sense of closure.[99] For example, the CONADEP findings were fundamental in exposing the truth about the fate of thousands of individuals disappeared in Argentina, providing their relatives and friends with the answers they were long denied, and allowing them to finally mourn for their losses.[100] This social dimension of healing is directly recognised by the TRC, which among the four notions of truth distinguished in its report identifies a "healing truth", consisting in "the kind of [subjective] truth that places facts and what they mean within the contest of human relationships – both amongst citizens and between the State and its citizens [in order to] contribute to the reparation of the damage inflicted in the past and to the prevention of the recurrence of serious abuses in the future".[101]

One important step in the process of healing the South African nation was the recovering of the traditional concept of *ubuntu*. This term expresses the concept that human beings are human through other human beings; as such, it manifests a holistic comprehension of society, as it stresses the importance of the community, and the belief that human beings find the core of their identity (and value) only in the empathic relation with other human beings.[102] As this relation was jeopardised and disrupted during the Apartheid era, the members of the TRC believed that "the nation would be healed by recuperating a notion of human mutuality imagined in the past but disabled by the wounds inflicted by the indignities of the Apartheid".[103] In other words, the only way to heal, individually and collectively, was in the eyes of the Commission through disclosure and truth, admission of responsibility, acknowledgment of humanity both in oneself and in the others – so as to become a one, united body.[104]

Caught Between Wrong Priorities and Unrealistic Expectations: A Critical Look at Truth Commissions

In spite of (and maybe also because of) extremely high hopes, these extraordinary and politically entrenched bodies have also shown several limitations, highlighted by the numerous criticisms received. Some among the most relevant ones – which strike at the core of the restorative project of truth commissions in general – are analysed in the following pages.

First, the ability of truth commissions to establish a full, undisputable truth is debated. Even leaving aside the (many) doubts concerning the effective possibility of knowing the full truth about past events,[105] several authors believe the truth presented by these bodies to be inevitably partial and biased. For example, Erin Daly in her article "Truth Skepticism: An Inquiry into the Value of Truth in Times of Transition" points out how, being these bodies created by a newly established government facing multiple challenges, they will likely offer a version of the events that discredits the past regime while uncritically providing legitimacy to the current executive, as well as to the transitional process they form part of.[106] This is in part caused by the fact that the commission members frequently represent, more or less directly, the new authorities, or more generally the "victorious side" of the conflict[107]; therefore – although they are not rarely flanked by internationally recognised figures – the risk is present that their truth-finding activities will be biased, maybe unwittingly, and maybe because of the very way in which the commission is designed. When this is the case, or more generally when the post-conflict society is still deeply divided (especially along ethnic lines), it will be extremely difficult for the version of truth presented by the commission to be accepted by the population.[108]

Moreover, some scholars specify how truth commissions do not discover, but rather *construct* one particular version of truth, as consequence of both the limitations they are being imposed and the choices they make. For what concerns the former, their activity is normally limited regarding the period of time, the geographical space and the categories of crimes they are mandated to investigate; besides, they operate with a limited amount of resources, staff and time,[109] often lacking any kind of coercive power.[110] About the latter, truth commissions adopt critical decisions, about – among others – who will "testify" and who will be excluded, who qualifies as victim, whether alleged perpetrators should be named in the final report.[111] All these "filters" influence the version of truth which is reconstructed, in such a way to, inevitably, shape it. Also, some authors believe these specificities to prevent the commissions from fully grasping with the deepest causes underlying the conflict.[112] As a result, instead of contributing to the establishment of peace and reconciliation, these bodies may appear as engaging in a sort of witch-hunt, thus eventually causing further divisions and violence. Furthermore, the omission from their investigations of specific events or topics can be harmful to some of the victims, who will feel as neither acknowledged nor represented by the narrative developed by the commission, their experience once again denied.[113]

Secondly, one of the most commonly raised criticisms is that truth commissions fail to provide accountability and justice, therefore being inadequate to guide the country towards a future in which human rights and the rule of law are respected. Indeed, these instruments often lack the power to impose penalties, directly award reparations, even ask for signs of remorse, and in general their efficacy rests more on civil persuasion and pressure than on laws or coercive measures[114]; as a consequence, they risk being employed as smokescreens, in alternative to (rather than as a complement of) more "substantial" and "impactful" mechanisms.[115]

Another weakness that many of these bodies seem to share with criminal prosecutions (domestic as well as supranational) is their inability – or unwillingness – to account for the role of international actors in causing, fostering and participating in conflicts.[116] The feeling of "missed justice" becomes even stronger in those situations in which laws are in place granting amnesties, when subjects who were clearly involved in the commission of crimes remain in positions of power, and/or when basic socio-economic needs of the population are left unaddressed. With regards to the latter point, although some countries were able to implement more inclusive and substantial reparation programs,[117] others, especially the poorest ones, could mostly grant merely symbolic support. This is also due to the fact that, while in contexts such as Argentina, the victims were more circumscribed and easier to identify, in situations such as South Africa discriminatory and segregationist policies were in place for generations, creating a social structure in which the majority of the population was constrained in cycles of poverty and denied the possibility to escape. In such scenarios, to effectively intervene with reparations or other individualised measures becomes more complex, while general economic and social reforms also are – or should be – a primary concern, with the aim of transforming the political, administrative, financial system that furthered the exploitation.[118] However, these interventions will eventually show their effects only in the long term, and thus tend to leave those most in need unsatisfied.[119] The South African transitional government addressed this issue by dedicating one of the TRC subcommittees, the RRC, to the formulation of proposals concerning reparations to the victims and reform programmes. While many sources depict South Africa to be better-off, as a result of the transitional process, at least in terms of social stability and respect for the fundamental rights of the population,[120] several studies actually found poverty, unemployment and inequality to be still widespread, and in such a way to reproduce the ethnic and racial discriminations typical of the Apartheid era.[121] The reasons for it are many and complex, and their analysis falls outside the space of this chapter; however, the fact that the RRC lacked the power to directly implement its proposals surely did not help.[122] Also on this issue, it is worth to mention how many truth commissions are increasingly criticised for their limited focus on violations of civil and political rights, which make them ill-suited to both investigate the deepest causes of conflicts (often residing in unequal power dynamics between races, classes and genders) and provide a meaningful justice to the victims; this aspect, however, will be the subject of the last two chapters of this book.

Other characteristics of these restorative organisms draw criticisms. For example, these bodies are often depicted as "touchy-feely", or excessively focused on those considered as the most symbolic and metaphorical aspects of a transition – such as reconciliation and healing – while failing to address more basic, practical needs of the population. In particular, many survivors get involved with truth commissions as they hope they will get some sort of reparation and material help in order to (re-)build their lives,[123] sometimes as these organs appear, on the ground, as the only "accessible" link between them and political-administrative bodies, the only forum where to express their grievances. This was the case in Sierra Leone, where, as already touched upon,[124] part of the disappointment of the population towards the local truth commission was related to the fact that many participated convinced, by the messages of the commission itself, that this institution would have given them practical help (more specifically, in the local culture terms like "help" and "encourage" are immediately linked to material support, rather than to a psychological or spiritual one).[125] In this way, by failing to tailor its message to the local context, the Commission provoked a misunderstanding that tainted its positive effects. This is not to claim that truth commissions should themselves be responsible for responding to every need of victims and survivors (this is the task of a comprehensive transitional project, of which these bodies can, and should, only be one of many components); however, these experiences manifest once again a problem of priorities, and reveal the importance, for truth commissions and for post-conflict bodies more in general, of effectively communicating with the local population, clarifying their role as well as their limits.

Faults in the Truth-as-Healing Paradigm

Finally, a more general critique of truth commissions as a model, introduced in the previous paragraph, is that such mechanisms might not be, at least to some extent, what the local population needs or wants, especially when the local culture envisages completely different instruments or ways to deal with traumatic events, both at the individual and at the social level.

For example, both Gearoid Millar and Rosalind Shaw[126] analysed the impact of the truth commission on Sierra Leone, revealing how the therapeutic truth paradigm that this body promoted and pursued collides with the local, traditional approach to trauma, that on the contrary values the act of forgetting – understood as "containment [of memories] in a form that would enable them to recover their lives"[127]; accordingly, in the Sierra Leonean culture what leads to reconciliation, at least in the narrow sense of non-violent social coexistence, is leaving the past behind in a sort of agreed amnesia. While such an approach is to some extent questionable, and might deserve to be problematised and potentially addressed, intervening out of the blue with an instrument centred around confession and narration of one's truth is likely to be destabilising, when not source of new tensions and conflicts. More generally, while several supporters of restorative justice mechanisms praise the supposed benefits of publicly narrating one's truth, a relevant number of authors and studies stress how such practices might eventually do more harm than good, both to the victims and to society as a whole.[128] In particular, the risk exists that recovering old, painful memories and sharing them with a wide and unfamiliar public causes a re-traumatisation, because of a lack of material and psychological support (regarding both past experiences and the narrative act itself) or because the local culture does not value confession as a therapeutic tool. Indeed, attaching healing effects to the practice of talking is, in the eyes of many, a typical Western assumption grounded in the modern psychoanalytical tradition,[129] and as such it might reveal detrimental to impose it within cultures that deal with traumas differently. A good case in point is, once again, the one of the Sierra Leonean Commission, analysed by Gearoid Millar while investigating possible shortcomings of the "therapeutic truth paradigm": the author concluded that the commission has had beneficial effects for the wealthiest sector of the population – more familiar with the international (Western) culture – while non-elite interviewees mostly reported negative outcomes.[130] Just as an additional example, several authors have revealed how the "pressure" that truth commissions sometimes put on women to talk about rape and sexual violence might cause a further traumatisation of the woman, which is brought to re-experience traumatic moments, as well as an exacerbation of her stigmatisation by the part of her community – without being able to support neither the woman nor the community.[131]

More generally, failing to properly prepare as well as follow-up the act of testifying can carry several negative consequences such as post-traumatic stress disorder and panic attacks.[132] Indeed, while getting to know, as well as narrating, the truth about one's past surely has several positive effects, it is also likely to create further needs – such as the desire for accountability, vengeance, repentance, material and psychological support – which post-conflict institutions are not always able, or willing, to provide. A related criticism is that the "international therapeutic paradigm […] obscures the material needs of survivors, pathologies war-affected nations, authenticates the political, social and moral claims of the powerful and *cultivates victims as vulnerable, infantile and in need of rescue*",[133] thus denying the victims empowerment and autonomy, and further entrenching – rather than dismantling – abusive dynamics between subjects. This risks happening especially in those situations in which truth commissions are used as a substitute for – rather than a complement to – criminal prosecutions, as while victims struggle with the psychological and practical consequences of past horrors, the subjects responsible for such acts are essentially allowed to move on with their lives, sometimes retaining their positions of power and influence.[134] This was a major issue in South Africa, where dozens of perpetrators admitted their misdeeds in front of the AC, often with indifference and absent any sign of remorse, and were awarded a fresh start, while victims could only passively assist to a show that forced them to move on, for the sake of a nation that for generations had just harmed them.[135]

The TRC foresaw the potentially harmful effects of exposing one's past or getting to know a repressed truth, and therefore put dedicated measures in place, such as training programs for its staff, and psychological support for the witnesses before and after the hearings. However, these initiatives – which are anyway exceptional for a truth commission – had a limited impact, for several reasons. First, everybody reacts to the narration of (or the exposure to) truth differently, and in ways that are only in part predictable; this makes the design of a general approach able to effectively manage these different needs complicated (According to the Trauma Centre for Victims of Violence and Torture in Cape Town, about half of the people it worked with faced grave psychological consequences and/or regretted the testimony in front of the Commission.)[136] Secondly, the number of persons who came in front of the HRVC or the AC is elevated, while the Commission lacked the resources and the staff to assist these subjects for the time necessary to heal their psychological wounds. Moreover, virtually every single person in South Africa was somehow affected by the work of this body, and to specifically address the different needs of millions of subjects, with different backgrounds, faiths, genders and experiences, was just impossible. As the Commission itself admitted,

> The Truth Commission has helped break the silence of past suffering, atrocities and abuses, in doing so, it has both released some traumatised ex-conscripts from the prison of silence and trapped them in the role of perpetrators of Apartheid. For some, the contradictions of their experience might prove intolerable."[137]

The Amnesty Process: Is Justice the Price for Peace?

> The adoption of this Constitution lays the secure foundation for the people of South Africa to transcend the divisions and strife of the past, which generated gross violations of human rights, the transgression of humanitarian principles in violent conflicts and a legacy of hatred, fear, guilt and revenge. These can now be addressed on the basis that there is a need for understanding but not for vengeance, a need for reparation but not for retaliation, a need for Ubuntu but not for victimization. In order to advance such reconciliation and reconstruction, *amnesty shall be granted in respect of acts, omissions and offenses associated with political objectives and committed in the course of the conflicts of the past.[. . .]* With this Constitution and these commitments we, the people of South Africa, open a new chapter in the history of our country.[138]

This unparalleled decision to offer amnesty to persons guilty of crimes and violence, envisaged in the Interim Constitution, and therefore prior to the establishment of the Commission itself, was undoubtedly the most controversial decision adopted in the design of the TRC, whose reasons can be discerned from the letter of the Postamble. In particular, amnesty was implemented as a necessary component of the post-Apartheid compromise,[139] determined by a desire for reconciliation and closure, as well as by practical considerations. First, as aforementioned, representatives and supporters of the old regime held powerful positions and would have never allowed for a peaceful transition, if that implied widespread criminal prosecutions, so that the country "would have been overwhelmed by the bloodbath that virtually everyone predicted as the inevitable ending for South Africa".[140] Secondly, resources were critically limited, while the subjects involved in the repression were just too numerous. Additionally, Nuremberg itself had shown the limitations of a purely judicial body in satisfactorily grasping with a comprehensive and pervasive system of abuses developed and furthered by the state with the complicity of the population. As a consequence, the retributive model was deemed in that specific context as not suitable to grant neither justice nor truth, which would instead be pursued through more inclusive means.[141] In turn, this implied finding instruments different from coercion to attract the perpetrators, and to convince them to play an active part in the transitional exercise.

The AC, competent for inquiring the applications for amnesty submitted to the TRC, followed several formal and factual criteria, among which the most relevant were 1) that the act or omission the subject asked pardon for qualified as "gross violations of human rights", 2) the motive of the offense, meaning that the act pursued a "political objective", and 3) that the applicant had made a "full disclosure" of such acts.[142] The procedure followed by the AC was an articulated one, and – for those applications who met the formal criteria envisaged in the Unity and Reconciliation Act – included a public hearing that had to be notified to the victims and other persons interested, in order to give them the possibility to participate and intervene.[143] In particular, during this hearing the applicant was asked to publicly confess what he had already admitted in the written statement, followed by testimonies of witnesses and/or other persons interested, and possible cross-examinations.[144] The adoption of such a complex and "sensitive" procedure was justified by the important consequences that the decision of the Committee had on the alleged perpetrator, the victims and the state itself. Indeed, the eventual granting of the amnesty, which followed the corroboration of the confessed acts by the Committee's investigative units, precluded not only criminal prosecutions but also civil liability concerning these same acts (although the names of those granted pardon were published)[145]; additionally, victims were precluded from suing the state or other organisations for the same crimes.[146] However, if the amnesty was denied, the applicants risked to be held accountable both criminally and in civil courts.[147] According to the final report, applications were filed by more than 7000 people, but more than 5000 were rejected[148]; the Committee addressed through public hearing around 1700 cases, and conceded amnesties, full or partial, in about 1300, the main reason for rejection being the absence of a "genuine" political motive.[149]

As discussed in the first part of this book,[150] the impact of amnesties is highly dependent on the other transitional mechanisms put in place and their efficacy, as well as on the local attitude. In South Africa, the amnesty process was criticised both as such, in its ideological justifications, and because of some peculiarities, such as the preclusion of any kind of legal liability, the very limited consideration of the victims' opinions, and the fact that the perpetrators were not asked for any sign of remorse or repentance.[151] As a consequence, sometimes this ritual of confession appeared as a formal step to be undertaken by the perpetrators – which not rarely maintained positions of power and wealth – in order to obtain a fresh start, while the burden of the truth rested all on the victims.[152]

However, other authors believe that the potential justice deficit created by the amnesties was filled by the "justice" and pacification the TRC fostered[153]: amnesty was the price for truth, justified by the absence of satisfying alternatives[154]; by stubbornly excluding it in name of a retribution which was practically not feasible, there would have been neither peace nor accountability, and consequently no justice. Accordingly, the Commission had the merit of developing a balanced compromise between blanket pardon and strict punishment. In particular, the idea of conditioning the amnesty to the exercise of full disclosure appeared at the time as the most acceptable way to provide accountability without impinging on pacification. Thanks to this requirement, amnesty was perceived by many not as an escape from justice, but rather as a realistic alternative given to perpetrators: they were offered the possibility to come forward and participate in the process of reconciliation, thus playing a constructive role in the creation of the new nation, or they could passively face criminal prosecutions.[155]

Conclusions

The South African experiment was a fortunate one, which could enjoy an amount of resources and support – both domestic and international – which are exceptional for a transitional mechanism. It was only one element of a broader project of structural reform, and it was carefully crafted and implemented in order to respond to that specific situation, with all its peculiarities, analysed above; among others, the pervasiveness of the Apartheid system, its insinuation in every fold of the social fabric, which required – as a response – an inclusive project of pacification between estranged and opposed groups; the need to completely refashion the society as well as public institutions, rather than only focusing on few individuals, which inevitably represent only the tip of a much more entrenched iceberg of abuses and discrimination, whose eradication requires not only criminal punishment but also comprehensive interventions at the political, economic and social level.

Furthermore, the Commission proved that reconciliation – or anyway a peaceful coexistence among former enemies – requires truth, not only blame.[156] One of the core challenges of transitional justice is precisely to find the right way to get former opponents to live together again, preventing future conflicts. With the TRC, and with the development of the restorative justice model in general, the hypocrisy is dismantled that post-conflict scenarios are characterised by a struggle between absolute evil and absolute good, and therefore that the mere punishment of few individuals is sufficient in creating a new, inclusive society.[157] Accordingly, these instruments "transcended the single-minded focus on individual accountability in favour of a more communitarian conception",[158] with legal terms and instruments blending with the rhetoric of confession, ritual and healing. Beyond its effects on the ground, the South African experiment also proved mostly successful in providing an alternative, a "realistic" one, to criminal prosecutions as the post-conflict instruments par excellence; in showing that justice is not merely – or necessarily – equated with retribution, nor the exclusive domain of the lawyer and the judge. Indeed, the TRC process is considered as a fair and substantially impartial one that provided at least a degree of accountability and contributed to the creation of a more inclusive society, teaching citizens to see and accept the humanity in oneself and in the other, and to be active parts of the society. Particularly interesting on this point is the perspective of Andrea Lollini, who rejects the assertion that the Commission fostered impunity, believing instead that the TRC eluded the punishment/justice – not punishment/impunity dichotomy, proving that effective forms of transitional justice exist outside the retributive model[159]; forms based on inclusion rather than exclusion, on acceptance rather than guilt, focused not only on the wrongs of the past but also on building a new society, in whose development also the offenders play a meaningful part. Understood in this way, truth commissions assume a constitutive force.[160]

Nevertheless, both the TRC and truth commissions in general are neither perfect instruments nor the solution to the many needs and grievances of societies post-conflict; in the words of Priscilla Hayner,

> Truth commissions are difficult and controversial entities; they are given a mammoth, almost impossible task and usually insufficient time and resources to complete it; they must struggle with rampant lies, denials, and deceit and the

> painful, almost unspeakable memories of victims to uncover still-dangerous truths that many in power may well continue to resist.[161]

They provide an inclusive and understanding environment, but they are substantially dependant on the support of the state and the civil society, and therefore they need cooperation in implementing what they can only draft. Moreover, they are not rarely overburdened by unrealistic goals and expectations, which do not adequately consider their limitations in resources and personnel, the fragile environment they move in, and the time required to discover the truth and promote reconciliation. Another potential weakness of truth commissions lies in one of its key peculiarities, meaning their being centred on the victims, and on narrative rituals: often, they risk opening a Pandora's box without having the ability, the resources and the expertise to deal with its consequences. Similarly, because of their steady presence at the core of the transitional "toolbox" promoted by international actors in post-conflict scenarios, they are not rarely instituted unreflectively, and without taking into adequate consideration the needs, traditions and grievances of the local population, in this way risking worsening an already severe situation.

In relation to the latter point, and on a more general level, truth commissions are also increasingly criticised as manifestations of that same legalistic, one-size-fits-all approach promoted by the international community, from which criminal trials themselves emerged: similarly to these bodies, they also are perceived as prioritising violations of civil and political rights, at the expenses of a more substantial attention to structural inequality and economic issues; they appear to focus – almost blindly – on abuses unfolded in the public sphere, while unconcerned with violations experienced in the private sphere[162]; also, at a closer look, they appear dominated by legalistic rhetoric and professionals. These criticisms, which strike at the core of transitional justice as a field, will be the protagonists of the next two chapters.

Notes

1. Ruti G. Teitel, "Transitional Justice Genealogy", *Harvard Human Rights Journal* 16 (2003): 78
2. Audrey R. Chapman and Patrick Ball, "The Truth of Truth Commissions: Comparative Lessons from Haiti, South Africa, and Guatemala", *Human Rights Quarterly* 23 (2001): 2
3. Priscilla B. Hayner, *Unspeakable Truths: Confronting State Terror and Atrocity* (New York: Routledge, 2001), 27

4. For a full list of truth commissions established up to now, see "Truth Commission Digital Collection", United States Institute of Peace, accessed December 13, 2016, http://www.usip.org/publications/truth-commission-digital-collection.
5. James L. Gibson, "On Legitimacy Theory and the Effectiveness of Truth Commissions", *Law and Contemporary Problems* 72 (2009): 125
6. Andrea Lollini, *Constitutionalism and Transitional Justice in South Africa* (Oxford: Bergham Books, 2011), 270
7. Nelson Mandela, *Long Walk to Freedom: The Autobiography of Nelson Mandela* (London: Little, Brown & Co: 1995), 71
8. William Beinart and Saul Dubow, eds., *Segregation and Apartheid in Twentieth-Century South Africa* (London and New York: Routledge, 1995), 7
9. See Martin Legassick, "British Hegemony and the Origins of Segregation in South Africa, 1901–14", in William Beinart and Saul Dubow, eds., *Segregation and Apartheid in Twentieth-Century South Africa* (London and New York: Routledge, 1995), 43. Particularly telling is the analysis of the concept of "native assisted evolution."
10. Harold Wolpe, "Capitalism and Cheap Labour Power in South Africa", in William Beinart and Saul Dubow, eds., *Segregation and Apartheid in Twentieth-Century South Africa* (London and New York: Routledge, 1995), 60
11. Legassick, "British Hegemony and the Origins of Segregation in South Africa", 48
12. Michael Humphrey and Estela Valverde, "Human Rights Politics and Injustice: Transitional Justice in Argentina and South Africa", *The International Journal of Transitional Justice* 2 (2008): 85
13. Wolpe, "Capitalism and Cheap Labour Power in South Africa", 81
14. Abdullah Omar, "Truth and Reconciliation in South Africa: Accounting for the Past", *Buffalo Human Rights Law Review* 4 (1998): 7
15. Stephen Zunes, "The Role of Non-Violent Action in the Downfall of Apartheid", *The Journal of Modern African Studies* 37(1) (1999): 153
16. Derek Powell, "The Role of Constitution Making and Institution Building in Furthering Peace, Justice and Development: South Africa's Democratic Transition", *The International Journal of Transitional Justice* 4 (2010): 238
17. Paul Lansing and Julie C. King, "South Africa's Truth and Reconciliation Commission: the Conflict between Individual Justice and National Healing in the Post-Apartheid Age", *Arizona Journal of International and Comparative Law* 15(3) (1998): 756
18. Nickname of Umkhonto we Sizwe ("Spear of the Nation"); For more on the MK and the approach of Mandela to violent resistance, see Mandela, *Long Walk to Freedom,* 164

19. James L. Gibson, "The Contributions of Truth to Reconciliation. Lessons from South Africa", *Journal of Conflict Resolution* 50 (2006): 421
20. Ibid.
21. See Zackie Achmat, "Law, Politics and Social Transformation", *International Journal of Legal Information* 32 (2004): 237–242
22. Beinart and Dubow, eds., *Segregation and Apartheid in Twentieth-Century South Africa,* 4
23. Powell, "The Role of Constitution Making and Institution Building in Furthering Peace", *Justice and Development,* 237
24. Ibid.
25. Mandela, *Long Walk to Freedom,* 71
26. Beinart and Dubow, eds., *Segregation and Apartheid in Twentieth-Century South Africa,* 20
27. Ibid.
28. Lansing and King, "South Africa's Truth and Reconciliation Commission", 757
29. Ibid., 757
30. Among others, see Lansing and King, "South Africa's Truth and Reconciliation Commission"; Omar, "Truth and Reconciliation in South Africa: Accounting for the Past": 5–14
31. Zunes, "The Role of Non-Violent Action in the Downfall of Apartheid", 138
32. Lansing and King, "South Africa's Truth and Reconciliation Commission", 759
33. Ibid., 785
34. Richard J. Goldstone, "Past Human Rights Violations: Truth Commissions and Amnesties or Prosecutions", *Northern Ireland Legal Quarterly* 51(2) (1999): 166
35. *Promotion of National Unity and Reconciliation Act*: Act 34 of 1995, Statutes of the Republic of South Africa – Constitutional Law, 801–854
36. Sam Garkawe, "The South African Truth and Reconciliation Commission: A suitable Model to Enhance the Role and Rights of the Victims of Gross Violations of Human Rights", *Melbourne University Law Review* 27 (2003): 348
37. South African citizens were invited to submit nominations: these were then scrutinised by a selection panel, which compiled a list of 25 candidates, from which the President picked the final names. Truth and Reconciliation Commission, "Truth and Reconciliation Commission of South Africa Report" (Cape Town: Juta and Co., 1998) (hereinafter: TRC Report): Vol.1, Chapter 4, Par. 23
38. Peter Schey, Dinah Shelton and Naomi Roht-Arriaza, "Addressing Human Rights Abuses: Truth Commissions and the Value of Amnesty", *Whittier Law Review* 19 (1997): 327

39. *Promotion of National Unity and Reconciliation Act*, Chapter 1, Par. 1 (ix) [emphasis added]
40. Ibid., Vol.1, Chapter 2
41. Ibid., Chapter 2, Par. 3
42. The TRC included a chapter on recommendations in Volume 5 of the Report, Chapter 8
43. TRC Report, Vol.1, Chapter 4, Par. 32
44. Chapman and Ball, "The Truth of Truth Commissions", 15
45. TRC Report, Vol.1, Chapter 10, Par.1
46. Garkawe, "The South African Truth and Reconciliation Commission", 367
47. TRC Report, Vol.1, Chapter 6, Par. 21ss
48. Lansing and King, "South Africa's Truth and Reconciliation Commission", 765
49. Garkawe, "The South African Truth and Reconciliation Commission", 366
50. Ibid., 374
51. Lansing and King, "South Africa's Truth and Reconciliation Commission", 764
52. Goldstone, "Past Human Rights Violations", 173
53. Hayner, *Unspeakable Truths*, 25
54. Erin Daly, "Truth Skepticism: An Inquiry into the Value of Truth in Times of Transition", *The International Journal of Transitional Justice* 2 (2008): 26
55. Nenad Dimitrijevic, "Justice beyond Blame. Moral Justification of (The Idea of) a Truth Commission", *Journal of Conflict Resolution* 50 (2006): 379
56. Volume 4 of the TRC report is focused on the involvement and the role of constituencies such as the media, the legal community, the health and the prison systems.
57. TRC Report, Vol.5, Chapter 6, Par. 162
58. TRC Report Vol.1, Chapter 5, Par. 108
59. Hayner, *Unspeakable Truths*, 94
60. Eric Brahm, "Uncovering the Truth: Examining Truth Commission Success and Impact", *International Studies Perspectives* 8 (2007): 21
61. Hayner, *Unspeakable Truths,* 106
62. Hayner, *Unspeakable Truths*, 108 analyses in depth the opportunity of naming the subjects found guilty by truth commissions, and recalls some examples.
63. Lansing and King, "South Africa's Truth and Reconciliation Commission", 781
64. Among others, TRC Report Vol.1, Chapter 1, Par. 22
65. Brahm, "Uncovering the Truth", 24
66. This issue will be discussed in more depth in the following paragraphs

67. Among others, see Powell, "The Role of Constitution Making and Institution Building in Furthering Peace, Justice and Development": 230–250
68. Garkawe, "The South African Truth and Reconciliation Commission", 375
69. See infra, Chapter 4
70. Gibson, "The Contributions of Truth to Reconciliation", 414
71. Gibson, "On Legitimacy Theory and the Effectiveness of Truth Commissions", 136
72. TRC Report Vol.5, Chapter 9, Par. 112
73. Hayner, *Unspeakable Truths*, 155
74. Ibid., 160
75. Ibid., 155
76. The TRC stresses, in its report, how all the factions were responsible for violence and misdeeds, with some sections – such as Chapters 4 and 6 of Volume 2 – specifically dedicated to the wrongdoings of the resistance and liberation movements. Notably, this was itself subject to criticisms, in that it appeared to imply a similarity in the abuses suffered by the two sides, which were in fact very different in scale and justifications.
77. TRC Report Vol.5, Chapter 9, Par. 1
78. Lansing and King, "South Africa's Truth and Reconciliation Commission", 780
79. Anita Isaacs, "At War with the Past? The Politics of Truth Seeking in Guatemala", *The International Journal of Transitional Justice* 4 (2010): 261
80. Garkawe, "The South African Truth and Reconciliation Commission", 350
81. TRC Report Vol.1, Chapter 5, Par. 89
82. Gearoid Millar, "Assessing Local Experiences of Truth-Telling in Sierra Leone: Getting to 'Why' through a Qualitative Case Study Analysis", *The International Journal of Transitional Justice* 4 (2010): 480
83. Chapman and Ball, "The Truth of Truth Commissions", 35
84. Ibid., 11
85. Goldstone, "Past Human Rights Violations", 168
86. Schey, Shelton and Roht-Arriaza, "Addressing Human Rights Abuses", 334
87. Nneoma v. Nwogu, "When and Why It Started: Deconstructing Victim-Centered Truth Commissions in the Context of Ethnicity-Based Conflict", *The International Journal of Transitional Justice* 4 (2010): 282
88. Isaacs, "At War with the Past? The Politics of Truth Seeking in Guatemala", 269
89. Millar, "Assessing Local Experiences of Truth-Telling in Sierra Leone", 478
90. Garkawe, "The South African Truth and Reconciliation Commission", 369
91. Hayner, *Unspeakable Truths*, 133
92. Millar, "Assessing Local Experiences of Truth-Telling in Sierra Leone", 481

93. Hayner, *Unspeakable Truths*, 133
94. Rebecca Horn, Simon Charters and Saleem Vahidi, "Testifying in an International War Crimes Tribunal: The Experience of Witnesses in the Special Court for Sierra Leone", *The International Journal of Transitional Justice* 3 (2009): 117
95. Hayner, *Unspeakable Truths*, 134
96. Lollini, *Constitutionalism and Transitional Justice in South Africa*, 261
97. Lansing and King, "South Africa's Truth and Reconciliation Commission", 782
98. TRC Report Vol.1, Chapter 6, Par. 34. Also, see Vol.5, Chapter 9 for examples of beneficial effects
99. Lansing and King, South Africa's Truth and Reconciliation Commission, 769
100. James L. Gibson, "Overcoming Apartheid: Can Truth Reconcile a Divided Nation?", *Politikon* 31 (2004): 132
101. TRC Report Vol.1, Chapter 5, Par. 43–44
102. Lollini, *Constitutionalism and Transitional Justice in South Africa*, 246
103. Deborah Posel, "History as Confession: The Case of South African Truth and Reconciliation Commission", *Public Culture Winter* 20 (2008): 129
104. Ibid.
105. See Infra Chapter 3 on different positions regarding the "existence" and possibility to reconstruct a one, objective truth
106. Daly, "Truth Skepticism", 26 & 39
107. Ibid., 28
108. Ibid., 38
109. Hayner, *Unspeakable Truths*, 73
110. The TRC was an exception, as it was granted several quasi-judicial powers. See Chapman and Ball, "The Truth of Truth Commissions", 14
111. Ibid., 8 on the choice of the TRC to focus on some "window cases"
112. Nwogu, "When and Why It Started", 276
113. Hayner, *Unspeakable Truths*, 73; Also, the argument is discussed infra, in Chapter 2
114. Brahm, "Uncovering the Truth", 28
115. Hayner, *Unspeakable Truths*, 86
116. Ibid., 75
117. See Ibid., 177 on the case of Argentina
118. Powell, "The Role of Constitution Making and Institution Building in Furthering Peace, Justice and Development", 237
119. Ibid.
120. Among others, see Gibson, "Overcoming Apartheid", 129–155
121. Powell, "The Role of Constitution Making and Institution Building in Furthering Peace, Justice and Development", 245

122. Garkawe, "The South African Truth and Reconciliation Commission", 368
123. Hayner, *Unspeakable Truths*, 172
124. See Infra, Chapter 8
125. Millar, "Assessing Local Experiences of Truth-Telling in Sierra Leone", 491
126. Rosalind Shaw, "Memory Frictions: Localizing the truth and Reconciliation Commission in Sierra Leone", *The International Journal of Transitional Justice* 1 (2007): 183–207
127. Ibid., 194
128. Millar, "Assessing Local Experiences of Truth-Telling in Sierra Leone", 492
129. Ibid., 493
130. Ibid., 495
131. Shana Tabak, "False Dichotomies of Transitional Justice: Gender, Conflict and Combatants in Colombia", *International Law and Politics* 44 (2011): 124
132. Hayner, *Unspeakable Truths*, 141–145
133. Vanessa Pupavac, "International Therapeutic Peace and Justice in Bosnia", *Social and Legal Studies* 13(3) (2004) as quoted in Henry, "Witness to Rape", 118 [emphasis added]
134. Lansing and King, "South Africa's Truth and Reconciliation Commission", 771
135. Ibid., 772
136. Hayner, *Unspeakable Truths*, 144
137. TRC Report, Vol.5, Chapter 9, Par.26
138. *Interim Constitution of South Africa* (1993), Postamble (Chapter 16) [emphasis added]
139. Omar, "Truth and Reconciliation in South Africa: Accounting for the Past", 9
140. TRC Report Vol.1, Chapter 1, Par. 22
141. This concept was clearly stated by the Constitutional Court of South Africa in the Biko Case: *The Azanian People's Organization (AZAPO) v The President of the Republic of South Africa* CCT 17/96 (25 July 1996)
142. *Promotion of National Unity and Reconciliation Act*, Chapter 2, Par.3
143. TRC Report, Vol.1, Chapter 10, Par. 9
144. Lollini, *Constitutionalism and Transitional Justice in South Africa,* 183
145. *Promotion of National Unity and Reconciliation Act*, Chapter 4, Par. 7(a)
146. Ibid., Par. 7(c)
147. Garkawe, "The South African Truth and Reconciliation Commission", 354
148. TRC Report Vol.1, Chapter 10, statistical information
149. Ibid.
150. See Infra, Chapter 5
151. Garkawe, "The South African Truth and Reconciliation Commission", 370

152. Lansing and King, "South Africa's Truth and Reconciliation Commission", 772
153. Gibson "Overcoming Apartheid", 149
154. TRC Report, Vol.1, Chapters 1 and 5, Par. 71
155. Schey, Shelton and Roht-Arriaza, "Addressing Human Rights Abuses", 342
156. Gibson "Overcoming Apartheid", 142
157. Gibson, "The Contributions of Truth to Reconciliation", 44
158. Teitel, "Transitional Justice Genealogy", 80
159. Lollini, *Constitutionalism and Transitional Justice in South Africa,* 217
160. Ibid., 262
161. Hayner, *Unspeakable Truths*, 23
162. Tabak, "False Dichotomies of Transitional Justice", 124

CHAPTER 10

Adapting the Perspective: The Role of Bottom-Up Initiatives

Introduction

The previous chapters presented the main instruments used in transitional contexts – namely tribunals and truth commissions – as expressions of two distinct and contrasting approaches to justice, namely the retributive and the restorative one. However, at a closer look these mechanisms share several characteristics, in terms of priorities, rhetoric and organisation, due – at least according to critical voices – to their being expression of a "one-size-fits-all" approach developed at the international level and uncritically applied in the most diverse of circumstances.

The last two chapters address this and other issues through a more critical perspective on the transitional enterprise as such, analysing more in-depth limitations and blindspots that already emerged, more or less implicitly, throughout the book; they follow a common thread and introduce similar arguments, but they also have two different focuses. In particular, while the next chapter reserves more attention to the theme of development, and to the continuities between pre- and post-conflict violence and inequality, hereby the themes of the ownership and context sensitivity of the process are more thoroughly addressed, especially pausing on the dynamics between local and international actors.

In particular, transitional justice programmes are often criticised for adopting a top-down dynamic, and for being largely internationally driven: external actors, such as foreign countries, the UN and international NGOs

G. Girelli, *Understanding Transitional Justice*,
Philosophy, Public Policy, and Transnational Law,
DOI 10.1007/978-3-319-53606-4_10

are perceived as sponsoring a "one-size-fits-all" approach to transitions, intervening in different situations with the same instruments, forged around Western values, while ignoring local dynamics and needs[1]; in this way, few schemes of intervention are being developed, which are implemented in every scenario, while the local communities are only involved in the final implementation stage, and denied ownership of the justice process.[2]

The following paragraphs outline the many criticisms moved to this top-down, "one-size-fits-all" approach to transitions, specifically focusing on the perceived imperialistic influence of foreign actors, and on the uncritical preference for purely legal instruments. Because of the sheer amount of different arguments, studies and positions on this issue, it is only possible to provide a brief overview of some of the main critiques, which several authors have more thoroughly developed. Following, building on the example of *Fambul Tok* the realm of grassroots initiatives will be addressed, being these mechanisms often praised as the key solution to this problem, thanks to their close relation to the local context and culture, and to their perceived efficacy and legitimacy. After an assessment of their main potential or actual benefits (aware of the complexity and variegated nature of the category) some limitations will also be considered, some of which are related to the nature of these instruments, while others appear to be caused by their employment in extraordinary scenarios like the post-conflict ones.

The Colonising Nature of Post-Conflict Interventions

The introduction briefly outlined some among the main criticisms moved to traditional post-conflict initiatives, rooted in the observation that most post-conflict interventions occur in "developing", non-Western countries, and experience a dominating presence of the international community and of foreign powers, both directly – through official interventions – and more indirectly, represented in the many rules, standards, mechanisms and objectives that characterise transitional efforts. As a consequence, the transitional machinery is by some accused of treating domestic governments and populations with asymmetry and paternalism,[3] as "the West arrogates the universal to itself and then brings all others into its fold of humanity",[4] valuing locals as either weak victims or violent criminals lacking a sense of order and pacific coexistence, in need for civilisation and help.[5] Makau Mutua described this dynamic in a particularly effective and evocative way in his article "Savages, Victims and Saviors: The Metaphor of Human Rights",[6] where he questions the attitude of

Western states, organisations and academics, which intervene in conflict and post-conflict situations as saviours of weak, disempowered subjects perceived and depicted as victims of a savage state; what makes this state barbaric is, in the eyes of the (typically white and male) rescuer, its rejection of the civilising call of human rights and Western culture, while the "elevation to 'savior' status may simply obscure the involvement of the 'saviors' in creating the 'savage'".[7]

As the essence of the savage state lies in its barbaric and illiberal culture, in the aftermath of conflicts the international community takes over the failed and unsovereign (because illiberal) government by following and imposing its own standards and conceptions, appreciated as natural sources of peace and democracy, with the consequence that local mechanisms are either discarded or exploited as legitimising tools, while at the core of transitional processes stand the universal symbols of justice: criminal tribunals. While trials often play a fundamental role post-conflict, their uncritical adoption as the key instrument to confront complex and heinous wars reveals not only an assumed narrative of past events and responsibilities but also an unspoken hierarchy between different instruments of justice and their underlying priorities and values, in favour of legal, technical approaches and against more participative and informal processes.[8] This manifestation of ideological power is problematic both in theory, as it reveals a prejudice against popular mechanisms, and in practice, as it has led to the blind implementation of instruments which are just out of focus, inadequate to address the specific issues faced by the target countries. For example, authors such as Abdullahi An-Na'im criticised, with regards to Darfur, the obsession of the international community with individual criminal accountability (at the international level) to confront a situation generated by long-standing conflicts over resources and inequality and exacerbated by colonialism, elitism, ethnic polarisation and even climate change.[9] Such an insensitive approach proved not only inadequate but also, eventually, detrimental to the peace process.

Underlying these criticisms is a more general perception of the presumed neoliberal character of post-conflict interventions: irrespective of different origins or characterisations, most (if not all) transitional processes are dominated by a peculiar, although at the same time universalised, understanding of justice and peace: specific instruments, priorities and goals are thus presented as neutral, inevitable and necessary, while in fact being influenced by Western neoliberal thought and by legalistic approaches.

The "global transitional justice industry"[10]

This neoliberal paradigm presents a set of characteristics which can be found, although in different degrees and sometimes under different guises, in virtually every transitional process implemented up to now. For example, and as more thoroughly elaborated upon in the next chapter, the post-conflict machinery tends to concentrate on violations of civil and political rights, while underestimating violations of economic and cultural rights,[11] as well as the role of socio-economic inequality as root cause of conflicts[12]; as a consequence, individual perpetrators of violent crimes are the main targets of punitive measures, while the responsibilities of foreign political and economic powers are normally overlooked. This pattern unfolded, among others, in Iraq, where the transitional justice process focused on the brutal crimes and the acts of repression of the Hussein regime, while the themes of the foreign military intervention, the war on terror, and the internal resistance were largely avoided.[13] Similarly, these mechanisms often fail to acknowledge the impact of past experiences of colonisation – as well as abusive decolonisation processes – on breeding instability and violence.[14] As a consequence, the transitional project risks only focusing on the "tip of the iceberg", criminalising the final product of a long-standing abusive system, while ignoring its origins and deepest causes – in this way being incapable of fostering a positive and long-lasting peace.

Post-conflict interventions are also criticised because of a perceived attitude to confront their target contexts through a Western perspective,[15] whose features can be highly discordant with those of the local mind-set. One of these features is its individualism, understood as focus on the individual as "basic and irreducible unit of society",[16] in contrast with more holistic approaches of many Asian and African cultures, in which individuals find their locus and meaning within their community, which regulates their daily life, also determining their social status, and whose needs are prioritised.[17] In such a context, interventions focused primarily on the subject (both as responsible for violence and as victim of abuses and hardships) in its individual dimension risk revealing ineffective, because of a resulting failure to address those underlying power dynamics which fostered the conflict, as well as a potential misperception of individual and social needs and priorities post-conflict.[18]

This bias can also be perceived in the interpretation of key notions employed in the transitional rhetoric, such as that of "healing". As previously outlined,[19] several post-conflict initiatives are implemented with the purpose of providing healing to the population, consequently privileging processes of truth-telling, discussion, sharing of traumatic experiences.[20] However, although presented as neutral and universal, and thus replicated with only few adjustments in different countries, this approach to mental health (as well as to grief and guilt) finds its roots in the Western psycho-analytical tradition. On the contrary, it revealed to be less appropriate and responsive in other cultures, such as the Sierra Leonean one, which attach greater importance to silence and forgetting, or whose members reserve less value to confession as an instrument of spiritual relief.[21]

A similar line of criticism of these top-down initiatives concerns their tendency to impose a peculiar idea of progress, a specific and inevitable objective: democratic governance, through the adoption of Western-like state institutions,[22] and development as naturally flowing from the adoption of a liberal market economy, which are normally constitutive elements of the post-conflict "package"[23]: political and economic liberalisation is the recipe through which the savage state will move towards and into the community of civilised nations. As a consequence, "wider geo-political and economic interests [. . .] shape what tend to be represented as politically and economically neutral post-conflict and transitional justice initiatives".[24] This fosters, as a further consequence, a strong focus on state-level institutions, assumed as the source and the core of state power and legitimacy, and therefore as the engines of order and development: state-building is therefore conceived of in terms of establishment and development of formal institutions.[25] This overlooks the reality that, in many (if not most) countries undergoing a transition, the central level shows an extremely weak ability and reach, in favour of local authorities, which have a much stronger grasp and control of the territory.[26] This is often the by-product of historical factors, such as traditional organisation into local communities and tribes, and it is sometimes also influenced by the fact that the central state is perceived (this also for historic reasons) as corrupt or discriminatory, and/or as responsible for violence and instability.[27]

The state level is also typically of limited accessibility and availability to traditionally marginalised constituencies[28]; as a consequence, failing to engage with the local dimension also risks furthering their exclusion and silencing, thus manifesting a lack of context sensitivity and resulting in a transitional process which is ineffective, or even detrimental, as this potentially provokes tensions between different sources and levels of power.[29] In this kind of contexts, therefore, rebuilding or reforming state institutions is of limited use, when not integrated by initiatives dedicated to redistribution of resources, tackling of corruption and indirect systems of discrimination, promotion of political representation and participation of traditionally marginalised subjects (such as, in many cases, women or ethnic minorities). Notably, focusing on the community level is not only potentially more inclusive but can also help restoring local ways of establishing rules and standards, as well as local deliberative processes, thus fostering emancipation and empowerment.[30]

Finally, a typical feature of this neoliberal paradigm which is worth pausing on is its legalism, as over-reliance on law and legal instruments to confront the legacies of violence and conflict,[31] while underestimating the potential benefits of non-legal practices. This biased approach (which supported – while at the same time strengthening – the aforementioned primary focus on violations of civil and political rights) is rooted in an appreciation of law – especially state law – as a purely technical and neutral tool, gifted with an element of universality, and consequently praised as the primary and essential instrument to employ in order to achieve a peaceful and democratic future.[32] Justice is therefore equated with law (and in particular with legal criminal accountability), and reconstruction is predominantly pursued through legal reforms, while other approaches are marginalised or perceived as merely complementary.[33] As a consequence, the field itself is dominated by legal scholars and practitioners,[34] while other disciplines and experts (such as anthropologists, sociologists, psychologists, but also engineers or agriculturalists), which could prioritise other needs or initiatives, are too often only included as ancillary.

A fundamental element of this legal project is the concept of the "Rule of Law", whose promotion is often presented as one of the key objectives of post-conflict interventions. Indeed, this well-established principle is (similarly to others) praised as something technical, neutral, inherently positive and culture-less, as a value and a goal naturally and universally shared by all peoples,[35] while in fact being interpreted through Western lens; as such, it is inextricably linked to culture-specific values and instruments, such as those of democratic governance and written law.[36] As mentioned, to be problematic is not the concept per se', but rather its elevation as a technical and universal standard, with the effect that law is abstracted from the context, and consequently not critically approached and evaluated in its nature as manifestation and shaper of power dynamics (at the local, national and international levels alike).[37]

This overreliance on law as the technical tool par excellence – which also makes everything else appear marginal, imperfect, expression of less civilised and advanced cultures – is influenced by the widespread perception of law as an instrument able to bring harmony in the chaos, to rationalise the irrational, through a linear process of labelling and defining, in this way clearly distinguishing innocence from guilt, right from wrong.[38] However, for the same reason, a purely legal narrative also risks essentialising the context. Indeed, precisely because of this binary approach to reality, law is ill-equipped to efficiently engage with complex identities (such as in the case of child soldiers),[39] as well as to adequately account for and confront long-standing inequalities, complex stories of colonialism, ethnic rivalries and scarcity of resources.[40] In other words, the adoption of a legal language depoliticises essentially political issues and processes,[41] while at the same time depoliticising law itself.

In sum, post-conflict instruments are criticised for adopting initiatives presented as purely technical and apolitical, and therefore not even in need of scrutiny, while at a closer look being grounded on the ideological assumptions of Western liberalism, and aiming at ensuring compliance by the "liberated" and "civilised" country to international political and economic norms.[42] At the same time, traditional practices that could potentially have a stronger impact on the population, being closely related to their cultural and historical heritage, are discarded for failing to meet international standards of human rights and development which were themselves predominantly defined – at least according to some – by the West[43]: Kieran McEvoy defines this process as "Westoxification", defined as the imposition, by the part of Western powers, of standards and principles that the international community itself fails to respect and uphold.[44]

For these reasons, several authors criticise transitional justice as a *colonising field*,[45] instrumental to the self-appointed civilising mission of the West as donor of universal standards of justice and dignity to savage non-Western countries, whose informal mechanisms, rituals and oral customs are an expression of their inferior culture.[46] Like colonialism, transitional justice is criticised for overlooking or dismissing different experiences and understandings – of justice, peace and development – as sub-civilised[47]; even when local and customary mechanisms are allowed within the post-conflict machinery, these are hybridised and contaminated with foreign values and priorities, as only what responds to the coloniser's parameters and standards is tolerated (one among many examples is that of the opposition to traditional mechanisms of conflict resolution for failing to meet "due process" standards).[48]

Additionally, like colonialism this kind of intervention denies itself, or at least its responsibilities, its failures and potential negative consequences.[49] Not by chance, the aforementioned legalistic approach, as well as the limiting focus on individual responsibility, conveniently remove the international community from the conflict and post-conflict narrative, if not as saviour and protector.

Finally, just like colonialism, this artificial universality and paternalism,[50] besides provoking disempowerment, also fosters resistance and rejection.

Is Another Transition Possible? Framing Grassroots Initiatives

Before delving further into the multifaceted realm of grassroots mechanisms and approaches, a caveat is necessary, as any analysis of these instruments is in itself problematic from its inception, in the choice of the terminology.

Indeed, these mechanisms are described through several terms: traditional, grassroots, informal, customary are just some among the many possibilities – and each of these concepts, while grasping with some key characteristics of these instruments, also have potentially problematic implications. Particularly interesting is An-Na'im's notion of "indigenous formations of justice",[51] which conveys particularly well the idea of mechanisms crafted upon an understanding of justice, both as a process and as a product, shaped by local values and priorities. However, the term "indigenous" also risks transmitting, to the biased ear, the image of a simple and underdeveloped, almost folkloristic mechanism, while in fact local systems of justice can be incredibly complex and advanced.

Secondly, due to the extremely variegated nature of these phenomena, which in itself is one of their defining characteristics, a certain level of generalisation in addressing their strengths and weaknesses results unavoidable. The mechanisms commonly referred to as traditional, indeed, are often very different from each other, under many profiles – such as their objectives and emphasis, the degree of participation of the community, their level of hybridity.[52] Additionally, customary justice systems are typically more flexible and dynamic than their formal counterparts, following well-established customs but also constantly adapting to the context and mirroring the evolution of the community; as such, they are never the same, and traumatic experiences like conflicts have an extremely strong impact on their organisation and functioning.[53] Therefore, any reconstruction, opinion and conclusion on the issue does not constitute a definitive and "always-true" assessment of these mechanisms.

Aware of these criticalities, in the next paragraph the terms "grassroots", "traditional" and "bottom-up" will be employed to refer to instruments which have a basis, in terms of custom and/or pre-existent practice, in the culture of the communities experimenting the transitions, and which have a substantially informal nature: they emerge from the experience of the local communities – although the state might play a role in their implementation, or in different ways acknowledge and incorporate them in the formal structure.[54] Also typical of most of these mechanisms is their holistic approach, as focus as a final objective on the protection and restoration of the harmony within the community, also when presenting punitive features.[55]

The Importance of Focusing on the Community

Communities, as social conglomerates, are fundamental because they are the locus where former enemies confront and coexist with each other (willingly or because of the circumstances of life), where the extraordinary meets the ordinary.[56] This is the dimension of daily life, where collective memories are shaped and tensions and prejudices often get reinforced by coexistence, and consequently can also be potentially addressed with the most efficacy. Additionally, especially in those contexts in which the state lacks a strong formal, centralised structure, local power dynamics determine the social status of individual and groups, and traditional authorities essentially maintain law and order in the territory, being the primary sources and providers of justice. Notably, coexistence is often also a source of solidarity, as individuals cooperate with the final objective of maintaining peace and stability in the community. One of the consequences is that internal conflicts are addressed not merely in their interpersonal dimension, but rather primarily as episodes that impinge on the harmony of the group, which is carefully preserved.[57]

As a result, communities are increasingly appreciated as a crucial, if not the primary, level of intervention, where post-conflict mechanisms must be implemented, in order to ensure the success of the whole process. However, these should not be integrated uncritically, as idyllic spaces where all contrasts are solved through dialogue and everybody lives in harmony and equality.[58] On the contrary, communities are often privileged spaces for abuse and violence, where differences are sharpened and conflicts and acts of violence originate.[59] Indeed, any social group (in any part of the world) rests upon deep-rooted power dynamics which are often unequal, exclusionary and discriminatory, especially of traditionally weaker subjects, such as children, or minorities: within a community some voices are louder than others, and this can lead to the marginalisation, when not abuse, of certain individuals or groups, which in turn also prevents positive change.[60]

Additionally, as introduced, communities as such are often traumatised by violence and conflicts (especially domestic ones, as most conflicts today): killings, displacement and migration have reshaped them, while distrust, suspect and fear dominate[61]; also, constitutive dynamics have been disrupted, with local authorities often losing power or facing accusations, and other subjects – such as women[62] – emerging, scarred but empowered, on the public scene, determine to play a role in the reconstruction process. Communities are therefore wounded and fragmented actors, often less cohesive than imagined, and looking for a new identity.

As a consequence, in involving this level there should be no hypocrisy. However, at the same time, awareness of these limitations should not cause the exclusion of these collectivities from the process. On the contrary, it is also because of their flaws that communities are important spaces where to confront legacies of violence – striving to strike a balance between local perceptions and standards on one side, and fundamental rights on the other.

Doing Justice on the Ground: The Experience of Fambul Tok

One of the grassroots processes which have attracted more praise is Fambul Tok,[63] originated in Sierra Leone building upon traditional conflict resolution mechanisms to confront the trail of pain and neediness left by the civil war, and to integrate the work of the official mechanisms – which were struggling to generate a positive impact on the ground – with a restorative approach.[64] Fambul Tok works for several months in the chosen village, engaging its constituencies and the different local leaders; notably, not only traditional and religious leaders are involved but also respected representatives of women and young people, who were traditionally marginalised and excluded[65]. One of the most awaited and significant moments is the bonfire ceremony in which the community gathers around a fire and both survivors and alleged perpetrators share their experiences, debate, ask for forgiveness and in some cases reconcile.[66] This ceremony is marked by singing and dancing and typically lasts several hours, and it is often complemented or followed by a cleansing ceremony, which may include sacrifices and purification rituals.[67] Fambul Tok keeps operating in the community afterwards, by developing and implementing long-term reconciliation projects, often with a practical use, aimed at fostering cooperation and integration:[68] many establish a community garden or a farm, and in some cases the revenues from these activities are then further re-invested in communal projects.[69] Therefore, beyond their symbolic undertones, these projects also aim at fostering peace and socio-economic development from the bottom-up.

Fambul Tok builds upon the traditional *family talk* (which in the aftermath of the conflict was hardly ever practiced),[70] but was crafted and implemented by a local human rights organisation in cooperation with a US-based foundation, introducing several innovations which distance it from the original tradition[71]: as such, it can be – and it is – described not only as a bottom-up instrument but also as a hybrid mechanism, in which traditional ceremonies and external standards are merged, mostly to overcome discriminatory inclinations of the original model, from which women and youth were excluded.[72] In this way, Fambul Tok was implemented not only with the purpose of reconstructing some truths and provide accountability at the local level but also hoping to reshape abusive power dynamics which had characterised several Sierra Leonean communities for long before the conflict, and which had played a role in exacerbating pre-war tensions.[73] The positive character of these mechanisms resides in the fact that these "innovative" standards and procedures are not imposed a priori on the supposed beneficiaries; rather, they are proposed and then shaped with the participation of the local authorities and leaders, and standing the final test of the local community: its success is strictly dependent on the favourable reception and voluntary participation of the individuals on the ground, which has been largely reported as positive.[74]

Although just briefly introduced, Fambul Tok is a good example of a bottom-up initiative, as it illustrates many of the benefits that are often attached to these mechanisms.

Informal Mechanisms: A Cure-All Solution for Transitional Issues?

Grassroots initiatives are appreciated for their many, actual or potential, virtues.

For example, these instruments are believed to be more affordable and sustainable than their formal counterparts: they build on a structure that already exists at the local level and have relatively limited costs, as often there is no need for infrastructures or involvement of paid professionals; at the same time, they are fast in reaching decisions and readily accessible to the population[75]: ideally, they do not require extensive travel or a legal representative, and participating does not negatively affect the working patterns of the local population. Accessibility also fosters participation, together with the plain language used. This generates a feeling of ownership which in turn enhances the credibility and legitimacy of the process, as the same subjects who endured the violence of war are now called to shape and witness justice happening.[76] In addition, these mechanisms often envisage spaces for the active participation of both victims – who can thus overcome feelings of passivity and feel empowered in their new active role in society – and perpetrators, who have an opportunity to plead their cases and ask for forgiveness, thus ideally being more sincerely readmitted within their community.

Unlike criminal trials and commissions, which restrain most of the participants to an essentially passive role (as spectators), informal justice processes are built around the involvement of the whole community: they follow familiar customary rules which are consistent with local cultural beliefs, and a crucial role is played by religious and traditional leaders, which are trusted and respected by the population.[77] As a consequence, these mechanisms carry a strong potential of strengthening the community as such[78]; indeed, debates, rites and ceremonies, even contestation and disputes – as forms of inclusion – eventually provide legitimacy and credibility, and contribute to rebuilding communal support structures.

Concurrently, these processes ideally foster the recovery and/or reshaping of individual and communitarian identities.[79] As aforementioned, communities are often a privileged space for conflict and abuse, and most conflicts today are fought at the local level, often exacerbated by ethnic tensions which inflame intracommunity dynamics, insomuch that in their aftermath, communities are lacerated and traumatised, its traditional structure often destroyed. In such a scenario, customary mechanisms can play a fundamental role in reuniting communities around traditional values, memories and rites, also helping to critically reflect on biased understandings of "the other" – by stressing commonalities between subjects and groups and humanising the conflict: when opposing factions confront and interact, they can recognise themselves in the experiences of suffering, loss and exploitation of the other.

Another strength of these instruments is their flexibility. As customary mechanisms are by nature dynamic, evolving and adapting to the specific context, these can easily be reshaped, while staying loyal to their core values, to confront violations which go beyond their classical competencies.[80]

All these strengths would have the further result of ensuring the effectiveness of local mechanisms, on several levels. On one side, they are ideally more "on point": their local dimension and the broad involvement of the population ideally guarantees the appropriateness of the instruments when adopted post-conflicts, as well as of their priorities. Indeed, incorporating local mechanisms in the transitional process ideally ensures that the voices of the locals – which at the national level get easily lost – are heard more clearly; this in turn allows for shaping a justice more responsive, both culturally and practically, to their priorities and necessities,[81] in this way also investing already scarce resources in a more effective way.[82] Therefore, building justice from the bottom-up also means focusing on the daily problems and necessities of those most in need (such as safe food, water and infrastructure), which risk getting lost amidst grand projects for criminal accountability and national reconciliation. Andrew Iliff adopted the notion of "localised devolution",[83] to refer to a more flexible and modest transitional model which, however, also has more chances of producing real, practical effects on the ground, thus working towards eliminating the very root causes of conflicts and shaping a solid basis on which to implement the post-conflict process, in turn fostering stability. Therefore, paying more attention to the local dimension also ideally enhances effectiveness in the long term, as it helps making the whole transitional discussion more "practical".[84] Just as a way of example, the choice of imprisoning suspects found guilty in trials – especially for minor wrongdoings – is sometimes criticised for its negative consequences on the defendants' family or community: in the aftermath of violent and disrupting conflicts, these subjects might be their families' breadwinners, and might be needed in the reconstruction process; in those situations, engaging the local constituencies helps realising how other kind of sanctions, such as community work, might be more adequate.

On the other side, effectiveness is enhanced by a stronger enforcement potential: as the population itself defines its priorities and mechanisms, these are more likely to be embraced, and their outcomes respected; additionally, the whole community becomes an enforcer of the justice that is being made, and often the mere threat of sanctions –together with the ensuing social pressure – are sufficient to ensure compliance.[85]

Finally, incorporating local mechanisms appears to many – sometimes irrespective of perceived benefits or shortcomings – as the "realistic choice". As seen, countries emerging from periods of conflict are often characterised by legal pluralism and by a weak central state, most likely perceived as responsible for heinous abuses. On the contrary, customary mechanisms are already in place and enjoy a strong level of legitimacy and authority[86]; also, devolution and delegation allow to relieve stress from the formal state structure, which in this phase typically struggles to cope with the many emergencies.[87] Local initiatives are therefore often adopted in order to fill a seemingly inevitable justice gap. In terms of realism, it is also noteworthy that the many perceived benefits of local justice systems make them particularly appealing to donors, which have witnessed the many failures of tribunals and other formal mechanisms, and might encounter difficulties in justifying funding similar initiatives. At the same time, incorporating traditional mechanisms can help to more adequately counter attempts to discredit the transitional process, especially when based on their perceived political and imperialistic character.[88]

"*All that Glitters is not Gold:*"[89] Risks and Limitations of Customary Mechanisms

The previous paragraph has briefly introduced some of the main assumptions about the many beneficial effects of grassroots mechanisms when employed in transitional justice processes. However, these are also increasingly scrutinised and met with criticism.

Firstly, while largely perceived and presented as organic, harmonic and broadly embraced instruments, they are often in fact fragmented, resisted and contested,[90] and even more so in the aftermath of conflicts. As previously mentioned, during a period of instability these mechanisms are sometimes disrupted, traditional authorities contested or removed. Concurrently, the community experiences crucial changes: some have left or have been killed, many are grieving, others are guilty or suspected so; new subjects might be present, maybe migrated from other territories, bringing with them their own traditions; power dynamics are being questioned and reshaped.[91] In other words, the community as traditionally known just does not exist anymore, and this inevitably affects its traditional conflict resolution tools, which themselves often need to be re-established and reformed.

Another characteristic of these mechanisms is their lack of coercive tools for enforcement, which rests primarily on social pressure and voluntary compliance.[92] Investigative powers are equally limited, being these processes mostly based upon discussion and testimonies. These characteristics can impinge on their efficacy in establishing the truth and providing accountability,[93] while the risk is present of condemning and punishing innocents – maybe on the basis of pre-existing tensions, with very limited possibilities of supervision and appeal. (This is one of the most typical criticisms moved to customary justice systems by human rights organisations, concerned about the lack of due process guarantees; however, notably, any attempt of correcting these limitations also risks fatally corrupting these mechanisms.) For these same reasons, it is questioned whether traditional instruments are at all adequate to cope with legacies of extraordinary violence.[94] Indeed, many of these mechanisms were originally developed in order to solve everyday controversies, especially concerning lands or property, and family disputes. However, during a transition they are often refashioned and employed with the task of determining the responsibility of individuals – sometimes with very significant consequences – for heinous and complex crimes, which not only are extremely distant from their normal "jurisdiction", but whose reconstruction is typically strenuous: crimes during conflicts are not rarely committed by groups, they are often part of a larger pattern of abuses and they unfold in an extremely uncertain context, where ideology and/or poverty play a defining role and with a heightened potential for lack of strongly reliable witnesses.

Also noteworthy is that an excessive devolution or localisation of the traditional process can lead to distortions in the reconstruction of the conflict and its root causes, which can be excessively "horizontalised"[95]; in other words, a strong focus on the local dimension – especially when coupled with the lack of a comprehensive project – risks creating a too limited attention on local events, while underestimating or overlooking larger dynamics, as well as the responsibilities and failures of the state as well as of foreign actors.

However, among the most significant criticisms are those that address the very nature of these initiatives: customary justice mechanisms – as all justice mechanisms – are a manifestation of underlying, often unequal, power dynamics, and as a consequence they might perpetuate, rather than confront, the very marginalisation and abuse which often contributed to the explosion of violence in the first place. For example, women are sometimes excluded from actively participating in these processes, as a result of underlying patriarchal ideologies, and young men might be similarly left out.[96] As a consequence, an uncritical adoption of these mechanisms post-conflict might further entrench abusive dynamics and fatally limit their potential to bring about constructive change and positive peace, while also failing to take into adequate account the different dynamics and relations of powers emerging from the conflict itself. Tradition, therefore, is a double-edged sword: while being source and ground for authority, it might also evoke abusive practices and dynamics, and the silencing of precisely the subjects who need more support, protection and inclusion in the post-conflict project.

This also leads to reconsidering the benefits inherent in the often praised flexibility of these mechanisms, as well as their being rooted in oral customs: these elements guarantee a very strong discretion to those who are admitted to play an active role in the processes, in particular local authorities, which however might abuse it – adopting unfair decisions – or simply lack consistency, especially at the expenses of marginalised and silenced (in that powerless) members of community. This precise issue was acknowledged in several Fambul Tok projects, which struggled with the potential inclusion of local chiefs: while these subjects would have conferred a strong authority to the process, they were also increasingly opposed by some communities, by which they were considered – already since before the war – corrupt and biased, especially towards young people; indeed, many resented local chiefs for inflicting unfair or humiliating punishments, or excessive fines, and in general for discriminating against certain members of the community.[97] Eventually, the decision was taken of involving them, because as "chiefs were part of the problem, they also need to be part of the solution, because they are part of the family"[98]; however, other authoritative figures were also included in the projects, in particular women and youth leaders, to represent traditionally excluded categories and thus ideally ensure more balanced and respectful processes.[99] This case, while showing that these mechanisms can be reshaped in a way that is sensitive to the context, however also calls for careful reflection in choosing which mechanisms to implement and validate on the ground, as well as which goals to pursue. In particular, objectives such as *re*building and *re*constructing, when understood as returning to a pre-existing situation, might actually be problematic for those subjects who before the conflict were in a position of marginalisation or exploitation.

Additionally, while flexible under these profiles, customary systems are at the same time fairly rigid, precisely because of their extremely close ties to the social group they are employed by. This has revealed problematic in transitional contexts where communities have been reconfigured by migration, as they might provoke exclusion or discrimination against members of different communities of origin; for the same reasons, in some cases they have been considered as non-suitable to satisfactorily address disputes that involve members of different ethnic, religious or territorial groups.[100]

Finally, it is worthy to introduce a further issue, related not so much to these mechanisms per se', but rather to the choice – especially by the part of the state or foreign actors – to integrate them into the transitional process – meaning their potential instrumentalisation and distortive officialisation. The most renowned (as well as debated) example is that of the Rwandan Gacaca courts, which are by many authors approached as a distortion of informal, traditional mechanisms by the part of the central state, through formalisation and cooptation, with the final purpose of reinforcing its power and reach on the territory, thus providing an aura of legitimacy to its supremacy. In general, their many perceived benefits – and in particular their assumed effectiveness and legitimacy – might propel the state to exploit local mechanisms as a smokescreen for its inability to establish post-conflict initiatives which are effective and respectful of fundamental rights, or with the primary purpose of attracting donors and enhancing their international credibility.[101]

Conclusions

The field of transitional justice has experienced a fast-paced development, constantly adapting to different contexts while attempting to maintain certain core values and standards. At the same time, conflict scenarios are by their very nature sites of contestations and tensions between actors and priorities, and striking a balance between local ownership and legitimacy on one side, and international resources and guarantees on the other, appears almost utopic, especially in light of perceived neo-colonial tendencies underlying post-conflict interventions. As introduced, these are often resisted and criticised as top-down intrusions of foreign actors who deny their direct or indirect responsibilities and operate as civilisers of the savage state, by bringing the "right" values, beliefs and models of socio-economic development. A stronger role of grassroots mechanisms is thus increasingly advocated as the key solution to this issue, thanks to their many potential benefits, both practical (accessibility and sustainability) and as a model of justice developed by and for the local community, striving to re-establish harmony and support the reconstruction of the social group. Local instruments are therefore appreciated as more respectful of the context in which they operate, and substantially more effective: being more familiar and authoritative, they encounter less resistance, and answer to the right questions; ideally, they make peace a thing of the people, to be built and preserved through daily struggles, thus fostering empowerment, participation and ownership.

However, customary justice systems also present several limitations; for example, they are crafted by and respond to underlying power dynamic, which are often exclusionary and abusive in nature, therefore their adoption in transitional phases might further entrench, or even strengthen, some of the very issues they are called to confront. Also, local mechanisms have been critically traumatised by conflict, which have altered social dynamics and sometimes caused their disruption – and even when still operational, their ability to adequately deal with mass crimes and exceptional violence is strongly questioned.

The scrutiny of these issues shows, once more, the impossibility of reaching easy answers and solutions, and the necessity to approach justice practically in the context in which this is developed, in a difficult balance between idealism and realism. A transition will never be purely local, at the very least because no conflict is such: nowadays, even the most territorially limited conflict is more or less directly influenced by transnational social, economic and political dynamics, and it reverberates beyond its territorial borders. Therefore, a total localisation of post-conflict processes risks overlooking these supranational dynamics, thus reproducing some of the very issues that these attempt to solve. Additionally, international actors play very often a fundamental role in the resolution of conflicts, and in supporting the transitional project. In conclusion, to be problematic is primarily not the "if" of international interventions, but rather the "how": the imposition of concepts, values and objectives which are foreign to the target context. This clearly emerges in the approach to the concept of *justice* typical of post-conflict scenarios.

Indeed, at least in some parts "the conception of justice in periods of political change is extraordinary and constructivist: it is alternately constituted by, and constitutive of, the transition. The conception of justice that emerges is contextual: what is deemed just is contingent and informed by prior injustice".[102] Too often, however, a specific conception of justice is imposed as natural and universal while in fact promoting and requiring the adoption of specific (legal) mechanisms and objectives (democratic governance and economic liberalisation), without taking into adequate consideration local understandings and priorities. The core issue is therefore not the intervention of foreign actors or the adoption of legal mechanisms as such – but rather the aura of neutrality, universality and ineluctability they are invested with, as well as the artificial estrangement, detachment from cultural and social context; in other words, the de-politicisation of transitions as essentially political processes.[103]

Therefore, what is really critical is that the conception of justice adopted – which is crucial in influencing the choice of the post-conflict mechanisms – is sensitive and responsive to the local context and experience. In the words of Abdullahi An Na'im, justice should be approached "in the indigenous terms of every society all the time *as a matter of self-determination* and not as dictated by some presumed neo-colonial progression in transition".[104] Transitional phases are therefore to be conceived of as an opportunity – although in the most dire of circumstances – for the state and the local community to set their own course – through a process that inevitably involves missteps, errors, resistance, as well as support by the international community. For the same reason, key narrative devices such as the concepts of *re*construction and *re*building need to be thoughtfully reflected upon.[105]

This theme of justice as an inevitably political effort – both as a process and as an ideal objective – will be further analysed in the next chapter.

Notes

1. Among many others, see Stephanie Vieille, "Transitional Justice: A Colonizing Field?", *Amsterdam Law Forum* 4(3) (2012): 58–68 and Kora Andrieu, "Civilizing Peacebuilding: Transitional Justice, Civil Society and the Liberal Paradigm", *Security Dialogue* 41 (2010): 537–557
2. Patricia Lundy and Mark McGovern, "Whose Justice? Rethinking Transitional Justice from the Bottom Up", *Journal of Law and Society* 35 (2) (2008): 266
3. Rosemary Nagy, "Transitional Justice as a Global Project: Critical Reflections", *Third World Quarterly* 29(2) (2008): 282
4. Ibid., 281
5. Lundy and McGovern, "Whose Justice?", 278
6. Makau Mutua, "Savages, Victims and Saviors: The Metaphor of Human Rights", *Harvard International Law Journal* 42(1) (2001): 201–245

7. Mark A. Drumbl, "Restorative Justice and Collective Responsibility: Lessons for and from the Rwandan Genocide", *Contemporary Justice Review* 5(1) (2002): 12
8. For an in-depth discussion of the dominance of law in transitional justice, see Kieran McEvoy, "Beyond Legalism: Towards a Thicker Understanding of Transitional Justice", *Journal of Law and Society* 34 (4) (2007): 411–440
9. Abdullahi An-Na'im, "Editorial Note: From the Neocolonial Transitional to Indigenous Formation of Justice", *The International Journal of Transitional Justice* 7 (2013): 200
10. Kimberly Theidon, "Editorial Note", *The International Journal of Transitional Justice* 3 (2009): 296
11. Nagy, "Transitional Justice as a Global Project", 278
12. Among others, see Nagy, "Transitional Justice as a Global Project", 284 and Dustin N. Sharp, "Interrogating the Peripheries: The Preoccupation of Fourth Generation Transitional Justice", *Harvard Human Rights Journal* 26 (2013): 157
13. Nagy, "Transitional Justice as a Global Project", 280
14. Among others, see the examples of Darfur and Rwanda, where the process of radicalisation and fixation of ethnic identities undergone by the colonial powers played a crucial role in leading to the conflicts. See Mahmood Mamdani, *When Victims Become Killers: Colonialism, Nativism and the Genocide in Rwanda* (Princeton: Princeton University Press, 2002)
15. Vieille, "Transitional Justice: A Colonizing Field?", 60
16. Ibid., 60
17. McAuliffe, "Romanticization Versus Integration?", 51
18. McEvoy, "Beyond Legalism", 438
19. See Infra, Chapter 3
20. Marita Eastmond and Johanna Mannergren Selimovic, "Silence as Possibility in Postwar Everyday Life", *The International Journal of Transitional Justice* 6 (2012): 503
21. See Infra, Chapters 3 and 8
22. Sharp, "Interrogating the Peripheries", 157
23. Lundy and McGovern, "Whose Justice?", 276
24. Ibid., 276
25. Peter Albrecht and Helene Maria Kyed, "Non-State and Customary Actors in Development Programs", in Peter Albrecht, Helene Maria Kyed, Deborah Isser and Erica Harper, eds., *Perspectives on Involving Non-State Actors in Justice and Security Reform* (Rome: IDLO, 2011), 4
26. An-Na'im, "From the Neocolonial Transitional to Indigenous Formation of Justice", 202

27. Noah Coburn, "The International Community and the 'Shura Strategy' in Afghanistan", in Peter Albrecht, Helene Maria Kyed, Deborah Isser and Erica Harper, eds., *Perspectives on Involving Non-State Actors in Justice and Security Reform* (Rome IDLO, 2011): 11
28. Andrew R. Iliff, "Root and Branch: Discourses of Tradition in Grassroots Transitional Justice", *The International Journal of Transitional Justice* 6 (2012): 255
29. Sharp, "Interrogating the Peripheries", 163
30. Vieille, "Transitional Justice: A Colonizing Field?", 65
31. Lundy and McGovern, "Whose Justice?", 266
32. Vieille, "Transitional Justice: A Colonizing Field?", 62
33. Sharp, "Interrogating the Peripheries", 159
34. McEvoy, "Beyond Legalism", 420
35. Vieille, "Transitional Justice: A Colonizing Field?", 62
36. Ibid., 61
37. Ibid., 62
38. McEvoy, "Beyond Legalism", 419
39. Iliff, "Discourses of Tradition in Grassroots Transitional Justice", 254
40. McEvoy, "Beyond Legalism", 416
41. Ibid., 418
42. Nagy, "Transitional Justice as a Global Project", 278
43. An-Na'im, "From the Neocolonial Transitional to Indigenous Formation of Justice", 197
44. McEvoy, "Beyond Legalism", 418
45. Among others, see An-Na'im, "From the Neocolonial Transitional to Indigenous Formation of Justice": 197–204 and Vieille, "Transitional Justice: A Colonizing Field?": 58–68
46. An-Na'im, "From the Neocolonial Transitional to Indigenous Formation of Justice", 197
47. Ibid.
48. Vieille, "Transitional Justice: A Colonizing Field?", 67
49. Nagy, "Transitional Justice as a Global Project", 281–283
50. Ibid., 282
51. An-Na'im, "From the Neocolonial Transitional to Indigenous Formation of Justice": 197–204
52. Tim Allen and Anna MacDonald, "Post-Conflict Traditional Justice: A Critical Overview" (The Justice and Security Research Programme, Paper 3, 2013): 12
53. Luc Huyse and Mark Salter, eds., *Traditional Justice and Reconciliation after Violent Conflict: Learning from African Experiences* (Stockholm: International IDEA, 2008), 8

54. Augustine S.J. Park, "Community-based Restorative Transitional Justice in Sierra Leone", *Contemporary Justice Review* 13(1) (2010): 195
55. For an in-depth analysis of these instruments and their characteristics, see Padraig McAuliffe, "Romanticization Versus Integration?: Indigenous Justice in Rule of Law Reconstruction and Transitional Justice Discourse", *Goettingen Journal of International Law* 5 (2013): 49
56. Juan Diego Prieto, "Together after War While the War Goes On: Victims, Ex-Combatants and Communities in Three Colombian Cities", *The International Journal of Transitional Justice* 6 (2012): 544
57. Ibid., 530
58. Ibid.
59. Andrieu, "Civilizing Peacebuilding", 553
60. Cassandra Balchin, "Strenghtening International Programming on Access to Justice for the Poor and Women: Lessons learnt from Pakistan's Musalihat Anjumans and other Programmes", in Peter Albrecht, Helene Maria Kyed, Deborah Isser and Erica Harper, eds., *Perspectives on Involving Non-State Actors in Justice and Security Reform* (Rome: IDLO, 2011), 93
61. Huyse and Salter, eds., *Traditional Justice and Reconciliation after Violent Conflict,* 76
62. See Infra, Chapter 2
63. Iliff, "Discourses of Tradition in Grassroots Transitional Justice", 261
64. Park, "Community-based Restorative Transitional Justice in Sierra Leone", 113
65. Iliff, "Discourses of Tradition in Grassroots Transitional Justice", 263
66. Ibid.
67. Ibid.
68. Ibid.
69. Lyn S. Graybill, "Traditional Practices and Reconciliation in Sierra Leone: The Effectiveness of Fambul Tok", *Conflict Trends* 3 (2010): 46
70. Ibid., 44
71. See "Fambul Tok International: What is Fambul Tok?", last updated December 5, 2016, http://www.fambultok.org/what-is-fambul-tok
72. This example also shows how, in a context of emergency and lack of resources, hybridity is practically inevitable; what really makes the difference is the way hybridity is managed.
73. Iliff, "Discourses of Tradition in Grassroots Transitional Justice", 271
74. Graybill, "Traditional Practices and Reconciliation in Sierra Leone", 44–50
75. Danish Institute for Human Rights, "Informal Justice Systems. Charting a Course for Human Rights-Based Engagement" (New York: UNDP, UNICEF and UN Women, 2013): 8

76. Erin Daly, "Between Punitive and Reconstructive Justice: The Gacaca Courts in Rwanda", *New York University Journal of International Law and Politics* 34 (2002): 377
77. Lundy and McGovern, "Whose Justice?", 290
78. Daly, "Between Punitive and Reconstructive Justice", 376
79. Huyse and Salter, eds., *Traditional Justice and Reconciliation after Violent Conflict*, 115
80. Danish Institute for Human Rights. "Informal Justice Systems", 10
81. Sharp, "Interrogating the Peripheries", 164
82. Among many examples, see Infra, in Chapter 8, the discussion about the decision to build a new, state-of-the-art tribunal for the Special Court of Sierra Leone.
83. Iliff, "Discourses of Tradition in Grassroots Transitional Justice", 254
84. Huyse and Salter, eds., *Traditional Justice and Reconciliation after Violent Conflict*, 112
85. Ibid., 14
86. Allen and MacDonald, "Post-Conflict Traditional Justice", 3
87. Huyse and Salter, eds., *Traditional Justice and Reconciliation after Violent Conflict*, 182
88. See Infra, Chapter 7, with regards to ICTY
89. William Shakespeare, *The Merchant of Venice*, Act 2, Scene 7, Page 3
90. Iliff, "Discourses of Tradition in Grassroots Transitional Justice", 256
91. Ibid.
92. Huyse and Salter, eds., *Traditional Justice and Reconciliation after Violent Conflict*, 113
93. Lundy and McGovern, "Whose Justice?", 290
94. Allen and MacDonald, "Post-Conflict Traditional Justice", 16
95. Ibid.
96. Ibid.
97. Iliff, "Discourses of Tradition in Grassroots Transitional Justice", 264
98. Graybill, "Traditional Practices and Reconciliation in Sierra Leone", 45
99. Ibid.
100. Among others, Huyse and Salter, eds., *Traditional Justice and Reconciliation after Violent Conflict*, 144
101. Allen and MacDonald, "Post-Conflict Traditional Justice", 4
102. Ruti Teitel, "Transitional Jurisprudence: The Role of Law in Political Transformation", *The Yale Law Journal* 106(7) (1997): 2014
103. Nagy, "Transitional Justice as a Global Project", 279
104. An-Na'im, "From the Neocolonial Transitional to Indigenous Formation of Justice", 2 [emphasis added]
105. Allen and MacDonald, "Post-Conflict Traditional Justice", 15

CHAPTER 11

"No Hay Paz Sin Trabajo": Incorporating Indigenous Perspectives in the Struggle for a More Meaningful Justice

Introduction

Indigenous peoples are subject to violations and abuses in many areas of the world;[1] although often marginalised and denied institutional representation and participation, they have become increasingly vocal at the local, national and international levels, fighting for their recognition and the redress of historical injustices, insomuch that they are now reckoned with as a potentially revolutionary force in the international law arena, and in particular in the human rights domain. In recent times, an increased activism of indigenous groups has also been witnessed in transitional justice scenarios, with the effect of pushing classical boundaries of the discipline[2]; indeed, indigenous peoples' perceptions of conflicts and regimes of oppression – understood as inextricably linked to ongoing experiences of discrimination and expropriation – pose some fundamental challenges to this machinery, both in the practice (by requiring an adjustment of the functioning of typical mechanisms, for example with regards to the language used and the processes of conflict resolution adopted)[3] and in its very appreciation of justice. As a consequence, their involvement in the transitional justice discourse encourages a critical reassessment of the predominant understanding of some key traditional parameters of the field, such as the temporal limitations of transitional mechanisms, their focuses and objectives, as well as of crucial concepts such as violence, truth, peace – and transition itself.

G. Girelli, *Understanding Transitional Justice*,
Philosophy, Public Policy, and Transnational Law,
DOI 10.1007/978-3-319-53606-4_11

Aware of this plurality of issues, the following paragraphs persevere on the path undertaken in the previous chapter, going back to the themes of ownership and of the dominant paradigm of transitional justice: looking at conflicts and transitions through an indigenous perspective reveals precisely the constructed and culture-specific nature of many concepts and objectives typically promoted in post-conflict scenarios as universal and inevitable. However, this chapter will pause more specifically on structural violence and inequality, and on the links between transitional justice and development. In particular, as long-standing abusive patterns, ingrained in the political and socio-economic system, are often identified by indigenous peoples as the most profound causes of conflicts and violations, particular attention will be reserved to the capacity (and adequacy) of post-conflict mechanisms to address – and ideally redress – these dynamics, thus laying the foundation for a peaceful future. This issue is not merely theoretical; on the contrary, it is highly relevant today, as inevitably emerging in all those (numerous) situations in which conflicts are identified as grounded in similar patterns of oppression, racism and economic violence.[4]

After an introduction to key defining features of indigenous peoples' experiences and approaches to justice, some typical characteristics of the traditional paradigm of transitional justice will also be outlined, and then compared and contrasted with the indigenous understanding of these same aspects. (The choice of saving a definitional paragraph on transitional justice for the last chapter of the book, although seemingly counter-intuitive, was not casual; on the contrary, confident that experiencing something is often better than having it described or defined, this book presented and assessed some of its most crucial themes and paradigmatic experiences, with the further aim of conveying an idea, a sense of what this field "is" – what it aims to and how it operates. This sense will now be called into question.)

Following, the case of Guatemala will be briefly considered, through an overview of the armed conflict, its root causes and their impact on indigenous communities – while also pausing on some peculiarities of the post-conflict process. The final paragraph is dedicated to investigating, on a more theoretical level, whether transitional processes are, or hold the potential to be, an adequate forum in which to address the plight of indigenous peoples and provide a meaningful justice, as basis for a lasting peace and more equitable social relations. This reflection will provide some valuable cues for this volume's final conclusions.

Indigenous Peoples and Transitional Justice: Lost in Translation?

Almost 400 million people today form part of "indigenous", "native" or "tribal" communities[5] – each one with its own history, traditions and struggles. Therefore, any discussion of "indigenous peoples' issues" promises to be complex, always at risk of overgeneralising, or over particularising. Indigenous peoples are also increasingly vocal in local and international fora: they are now established as important actors in the human rights field, and they contributed to innovative reflections as well as pioneering applications of transitional mechanisms in "settler-states scenarios" and "conflicted democracies",[6] where typical transitional instruments – such as truth commissions – have been adopted in order to confront the legacies of colonisation and discriminatory state policies.[7] This growing activism of indigenous peoples allowed to identify some characteristics these communities share, with regards to their cosmovisions, their social organisation, their claims and priorities.

Defining Indigenous: An History of Expropriation, Racism and Resilience

Indigenous communities throughout the world share a position of marginalisation, discrimination and abuse, cornered in conditions of poverty and often figuring among the main targets of violence. In addition, they are frequently denied participation in the political and social life of the country they live in, as well as acknowledgment of their entitlements. As such, they are often silenced, unheard in formal structures. At the same time, indigenous groups are among those most fiercely resisting structures of oppression, and over the past decades they have increasingly emerged in the international arena, adopting the languages of self-determination and human rights to present their claims to a plethora of actors[8]; these processes led to the adoption of important measures at the local, national and international level, such as the United Nations Declaration on the Rights of Indigenous Peoples,[9] as well as to several judgments by regional human rights courts, that expand on regional human rights conventions and recognise, in favour of tribal communities, specific and innovative rights (such as the right to communal ownership of lands and resources.)[10]

This increased recognition and activism brought to the forefront the problem of defining indigenous peoples, in a way that acknowledges peculiar worldviews and social orders, does justice to histories of oppression and exploitation and respects the uniqueness of every community, while also avoiding depicting indigenous peoples as merely victims, or folkloristic characters. Nowadays a mixed approach is generally adopted in the theory and in the practice, which accords primary relevance to self-identification (indigenous peoples' right to characterise themselves as such),[11] combined with the presence of "typical" characteristics – such as: historical continuity with the "pre-invasion" period and a strong, vital, connection – both spiritual and material – to the land[12]; voluntary and conscious perpetuation of the community's cultural distinctiveness; non-dominant position in society, linked to experiences of marginalisation and exclusion.[13] Also distinctive is a social order built on and around the community, perpetuated through the oral transmission of a complex system of customary rules, from which also flows an understanding of justice strictly dependent on the (restoration of) harmony within the group.[14] A defining feature of indigenous peoples, therefore, is precisely their being the object of long-standing abuses, violence and disempowerment, which started with forms of colonisation. This, together with the very fact that the term "indigenous" is now synonymous of minority and marginalised, expresses the faults of colonialism, assimilationist policies and exploitation. This structural condition of poverty and subjugation also strongly affects indigenous peoples' perceptions of conflicts, violence and transitions, in such a way to call into question the predominant model of transitional justice and its key tenets.

Subjective and Systemic Violence: Is Transitional Justice Treating the Symptoms or Curing the Illness?

Transitional justice,[15] as a discipline, is strictly intertwined with human rights and international criminal law, as emerging from the same cultural and ideological background.[16] As such, many similarities can be found in the conceptualisation of conflict and violence, as well as in the proposed responses to them –that often clash with indigenous perceptions and priorities.

As (hopefully) emerging from the previous chapters, transitional justice has undergone a rapid and restless development and faced innumerable challenges, always striving to achieve complex and ambitious objectives in diverse and demanding scenarios; under the "transitional justice" umbrella very different experiences and outcomes have been accommodated, and this field has significant links with other disciplines (such as development, peacekeeping and international criminal law): for all these reasons, the field eludes definitive and comprehensive definitions. While countless definitions have been proposed and adopted, the most widely accepted[17] is probably the one coined by Ruti Teitel – who refers to "the conception of justice associated with periods of political change, characterized by legal responses to confront the wrongdoing of repressive predecessor regimes"[18]; similarly, the "United Nations Approach to Transitional Justice", aimed at informing a common understanding of the discipline in the practice, defines this field of law as the

> Full range of processes and mechanisms associated with a society's attempt to come to terms with a legacy of large-scale past abuses, in order to ensure accountability, serve justice and achieve reconciliation.[19]

An in-depth analysis of the different approaches to this discipline and their implications goes beyond the space of this chapter. However, some typical features of this "paradigmatic model" of transitional justice[20] can be identified, all intertwined, and almost all disputed by alternative indigenous experiences and understandings.

For example, virtually all defining transitional processes, such as the ones employed in post-apartheid South Africa, post-genocide Rwanda or post-junta Argentina, were developed in order to confront periods of exceptional violence and often institutionalised crime, with state forces being the main (although not the only) responsible for massacres and abuses. As a consequence, transitional mechanisms have traditionally primarily dealt with violations of human rights and humanitarian law such as killings, forced disappearances, sexual abuses and torture,[21] informed by a specific understanding of violence as violation of physical integrity, and heavily borrowing concepts from international criminal law.[22] In other words, transitional mechanisms have classically focused on what Slavoj Žižek categorises as "subjective violence": physical harm "performed by an easily identified and often individualized agent imbued with qualities of rationality and culpability".[23] This focus, although legitimate and necessary, however often distracts from addressing underlying, less visible but equally vicious forms of violence inherent in the social, political and economic systems – defined by the Slovenian author as "systemic violence"[24] – which in many cases constitute the root causes of conflicts.

These different types of violence, and the causal relations between them, are clearly manifested in indigenous experiences, which show a continuity of violence, in the form of a "politico-economic context of historic and ongoing dispossession and of contemporary deprivation and poverty",[25] which survive and exacerbate during phases of armed conflict. Consequently, as evident from the upcoming example of Guatemala, wars and conflicts are frequently perceived by native communities not as sudden and exceptional breaks from a peaceful past, but rather as a continuation, often with a heightened intensity and with an increase in physical harm, of pre-existing patterns of systemic violence, which appear ingrained in society and solidified throughout the centuries.

One of these patterns is the ongoing expropriation and exploitation of lands and resources. As outlined above, such communities are characterised by a strong attachment to ancestral lands, which plays a fundamental role in the construction of individual and collective identities. However, the plunder of ancestral territories by settlers first, and by private and public companies afterwards, is another common trait of indigenous experiences around the world,[26] worsened by a current economic paradigm grounded on individual private property, which clashes with tribal communal systems of ownership of lands and resources. Ongoing expropriation in turn determines high levels of poverty and marginalisation, further aggravated by widespread violations of socio-economic rights, resulting in low levels of education, unemployment and lack of access to basic needs.[27] As a consequence, the struggle for autonomy, restitution and protection of ancestral lands, as well as for the recognition of communal property, is one, if not the most, crucial fight of indigenous peoples today, both in "ordinary" times (often capitalising upon human rights norms), and in post-conflict scenarios.[28]

Systemic violence is also manifested in the marginalisation and exclusion of indigenous communities from political participation, and in general from society: indigenous peoples often lack representation in the public sphere, while access to fundamental services is in many scenarios obstructed because of practical limitations (such as absence of infrastructures and non-recognition of indigenous languages) as well as lack of recognition of indigenous peoples' rights. A striking example is the difficulty of natives around the world in accessing formal courts of law.[29]

Another form of violence is represented by widespread racism, in many contexts sanctioned at the institutional level.[30] As the history of countries such as Australia and Canada show,[31] discriminatory approaches towards the natives often evolve into the adoption of assimilationist, and sometimes genocidal, policies: tribal communities are attacked in their identity, their culture targeted as inferior and thus to be eliminated, and their people perceived (borrowing Mutua's words)[32] as savages that in need of being civilised through integration into the prevalent (ideally Western-like and patriarchal) culture.

All these recurring patterns of underlying, systemic violence have strong and lasting effects on indigenous communities, both in spiritual and in material terms,[33] also affecting their understanding and conceptualisation of violence and conflict, and consequently of the measures which are deemed by these same groups necessary in order to "transition", to address and redress a history of violence and move towards a peaceful and dignified future.

By Other Means: Reframing Transitions' Cardinal Points

The previous chapter paused on the dominance, in transitional justice, of legalistic approaches and responses, which also foster a partial focus on (violations of) civil and political rights, and on individuals – both as perpetrators and as victims; such a limited emphasis can reveal particularly problematic for indigenous peoples, when it detracts attention from broader structures of discrimination that both were caused by and led to the conflict, from broader societal responsibility,[34] and from the abusive role of traditionally overlooked actors such as private companies[35]; at the same time, this individualistic approach also influences the prevalent perception of victims as idealised individuals, removed from space and time, avulse from their community and socio-economic situation.[36] This risks not only narrowing the reconstruction of the events – as larger and more subtle systems of abuse are left unseen and untouched[37] – but also to obstacle the acknowledgment and involvement, as victims, of indigenous communities as such.[38]

The participation of tribal peoples in transitional processes can be further hindered by their peculiar, collective conception of justice, conceived first and foremost as restoration of the harmony within the group, and with the natural and spiritual world; consequently, specific methods of conflict resolution are adopted, which typically involve traditional ceremonies, and in which subjects often participate as members of the group, rather than in their individuality[39]; in addition, the aforementioned perception of violence as a systemic pattern of abuses leads to conceiving of meaningful justice as necessarily requiring the redressing of those very structural inequalities. Indigenous claims post-conflict are thus often not limited to assigning responsibilities for massacres and crimes, but rather include calls for collective reparations, restitution or redistribution of lands, structural reforms of the justice and education systems, as well as of the political structure – measures that are often considered as foreign to the realm of transitional justice as strictly and traditionally comprehended.

The described prioritisation, by most transitional mechanisms, of physical violence plays a crucial role in informing the common understanding of transitions as clear passages from a situation of repression and abuses (mostly conceived of as physical harms) to one of peace (whose most visible characteristic is indeed a reduction, if not the absence, of that same physical violence). As wars and authoritarian regimes are perceived as exceptional phases in the history of the country, also transitional mechanisms are considered as inherently exceptional, with a dichotomy being developed between transitional and ordinary justice.[40] What follows is that transitional justice instruments are characterised by multiple (and often self-determined) temporal limitations[41]: they are supposed to operate for a limited period of time, and they focus on a limited timeframe. Indigenous peoples' involvement, however, calls this framing of transitions into question. Indeed, although conflicts are surely exceptionally violent and tragic periods, indigenous communities are more likely to perceive the abuses suffered in these phases not as the result of sudden breaks from a peaceful past, but rather in a "continuum of violence",[42] as an expression of "structures of oppression"[43] enduring since colonisation. It is precisely this different perception of conflicts that "justifies" the use of transitional instruments to address the wrongdoings of settler states, which do not emerge from an experience of conflict as commonly defined, but whose policies towards native communities clearly manifest the aforementioned systemic violence. Also, this helps explaining potential discrepancies, in post-conflict scenarios, between the temporal references adopted by transitional instruments and those of indigenous peoples: as the "pre-conflict" past is not perceived as peaceful, so the prevalent understanding of when the conflict began and ended might be questioned, and – enduring underlying structures of abuse and discrimination – indigenous peoples might even disagree that the conflict has ceased.[44]

Similarly, indigenous peoples approach to justice calls into question dominant prioritisations of transitional objectives. As introduced in the previous chapter, post-conflict projects often promote political and economic liberalisation (the latter being centred around exclusive property), as naturally and inevitably leading to peace.[45] This bias would be in turn influenced by political and historical contingencies,[46] and by a general "dominance of the neoliberal free market global paradigm, which is perceived as the only viable path to development and human well-being".[47] Also, this economic dimension of transitions has only recently become object of debate,[48] while traditionally transitions were approached as essentially political events,[49] as passages from a repressive to a democratic political regime, with economic alterations (ideally towards market economy) as a sort of natural corollary. On the contrary, indigenous peoples might conceive of a meaningful transition to a positive peace as a primarily economic endeavour, ideally entailing recognition of forms of collective property, redistributive policies, as well as measures pursuing the realisation of socio-economic rights, with structural reforms of the political and administrative systems required as instrumental to achieving social and economic justice.

In sum, the dominant paradigm of transitional justice often appears to

> Fall short of offering meaningful avenues for rectifying ongoing injustices centred on land dispossession and self-determination that impact some 350million indigenous peoples residing in 70 states around the world.[50]

What are the reasons for these limitations? How can these be redressed? And, are transitional justice mechanisms really an adequate forum for tackling dynamics of oppression entrenched in the socio-economic system? In the following paragraphs the case of Guatemala will be analysed, as a fascinating example of the experience of indigenous peoples, and of the tensions highlighted above between different conceptions of history, violence and justice.

Post-colonial Guatemala: Institutionalised Racism and Economic Elitism, in a Continuum of Violence

Guatemala's Native Tribes: An Oppressed and Disempowered Majority

As in many Latin American countries, indigenous peoples in Guatemala represent a significant portion of the population – constituting (according to inevitably inaccurate surveys, due to definitional discrepancies) between 40 per cent and 75 per cent of the country's inhabitants[51] – and mainly live (at least traditionally) in rural areas.[52] Throughout the centuries a social polarisation has increasingly crystallised, opposing Mayans on one side, and ladinos, or *mestizos* – "mixed-race descendants of indigenous groups, Spanish settlers and other immigrant"[53] – on the other (although both communities, especially in rural territories, have suffered the effects of colonisation and elitism)[54]: they live in different territories, wear different clothes, speak different languages – with a relevant portion of the indigenous population excluded from education, and often not fluent in Spanish, which is the country's official language.[55]

These communities, although all unique, also share (between each other and with most indigenous peoples around the world) a peculiar cosmo-vision, a crucial attachment to the land, and a position of poverty, exploitation and marginalisation within society; also, indigenous peoples' identity is structured around the community, which is built upon cooperation, customary laws and traditional ceremonies, together with oral transmission of education and traditional knowledge.[56]

Fundamental to Mayan communities is the land – on at least three levels. Firstly, ancestral lands are of enormous symbolic importance, as "the place where one can approach the supernaturals",[57] the traditional foundation of the identity, solidarity and continuity of the community. Secondly, land was traditionally a source of local power and authority.[58] At the same time, the land was (and often still is) the primary, if not the only, means of survival and subsistence of both individuals and communities, source of economic autonomy, development and thus dignity. Land is therefore one, if not the, key element around which the indigenous identity is formed, crucial to individuals' and communities' physical and cultural survival.[59] However, since colonisation land has constantly been object of plunder and abuse, which figure among the primary causes of the socio-economic situation ofindigenous peoples in today's Guatemala, which is one of marginalisation and exclusion: substantially denied full citizenship and political participation, Mayans have been gradually expropriated of their ancestral territories (first by colonisers and then for intensive exploitation) – with profound consequences on their identity and development opportunities – while also often exploited as cheap workforce in plantations.[60]

Tribal peoples' survival as distinct groups, manifested in autonomous (or semi-autonomous) legal systems and forms of local administration, has also been constantly threatened by assimilationist or abusive policies, which were opposed through the "development of a pervasive Mayan culture of preservation, syncretism and resistance",[61] including – in more recent times – increasing politicisation and growing ties with other social movements[62]: these strategies revealed crucial to resist the vicious, destructive and eventually genocidal policies pursued by successive authoritarian governments during one of twentieth century's most violent internal conflicts.

A State-Led Strategy of Brutalization and Annihilation: La Violencia

Between late 1950s and 1996, Guatemala has endured a protracted, complex and exceptionally violent internal conflict.[63] Although some authors trace its origins back to the nineteenth (or even the sixteenth) century,[64] a fundamental turning point was the 1954 CIA-backed coup d'état, which abruptly halted a reformist decade of social progress and land redistribution, and installed the first of many military regimes.[65] The United States intervention in the country was "justified" not only as strategic in the context of the Cold War[66] but also to protect the interests of US companies (mostly agrarian) in Guatemala, which were being jeopardised by progressive reforms regarding land distribution and exploitation, aimed at benefitting the rural population and the indigenous communities, at the expenses of the economic elite.[67]

The conflict, whose main actors were the military and the *Unidad Revolucionaria Nacional Guatemalteca* (URNG) – increasingly supported by social movements and Mayan communities – saw different stages of violence and repression, which culminated in the 1980s (in the period known as *la violencia*), when successive governments adopted and then ruthlessly implemented the doctrine of the "internal enemy": all political opponents, as well as everyone perceived as a threat to national security – with no distinction between combatants and civilians – became the target of scorched-earth operations, executions and forced displacement.[68] Indigenous communities were among the main objectives, not only because of their role as an important support structure for rebel movements but also on the basis of a racist ideology: Mayan culture had to be destroyed, once and for all.[69]

As a result of the 40-year long armed confrontation, more than 200,000 Guatemalans lost their lives, of which more than 80 per cent were identified as belonging to indigenous tribes, while more than one million people were forcibly displaced.[70] The impact of the conflict on indigenous peoples was tremendous, both at the individual and at the community level. In particular, the indiscriminate strategy of persecution adopted by the state against the indigenous population included (but was not limited to): massacres, executions, forced disappearances[71] and selective killings of social leaders[72]; widespread rape and horrendous acts of sexual violence and abuse – aimed at instilling fear,[73] destabilise the community, and deprive it of the fundamental role women traditionally play as keepers and transmitters of Mayan worldview[74]; looting and destruction of villages so to displace the local population, forced to live in inhuman conditions.[75] Such a campaign deprived indigenous communities of any possibility for economic subsistence and development, already undermined by increasing migration[76] and by state policies aimed at creating a situation of economic dependence of the natives from the state and the army.[77] More specifically, traditional dynamics within Mayan communities were further disrupted by submission and militarisation[78]– through the adoption of mechanisms such as the Patrullas de Auto defensa Civil (PACs), paramilitary forces created by the army to maintain order in the villages and responsible for some of the most heinous abuses recorded[79]: most Mayans were threatened or forced into joining and "to inform on others, to inflict punishment [. . .] even to the point of killing their own fellow members of the Maya Ixil ethnic group",[80] with the further objective of destabilising communities, depopulating indigenous territories[81] and tearing apart a traditionally cohesive and supporting social fabric,[82] in this way also curtailing aid to the insurgency.[83] In its attempt to obliterate Mayan culture, the state also attacked its traditions and symbols, sometimes destroying them, sometimes misappropriating them, so to corrupt them[84]; similarly, forced disappearances and other crimes prevented Mayan communities from providing proper burial to their members, thus attacking a fundamental tenet of their culture. More generally, racism and discrimination were institutionalised, insomuch that any expression of Mayan culture (such as wearing traditional clothing or speaking the tribal language) was potentially fatal.[85]

In sum, during the internal conflict in Guatemala, the state did not just implement a counter-insurgency strategy with the purpose of quashing the rebel forces; rather, it developed a comprehensive, twisted and genocidal[86] national security policy of institutionalised racism and terror, aimed at obliterating indigenous communities by attacking their identity, their means of economic survival and development and by generating mistrust, isolation and stigmatisation within, scattering its members[87]; the objective was the final and irreversible compromising of a social fabric that had already been critically weakened in the past centuries, so to create a situation of dependency of native communities from the government,[88] assimilate their surviving members into the dominant culture and eradicate any resistance to elitist policies of land (and labour) exploitation.

The War That Always Was

Beyond the extremely grave consequences on individual victims, the destructive strategy adopted by the state had the further effect of destabilising and traumatising communities, resulting in increased fear, undergrounding of culture,[89] distrust of state structures and lack of political participation[90]– thus reinforcing a structural condition of marginalisation and exclusion of Mayans from the public life of the country.

Indeed, these dynamics of violence, marginalisation and inequality were neither novel nor casual. On the contrary, the patterns of systemic violence described in the previous paragraphs can all be observed unfolding throughout the history of Guatemala, and they appear to constitute the structural causes of the conflict – which, in the eyes of indigenous peoples, is thus best understood in a heightened continuum of violence, rather than as a sudden and exceptional break from an ordinary and predominantly non-violent situation. Indeed, since colonisation Guatemala has been characterised by profound social and economic inequality and lack of democracy, with authoritarian governments and the economic elite protecting each other's interests: power, wealth and resources (land in primis) were concentrated in the hands of a "small elite identifying itself as ethnically and culturally distinct"[91]: Mayan communities were gradually but constantly dispossessed of territories they valued as sacred, and which constituted their primary source of subsistence, in favour of local and foreign companies colluding with abusive regimes[92]; indigenous peoples (as well as many rural ladinos) were then further exploited and disempowered, employed as cheap workforce in those same plantations.[93] To sustain this system grounded on racism, elitism and increased privatisation, the state resolved to rule through violence and repression rather than law, and human rights violations became a "key element of governance".[94] This resulted in a normalisation of violence,[95] coupled with an extremely unequal distribution of land, 70 per cent of which was owned by less than 3 per cent of the population, with a strong ethnic characterisation.[96]

The continuity of violence before and during the conflict is thus particularly apparent, in the experience of indigenous peoples. For example, the genocidal strategy pursued by the state represents an "evolution" of long-standing assimilationist policies which endured since colonisation, pursued by political and economic elites against the local population, and aimed at the "removal of indigeneity"[97]; forced displacement and looting constitute a new phase in a long history of exploitation of lands and denial (when not active removal) of development opportunities, coupled with the inevitably violent effects of imposed economic liberalisation; even massacres and abuses against women can be understood as renewed attempts of denial and abuse of indigenous personhood and bodies, and as manifestations of ingrained and unequal gendered power relations.[98]

Guatemala's Transitional Process: Innovative Aspirations Within a Conservative Model

Guatemala's transitional phase, prompted during the 1980s by a mix of internal conditions[99] and international pressures,[100] was crafted through complex negotiations between warring parties, influenced by external actors and supervised by the UN, and resulted in the adoption of several instruments, forming a multifaceted and comprehensive transitional machinery.

As a complete description and analysis of the whole Guatemalan transitional process and its results[101] exceed, regrettably, the space of this chapter, the following paragraphs only provide an overview of some instruments, which more directly address (at least potentially) indigenous peoples' grievances, and which better manifest the approach adopted by the Guatemalan post-conflict machinery towards socio-economic issues and structural patterns of abuse, as well as its limitations. In particular, analyses of these initiatives show how several of the actors and bodies involved appreciated this phase as a transformative opportunity not only to address the violence committed during the conflict but also, beyond that, to lay the basis for a structural change in Guatemala's societal and institutional framework.[102] This was particularly significant for indigenous peoples, who – although limited in their direct participation[103] – saw in this process a unique forum where to advocate for social and political inclusion, as well as for democratisation[104]; as a chance to address – and redress – ingrained discrimination and violence.[105] As such, indigenous peoples' demands focused on participation and integration, political autonomy and recognition of land rights, both with regards to ancestral lands and in terms of a more equitable distribution.[106]

Awareness of the most profound causes of the conflict is reflected in the 1996 Peace Accords,[107] developed with the final purpose of not only ending the armed confrontation but also of reconfiguring Guatemalan society.[108] Among the 11 agreements negotiated between the parties, two stand out. One, the Agreement on Identity and Rights of Indigenous Peoples,[109] acknowledges the discrimination, exploitation and abuses that these communities endured not only during but also prior to the conflict,[110] and consequently outlines a comprehensive set of initiatives at the social, political and cultural levels, deemed necessary to transform the position of indigenous communities within Guatemalan society; among these, the Agreement provides for the promotion of indigenous languages in administration and education, recognition of customary law, strengthening of local autonomy.[111] Equally ambitious is the Agreement on Socio-Economic Aspects and the Agrarian Situation (Socio-Economic Accords),[112] which – at least apparently – addresses the very roots of socio-economic violence and inequality in the country, envisaging structural reforms in the realms of education, health, labour rights, welfare and access to land.[113]

Another key mechanism, established by the 1994 Oslo Accords,[114] is the Comisión para el Esclarecimiento Histórico (Commission for Historical Clarification, CEH), the truth commission mandated with investigating violations "that have caused the Guatemalan population to suffer, connected with the armed conflict".[115] In order to provide a better understanding of the internal conflict, this body went beyond merely documenting acts of violence committed during this period, and also covered those which were considered the most profound causes of the conflict – identified in the "structure and nature of economic, cultural and social relations in Guatemala [which are] marked by profound exclusion, antagonism and conflict",[116] supported by authoritarian and racist regimes which ruled through violence and dispossession.[117] The commission's innovative approach brought

> To the fore the epistemological tensions between a strictly judicial framing of the violence and diverse social and historical understandings of the structural and processual dynamics that fed the conflict,[118]

stressing the damages caused by colonisation, land expropriation and exploitation (especially in the interest of large-scale production and export) and abuse of native workforce.[119]

Also noteworthy is the National Reparation Program (PRN), created in 2003 by the government to provide individual and collective reparations to those affected by the conflict.[120] This programme holds great potential for indigenous peoples, as it envisages several kinds of reparations, among which material (housing and sources for development) and cultural ones – aimed at recovering native culture and strengthen multiculturalism.[121]

In sum, the Guatemalan post-conflict process seems to expand on the traditional purposes and reach of transitional instruments, by going beyond the classic contents of a ceasefire and peace agreement, and the mere addressing of abuses committed during the armed confrontation – in two directions: looking back, the impact of colonisation, exploitation and inequality is acknowledged in leading to and fuelling the conflict; looking forward, peace is explicitly linked with development, by committing to creating the conditions for a refashioning of Guatemalan society, through human rights and social reform.[122]

Forgotten Promises

Because of this peculiar approach, the Guatemalan peace and post-conflict process is by many lauded as a fundamental step towards enhancing inter-ethnic relations in the country, and as more far-reaching and ambitious than most transitional processes.[123] However, its merits are called into question by the substantially unaltered social and economic situation of indigenous peoples in the country. Indeed, nowadays the Mayan population is still broadly suffering from discrimination, oppression and exclusion[124]: almost 75 per cent of natives are still living in poverty, with no access to basic necessities,[125] denied education and opportunities[126]; land distribution and ownership are still extremely unequal, with 1 per cent of the farmers reported as owning around 75 per cent of the (best) land (making Guatemala one of the countries with the most unequal land distribution in Central and Latin America)[127]; Mayan individuals and organisations still face discrimination and prejudicial treatment by the part of state organs, in the political arena and in the administration of justice.[128] Also, violence and impunity are still widespread, although in partially mutated forms, and in some cases they appear to have intensified with respect to the pre-conflict situation.[129]At the same time, the economic, military and political elites have succeeded in maintaining their position of wealth and influence,[130] with the state largely responding to private interests, rather than pursuing the benefit of the whole population.[131]

As briefly described in the previous paragraph, the content and purpose of Guatemalan transitional instruments appear broad and ambitious in addressing socio-economic issues. Such a commitment is important in terms of acknowledgment, for a more complete reconstruction of the truth, and to symbolically set a new course for the society and the country. However, it also risks creating false hopes and resentment, when implementation is inadequate, as precisely in the case of Guatemala, where the majority of the provisions addressing key socio-economic concerns contained in the Peace Accords, as well as in the CEH recommendations, are reported as largely unimplemented.[132]

On a closer look, initiatives designed to address indigenous peoples' grievances have been fragmented, weak and marginal to governmental plans,[133] as well as implemented with a very limited involvement of indigenous representatives.[134] With regards to land, no specific legal mechanisms have been established to adequately acknowledge and protect indigenous territories – in violation of well-affirmed international human rights standards regarding recognition of ancestral land ownership,[135] and according to several sources many key policies adopted by post-conflict governments (also influenced by aid conditionality)[136] actually strengthen the positions of private owners[137]; at the same time, several displaced communities are still prevented from returning to their lands, while others are already being forcefully evicted, sometimes to make space for intensive agriculture.[138]

The reasons for this lack of structural changes are many and complex. However, beyond practical obstacles and contingencies (such as lack of resources), some criticalities of the transitional process per sé can be identified, which impinged on its potential to redress past violations and abuses, and thus to address the grievances of the country's indigenous population. In particular, although being somewhat progressive and innovative, the Guatemalan process ultimately appears to suffer from the same limitations outlined in these last two chapters with regards to traditional transitional processes, in turn grounded in the preservation of a peculiar prioritisation of concerns and understanding of key concepts and objectives, which contrast with indigenous perceptions and priorities.

For example, the Guatemalan transitional machinery appears to be, in practice, characterised by the same individualistic approach also registered in other post-conflict experiences. This bias is at the same time influenced by and reinforcing a primary focus on subjective violence, and on violations of civil and political rights, at the expenses of a more solid attention to violations of economic, social and cultural rights. This partiality of the developed narrative can be witnessed in the CEH report: although lauded for acknowledging the fundamental causal role of systemic violence in leading to the conflict, some authors highlight how socio-economic inequalities were in fact addressed almost exclusively in the sections reconstructing the historical background, rather than as actual violations of fundamental rights.[139] By describing them as unfulfilled obligations of the state,[140] rather than merely contextual, less flexibility would have been left to political leaders in designing the new Guatemala. Instead, the Commission substantially maintained the same primary focus on episodes of physical harms and the same legalistic approach witnessed in the work of most commissions around the world, in this way also reinforcing the preconceived idea of victims as individualised subjects, thus also making it harder to grasp with the combined effects of crimes and abuses on tribes as collectivities. At the same time, the Commission has been criticised for failing to overturn the regime's narrative with regards to Guatemala's ideal social structure: in particular, as the military governments had stressed the goal of national unity as justification for assimilationist and then genocidal policies, also the CEH – rather than fully recognising Mayan autonomy, identity and nationhood – essentially maintained a focus on social integration and unity, which according to some critics perpetuates (although unwittingly) the same post-colonial narrative of assimilation and reduction of indigenous experiences within pre-defined official structures.[141]

In addition, the transitional process appears to promote, as one of its final objectives, the political and economic liberalisation of the country, thus being unable to satisfy some of the key demands of the indigenous population – especially those concerning the land. This inclination transpires (among others) from the Socio-Economic Accords, which, although acknowledging the centrality of the issue of land, ultimately fail to envisage structural changes, and on the contrary

> Implicitly indicate[s] that resolution of the agrarian problem is understood as a process of reallocating resources within a marginally reformed institutional context based on private ownership and the market.[142]

As a result, instead of laying the basis for a meaningful, substantial transition to an economic model which is responsive to the needs of the indigenous communities (and, more generally, of the social groups most gravely affected by the conflict), the prevailing neoliberal model of market economy was reconfirmed, with private property at its core,[143] while no substantial redistributive policies were outlined, able to counter the unequal distribution and exploitation of lands and resources.[144]

The limitations concerning the economic dimension of the transition also emerge in the implementation of the PRN: although reparations were designed in a comprehensive and progressive way, in the practice the program has been focusing on monetary compensations to individual victims,[145] while side-lining measures which would have benefitted communities as a whole[146]; also, those who suffered physical harm (or whose relatives were killed or forcibly disappeared) were prioritised in the awarding of reparations, while victims of dispossession or displacement were essentially excluded.[147] Although reparations are extremely important for the victims and their families, the program ultimately failed to adequately meet the needs of the indigenous population – both material (as restitution of plundered lands and resources) and spiritual (compensation is largely perceived as a pay-off for the loss of beloved members of the family or tribe, thus causing a sense of guilt),[148] while also generating tensions within communities.[149]

In conclusion, the Guatemalan transitional experience is in part a positive one, in that long-standing patterns of inequality and discrimination were identified among the root causes of violence against indigenous peoples, which culminated in genocidal policies. Such recognition is a step forward, in that it goes beyond what done by many other transitional instruments, by expanding the focus beyond violations occurred during the conflict and in this way potentially encouraging a discussion on the legacies of colonisation as integral to the post-conflict process. Also positive is the inclusion in peace agreements – traditionally quite limited instruments, focused on the cessation of armed confrontations – of provisions on socio-economic rights, which confirm how fundamental their realisation was considered in promoting a lasting peace in the country.

However, the Guatemalan project also manifests severe limitations, clearly emerging from the practice, and related to an unwillingness – or inability – to move beyond a predominant model of transitional justice which is "part of a hegemonic discourse that links development and peace building to a liberal state-building project that sees liberal democracy as its endpoint".[150] In other words, the Guatemalan transitional process, although showing an increased sensitivity to the plight of marginalised communities, remains influenced by an excessive focus on civil and political rights, legalism, individualism and uncritical preference for economic liberalisation – and as such limited in its potential to satisfactorily confront violence and abuses targeting indigenous populations. As a result, by maintaining a restricted approach to justice as primary political and at the same time depoliticised (as detached from structural reform and redistributive policies), the transitional process appears to be "serving a few individuals in the name of the entire citizenry".[151]

This ultimate failure in responding to indigenous peoples' demands post-conflict, coupled with the many flaws characterising transitional enterprises, pose a more general issue of whether transitional mechanisms, and the field as such, hold any potential of satisfactorily addressing violations of socio-economic rights and structural violence – which are increasingly acknowledged as root causes of many intrastate conflicts – or whether the highlighted limitations are intrinsic to the field, and as such insurmountable.

Rethinking Transitions: Same Objectives, New Sensitivities, for a More Ambitious Justice

The last two chapters of this volume aimed at illustrating how the field of transitional justice presents some (apparently inherent) conceptual limitations, linked to its ideological and cultural development, which can impair its ability to adequately address, in post-conflict scenarios, the demands of its intended beneficiaries, and in general to successfully intervene in all those situations in which conflicts and oppression are rooted in structural conditions of inequality and discrimination. A reconceptualization of some key objectives and instruments is thus increasingly discussed, and advocated for, in the academia and in the practice, as "naturally" flowing from the incorporation, in post-conflict discourses, of the indigenous understandings of violence and peace outlined above, and more in general of local perceptions, priorities and mechanisms.

Necessary Development or Excessive Stretching?

Before considering how transitional processes can, or should, be adapted in order to incorporate a notion of justice more responsive to indigenous peoples' needs and priorities, however, it is necessary to address critical and dissenting opinions. Indeed, some authors stress how transitional processes are, and should be, employed exclusively in exceptional and temporary situations with the purpose of reconstructing the events of the past and, if possible, identifying those to be held accountable, as well as to outline means for responding to victims' needs. As such, requiring transitional mechanisms to redress long-standing socio-economic violations, or to outline developmental and economic policies, exceeds this "natural" mandate of transitional bodies,[152] and would thus risk creating unrealistic expectations[153]; rather, these concerns should be left to other phases (such as the post-transitional one), other disciplines (such as development), other actors.

However, such an approach to transitional justice appears grounded in the debatable assumption that post-conflict processes do not have any distributional or developmental effects,[154] and in an essentially artificial distinction between foreground and background violations, this also supported by that specific understanding of violence and conflict outlined in the previous chapters. On the contrary, it is evident looking at the practice (Guatemala is only one among many examples)[155] that entrenched patterns of violence have a crucial impact on causing conflicts, and that violations of civil and political rights on one side, and socio-economic rights on the other, are intrinsically intertwined. There are therefore several reasons justifying (when required by the context and features of a conflict) a renewed approach to the classical understanding of transitional mechanisms and objectives.

Firstly, investigating and addressing the most profound sources of violence is a fundamental step in realising key objectives of transitional justice mechanisms, such as reconstructing the *full* truth with regards to the events of the past, establishing accountability, ensuring (as much as possible) the non-repetition of violations and crimes: investigations into the past are the most truthful when they identify the origins of violence and conflicts, thus also accounting for historical continuities, and post-conflict mechanisms prove to be the most effective when such root causes are confronted and addressed. On the contrary, only focusing on the most recent (and visible) manifestations of violence, while ignoring underlying social and economic dynamics, would inevitably result in sanctioning a partial truth, in this way potentially fostering resentment and frustration, and consequently facilitating the resurgence of violence.[156]

Secondly, transitional justice mechanisms should strive to be as responsive as possible to the needs and demands of the victims, which should be granted central and substantial participation throughout all the phases of the process. In contexts such as Guatemala, indigenous victims have been vocal and clear in specifying how justice and peace are necessarily dependent on the acknowledgment and redress of their historical position of marginalisation, poverty and unemployment.[157] As a consequence, the very fact that those most affected by the conflict perceive it as rooted in patterns of social and economic violence, and the redressing of these patterns as an inevitable step in their satisfaction,[158] should be a sufficient justification for adjusting the target.

Additionally, transitions are inherently transformative phases, exceptional periods in which key pillars of the state structure are potentially open to renegotiation; a time in which the country is under international spotlight, and in which participation of the civil society is, at least ideally, enhanced. As such, they might constitute, in practice, the only chance for traditionally marginalised and silenced subjects of having their concerns heard and addressed at the institutional level. Transitions are ultimately a "definitional project",[159] in which authoritative and lasting narratives, on the past as well as on the future, are formed; as such, transitional mechanisms have the invaluable opportunity to define the conflict in its significance and causes, to identify and name these underlying structures of oppression, to acknowledge the responsibilities of the state (and of society as large), and to dispel the myth of indigenous peoples – and more in general of local societies and populations – as naturally inferior, on the contrary stressing the role of colonisation, imposed economic modernisation and long-standing discriminatory policies,[160] thus reconfirming how "rights violations are not [. . .] random in distribution or effect. Rights violations are, rather, symptoms of deeper pathologies of power".[161] Simultaneously, transitional bodies can play a pivotal role in framing the future of the country, in a way that reconfigures the social and economic position of traditionally marginalised and oppressed groups. However, when wars and transitions are presented as "stories of political and legal change and of physical violence rather than as tales of economic liberalization or structural violence",[162] then transitional instruments and the narrative they compose can have the effect of perpetuating those very patterns of abuse and marginalisation, by de-linking peace from historic, economic, and in many scenarios ethnic, justice.

Expanding Categorisations and Practical Responses: Reports, Reparations and Reconciliation

It is therefore because of their exceptional status as founding experiences that post-conflict mechanisms not only can, but should – when so urged by the victims and the local population – undergo a process of rethinking of the predominant (and seemingly innate) understanding of their fundamental objectives and purposes, and consequently work to overcome their classical boundaries, by expanding their focus and reach.

As described in previous paragraphs, the report of the Guatemalan truth commission is largely praised as innovative and progressive, as it acknowledged, as historical background, underlying patterns of violence and discrimination. While this represents a significant step forward, equally important should be the recognition of the historical and ideological continuities between those underlying structures and the abuses committed during the conflict, as well as of the violence inherent to forced economic modernisation, and the responsibilities of private actors; this would allow to do justice to the experience of indigenous peoples (and victims more in general) and stress the importance of addressing those underlying issues in order to pursue a positive peace,

> Which involves not just the silence of AK-47s and the absence of the direct violence of hot conflict, but also the absence of more indirect forms of violence, including forms of structural violence such as poverty, corruption, radical economic, social, civil, and political inequalities, and other forms of social injustice.[163]

One way to achieve these goals is by intervening on the narrative. Notably, most truth commissions employ, in their reconstruction of the events and in framing recommendations, concepts developed in human rights law (with a focus on civil and political rights) or international criminal law. While the adoption of this inevitably legalistic language presents several benefits, in terms of clarity, comparability, appeal to the general public (and to donors),[164] it also risks perpetuating an almost voyeuristic focus on physical harm, while distracting from other violations and experiences.[165] This prejudicial attention is particularly apparent in reports concerning violence against women – especially when targets are indigenous women and girls – whose narrative often appears affected by a de-contextualisation of the person from her social and cultural structure, as well as by a tension

> Between, on one hand, an occlusion of the cultural, historical and structural gendered dimension of violence and, on the other, the hyper visibility given to experiences of sexual violence. The dualities of occlusion and hyper

> visibility contribute to the continued monolithic representation of women, and in particular racialized women, as victims.[166]

Therefore, an expansion of the discourse could prove beneficial, which integrates in the post-conflict rhetoric other concepts and categories, such as those of socio-economic and cultural rights, corruption[167] and poverty,[168] development and self-determination[169]; this would make it easier to also acknowledge long-standing structures of oppression, as well as the violence inherent to (post-)colonialism and economic modernisation, and to more forcefully advocate for their overcoming.

Moreover, such a widened narrative could have further beneficial effects. Ideally, it would lay the foundation for open discussion, in society and at the institutional level, on the legacies of colonialism, its victims and beneficiaries,[170] and the interventions needed to overcome its long-standing effects, with a more substantial appreciation of the needs of the population, and of the collective dimension of victimhood as experienced by tribal groups. Additionally, it could have a trigger effect on the design and implementation of other fundamental transitional instruments, such as reparations and reconciliatory measures.

With regards to the former, reparations often figure among the primary instruments proposed to address indigenous peoples' demands, because of their symbolic potential as forms of acknowledgment, and thanks to their ability to provide much-needed material help.[171] However, as experienced in Guatemala, too often reparations programmes appear limited both in their focus and in their design,[172] as characterised by a preference for monetary compensations to individuals, which revealed inadequate as a response to indigenous peoples' grievances (at least when not complemented by redistributive measures). In particular, this kind of interventions can generate tensions within the community, and risk being perceived as a surrogate for redistribution,[173] while also in many cases strengthening oppressive dynamics of dependence and even legitimising the dispossession[174]; indeed,

> Offering a rigid economic framework through which to explore the potential of healing, belonging, identity and culture reinforces Western economic hegemony and side lines indigenous voices.[175]

On the contrary, reserving more attention to structural abuses when shaping reparations programmes could result in instruments more respective of victims' worldviews and priorities, through the inclusion of means for restitution, redistribution of land and resources, culture revitalisation.[176] This in turn could reveal crucial in empowering and emancipating the victims, and consequently in refashioning a traditionally oppressive society.

For what concerns reconciliation, a more substantial appreciation of the experiences of indigenous communities prior and during the conflict would lead to a redefinition of the "real" meaning of this key objective of transitional instruments, as well as of the mechanisms which better allow to achieve it.[177] As outlined throughout the book,[178] the rhetoric of reconciliation as broadly employed in post-conflict scenarios is increasingly criticised for being excessively artificial and ultimately instrumental to reinforcing state legitimacy,[179] in that it often encourages the society to "move on", while silencing critical voices.[180] In the eyes of indigenous communities, reconciliation is inconceivable without forms of acknowledgment of the underlying causes of conflicts, the history of marginalisation and denial of opportunities,[181] the plunder of lands and resources, and if not accompanied by a broad set of measures aimed at redressing those same root causes – such as reparations and reforms of state structure,[182] and which also incorporate indigenous concepts of healing.[183] Some voices even link reconciliation and decolonisation,[184] thus engaging with transitions as sites of struggle of tribal communities, towards the definitive overturn of ingrained dynamics of subjugation and abuse of power. In this renewed framework, reconciliation is thus also understood as a shift in narrative, as a process of emancipation of the indigenous experience from colonisation as its main – if not only – definitional parameter.[185]

Transformation of the Political, Economic and Legal Systems

Another fundamental step in reshaping the transitional experience in a way that is more responsive to indigenous peoples consists in the adoption of a more inclusive understanding of *transition* as such, which in turn requires rethinking several paradigmatic axioms of transitions, many of which introduced in the previous chapters.

One of these defining parameters is surely time. As aforementioned, post-conflict processes face several temporal constraints, limiting the operational time that transitional bodies are accorded, as well as the timespan they are mandated to investigate. These limitations are justified by limited resources and by the need – in a traumatised society – to provide responses and accountability in a short period of time; however, they also impinge on the ability of post-conflict instruments to satisfactorily reconstruct and account for the role of structural violence in leading to and fomenting the conflict, as well as to reframe the political and social structure of the country. More generally, too often transitions are approached as short-term limbos between an undemocratic and a democratic political order, characterised by "minor reforms and accommodation within existing dominant culture structures".[186] However, if conceived more ambitiously as phases of transformation, and as machineries for conflict prevention,[187] the full potential of transitions emerge for addressing chronic patterns of violence and not merely for reinforcing, but rather for constructively challenging, traditional state structures, with the final purpose of transitioning "from unjust relations to just relations and the transformation of the social, political, economic and legal framework".[188]

Consequently, a central role should be played by constitutional and legal reform, developed with the involvement of traditionally excluded groups and focused on addressing institutionalised discrimination, often manifested in aspects such as the electoral system, the administration of justice, and local government. Transitional processes should therefore at least outline a comprehensive strategy towards a reformed political order, also envisaging substantial participation of indigenous communities at the institutional level, as well as enhanced systems of autonomous local administration.[189]

At the same time, once justice is valued not merely as accountability (which is however a fundamental factor) but also as redress,[190] as instrumental to refashioning society as a whole, inevitably the economic dimension of the process acquires central relevance. In particular, in transitional scenarios involving indigenous peoples the issue of land cannot be ignored, being it one – if not the – central plight of tribal communities.[191] Therefore, addressing this issue is fundamental both symbolically and in practice: it is necessary in order to confer legitimacy and credibility to the whole transitional process, and for providing ultimate meaning and substance to concepts such as justice and reconciliation; at the same time, it potentially constitutes one of the most empowering interventions for the victims,[192] as a form of recognition of an individual and collective identity for long denied and/or attacked, while also providing an opportunity for tribal groups to take development, and reconstruction of the community, into their own hands – thus breaking the cycle of displacement and forced dependence on an abusive state. In addition, a substantial focus on land would also send an important message, to the population and to the different constituents of the post-conflict process, that the route to justice, reconstruction and development is neither pre-determined nor inevitably dependent on a certain path, but rather first and foremost shaped by the perspective and the demands of the locals. On the contrary, ignoring the issue of land would result in a transitional machinery which appears to selectively confront some wrongdoings of the past while leaving the conditions of inequality, dispossession and forced passivity essentially untouched. The centrality of this issue therefore explains why envisaging interventions with regards to land, for how complex in a context of emergency and reconstruction, cannot be left to the post-transitional phase, neither entirely delegated to other fields.

Addressing policies and patterns of plunder, exclusion and denial of protection requires a comprehensive approach. On one side, land issues should inform the work of classical post-conflict instruments: for example, truth commission should consider acknowledging the impact of policies and experiences of dispossession on the emergence of violence, also recognising the faults of private economic actors and beneficiaries (too often ignored by transitional instruments)[193]; reparation programmes should envisage forms of land redistribution and restitution and – when not possible – compensation[194]; apologies should be expressed by the government.[195]

Concurrently, targeted initiatives need to be at least discussed (with the involvement of indigenous groups) and outlined; among these, noteworthy are land reforms and interventions on land tenure, in particular towards the acknowledgment of communal forms of ownership, as well as of rights of marginalised individuals, also incorporating a gender perspective (e.g., Mayan women in Guatemala still face relevant challenges in accessing lands and in obtaining recognition of property); redistributive schemes should be envisaged, also connected to solid employment policies, and potentially forms of microcredit. Additionally, the transitional phase, representing a fresh start, is also a perfect opportunity to lay the foundation for agrarian reform informed by the goal of sustainable development, thus reversing patterns of intensive land exploitation. In this regard, indigenous peoples are increasingly recognised as key players in the fight against deforestation and climate change, thanks to a centuries-old knowledge of the natural world and a strong sensitivity towards conservation and preservation.[196] A meaningful step towards the involvement of these communities in the national machinery, within and beyond the transitional phase, could thus be the promotion of their participation in the design of targeted environmental and agrarian policies and interventions. This would also foster a shift in the narrative around indigenous peoples, contributing to overcome common perceptions of the natives as either uncivilised subjects or victims to be pitied, towards their recognition as communities with valuable scientific and organisational skills.

In Search of a New Paradigm?

Because of the many practical changes, conceptual and ideological adjustments, refocusing and rebranding of several key instruments and concepts, necessary to better confront the legacies of violence and discrimination, some authors conclude that the field of transitional justice per sé is just unable to accommodate these concerns. Underlying is the belief that "transitional justice is inherently short-term, legalistic and corrective. As such, it should focus on accountability for gross violations of civil and political rights",[197] while it should not be preoccupied with violations of social, economic and cultural rights nor ingrained patterns of violence. Consequently, either these issues should be left to other disciplines, or the field as such should be substantially redefined, or replaced by another model. Paul Gready and Simon Robins, for example, advocate for a renewed conceptualisation of transitional justice as "transformative justice", described as a form of "emancipatory peace-building"[198] grounded on the needs of the local population as expressed by them, and ideally resulting in a hybridised machinery",[199] potentially more efficient because rooted in the local context and culture. This enhanced model proposed by Gready, as well as other practitioners,[200] presents several positive features: it appears to be more attentive to the local context, and to the demands and needs of the victims, while also linking peace with development, and thus striving to overcome artificial separations between strictly intertwined disciplines.

However, the adoption of a more responsive approach does not require, in my opinion, a re-conceptualisation of the field; indeed, such an intervention would have the effect of reinforcing the above mentioned assumption that transitional justice is inescapably limited in its reach and scope, unable to develop beyond its classical boundaries, and therefore to confront forms of violence rooted in the social and economic systems; as such, the field would be of limited utility in addressing contemporary violence and strives, which are more and more evidently rooted in conflicts over resources. On the contrary, the definition of transitional justice as a field has always been flexible, and a more holistic understanding of what a transition is and entails is easily reconcilable with transitional justice's key tenets; in fact, what this chapter has tried to illustrate is that once core concepts such as conflict, violence, reconciliation and justice are interpreted according to the indigenous (and more generally local) perspective, and transitional justice is fully appreciated as a transformative opportunity and a tool for conflict prevention, then all the aforementioned interventions appear as necessary and instrumental for a meaningful pursue of transitional justice's key objectives. In other words, what the field of transitional justice needs, in order to remain relevant and responsive, is not the incorporation of new concepts and objectives, but rather the adoption of a renewed *understanding* of traditional transitional concepts and goals, more sensitive to the context, and which takes into primary consideration the perspective of victims and beneficiaries.

Conclusions

Indigenous peoples are a dissonant element in the current international legal and political order, out of place and focus: their holistic social organisation, with community at its core, contrasts with an international system composed of clearly (and often artificially) bordered nation-states, dominated by an individualistic paradigm; orally transmitted customary law, approaching the human, natural and spiritual worlds as part of the same continuum, does not easily dialogue with highly formal and legalistic systems; the scarce value attributed to money and exclusive property, as well as the preservation of an economic system based on communal ownership of land and resources, is in tension with the predominant model of economic liberalism based on trade and private property. More in general, their present condition of marginalisation and poverty constitutes a living testimony to the faults of colonialism and Western cultural hegemony, imposed economic liberalisation, and globalisation. Consequently, any call for indigenous self-determination results almost impossible to accommodate, without first rethinking the predominant narrative with regards to modernisation and development, and critically reassessing the (post-) Westphalian model of international relations.

A discussion of the intersections between indigenous peoples' issues and transitional justice has been reserved for the last chapter of the book, because it clearly manifests the fundamental role this field plays, at least potentially, in the progression of a country and a society, its evolution, its complexities and critical profiles, both in the theory and in the practice. Indeed, indigenous peoples' increased activism for recognition and respect calls into question seemingly innate linchpins of international law, human rights and post-conflict processes, compelling an intervention on the practical features and functioning of transitional mechanisms, in such a way to ensure the substantial participation of the natives; also, at a more epistemological level, it forces a rethinking of supposedly natural and unproblematic understandings of key concepts such as justice, reconciliation, truth – even time; it compels us to look under the surface towards the most profound causes of violence and inequality, and thus to appreciate how perceptions of peace and conflict prevalent today at the international level are in fact constructed, arising from a specific historical and cultural background, and often informed by colonial and post-colonial narratives.

This chapter thus aimed at illustrating how by assuming the perspective of the victims and the locals – in this case indigenous communities – traditional concepts and objectives of the transitional justice field are invested with new meanings. For example, peace is regarded as necessarily posited on substantial equality, as well as linked with development; as a consequence, the transitional process will in many cases be conceived not merely as political but also, inevitably, as a struggle for the socio-economic transformation of the country; as an opportunity to acknowledge, discuss and ideally address enduring and ingrained racism, exploitation and marginalisation. Similarly, reconciliation is often perceived as meaningful and sincere only if part of a broader set of interventions aimed at addressing long-standing violations, in the context of a broader discussion on the origins of systemic violence and on the responsibilities of society as a whole. Pursuing these objectives in turn requires the inclusion of indigenous communities in laying the foundations for a new, more inclusive political and economic system, which recognises and preserves spaces for autonomy, if not self-determination, and in which traditional barriers to education and justice are removed. In particular, central attention should be reserved to the issue of land, whose expropriation and exploitation figure among the main causes of indigenous peoples' contemporary situation: the struggle for restitution, ownership and protection of land is the fundamental fight of indigenous peoples today – and no mechanism of justice and reform will be perceived as meaningful and fair in the eyes of tribal communities, that does not at least take up this issue.

Additionally, the transitional phase is the perfect opportunity for a shift in the narrative, and in the institutional language: indigenous peoples should therefore be recognised and included in the project not only as victims but also as organised communities with an own system of order and justice, holders of an articulated and comprehensive system of knowledge concerning the natural world, who can thus play a fundamental role in the political and economic life of the country, as well as in the struggle against key contemporary challenges, such as deforestation and climate change, and therefore towards lasting peace and sustainable development.

In conclusion, a reflection on indigenous experiences prior, during and in the aftermath of conflicts confirms the limitations of the dominant paradigm of transitional justice, but also, at the same time, this field's potential; all that might be needed to realise it is a more optimistic and ambitious approach to justice, and to transitions as definitional and transformative phases, and as crucial not only towards accountability and redress but also for the prevention of conflicts.

Notes

1. Jennifer L. Burrell, *Maya After War. Conflict, Power Politics in Guatemala* (Austin: University of Texas Press, 2013), 86
2. Nicola Henry, "From Reconciliation to Transitional Justice: The Contours of Redress Politics in Established Democracies", *The International Journal of Transitional Justice* 9 (2015): 214
3. For an analysis of the necessary adjustments, in this case in the work of truth commissions, see: Paige Arthur; Eduardo Gonzalez; Yukyan Lam; Joanna Rice; Cesar Rodriguez-Garavito and Deborah J. Yashar (hereinafter: ICTJ), "Strengthening Indigenous Rights through Truth Commissions: *A Practitioner's Resource*". New York: ICTJ, 2012

   "Strengthening Indigenous Rights through Truth Commissions: A Practitioner's Resource" (New York: ICTJ, 2012)
4. Darfur is one among many examples of the "typical" contemporary conflict: intra-state, characterised by an exacerbation of pre-existing tribal, ethnic or political tensions, and object of belated international attention, when physical violence reaches such a gravity that it becomes the only possible focus, and military intervention the only conceivable solution. See: Dustin N. Sharp, "Addressing Economic Violence in Times of Transition: Toward a Positive-Peace Paradigm for Transitional Justice", *Fordham international Law Journal* 35(3) (2012): 780–814
5. "Indigenous Peoples", Food and Agriculture Organization of the United Nations, accessed 13 July 2016. http://www.fao.org/indigenous-peoples/en/
6. Fionnuala Ní Aoláin and Colm Campbell, "The Paradox of Transition in Conflicted Democracies", *Human Rights Quarterly* 27(1) (2005): 172–213

7. Typical examples are those of Canada and Australia. For more information, see: Courtney Jung, "Canada and the Legacy of the Indian Residential Schools: Transitional Justice for Indigenous Peoples in a Non-Transitional Society", in Paige Arthur, ed., *Identities in Transition: Challenges for Transitional Justice in Divided Societies* (Cambridge: CUP, 2010)
8. Karen Engle, "On Fragile Architecture: The UN Declaration on the Rights of Indigenous Peoples in the Context of Human Rights", *The European Journal of International Law* 22(1) (2011): 146–162
9. *United Nations Declaration on the Rights of Indigenous Peoples*, New York, 13 September 2007, A/61/L.67/Annex
10. As an example, see the evolution in the interpretation of the right to property promoted by the Inter-American Court of Human Rights, so as to accommodate and protect communal ownership of lands and resources. For an in-depth analysis, see Maria Dolores Mino, "Traditional Knowledge Under International Human Rights Law: Applying Standards of Communitarian Property Over Ancestral Land to Traditional-Knowledge Related Claims", *ExpressO* (2001): 1–28
11. Ilias Bantekas & Lutz Oette, *International Human Rights Law and Practice* (Cambridge: CUP, 2013), 436
12. ICTJ, "Strengthening Indigenous Rights Through Truth Commissions", 8
13. Bantekas and Oette, *International Human Rights Law and Practice,* 437
14. Taiaiake Alfred and Jeff Corntassel, "Being Indigenous: Resurgences Against Contemporary Colonialism", *Government and Opposition* 40(4) (2005): 609
15. Lisa Laplante, "Transitional Justice and Peace Building: Diagnosing and Addressing the Socioeconomic Roots of Violence through a Human Rights Framework", *The International Journal of Transitional Justice* 2 (2008): 335
16. Lars Waldorf, "Anticipating the Past: Transitional Justice and Socio-Economic Wrongs", *Social & Legal Studies* (2012): 174
17. As the one which appears to be most commonly cited and referred to.
18. Ruti G Teitel, "Transitional Justice Genealogy", *Harvard Human Rights Journal* 16 (2003): 69
19. United Nations, "Guidance Note of the Secretary-General: UN Approach to Transitional Justice" (United Nations, 2010)
20. This volume refers to a "paradigmatic", "prevalent", "traditional" model of transitional justice, with some typical characteristics identified in the literature and in the practice, aware of the many differences between transitional experiences on the ground. Several authors have identified key features of this model, among which Henry, "From Reconciliation to Transitional Justice", 207
21. Waldorf, "Anticipating the Past", 176

22. Diana Sankey, "Towards Recognition of Subsistence Harms: Reassessing Approaches to Socioeconomic Forms of Violence in Transitional Justice", *The International Journal of Transitional Justice* 8 (2014): 132
23. Henry, "From Reconciliation to Transitional Justice", 215
24. Slavoj Žižek, *Violence: Six Sideways Reflections* (London: Profile Books, 2009), 1. Other authors present a similar reconstruction: among others, see Paul's Farmer's notion of structural violence, elaborated upon in Paul Farmer, *Pathologies of Power: Health, Human Rights, and the New War on the Poor* (Berkeley: University of California Press, 2004)
25. Alfred and Corntassel, "Being Indigenous", 599
26. See Aoife Duffy, "Indigenous Peoples' Land Rights: Developing a *Sui Generis* Approach to Ownership and Restitution", *International Journal on Minority and Group Rights* 15 (2008): 505–538
27. On the case of Guatemala, see Inter-American Commission on Human Rights (Inter-American Commission), "Situation of Human Rights in Guatemala: Diversity, Inequality and Exclusion" (Washington DC: Organization of American States, 2015)
28. Bantekas and Oette, *International Human Rights Law and Practice,* 438
29. Rachel Sieder and Marìa Teresa Sierra, "Indigenous Women's Access to Justice in Latin America" (Working Paper, Chr Michelsen Institute 2010): 10
30. Ibid., 15
31. Henry, "From Reconciliation to Transitional Justice", 202
32. Makau Mutua, "Savages, Victims and Saviors: The Metaphor of Human Rights", *Harvard International Law Journal* 42(1) (2001): 201–245
33. Sieder and Sierra, "Indigenous Women's Access to Justice in Latin America", 10
34. Rosemary L Nagy, "The Scope and Bounds of Transitional Justice and the Canadian Truth and Reconciliation Commission", *The International Journal of Transitional Justice* 7 (2013): 53
35. ICTJ, "Strengthening Indigenous Rights through Truth Commissions", 19
36. Elizabeth Oglesby, "Educating Citizens in Postwar Guatemala: Historical Memory, Genocide, and the Culture of Peace", *Radical History Review* 97 (2007): 80
37. Jeff Corntassel and Cindy Holder, "Who's Sorry Now? Government Apologies, Truth Commissions, and Indigenous Self-Determination in Australia, Canada, Guatemala and Peru", *Human Rights Review* 9(4) (2008): 472
38. Zinaida Miller, "Effects of Invisibility: In Search of the 'Economic' in Transitional Justice", *The International Journal of Transitional Justice* 2 (2008): 281

39. Victor Igreja, "Multiple Temporalities in Indigenous Justice and Healing Practices in Mozambique", *The International Journal of Transitional Justice* 6 (2012): 405
40. Henry, "From Reconciliation to Transitional Justice", 208
41. Miller, "Effects of Invisibility", 277
42. The notion of wars and conflicts as being perceived in a "continuum of violence" with the pre-conflict situation has been primarily developed and reflected upon with relation to violence against women. See Ulrike Krause, "A Continuum of Violence? Linking Sexual and Gender-based Violence During Conflict, Flight, and Encampment", *Refugee Survey Quarterly* (2015): 1–19
43. Nagy, "The Scope and Bounds of Transitional Justice", 57
44. ICTJ, "Strengthening Indigenous Rights through Truth Commissions", 19
45. Waldorf, "Anticipating the Past", 174
46. Laplante, "Transitional Justice and Peace Building", 335
47. Ismael Muvingi, "Sitting on Powder Kegs: Socioeconomic Rights in Transitional Societies", *The International Journal of Transitional Justice* 3 (2009): 167
48. An interesting review of the silences in the literature and institutional reporting is provided by Miller, "Effects of Invisibility", 272–278
49. Among others, see Miller, "Effects of Invisibility", 280; Henry, "From Reconciliation to Transitional Justice", 199–218
50. Corntassel and Holder, "Who's Sorry Now?", 468
51. Inter-American Commission, "Situation of Human Rights in Guatemala", 39
52. Ibid., 39
53. Rachel Sieder, "Reframing Citizenship: Indigenous Rights, Local Power and the Peace Process in Guatemala", in Rachel Sieder and Richard Wilson, eds., *Negotiating Rights: The Guatemalan Peace Process* (London: Conciliation Resources, 1997), 68
54. Sabine Kurtenbach, "Guatemala's Post-War Development. The structural failure of low intensity peace" (Project Working Paper No. 2, Institute for Development and Peace, 2008): 5
55. Kurtenbach, "Guatemala's Post-War Development", 3
56. Ibid., 4
57. Burrell, *Maya After War*, 43
58. Ibid., 66
59. Kurtenbach, "Guatemala's Post-War Development", 4
60. Ibid., 9
61. Patrick Costello, "Historical Background", in Rachel Sieder and Richard Wilson, eds., *Negotiating Rights: The Guatemalan Peace Process* (London: Conciliation Resources, 1997), 12

62. Costello, "Historical Background", 12. See also Sieder, "Reframing Citizenship", 67 for a reconstruction of the evolution of indigenous movements in Guatemala
63. For a more complete reconstruction of the conflict in Guatemala and the role played by national and international actors, see: Daniel Rothenberg, ed., *Memory of Silence: The Guatemalan Truth Commission Report* (New York: Palgrave Macmillan, 2012)
64. Laura Arriaza and Naomi Roht-Arriaza, "Social Reconstruction as a Local Process", *The International Journal of Transitional Justice* 2 (2008): 154
65. Burrell, *Maya After War,* 24
66. Rothenberg, *Memory of Silence,* XXVII
67. Ibid., XXI
68. Burrell, *Maya After War,* 26
69. Rothenberg, *Memory of Silence,* 185
70. Ibid., 179 & 34
71. Ibid., 9
72. Kurtenbach, "Guatemala's Post-War Development", 16
73. *Rigoberta Menchu et al v Ríos Montt et al* (Judgment) Constitutional Court of Guatemala Exp 1904–2013 (20 May 2013) (Rios Montt judgment), par A.2.31
74. Ibid., ar.III.43
75. Among others, see Ibid., Par.8.2
76. Burrell, *Maya After War,* 86
77. See Kurtenbach, "Guatemala's Post-War Development", 16
78. Rothenberg, *Memory of Silence,* 36–42
79. Arriaza and Roht-Arriaza, "Social Reconstruction as a Local Process", 155
80. Rios Montt judgment, par.A.4
81. Costello, "Historical Background", 14
82. Arriaza and Roht-Arriaza, "Social Reconstruction as a Local Process", 156
83. Rothenberg,*Memory of Silence,* XXII
84. Lieselotte Viaene, "Life Is Priceless: Mayan Q'eqchi' Voices on the Guatemalan National Reparations Program", *The International Journal of Transitional Justice* 4 (2010): 10
85. Rothenberg, *Memory of Silence,* 185
86. Inter-American Commission, "Situation of Human Rights in Guatemala", 176
87. Kurtenbach, "Guatemala's Post-War Development", 14
88. For more details,see Rothenberg, *Memory of Silence,* XXXI
89. Burrell, *Maya After War,* 59
90. Rothenberg, *Memory of Silence,* 187
91. Ibid., XX
92. Sieder, "Reframing Citizenship", 74
93. Rothenberg, *Memory of Silence,* XXVI

94. Ibid., XXI
95. Ibid., XVI
96. Costello, "Historical Background", 12
97. Alison Crosby and M Brinton Lykes, "Mayan Women Survivors Speak: The Gendered relations of Truth Telling in Postwar Guatemala", *The International Journal of Transitional Justice* 5 (2011): 472
98. Paul Gready and Simon Robins, "From Transitional to Transformative Justice: A New Agenda for Practice", *The International Journal of Transitional Justice* 8 (2014): 353
99. Kurtenbach, "Guatemala's Post-War Development", 13
100. For more details, see Costello, "Historical Background", 16
101. For a more complete reconstruction, see Rothenberg, *Memory of Silence*; an analysis of the implementation of the peace agreements is offered by Hilde Salvesen, "Guatemala: Five Years After the Peace Accords. The Challenges of Implementing Peace" (Oslo: International Peace Research Institute, 2002)
102. Kurtenbach, "Guatemala's Post-War Development", 3
103. Sieder, "Reframing Citizenship", 68
104. Ibid., 66
105. Kurtenbach, "Guatemala's Post-War Development", 2
106. Rachel Sieder, "Rethinking Democratisation and Citizenship: Legal Pluralism and Institutional Reform in Guatemala", *Citizenship Studies* 3(1) (1999): 105
107. The full text of the Agreements can be found here: United States Institute of Peace, "Peace Agreements: Guatemala", available at <http://www.usip.org/publications/peace-agreements-guatemala >
108. Rothenberg, *Memory of Silence*, XXXIII
109. *Agreement on Identity and Rights of Indigenous Peoples* (Mexico City, 31 March 1995), available at <www.un.org/Depts/minugua/paz7.htm> (accessed 29 July 2016)
110. Salvesen, "Guatemala: Five Years After the Peace Accords", 13
111. Sieder, "Rethinking Democratisation and Citizenship", 106
112. *Agreement on Socio-Economic Aspects and the Agrarian Situation* (Mexico City, 6 May 1996), available at <www.un.org/Depts/minugua/paz8.htm >
113. Rothenberg, *Memory of Silence*, XXXIII
114. *Agreement on the Establishment of the Commission to Clarify Past Human Rights Violations and Acts of Violence That Have Caused the Guatemalan Population to Suffer* (Oslo, 23 June 1994), available at <http://peacemaker.un.org/guatemala-humanrightsinvestigation94>
115. Rothenberg, *Memory of Silence*, 253
116. Ibid., 180
117. Ibid.

118. Oglesby, "Educating Citizens in Postwar Guatemala", 78
119. Rothenberg, *Memory of Silence*, XXVI
120. Denis Martinez, Gabriela Flores and Oliver Rogers, "We Struggle With Dignity: Victims' Participation in Transitional Justice in Guatemala" (Research Report, Impunity Watch, 2016): 51
121. Martinez et al., "We Struggle With Dignity", 52
122. Rothenberg, *Memory of Silence*, XXXIV
123. For an overview, see Louise Arbour, "Economic and Social Justice for Societies in Transition", *International Law and Politics* 40(1) (2007): 1–27
124. Inter-American Commission, "Situation of Human Rights in Guatemala", 40
125. Rothenberg, *Memory of Silence*, XXI
126. Inter-American Commission, "Situation of Human Rights in Guatemala", 45. This source, at pages 46–53, also offers a concise but detailed reconstruction of the current situation of indigenous peoples in Guatemala, with regards to the key social, economic and cultural rights.
127. Salvesen, "Guatemala: Five Years After the Peace Accords", 15
128. Martinez et al., "We Struggle With Dignity", 19
129. Instituto Interamericano de Derechos Humanos, "Contribución de las políticas de verdad, justicia y reparación a las democracias en América Latina" (San Jose': IIDH, 2011): 194
130. Kurtenbach, "Guatemala's Post-War Development", 3
131. IIDH, "Contribución de las Políticas de Verdad, Justicia y Reparación a las Democracias en América Latina", 194
132. Ibid., 196
133. Inter-American Commission, "Situation of Human Rights in Guatemala", 55
134. Ibid., 56
135. For a reconstruction, with specific focus on the Inter-American system, see Mino, "Traditional Knowledge Under International Human Rights Law", 1–28; Inter-American Commission, "Situation of Human Rights in Guatemala", 193
136. International financial institutions are playing an increasingly influential role in the design of post-conflict processes, through the instrument of aid and peace conditionality. See Salvesen, "Guatemala: Five Years After the Peace Accords", 129
137. Gustavo Palma Murga, "Promised the Earth: Agrarian Reform in the Socio-Economic Agreement", in Rachel Sieder and Richard Wilson, eds., *Negotiating Rights: The Guatemalan Peace Process* (London: Conciliation Resources, 1997), 78
138. Inter-American Commission, "Situation of Human Rights in Guatemala", 195
139. Waldorf, "Anticipating the Past", 177
140. Laplante, "Transitional Justice and Peace Building", 334
141. Corntassel and Holder, "Who's Sorry Now?", 485

142. Murga, "Promised the Earth", 78
143. Sieder, "Reframing Citizenship", 72
144. Murga, "Promised the Earth", 74
145. Inter-American Commission, "Situation of Human Rights in Guatemala", 183
146. For more details see Viaene, "Life Is Priceless", 4–25
147. Martinez et al., "We Struggle With Dignity", 55
148. Viaene, "Life Is Priceless", 16
149. Ibid., 19
150. Gready and Robins, "From Transitional to Transformative Justice", 341
151. Miller, "Effects of Invisibility", 275
152. Ibid., 267
153. Waldorf, "Anticipating the Past", 180
154. Miller, "Effects of Invisibility", 267
155. See Arbour, "Economic and Social Justice for Societies in Transition", 9 on Darfur
156. Muvingi, "Sitting on Powder Kegs", 163
157. Gready and Robins, "From Transitional to Transformative Justice", 346
158. Burrell, *Maya After War,* 86
159. Miller, "Effects of Invisibility", 267
160. Henry, "From Reconciliation to Transitional Justice", 215
161. Farmer, *Pathologies of Power,* 7
162. Miller, "Effects of Invisibility", 268
163. Sharp, "Addressing Economic Violence in Times of Transition", 804
164. Sarah Bradshaw, "Is the Rights Focus the Right Focus? Nicaraguan Responses to the Rights Agenda", *Third World Quarterly* 27(7) (2006): 1336
165. Jennifer Balint, Julie Evans and Nesam Mcmillan, "Rethinking Transitional Justice, Redressing Indigenous Harm: A New Conceptual Approach", *The International Journal of Transitional Justice* 8 (2014): 214
166. Crosby and Lykes, "Mayan Women Survivors Speak", 463
167. Sharp, "Addressing Economic Violence in Times of Transition", 793
168. Gready and Robins, "From Transitional to Transformative Justice", 356
169. Laplante, "Transitional Justice and Peace Building", 333
170. An interesting analysis of the role of society as a whole as beneficiaries (and co-perpetrators) of colonisation and oppression of indigenous communities is offered by Paulette Yvonne Lynette Regan, "Unsettling the Settler Within: Canada's Peacemaker Myth, Reconciliation, and Transformative Pathways to Decolonization" (PhD diss., University of Victoria, 2006)
171. Sankey, "Towards Recognition of Subsistence Harms", 139
172. Arbour, "Economic and Social Justice for Societies in Transition", 13
173. Muvingi, "Sitting on Powder Kegs", 180
174. Duffy, "Indigenous Peoples' Land Rights", 524
175. Ibid., 523

176. Henry, "From Reconciliation to Transitional Justice", 214
177. Regan, "Unsettling the Settler Within", 144
178. See Infra, Chapter 4
179. Henry, "From Reconciliation to Transitional Justice", 204
180. James L Gibson, "Overcoming Apartheid: Can Truth Reconcile a Divided Nation?", *Politikon* 31 (2004): 150
181. Henry, "From Reconciliation to Transitional Justice", 210
182. Ibid.
183. Nagy, "The Scope and Bounds of Transitional Justice", 61
184. Ibid., 54
185. Corntassel and Holder, "Who's Sorry Now?", 472
186. Regan, "Unsettling the Settler Within", 190
187. Miller, "Effects of Invisibility", 287
188. Balint et al., "Rethinking Transitional Justice, Redressing Indigenous Harm", 214
189. Nagy, "The Scope and Bounds of Transitional Justice", 62
190. Laplante, "Transitional Justice and Peace Building", 333
191. With specific regard to Guatemala, see Charles R Hale, "Neoliberal Multiculturalism: The Remaking of Cultural Rights and Racial Dominance in Central America" *PoLAR* 28(1) (2005): 20. For a more general reconstruction of indigenous land rights, see Duffy, "Indigenous Peoples' Land Rights", 505–538
192. Nagy, "The Scope and Bounds of Transitional Justice", 62
193. Just as one among many examples, see on the omissions and silences of the Special Court for Sierra Leone: Charles Chernor Jalloh, "Special Court for Sierra Leone: Achieving Justice?", *Michigan Journal of International Law* 32 (2011):421
194. Duffy, "Indigenous Peoples' Land Rights", 522
195. Corntassel and Holder, "Who's Sorry Now?", 469
196. Among others, see Jan Salick and Anja Byg, "Indigenous Peoples and Climate Change" (Oxford: Tyndall Centre for Climate Change Research, 2007)
197. Waldorf, "Anticipating the Past", 180
198. Gready and Robins, "From Transitional to Transformative Justice", 351
199. Ibid.
200. Among others, see Wendy Lambourne, "Transitional Justice and Peacebuilding after Mass Violence", *The International Journal of Transitional Justice* 3 (2009): 28–48

CHAPTER 12

Conclusions: Justice Beyond Rhetoric

Transitional justice is a field of dilemmas and tensions – between seemingly irreconcilable perspectives, actors and needs, operating in contexts where everything is urgently needed, and nothing is easy to achieve. In this work, surely not exhaustive, the evolution of the field has been briefly retraced, focusing primarily, although not exclusively, on instruments employed to pursue justice as accountability. This choice was determined by the fact that transitional justice itself, although now incorporating several mechanisms and approaches, in its traditional paradigm conceives of justice primarily as punishment of those responsible for crimes and repression; as a consequence, adopting this focus allowed to better reconstruct this dominant paradigm and its evolution, while at the same time identifying its limitations.

More precisely, transitional justice was essentially born with the Nuremberg experiment, when, for the first time – marking a crucial step in the evolution of international law – the international community set up a highly innovative instrument (an international tribunal competent to determine the *individual* responsibility of persons carrying out acts of state) specifically to deal with a conflict which had brought horror and loss right at the heart of Europe. In this context, justice was understood strictly as providing accountability through retribution and punishment, as just desert, with the further consequence of removing few "bad eggs", while society as a whole was given the chance to atone for its sins by

G. Girelli, *Understanding Transitional Justice*,
Philosophy, Public Policy, and Transnational Law,
DOI 10.1007/978-3-319-53606-4_12

witnessing the cathartic act of blaming its representatives. Although the Tokyo and Nuremberg tribunals presented several problematic features – such as the limited jurisdiction to acts committed by the "losing side" and the relegation of victims to a passive role – this model was further developed in the following decades, especially with the establishment of the ad hoc international tribunals for Rwanda and former Yugoslavia, through which individual criminal accountability was officially exalted as necessary for preserving international peace and security. As analysed in the seventh chapter of this book, these courts mark a crucial phase in the evolution of transitional justice, representing at the same time the apex of humanity's faith in supranational justice and the clearer manifestation of its many weaknesses and limitations. As a result, awareness of the intrinsic inability of purely international tribunals to respond to the many and complex challenges of post-conflict scenarios prompted the development of innovative, more tailored instruments. On one side, hybrid courts were established, in an attempt to solve the issue of the distance – physical as much as cultural – of international tribunals from the local territory and population, which was fatally impinging on their ability to contribute positively to peace processes on the ground. On the other side, the excessive legalism and the lack of substantial involvement of the victims fostered the creation of truth commissions, which were firstly adopted prior to the ICTY and ICTR, but found their most mature version in the South African TRC, whose experience and legacy still inform the discourse and practice around commissions, and transitions more in general. Truth commissions, as manifestations of a restorative approach to justice, have the merit of being (when properly designed and implemented) less costly, more sensitive and more inclusive of the population, as well as more flexible and adaptable to the specific context. As such, they are better suited to manage and capitalise upon the tensions inherent to transitional phases.

However, neither tribunals, in their different versions, nor truth commissions managed to overcome critical limitations and shortcomings, which came to be increasingly perceived as inherent to transitional justice as a field, as an ultimately neoliberal and neo-colonial effort. More precisely, as analysed in Chapter 10, to be denounced is a perceived paternalism of Western-dominated (directly or ideologically) institutions and actors towards the post-conflict state and its domestic constituencies, manifested through the top-down imposition of foreign mechanisms, priorities and discourses. This one-size-fits-all model of transitional intervention is characterised by, among others: a prominent focus on violations of civil and political rights and on the public sphere, and an underestimation or overlooking of violations of social, economic and cultural rights and abuses endured in the private sphere, as a consequence also ignoring the deepest causes of conflicts and the continuity of violence and inequality before, during and after wars; an individualistic attitude, influencing the identification and characterisation of both victims and perpetrators; legalism, as overreliance on law and legal mechanisms, presented as the neutral, technical cure to the evil of politics; and a limited and unreflective understanding of progress everywhere and always as adoption of democratic governance and market economy.

The faith (and the resources) once reserved for international tribunals and truth commissions was therefore gradually granted to grassroots and local mechanisms, which came to be perceived, by many, as the solution to the many limitations which appeared as intrinsic to more structured interventions (although with a latent uneasiness concerning some of these instruments' poor human rights record). Indeed, bottom-up mechanisms are designed and implemented with a substantial involvement of the population, they are more familiar to the victims and the beneficiaries and they normally enjoy a degree of flexibility which allows them to adapt to different communities and contexts. However, as touched upon, grassroots mechanisms also present several weaknesses, either in themselves or because of their application in exceptional and extraordinary contexts, such as the transitional ones.

From this brief reconstruction of the evolution of the field, together with the many expectations and limitations characterising it, some key features emerge of the "dominant" paradigm of transitional justice, together with a critique of the same. In particular, a recurring theme throughout this volume has been the need to rethink, re-evaluate classifications and dichotomies. Indeed, categories are a fundamental narrative device, crucial for designing and evaluating projects and interventions, and as such they should not be abandoned (in many, if not most cases, a victim is clearly a victim, and a perpetrator is clearly a perpetrator). However, a more sensitive and reflective approach to defining categories shaping the transitional justice discourse is advocated for, which moves beyond black-and-white separations and classifications. In particular, throughout the book four dichotomies have been particularly recurrent, whose limitations and artificiality have emerged.

The first one is the distinction between victims and perpetrators. While these categories, whose line of demarcation is often painfully clear, are particularly indispensable, an unreflective or excessively rigid categorisation of subjects into the "victim" or "perpetrator" category can prove problematic, in that it risks photographing the present while overlooking one's past and future. Concerning the former, a thorough consideration of the story of a subject can reveal how blurred the line between victim and perpetrator is, and how subjects who commit acts violence have often themselves endured marginalisation and abuses (among the examples considered in this book, particularly relevant are those of child soldiers and of previously marginalised ethnic groups which commit crimes). Taking the past into consideration is not intended to result in a naively conciliatory, generalised forgiveness; on the contrary, it is critically important for designing justice processes that, rather than only envisaging punishment as civilised revenge, are more carefully tailored on the needs of that specific society, and thus have the potential to eradicate the root causes of violence and promote positive peace, rather than merely incapacitating and embitter the few who are caught to stand judgment. Regarding the future, it has been noted how strict categories tend to restrain victims in fixed, rigid identities, in this way obstructing constructive processes of redefinition of oneself as survivor, resister and citizen. Retracing the evolution of several transitional mechanisms also allowed to grasp with how limited and partial the prevalent conception of victims often is: victims are not exclusively individuals who suffered physical violence in the public sphere, during the conflict or by the hands of an authoritarian regime, but also those – individuals or groups – who underwent economic, historical and cultural violence (such as indigenous communities as such), as well as persons who endured violence in the private sphere, in the context of or consequently to wars. Once again, this reflection is not meant to cause an excessive and ultimately futile relativisation; on the contrary, it should be appreciated as instrumental to designing initiatives and interventions – from reparations to truth commissions and demobilisation programmes – which are the most adequate to create positive and lasting change for the largest number of people in society.

A second recurring distinction, in the transitional rhetoric, is the one between law and politics, which has been thoroughly problematised throughout the volume. This dichotomy is, in a sense, constitutive of transitional justice mechanisms; indeed, they were born as a way to deal non-politically, in a break with the past, with conflicts and their aftermath, and law still constitutes the dominant transitional language and dominant field of expertise; however, at the same time, they rest upon political agreements that are constituted by political bodies, and engage with ultimately political situations. More precisely, to be most problematic is not the differentiation between law and politics per se', but rather the misleading depiction of politics as the reign of evil and chaos, the ultimate source of conflict, and of law as its detached and independent alternative, the neutral, technical (rational) response to the irrationality of politics. At a closer look, indeed, the opposition between law and politics results artificial, as law, emerging from political processes of negotiation and deliberation, is itself always political. Denying this political character of law and justice is not only misleading but it can also produce negative consequences in the practice. Indeed, not only all legal mechanisms adopted within transitions (as in the case of every court analysed in this book) have been negatively affected in their legitimacy, credibility and efficacy precisely by the accuse of being political (and consequently partial) bodies; also, it risks excluding from the process precisely those actors which can contribute the most to the transitional process, at the benefit of bureaucrats and lawyers. Additionally, this dichotomisation contributes to the aforementioned limited conception of justice as a purely legal affair which results in a prioritisation of criminal accountability and of the language of human rights, at the expenses of interventions focused on the economic and social organisation of the polis, and on abusive power dynamics. Law and politics therefore are better appreciated as two sides of the same coin, which influence and shape each other in a dynamic relationship: revealing, acknowledging and capitalising upon this relation, while reacting to its detrimental effects is more helpful, in the practice, than reasoning through unrealistic binomials.

A third dichotomy, which constitutes a "pillar" of the discourse but proved equally worth problematising is the one opposing peace and justice as mutually incompatible objectives. Underlying is the conviction that justice (once again understood restrictively as prosecution and punishment, as blaming) is bound to destabilise an already fragile environment, while peace requires stability and political realism; accordingly, transitions are sometimes depicted as the less-than-optimal trade-off between the two. However, an alternative perspective is offered in Chapter 5, devoted to the analysis of amnesties, which in theory represent the repudiation of justice par excellence, while in fact they can prove crucial (when carefully tailored and part of a comprehensive machinery) in pursuing a meaningful justice. This proves how justice and peace are, at a closer look, less incompatible than apparent, and that the two objectives can be reconciled, pursued together. This, however, requires a renewed, more sensitive understanding of the two notions. On one side, justice should be interpreted not merely in retributive – ultimately legalistic – terms, but rather as contextual (in other words, more receptive of the victims' own understanding of justice) and as more holistically open to incorporating restorative elements. On the other side, peace should be understood not only in its negative dimension, as absence of active conflict, but rather as positive peace, defined as the absence of subtler forms of violence (poverty, denial of basic necessities, entrenchment marginalisation and exclusion of ethnic or social groups), which often play a decisive role in leading to or exacerbating conflicts.

Finally, a fourth distinction which shapes discourses and practices around transitions is the one between local and international (actors, mechanisms, priorities). This classification has been recurring in almost every chapter of the book, in different facets, leading to the realisation that transitional justice is never, nowadays, a purely domestic affair: on one side, contemporary conflicts always have an extra-national dimension, because of the role that supra-national actors play in causing, continuing, or disrupting conflicts, the influences of extra-national socio-political and economic phenomena and dynamics, and their producing effects which go beyond the state borders (e.g., by provoking mass migration and influencing the markets); on the other side, international and foreign actors are always present, shaping and supporting transitions. Therefore, perceiving local and international actors and interventions as clearly separated and opposed is just not realistic, and – as concluded in Chapter 10 – the key issue is not the "why" or the "if", but rather the "how" of international interventions. Also emerging throughout the volume is the need for a more careful consideration of these two levels, keeping in mind that "local" is not always synonym with "positive", nor "international" is always detrimental, and vice versa. However, what is equally undeniable is that transitions – just as conflicts – always carry a cultural element, or dimension: this emerged already in the second chapter, where culture was identified as strongly influencing the way in which victims are "understood", and understand themselves; in the third and fourth chapters, analysing how truth processes and the relationship between truth and healing are informed by culture, and how reconciliation means different things and has different underpinnings in different contexts; also, it was a common thread linking the chapters dedicated to practical cases and mechanisms: virtually every transitional project has experimented a tension between theoretical, universalised and essentialised understandings and priorities on one side, and concepts and grievances on the ground, insomuch that the evolution of the field can be understood as an attempt to reconcile internationally established values and priorities (such as human rights and democracy) with local needs and understandings. Context has therefore emerged as a fundamental element: in Jon Elster's words, "the context-dependence of the phenomena [are] an insuperable obstacle to generalization",[1] insomuch that the configuration is excluded of a transitional *law,* a set of rules and tools to apply in any post-conflict situation, while a more inclusive and responsive transitional machinery therefore escapes definition. However, this does not mean that everything is relative and exclusively case-sensitive. On the contrary, some key characteristics of post-conflict processes have been identified – in particular, the importance of a bottom-up approach, as substantial inclusion of local sensitivities, in such a way to reconcile the universal quest for peace and justice with its local declination and thus maximizing the transition's potential legitimacy and efficacy. As a consequence, in designing and implementing transitional processes, the starting point must always be the victims, and the local population, while "if it does not make sense to [...] the community, it is not justice".[2] More specifically, from a more nuanced re-evaluation of fixed categories and dichotomies a renewed understanding of transitional justice emerges, more context-sensitive and articulated, less compartmentalised, with two fundamental features.

First of all, transitions are best understood as (political) processes, and long-term ones, which not only seek justice but also acknowledge and plant the seeds for addressing root causes of conflicts and abuses, and where spaces are carved for traditionally marginalised subjects to express their grievances. Transitions should consequently be approached as a forum for debate, critique, redefinition. As touched upon in the last chapter of this volume, such an understanding of transitional justice would not require a re-conceptualisation of this discipline's key objectives and notions, nor its replacement with a different paradigm, but rather "only" a reinterpretation of the prevailing *understandings* of such objectives, which takes into full consideration the perceptions and experiences of the victims and the needs of those most directly affected by violence. In particular, key concepts such as truth, justice and reconciliation reveal their utmost potential once valued not merely statically, as objectives, but also dynamically, as themselves processes. For example, as seen, reconciliation and truth are best approached as never-ending struggles for dialogue and harmonising tensions, rather than as somewhat utopic goals.

Additionally, transitional justice should be appreciated as an opportunity, in at least three senses. First, as already thoroughly described, in its most traditional conception it represents an opportunity for retribution, rebuilding and redress.

Secondly, it also constitutes an opportunity for revolution: transitions are not necessarily an inevitably circumscribed passage from turmoil to relative peace, rather, they can constitute, more organically, a phase of transformation of the political and economic order – and of society as a whole; a chance for not merely re-creating the past, which contained in itself the seeds of violence, but for reshaping institutions and dynamics. As highlighted, often conflicts and authoritarianism are not a sudden, exceptional and clearly demarcated break from a peaceful past, but rather a continuation, with a heightened intensity and with an increase in physical harm, of pre-existing patterns of systemic violence, which are entrenched in society. Accordingly, a meaningful transition is one which aims not only at addressing the most visible effects of conflicts (physical violence) but also strives towards reshaping social dynamics and institutions as well as towards disrupting abusive patterns, thus not only going back to the situation preceding the war, but adjusting it, in this way promoting a lasting, positive peace. As Abdullahi An Na'im emphasised, transitions can be more ambitiously appreciated as processes of emancipation and self-determination.

Thirdly, and following from the first two, transitions can be best capitalised upon once they are understood as fundamental not only to respond to the legacies of violence, but also as an opportunity for conflict prevention. Indeed, once the nature of violence is revealed as expression and continuation of underlying and long-standing dynamics, it becomes apparent how justice processes should serve not only to ascribe responsibilities and pursue the satisfaction of the victims, but also to prevent the cyclical resurgence of conflicts. This is realised, among others, by acknowledging and addressing those aforementioned abusive power dynamics, and by entrusting the allocation of responsibilities and the rebuilding of the society to the local population, thus allowing the country to build antibodies, to design new, constructive ways in which to tackle conflicts at their inception.

As repeatedly mentioned throughout the book, this broadened approach to transitions, although challenging, does not in fact constitute an excessive and unrealistic stretching of the field; on the contrary, it appears to be naturally flowing from an appreciation of justice more sensitive to the needs of the local populations. Indeed, the transitional period, being intrinsically exceptional and reconstructive, can in practice constitute a unique –potentially the only – opportunity for traditionally marginalised groups to express their claims, to have their voice heard at the institutional level, and to advocate for substantial changes in society. It can be a sort of 'ground-zero', the definitive chance for a country to move beyond ingrained patterns of inequality and abuse, and to honestly confront the legacies of – among others – colonisation, institutionalised racism, forced economic liberalisation, thus linking peace with historic, economic, and ethnic, justice, through the design of comprehensive and inclusive political, social and developmental policies.

Notes

1. Jon Elster, *Closing the Books: Transitional Justice in Historical Perspective* (Cambridge: Cambridge University Press, 2004), 77
2. Abdullahi An-Na'im, "Editorial Note: From the Neocolonial 'Transitional' to Indigenous Formations of Justice", *The International Journal of Transitional Justice* 7 (2013): 199

Bibliography

Books

Albrecht, Peter; Kyed, Helene Maria; Isser, Deborah and Harper, Erica, eds. *Perspectives on Involving Non-State Actors in Justice and Security Reform.* Roma: IDLO, 2011

Arendt, Hannah. *Eichmann in Jerusalem: A Report on the Banality of Evil.* New York: The Viking Press, 1963

Arthur, Paige, ed. *Identities in Transition: Challenges for Transitional Justice in Divided Societies.* Cambridge: Cambridge University Press, 2010

Austin, Beatrix; Fischer, Martina and Giessmann, Hans J., eds. *Advancing Conflict Transformation. The Berghof Handbook II.* Opladen/Farmington Hills: Barbara Budrich Publishers, 2011

Austin, Beatrix; Fischer, Martina and Giessmann, Hans J., eds. *Advancing Conflict Transformation. The Berghof Handbook II.* Opladen/Farmington Hills: Barbara Budrich Publishers, 2011

Bantekas, Ilias and Oette, Lutz. *International Human Rights Law and Practice.* Cambridge: Cambridge University Press, 2012

Beinart, William and Dubow, Saul, eds. *Segregation and Apartheid in Twentieth-Century South Africa.* London and New York: Routledge, 1995

Blackburn, Simon and Simmons, Keith, eds. *Truth.* Oxford: Oxford University Press, 1999

Boister, Neil, and Cryer, Robert. *The Tokyo International Military Tribunal – A Reappraisal.* Oxford: Oxford University Press, 2008

Burrell, Jennifer L. *Maya After War. Conflict, Power and Politics in Guatemala.* Austin: University of Texas Press, 2013

G. Girelli, *Understanding Transitional Justice*,
Philosophy, Public Policy, and Transnational Law,
DOI 10.1007/978-3-319-53606-4

Chapman, Audrey E. and Van der Merwe, Hugo, eds. *Truth and Reconciliation in South Africa: Did the TRC Deliver?*. Philadelphia: University of Pennsylvania Press, 2008

Clark, Philip and Kaufman, Zachary, eds. *After Genocide: Transitional Justice, Post-Conflict Reconstruction, and Reconciliation in Rwanda and Beyond*. New York: Columbia University Press, 2009

Cooper, Frank and McGinley, Ann, eds. *Masculinities and Law: A Multidimensional Approach*. New York: NYU Press, 2011

Cruvellier, Thierry. *Court of Remorse. Inside the International Criminal Tribunal for Rwanda*. Madison: University of Wisconsin Press, 2010

Donnelly, Jack. *Universal Human Rights in Theory and in Practice*. Ithaca and London: Cornell University Press, 2003

Elster, Jon. *Closing the Books: Transitional Justice in Historical Perspective*. Cambridge: Cambridge University Press, 2004

Farmer, Paul. *Pathologies of Power: Health, Human Rights, and the New War on the Poor*. Berkeley: University of California Press, 2004

Fernandez-Armesto, Felipe. *Truth: A History and a Guide for the Perplexed*. New York: St. Martin's Press, 1997

Foucault, Michel. *Power/Knowledge: Selected Interviews and Other Writing, 1972–77*. Edited by Colin Gordon. Brighton: Harvester, 1980

Franzinelli, Mimmo. *L"amnistia Togliatti*. Milano: Mondadori, 2006

Freeman, Mark. *Necessary Evils. Amnesties and the Search for Justice*. Cambridge: Cambridge University Press, 2009

Futamura, Madoka. *War Crimes Tribunals and Transitional Justice. The Tokyo Trial and the Nuremberg Legacy*. New York: Routledge, 2008

Galtung, Johan. *After Violence: 3R, Reconstruction, Reconciliation, Resolution: Coping with the Invisible Effects of War and Violence*. Transcend, 1998

Gourevitch, Philip. *We Wish to Inform You That Tomorrow We Will be Killed With Our Families*. London: Picador, 1999

Habermas, Jürgen. *Moral Consciousness and Communicative Action*. Cambridge: Massachusetts Institute of Technology, 1990

Habermas, Jürgen. *The Theory of Communicative Action vol.1: Reason and the Rationalization of Society*. Boston: Beacon Press, 1984

Hayner, Priscilla B. *Unspeakable Truths: Confronting State Terror and Atrocity*. New York: Routledge, 2001

Hazan, Pierre. *Justice in a Time of War: The True Story Behind the International Criminal Tribunal for Former Yugoslavia*. College Station: Texas A&M University Press, 2004

Henckaerts, Jean-Marie and Doswald-Beck, Louise, eds. *Customary International Humanitarian Law. Volume I: Rules*. Cambridge: Cambridge University Press and International Committee of the Red Cross, 2009

Huyse, Luc and Salter, Mark, eds. *Traditional Justice and Reconciliation After Violent Conflict: Learning from African Experiences*. Stockholm: International IDEA, 2008

James, Allison and Prout, Alan, eds. *Constructing and Reconstructing Childhood: Contemporary Issues in the Sociological Study of Childhood*. London and New York: Routledge, 1997

Kelsall, Tim. *Culture Under Cross-Examination*. Cambridge: Cambridge University Press, 2009

Kerr, Rachel. *The International Criminal Tribunal for the Former Yugoslavia: An Exercise in Law, Politics and Diplomacy*. New York: Oxford University Press, 2004

Kirkham, Richard L. *Theories of Truth: A Critical Introduction*. Cambridge: MIT Press, 1995

Kritz, Neil. *Transitional Justice: How Emerging Democracies Reckon with Former Regimes, Vol. 3 Laws, Rulings, Reports*. Washington, DC: United States Institute of Peace Press, 1995

Kutnjak Ivkovich, Sanja and Hagan, John. *Reclaiming Justice: The International Tribunal for the Former Yugoslavia and Local Courts*. New York: Oxford University Press, 2011

Laban Hinton, Alexander, ed. *Transitional Justice: Global Mechanisms and Local Realities After Genocide and Mass Violence*. New Brunswick: Rutgers University Press, 2010

Lessa, Francesca and Payne, Leigh A., eds. *Amnesty in the Age of Human Rights Accountability: Comparative and International Perspectives*. Cambridge: Cambridge University Press, 2012

Lewandowski, Joseph D. and Znoj, Milan, eds. *Trust and Transitions: Social Capital in a Changing World*. Newcastle: Cambridge Scholars Publishing, 2008

Lollini, Andrea. *Constitutionalism and Transitional Justice in South Africa*. Oxford: Bergham Books, 2011

Luban, David; O'Sullivan, Julie and Stewart, David P. *International and Transnational Criminal Law*. New York: Aspen Publishers, 2010

Mamdani, Mahmood. *Saviours and Survivors: Darfur, Politics and the War on Terror*. London: Verso, 2009

Mamdani, Mahmood. *When Victims Become Killers: Colonialism, Nativism and the Genocide in Rwanda*. Princeton: Princeton University Press, 2002

Mandela, Nelson. *Long Walk to Freedom: The Autobiography of Nelson Mandela*. London: Little, Brown & Co, 1995

Mani, Rama. *Beyond Retribution: Seeking Justice in the Shadows of War*. Cambridge: Polity, 2007

May, Larry and Hoskins, Zachary, eds. *International Criminal Law and Philosophy*. Cambridge: Cambridge University Press, 2010

Mettraux, Guénaël, ed. *Perspectives on the Nuremberg Trial*. Oxford: Oxford University Press, 2009

Owen, James. *Nuremberg: Evil on Trial*. London: Headline Review, 2006

Roeling, Bernard Victor Aloysius and Cassese, Antonio. *The Tokyo Trial and Beyond*. Cambridge: Polity Press, 1993

Rothenberg, Daniel, ed. *Memory of Silence: The Guatemalan Truth Commission Report*. New York: Palgrave Macmillan, 2012

Sarkin, Jeremy. *Carrots and Sticks: The TRC and the South African Amnesty Process*. Antwerp and London: Intersentia, 2004

Schabas, William A. and Bérnaz, Nadia, eds. *The Handbook of International Criminal Law*. London: Routledge, 2010

Schabas, William. *The UN International Criminal Tribunals*. Cambridge: Cambridge University Press, 2006

Shahabuddeen, Mohamed. *International Criminal Justice at the Yugoslav Tribunal: A Judge's Recollection*. Oxford: Oxford University Press, 2012

Sieder, Rachel and Wilson, Richard, eds. *Negotiating Rights: The Guatemalan Peace Process*. London: Conciliation Resources, 1997

Swart, Bert; Zahar, Alexander and Sluiter, Goran, eds. *The Legacy of the International Criminal Tribunal of the Former Yugoslavia*. New York: Oxford University Press, 2011

Von Bogdandy, Armin and Dellavalle, Sergio. *Paradigmi dell'Ordine*. Torino: Trauben, 2010

Žižek, Slavoj. *Violence: Six Sideways Reflections*. London: Profile Books, 2009

Articles

Achmat, Zackie. "Law Politics and Social Transformation", *International Journal of Legal Information* 32 (2004): 237–242

Aiken, Nevan T. "Learning to Live Together: Transitional Justice and Intergroup Reconciliation in Northern Ireland". *The International Journal of Transitional Justice* 4 (2010): 166–188

Akhavan, Payam. "The International Criminal Tribunal for Rwanda: The Politics and Pragmatics of Punishment". *The American Journal of International Law* 90 (1996): 501–510

Alfred, Taiaiake and Corntassel, Jeff. "Being Indigenous: Resurgences Against Contemporary Colonialism". *Government and Opposition* 40(4) (2005): 597–614

Allo, Awol K. "The 'Show' in the 'Show Trial': Contextualizing the Politicization of the Courtroom". *Barry Law Review* 15 (2010): 41–72

Andrieu, Kora. "Civilizing Peacebuilding: Transitional Justice, Civil Society and the Liberal Paradigm". *Security Dialogue* 41 (2010): 537–557

Androff, David K. Jr. "Can Civil Society Reclaim Truth? Results from a Community-Based Truth and Reconciliation Commission". *The International Journal of Transitional Justice* 6 (2012): 296–317

An-Na'im, Abdullahi. "Editorial Note: From the Neocolonial Transitional to Indigenous Formation of Justice". *The International Journal of Transitional Justice* 7 (2013): 197–204

Arbour, Louise. "Economic and Social Justice for Societies in Transition". *International Law and Politics* 40(1) (2007): 1–27

Archibald, Steven and Richards, Paul. "Converts to Human Rights? Popular Debate about War and Justice in Rural Central Sierra Leone". *Africa* 72(3) (2002): 340–367

Arriaza, Laura and Roht-Arriaza, Naomi. "Social Reconstruction as a Local Process". *The International Journal of Transitional Justice* 2 (2008): 152–172

Arzt, Donna E. "Views on the Ground: The Local Perception of International Criminal Tribunals in the Former Yugoslavia and Sierra Leone". *Annals of the American Academy of Political and Social Science* 603 (2006): 226–239

Aukerman, Miriam. "Extraordinary Evil Ordinary Crime: A Framework for Understanding Transitional Justice". *Harvard Human Rights Journal* 15 (2002): 39–97.

Balint, Jennifer; Evans, Julie and Mcmillan, Nesam. "Rethinking Transitional Justice, Redressing Indigenous Harm: A New Conceptual Approach." *The International Journal of Transitional Justice* 8 (2014): 194–216

Barrett, John Q. "Opening the Nuremberg Trial: The Moment of November 20, 1945". *St. John Legal Studies Research Paper December* 1 (2015): 1–9

Barria, Lilian A. and Roper, Steven. "How Effective are International Criminal Tribunals? An Analysis of the ICTY and ICTR". *The International Journal of Human Rights* 9 (2005): 349–368.

Bell, Christine and O'Rourke, Catherine. "Does Feminism Need a Theory of Transitional Justice? An Introductory Essay". *The International Journal of Transitional Justice* 1 (2007): 23–44

Betts, Alexander. "Should Approaches to Post-Conflict Justice and Reconciliation be Determined Globally, Nationally or Locally?". *The European Journal of Development Research* 17(4) (2005): 735–752

Bilsky, Leora. "Transitional Justice as a Modern Oedipus: The Emergence of a Right to Truth". *Critical Analysis of Law* 2(2) (2015): 447–466

Bonacker, Thorsten. "Global Victimhood: On the Charisma of the Victim in Transitional Justice Processes". *World Political Science Review* 9(1) (2013): 97–129

Borgwardt, Elizabeth. "A New Deal for the Nuremberg Trial: The Limits of Law in Generating Human Rights Norms". *Law and History Review* 26(3) (2008): 679 – 705.

Borgwardt, Elizabeth. "Re-examining Nuremberg as a New Deal Institution: Politics, Culture and the Limits of Law in Generating Human Rights Norms". *Berkeley Journal of International Law* 23(2) (2005): 401–462

Bradshaw, Sarah. "Is the Rights Focus the Right Focus? Nicaraguan responses to the rights agenda". *Third World Quarterly* 27(7) (2006): 1329–1341

Brahm, Eric. "Uncovering the Truth: Examining Truth Commission Success and Impact". *International Studies Perspectives* 8(1) (2007): 16–35

Burke-White, William W. "Protecting the Minority: A Place for Impunity? An illustrated Survey of Amnesty Legislation, Its Conformity with International Legal Obligations, and Its Potential as a Tool for Minority-Majority Reconciliation". *Journal of Ethnopolitics and Minority Issues in Europe* 1 (2000): 1–53

Cahn, Naomi R. and Ní Aolain, Fionnuala D. "Gender, Masculinities and Transition in Conflicted Societies". *New England Law Review* 1 (2010): 101–123

Cassese, Antonio. "Reflections on International Criminal Justice", *Journal of International Criminal Justice* 9(1) (2011): 271–275

Celermajer, Danielle. "Mere Ritual? Displacing the Myth of Sincerity in Transitional Rituals". *The International Journal of Transitional Justice* 7 (2013): 286–305

Chapman Audrey R. and Ball, Patrick. "The Truth of Truth Commissions: Comparative Lessons from Haiti, South Africa, and Guatemala". *Human Rights Quarterly* 23 (2001): 1–43

Clark, Janine Natalia. "Reconciliation Through Remembrance? War Memorials and the Victims of Vukovar". *The International Journal of Transitional Justice* 7 (2013): 116–135

Clark, Janine Natalia. "The Limits of Retributive Justice". *Journal of International Criminal Justice* 7 (2009), 463–487.

Clarke, Kamari. "Rethinking Africa Through Its Exclusions: The Politics of Naming Criminal Responsibility. *Anthropological Quarterly* 83(3) (2010): 625–652

Cohen, David. "'Hybrid' Justice in East Timor, Sierra Leone and Cambodia: 'Lessons Learned' and Prospects for the Future". *Stanford Journal of International Law* 43 (2007): 2–38

Corntassel, Jeff and Holder, Cindy. "Who's Sorry Now? Government Apologies, Truth Commissions, and Indigenous Self-Determination in Australia, Canada, Guatemala and Peru". *Human Rights Review* 9(4) (2008): 465–490

Crenzel, Emilio. "Argentina's National Commission on the Disappearance of Persons: Contributions to Transitional Justice". *The International Journal of Transitional Justice* 2 (2008): 173–191

Crosby, Alison and Lykes, M. Brinton. "Mayan Women Survivors Speak: The Gendered Relations of Truth Telling in Postwar Guatemala". *The International Journal of Transitional Justice* 5 (2011): 456–476

Daly, Erin. "Between Punitive and Reconstructive Justice: The Gacaca Courts in Rwanda". *New York University Journal of International Law and Politics* 34 (2002): 355–396

Daly, Erin. "Truth Skepticism: An Inquiry Into the Value of Truth in Times of Transition". *The International Journal of Transitional Justice* 2 (2008): 23–41

Dana, Shahram. "The Sentencing Legacy of the Special Court of Sierra Leone". *Georgia Journal of International Comparative Law* 42(3) (2014): 616–686

Dickinson, Laura A. "The Promise of Hybrid Courts". *The American Journal of International Law* 97(2) (2003): 295–310

Dimitrijevic, Nenad. "Justice beyond Blame. Moral Justification of (The Idea of) a Truth Commission". *Journal of Conflict Resolution* 50 (2006): 368–382

Dougherty, Beth K. "Right-sizing International Criminal Justice: The Hybrid Experiment at the Special Court for Sierra Leone". *International Affairs* 80(2) (2004): 311–328

Drumbl, Mark A. "Restorative Justice and Collective Responsibility: Lessons for and from the Rwandan Genocide". *Contemporary Justice Review* 5(1) (2002): 5–22

Dube, Siphiwe Ignatius. "Transitional Justice Beyond the Normative: Towards a Literary Theory of Political Transitions". *The International Journal of Transitional Justice* 5 (2011): 177–197

Duffy, Aoife. "Indigenous Peoples' Land Rights: Developing a *Sui Generis* Approach to Ownership and Restitution". *International Journal on Minority and Group Rights* 15 (2008): 505–538

Duthie, Roger. "Toward a Development-sensitive Approach to Transitional Justice". *The International Journal of Transitional Justice* 2 (2008): 292–309

Dwyer, Susan. "Reconciliation for Realists". *Ethics & International Affairs* 13(1) (1999): 81–98

Eastmond, Marita and Mannergren Selimovic, Johanna. "Silence as Possibility in Postwar Everyday Life". *The International Journal of Transitional Justice* 6 (2012): 502–524

Elander, Maria. "The Victim's Address: Expressivism and the Victim at the Extraordinary Chambers in the Courts of Cambodia". *The International Journal of Transitional Justice* 7 (2013): 95–115

Elias, Jose Sebastian. "Constitutional Changes, Transitional Justice, and Legitimacy: The Life and Death of Argentina's 'Amnesty' Laws". *Yale Student Scholarship Papers* 57 (2007): 1–67

Engle, Karen. "On Fragile Architecture: The UN Declaration on the Rights of Indigenous Peoples in the Context of Human Rights". *The European Journal of International Law* 22(1) (2011): 146–162

Eppel, Shari. "'Bones in the Forest' in Matabeleland, Zimbabwe: Exhumations as a Tool for Transformation". *The International Journal of Transitional Justice* 8(3) (2014): 404–425

Eriksson, Anna. "A Bottom-Up Approach to Transformative Justice in Northern Ireland". *The International Journal of Transitional Justice* 3 (2009): 301–320

Evenson, Elizabeth M. "Truth and Justice in Sierra Leone: Coordination Between Commission and Court". *Columbia Law Review* 104 (2004): 730–767

Falk, Richard. "Telford Taylor and the Legacy of Nuremberg". *Columbia Journal of Transnational Law* 37 (1998–1999): 693–723.

Ferme, Mariane C. "Archetypes of Humanitarian Discourse: Child Soldiers, Forced Marriage, and the Framing of Communities in post-Conflict Sierra Leone". *Humanity* 4(1) (2013): 49–71

Fichtelberg, Aaron. "Fair Trials and International Courts: A Critical Evaluation of The Nuremberg Legacy". *Criminal Justice Ethics* 28(1) (2009): 5–24

Fields, Shawn. "Private Crimes and Public Forgiveness: Towards a Refined Restorative Justice Amnesty Regime". *International Journal of Civil Society Law* 5(2) (2007): 7–22

Findlay, Mark. "Activating a Victim Constituency in International Criminal Justice". *The International Journal of Transitional Justice* 3 (2009): 183–20

Franke, Katherine M. "Gendered Subjects of Transitional Justice". *Columbia Journal of Gender and Law* 15(3) (2006): 813–828

Furtado de Mendonça, Isabel. "Searching for Reconciliation in a Post Complex Political Emergency Scenario". *Naçao e Defesa* 105(2) (2003): 121–140

Gallagher, Karen. "No Justice, No Peace: The Legalities and Realities of Amnesty in Sierra Leone". *Thomas Jefferson Law Review* 23 (2000): 149–198

Gandsman, Ari Edward. "Retributive Justice, Public Intimacies and the Micropolitics of the Restitution of Kidnapped Children of the Disappeared in Argentina". *The International Journal of Transitional Justice* 6 (2012): 423–443

Garcia-Godos, Jemima. "Victim Reparations in the Peruvian Truth Commission and the Challenge of Historical Interpretation". *The International Journal of Transitional Justice* 2 (2008): 63–82

Garkawe, Sam. "The South African Truth and Reconciliation Commission: A Suitable Model to Enhance the Role and Rights of the Victims of Gross Violations of Human Rights". *Melbourne University Law Review* 27 (2003): 334–380

Gibson, James L. "On Legitimacy Theory and the Effectiveness of Truth Commissions". *Law and Contemporary Problems* 72 (2009): 123–141

Gibson, James L. "The Contributions of Truth to Reconciliation. Lessons from South Africa". *Journal of Conflict Resolution* 50 (2006): 409–432

Gibson, James L. "Truth, Reconciliation, and the Creation of a Human Rights Culture in South Africa". *Law & Society Review* 38(1) (2004): 5–39

Gibson, James L. "Overcoming Apartheid: Can Truth Reconcile a Divided Nation?". *Politikon* 31 (2004): 129–155

Glasius, Marlies and Meijers, Tim. "Constructions of Legitimacy: The Charles Taylor Trial". *The International Journal of Transitional Justice* 6 (2012): 229–252

Goldmann, Matthias. "Sierra Leone: African Solutions to African Problems?". *Max Planck Yearbook of United Nations Law* 9 (2005): 457–515

Goldstone, Richard. "Past Human Rights Violations: Truth Commissions and Amnesties or Prosecutions". *Northern Ireland Legal Quarterly* 51(2) (1999): 164–173

Graybill, Lyn S. "Traditional Practices and Reconciliation in Sierra Leone: The Effectiveness of Fambul Tok". *Conflict Trends* 3 (2010): 44–50

Gready, Paul and Robins, Simon. "From Transitional to Transformative Justice: A New Agenda for Practice". *The International Journal of Transitional Justice* 8 (2014): 339–361

Groome, Dermot. "The Right to Truth in the Fight Against Impunity". *Berkeley Journal of International Law* 29 (2012): 175–199

Groome, Dermot. "The Right to Truth: The Evolution of a Right". Available at *Social Science Research Network* (2015): 1–11

Hale, Charles R. "Neoliberal Multiculturalism: The Remaking of Cultural Rights and Racial Dominance in Central America". *PoLAR* 28(1) (2005): 10–28

Hamber, Brandon. "Masculinity and Transitional Justice: An Exploratory Essay" *The International Journal of Transitional Justice* 1 (2007): 375–390

Han, Sang Wook Daniel. "Transitional Justice: When Justice Strikes Back – Case Studies of Delayed Justice in Argentina and South Korea". *Houston Journal of International Law* 30(3) (2008): 653–701

Haque, Mozammel. "Hope for Gender Equality? A Pattern of Post-Conflict Transition in Masculinity". *Gender, Technology and Development* 17(1) (2013): 55–77

Hart, H.L.A. "Positivism and the Separation of Law and Morals". *Harvard Law Review* 71(4) (1958): 593–629

Haskell, John D. "The Complicity and Limits of International Law in Armed Conflict Rape". *Boston College Third World Law Journal* 29 (2009): 35–84

Helfman, Tara. "Francis Biddle and the Nuremberg Legacy: Waking the Human Conscience". *The Journal Jurisprudence* 15 (2012): 353–372

Henry, Nicola. "From Reconciliation to Transitional Justice: The Contours of Redress Politics in Established Democracies". *The International Journal of Transitional Justice* 9 (2015): 199–218

Henry, Nicola. "Memory of an Injustice: The 'Comfort Women' and the Legacy of the Tokyo Trial". *Asian Studies Review* 37(3) (2013): 362–280

Henry, Nicola. "Witness to Rape: The Limits and Potential of International War Crimes Trials for Victims of Wartime Sexual Violence". *The International Journal of Transitional Justice* 3 (2009): 114–134

Higonnet, Ethel. "Restructuring Hybrid Courts. Local Empowerment and National Criminal Justice Reform". *Yale Law School Legal Scholarship Repository* 1 (2005): 1–70

Horn, Rebecca; Charters, Simon and Vahidi, Saleem. "Testifying in an International War Crimes Tribunal: The Experience of Witnesses in the Special Court for Sierra Leone". *The International Journal of Transitional Justice* 3 (2009): 135–149

Humphrey, Michael and Valverde, Estela. "Human Rights Politics and Injustice: Transitional Justice in Argentina and South Africa". *The International Journal of Transitional Justice* 2 (2008): 83–105

Humphrey, Michael. "From Victim to Victimhood: Truth Commissions and Trials as Rituals of Political Transition and Individual Healing". *The Australian Journal of Anthropology* 14(2) (2003): 171–187

Igreja, Victor. "Amnesty Law, Political Struggles for Legitimacy and Violence in Mozambique". *The International Journal for Transitional Justice* 9(2) (2015): 239–258

Igreja, Victor. "Multiple Temporalities in Indigenous Justice and Healing Practices in Mozambique". *The International Journal of Transitional Justice* 6 (2012): 404–422

Iliff, Andrew R. "Root and Branch: Discourses of Tradition in Grassroots Transitional Justice". *The International Journal of Transitional Justice* 6 (2012): 253–273

Isaacs, Anita. "At War with the Past? The Politics of Truth Seeking in Guatemala". *The International Journal of Transitional Justice* 4 (2010): 251–274

Jacobson, Douglas. "A Break with the Past or Justice in Pieces: Divergent Paths on the Question of Amnesty in Argentina and Colombia". *Georgia Journal of International and Comparative Law* 175 (2006): 175–204

Jain, Neha. "Conceptualising Internationalisation in Hybrid Criminal Courts". *Singapore Year Book of International Law and Contributors* 12 (2008): 81–95

Jalloh, Charles Chernor. "Special Court for Sierra Leone: Achieving Justice?". *Michigan Journal of International Law* 32 (2011): 395–460

James, Matt. "A Carnival of Truth? Knowledge, Ignorance and the Canadian Truth and Reconciliation Commission". *The International Journal of Transitional Justice* 6 (2012): 182–204

January, Sativa. "*Tribunal Verite*': Documenting Transitional Justice in Sierra Leone". *The International Journal of Transitional Justice* 3(2009): 207–228

Jelin, Elizabeth. "Public Memorialization in Perspective: Truth, Justice and Memory of Past Repression in the Southern Cone of South America". *The International Journal of Transitional Justice* 1 (2007): 138–156

Jenks, Chris and Acquaviva, Guido "Debate: The Role of International Criminal Justice in Fostering Compliance with International Humanitarian Law". *International Review of the Red Cross* 96 (2014): 775–794

Karnavas, Michael G. "The ICTY Legacy: A Defense Counsel's Perspective", *Gottingen Journal of International Law* 3 (2011): 1053–1092

Karstedt, Susanne. "From Absence to Presence, From Silence to Voice: Victims in International and Transitional Justice since the Nuremberg Trials". *International Review of Victimology* 17 (2010): 9–30

Kaufman, Zachary. "The Nuremberg Tribunal V. The Tokyo Tribunal: Designs, Staffs, and Operations". *The John Marshall Law Review* 43 (2009–2010): 753–768.

Kelsall, Michelle Staggs and Stepakoff, Shanee. "When We Wanted to Talk About Rape: Silencing Sexual Violence at the Special Court for Sierra Leone". *The International Journal for Transitional Justice* 1 (2007): 355–374

Kelsen, Hans. "Will the Judgment in the Nuremberg Trial Constitute a Precedent in International Law?". *The International Law Quarterly* 1(2) (1947): 153–171

Kent, Lia. "Local Memory Practices in East Timor: Disrupting Transitional Justice Narratives". *The International Journal of Transitional Justice* 5 (2011): 434–455

Kohen, Ari. "The Personal and the Political: Forgiveness and Reconciliation in Restorative Justice". *Critical Review of International Social and Political Philosophy* 12(3) (2009): 399–423

Kohen, Ari; Zanchelli, Michael and Drake, Levi. "Personal and Political Reconciliation in Post-Genocide Rwanda". *Social Justice Research* 1 (2011): 1–22

Koskenniemi, Martti. "Between Impunity and Show Trials". *Max Planck Yearbook of United Nations Law* 6 (2002): 1–35

Koskenniemi, Martti. "Hersch Lauterpacht and the Development of International Criminal Law". *Journal of International Criminal Justice* 2(3) (2004): 810–825

Krause, Ulrike. "A Continuum of Violence? Linking Sexual and Gender-based Violence During Conflict, Flight, and Encampment". *Refugee Survey Quarterly* 34(4) (2015): 1–19

Lambourne, Wendy. "Transitional Justice and Peacebuilding After Mass Violence". *The International Journal of Transitional Justice* 3 (2009): 28–48

Lansing, Paul and King, Julie C. "South Africa's Truth and Reconciliation Commission: The Conflict Between Individual Justice and National Healing in the Post-Apartheid Age". *Arizona Journal of International and Comparative Law* 15(3) (1998): 753–789

Laplante, Lisa. "Transitional Justice and Peace Building: Diagnosing and Addressing the Socioeconomic Roots of Violence Through a Human Rights Framework". *The International Journal of Transitional Justice* 2 (2008): 331–355

Lawther, Cheryl. "Denial, Silence and the Politics of the Past: Unpicking the Opposition to Truth Recovery in Northern Ireland". *The International Journal of Transitional Justice* 7 (2013): 157–177

Leebaw, Bronwyn Anne. "The Irreconcilable Goals of Transitional Justice". *Human Rights Quarterly* 95 (2008): 95–118

Luban, David. "The Legacies of Nuremberg". *Social Research* 54(4) (1987): 779–829

Ludwin King, Elizabeth B. "Amnesties in a Time of Transition". *The George Washington International Law Review* 41 (2010): 577–618

Lundy, Patricia and McGovern, Mark. "Whose Justice? Rethinking Transitional Justice from the Bottom Up". *Journal of Law and Society* 35(2) (2008): 265–292

Maculan, Elena. "Prosecuting International Crimes at National Level: Lessons from the Argentine 'Truth-Finding Trials'". *Utrecht Law Review* 8 (2012): 106–121

Mallinder, Louise and McEvoy, Kieran. "Rethinking Amnesties: Atrocity, Accountability and Impunity in Post-Conflict Societies". *Transitional Justice Institute Research Paper* 11 (2011): 1–46

Mallinder, Louise. "Can Amnesties and International Justice be Reconciled?". *The International Journal of Transitional Justice* 1 (2007): 208–230

Manjoo, Rashida and McRaith, Calleigh. "Gender-Based Violence in Conflict and Post-Conflict Areas". *Cornell International Law Journal* 44 (2011): 11–31

McAuliffe, Padraig. "Hybrid Tribunal at Ten: How International Criminal Justice's Golden Child Became an Orphan". *Journal of International Law and International Relations* 1 (2011): 1–65

McAuliffe, Padraig. "Romanticization Versus Integration?: Indigenous Justice in Rule of Law Reconstruction and Transitional Justice Discourse". *Gottingen Journal of International Law* 5 (2013): 41–86

McCarthy, Emily H. "South Africa's Amnesty Process: A Viable Route Toward Truth and Reconciliation?". *Michigan Journal of Race and Law* 3 (1997): 183–253

McDonald, Avril. "A Right to Truth, Justice and a Remedy for African Victims of Serious Violations of International Humanitarian Law". *Law, Democracy and Development* 2 (1999): 139–180

McEvoy, Kieran and McConnachie, Kirsten. "Victimology in Transitional Justice: Victimhood, Innocence and hierarchy". *European Journal of Criminology* 9 (2012): 527–538

McEvoy, Kieran and McConnachie, Kirsten. "Victims and Transitional Justice: Voice, Agency and Blame". *Social & Legal Studies* 22 (2013): 489–513

McEvoy, Kieran. "Beyond Legalism: Towards a Thicker Understanding of Transitional Justice". *Journal of Law and Society* 34(4) (2007): 411–440

McMahon, Patrice C. and Forsythe, David P. "The ICTY's Impact on Serbia: Judicial Romanticism Meets Network Politics". *Human Rights Quarterly* 30(2) (2008): 412–435

Mégret, Frédéric. "The Legacy of the ICTY as Seen Through Some of Its Actors and Observers". *Goettingen Journal of International Law* 3 (2011): 1011–1052

Mendez, Juan E. "Accountability for Past Abuses". *Human Rights Quarterly* 19(2) (1997): 255–282

Mieth, Friederike. "Bringing Justice and Enforcing Peace? An Ethnographic Perspective on the Impact of the Special Court for Sierra Leone". *International Journal of Conflict and Violence* 7(1) (2013): 1–12

Millar, Gearoid. "Assessing Local Experiences of Truth-Telling in Sierra Leone: Getting to 'Why' Through a Qualitative Case Study Analysis". *The International Journal of Transitional Justice* 4 (2010): 477–496

Millar, Gearoid. "Disaggregating Hybridity: Why Hybrid Institutions Do Not Produce Predictable Experiences of Peace". *Journal of Peace Research* 51(4) (2014): 501–514

Miller, Zinaida. "Effects of Invisibility: In Search of the 'Economic' in Transitional Justice". *The International Journal of Transitional Justice* 2 (2008): 266–291

Mino, Maria Dolores. "Traditional Knowledge Under International Human Rights Law: Applying Standards of Communitarian Property Over Ancestral Land to Traditional-Knowledge Related Claims". *ExpressO* (2001): 1–28

Moon, Claire. "Prelapsarian State: Forgiveness and Reconciliation in Transitional Justice". *International Journal for the Semiotics of Law* 17(2) (2004):185–197

Møse, Eric. "Main Achievements of the ICTR". *Journal of International Criminal Justice* 3 (2005): 920–943

Mundis, Daryl A. "Completing the Mandates of the Ad Hoc International Tribunals: Lessons from the Nuremberg Process?". *Fordham International Law Journal* 28 (2004–2005): 592–615

Mutua, Makau. "Never Again: Questioning the Yugoslav and Rwanda Tribunals". *Temple International and Comparative Law Journal* 11 (1997): 167–187

Mutua, Makau. "Savages, Victims and Saviors: The Metaphor of Human Rights". *Harvard International Law Journal* 42(1) (2001): 201–245

Muvingi, Ismael. "Sitting on Powder Kegs: Socioeconomic Rights in Transitional Societies". *The International Journal of Transitional Justice* 3 (2009): 163–182

Nadler, Arie and Shnabel, Nurit. "Instrumental and Socio-Emotional Paths to Intergroup Reconciliation and the Need-Based Model of Socio-Emotional Reconciliation", in Arie Nadler, Thomas Malloy and Jeffrey D. Fisher, eds. *Social Psychology of Intergroup Reconciliation*. New York: Oxford University Press, 2008

Nagy, Rosemary. "The Scope and Bounds of Transitional Justice and the Canadian Truth and Reconciliation Commission". *The International Journal of Transitional Justice* 7 (2013): 52–73

Nagy, Rosemary. "Transitional Justice as a Global Project: Critical Reflections". *Third World Quarterly* 29(2) (2008): 275–289

Naqvi, Yasmin. "The Right to the Truth in International Law: Fact or Fiction?". *International Review of the Red Cross* 88 (2006): 245–273

Ní Aolain, Fionnuala and Campbell, Colm. "The Paradox of Transition in Conflicted Democracies". *Human Rights Quarterly* 27(1) (2005): 172–213

Ní Aolain, Fionnuala. "Political Violence and Gender in Times of Transition". *Columbia Journal of Gender and Law* 15 (2006): 829–849

Ní Aolain, Fionnuala. "Women, Security, and the Patriarchy of Internationalized Transitional Justice". *Human Rights Quarterly* 31 (2009): 1055–1085

Ní Aolain, Fionnuala; O'Rourke, Catherine and Swaine, Aisling. "Transforming Reparations for Conflict-Related Sexual Violence: Principles and Practice". *Harvard Human Rights Journal* 28 (2015): 98–146

Nicol-Wilson, Melron. "International Criminal Tribunals: A Comparative Study of the Tribunals in Former Yugoslavia, Rwanda and Sierra Leone". *Australian International Law Journal* 126 (2002): 126–149

Nielsen, Elizabeth. "Hybrid International Criminal Tribunals: Political Interference and Judicial Independence". *UCLA Journal of International Law and Foreign Affairs* 289 (2010): 289–326

Nouwen, Sarah M.H. "Hybrid Courts. The Hybrid Category of a New Type of International Crimes Court". *Utrecht Law Review* 2 (2006): 190–214

Nouwen, Sarah M.H. and Werner, Wouter G. "Doing Justice to the Political: The International Criminal Court in Uganda and Sudan". *The European Journal of International Law* 21(4) (2011): 941–965

Nwogu, Nneoma. "When and Why It Started: Deconstructing Victim-Centered Truth Commissions in the Context of Ethnicity-Based Conflict". *The International Journal of Transitional Justice* 4 (2010): 257–289

Oglesby, Elizabeth. "Educating Citizens in Postwar Guatemala: Historical Memory, Genocide, and the Culture of Peace". *Radical History Review* 97 (2007): 77–98

Ohlin, Jens David. "On the Very Idea of Transitional Justice". *The Whitehead Journal of Diplomacy and International Relations* 8 (2007): 51–68

Olsen, Tricia D.; Payne, Leigh A. and Reiter, Andrew G. "The Justice Balance: When Transitional Justice Improves Human Rights and Democracy". *Human Rights Quarterly* 32 (2010): 980–1007

Omar, Abdullah. "Truth and Reconciliation in South Africa: Accounting for the Past". *Buffalo Human Rights Law Review* 4 (1998): 5–14

Oosterveld, Valerie. "The Gender Jurisprudence of the Special Court for Sierra Leone: Progress in the Revolutionary United Front Judgments". *Cornell International Law Journal* 44 (2011): 49–74

Orentlicher, Diane. "Settling Accounts: The Duty to Prosecute Human Rights Violations of a Prior Regime". *Yale Law Journal* 100(8) (1991): 2537–2615

Park, Augustine S.J. "Community-based Restorative Transitional Justice in Sierra Leone". *Contemporary Justice Review* 13(1) (2010): 95–119

Parker, Robert. "Fighting the Sirens' Song: The Problem of Amnesty in Historical and Contemporary Perspective". *Acta Juridica Hungarica* 42 (2001): 69–89

Pensky, Max. "Amnesty on Trial: Impunity, Accountability, and the Norms of International Law". *Ethics & Global Politics* 1(1) (2008): 1–40

Peterson, Jenny H. "A Conceptual Unpacking of Hybridity: Accounting for Notions of Power, Politics and Progress in Analyses of Aid-Driven Interfaces". *Journal of Peacebuilding & Development* 7(2) (2012): 9–22

Pocar, Fausto. "The Proliferation of International Criminal Courts and Tribunals". *Journal of International Criminal Justice* 2 (2004): 304–308

Popkin, Margaret and Roht-Arriaza, Naomi. "Truth as Justice: Investigatory Commissions in Latin America". *Law & Social Inquiry* 20 (1995): 79–116

Porter, Antonia. "'What Is Constructed Can be Transformed': Masculinities in Post-Conflict Societies in Africa". *International Peacekeeping* 20(4) (2013): 486–506

Posel, Deborah. "History as Confession: The Case of South African Truth and Reconciliation Commission". *Public Culture Winter* 20 (2008): 119–141

Posner, Eric A. "Political Trials in Domestic and International Law". *Duke Law Journal* 55 (2005): 75–152

Powell, Derek. "The Role of Constitution Making and Institution Building in Furthering Peace, Justice and Development: South Africa's Democratic Transition". *The International Journal of Transitional Justice* 4 (2010): 230–250

Prieto, Juan Diego. "Together After War While the War Goes On: Victims, Ex-Combatants and Communities in Three Colombian Cities". *The International Journal of Transitional Justice* 6 (2012): 525–546

Propen, Amy and Schuster, Mary Lay. "Degrees of Emotion: Judicial Responses to Victim Impact Statements". *Law, Culture and the Humanities* 6 (2010): 75–104

Puechguirbal, Nadine. "The Cost of Ignoring Gender in Conflict and Post-Conflict Situations: A Feminist Perspective". *Amsterdam Law Forum* 4(1) (2012): 4–19

Ramji-Nogales, Jaya. "Designing Bespoke Transitional Justice: A Pluralist Process Approach". *Michigan Journal of International Law*, 32 (2010): 2–72

Rapp, Stephen J. "The Compact Model in International Criminal Justice: The Special Court for Sierra Leone". *Drake Law Review* 57 (2008): 11–49

Rigby, Andrew. "Reflections on Reconciliation". *Committee for Conflict Transformation Support Review* 29 (2005–2006): 1–4

Robins, Simon. "Towards Victim-Centred Transitional Justice: Understanding the Needs of Families of the Disappeared in Postconflict Nepal". *The International Journal of Transitional Justice* 5 (2011): 75–98

Robinson, Darryl. "Serving the Interests of Justice: Amnesties, Truth Commissions and the International Criminal Court". *European Journal of International Law* 14 (2003): 481–505

Roht-Arriaza, Naomi. "After Amnesties are Gone: Latin American National Courts and the New Contours of the Fight Against Impunity". *Human Rights Quarterly* 37(2) (2015): 341–382

Rubio-Marin, Ruth and de Greiff, Pablo. "Women and Reparations". *The International Journal of Transitional Justice* 1 (2007): 318–337

Sankey, Diana. "Towards Recognition of Subsistence Harms: Reassessing Approaches to Socioeconomic Forms of Violence in Transitional Justice". *The International Journal of Transitional Justice* 8 (2014): 121–140

Sarkin, Jeremy. "The Trials and Tribulations of South Africa's Truth and Reconciliation Commission". *South African Journal on Human Rights* 12 (1996): 617–639

Saunders, Rebecca. "Questionable Associations: The Role of Forgiveness in Transitional Justice". *The International Journal of Transitional Justice* 5 (2011): 119–141

Schapiro, Hernán. "Surgimiento de los 'Juicios por la Verdad' en la Argentina de los Noventa". *El vuelo de Ícaro* 2(3) (2001–2002): 359–401

Scharf, Michael and Kang, Ahran. "Errors and Missteps: Key Lessons the Iraqi Special Tribunal Can Learn from the ICTY, ICTR and SCSL". *Cornell International Law Journal* 38 (2005): 911–947

Schey, Peter; Shelton, Dinah and Roht-Arriaza, Naomi. "Addressing Human Rights Abuses: Truth Commissions and the Value of Amnesty". *Whittier Law Review* 19 (1997): 325–344

Schrag, Minna. "Lessons Learned from ICTY Experience". *Journal of International Criminal Justice* 2 (2004): 427–434

Sgroi, Susanna. "Il principio di retroattività e il processo di Norimberga". *Diritto & Questioni Pubbliche* 3 (2003): 313–329

Sharp, Dustin N. "Addressing Economic Violence in Times of Transition: Toward a Positive-Peace Paradigm for Transitional Justice". *Fordham International Law Journal* 35(3) (2012): 780–814

Sharp, Dustin N. "Interrogating the Peripheries: The Preoccupation of Fourth Generation Transitional Justice". *Harvard Human Rights Journal* 26 (2013): 149–178

Shaw, Rosalind. "Memory Frictions: Localizing the truth and Reconciliation Commission in Sierra Leone". *The International Journal of Transitional Justice* 1 (2007): 183–207

Sieder, Rachel. "Rethinking Democratisation and Citizenship: Legal Pluralism and Institutional Reform in Guatemala". *Citizenship Studies* 3(1) (1999): 103–119

Simpson, Kirk. "Victims of Political Violence: A Habermasian Model of Truth Recovery". *Journal of Human Rights* 6(3) (2007): 325–343

Skaar, Elin. "Reconciliation in a Transitional Justice Perspective". *Transitional Justice Review* 1 (2012): 54–103

Sloane, Robert D. "The Expressive Capacity of International Punishment: The Limits of the National Law Analogy and the Potential of International Criminal Law". *Stanford Journal of International Law* 43 (2007):39–94

Slye, Ronald C. "The Legitimacy of Amnesties Under International Law and General Principles of Anglo-American Law: 'Is a Legitimate Amnesty Possible?'". *Virginia Journal of International Law* 43 (2002): 174 – 247

Sriram, Chandra Lekha. "Wrong-sizing International Justice? The Hybrid Tribunal in Sierra Leone". *Fordam International Law Journal* 29 (2005): 472–506

Sterio, Milena. "Rethinking Amnesty". *Denver Journal of International Law & Policy* 34(3) (2006): 373–400

Subotìc, Jelena. "The Paradox of International Justice Compliance". *The International Journal of Transitional Justice* 3 (2009): 362–383

Szoke-Burke, Sam. "Searching for the Right to Truth: The Impact of International Human Rights Law on National Transitional Justice Policies". *Berkeley Journal of International Law* 33(2) (2015): 526–578

Tabak, Shana. "False Dichotomies of Transitional Justice: Gender, Conflict and Combatants in Colombia". *International Law and Politics* 44 (2011): 103–163

Teitel, Ruti G. "Transitional Justice Genealogy". *Harvard Human Rights Journal* 16 (2003): 68–94

Teitel, Ruti. "Transitional Jurisprudence: The Role of Law in Political Transformation". *The Yale Law Journal* 106(7) (1997): 2009–2080

Teitel, Ruti. "Transitional Justice: Postwar Legacies". *Cardozo Law Review* 27 (2006): 1615–1631

Theidon, Kimberly. "Editorial Note". *The International Journal of Transitional Justice* 3 (2009):295–300

Theidon, Kimberly. "Reconstructing Masculinities: The Disarmament, Demobilization, and Reintegration of Former Combatants in Colombia". *Human Rights Quarterly* 31 (2009): 1–34

Thomson, Susan and Nagy, Rosemary. "Law, Power and Justice: What Legalism Fails to Address in the Functioning of Rwanda's *Gacaca* Courts". *The International Journal of Transitional Justice* 5 (2011): 11–30

Tolbert, David. "The International Criminal Tribunal for the Former Yugoslavia: Unforeseen Successes and Foreseeable Shortcomings". *The Fletcher Forum of World Affairs* 7 (2002): 7–19

Trumbull, Charles P. "Giving Amnesties a Second Chance." *Berkeley Journal of International Law* 25(2) (2007): 284–345

Trumbull, Charles P. "The Victims of Victim Participation in International Criminal Proceedings". *Michigan Journal of International Law* 29 (2008): 777–826

Viaene, Lieselotte. "Life Is Priceless: Mayan Q'eqchi' Voices on the Guatemalan National Reparations Program". *The International Journal of Transitional Justice* 4 (2010): 4–25

Vieille, Stephanie. "Transitional Justice: A Colonizing Field?". *Amsterdam Law Forum* 4(3) (2012): 58–68

Waldorf, Lars. "'A Mere Pretense of Justice': Complementarity, Sham Trials, and Victor's Justice at the Rwanda Tribunal". *Fordham International Law Journal* 33(4) (2011): 1221–1277

Waldorf, Lars. "Anticipating the Past: Transitional Justice and Socio-Economic Wrongs". *Social & Legal Studies* 21(2) (2012): 171–186

Weinstein, Harvey M. "Editorial Note: The Myth of Closure, the Illusion of Reconciliation: Final Thoughts on Five Years as Co-Editor-In-Chief". *The International Journal for Transitional Justice* 5 (2011): 1–10

Wilke, Christiane. "Remembering Complexity? Memorials for Nazi Victims in Berlin". *The International Journal of Transitional Justice* 7 (2013): 136–156

Woodbury, Laura. "Reconstructing Gender Identity for Child Combatants in Post-Conflict African Societies". *Journal of International Service* 1 (2011): 20–33

Young, Graeme. "Transitional Justice in Sierra Leone: A Critical Analysis". *United Nations Peace and Progress* 1 (1) (2013): 3–17

Zunes, Stephen. "The Role of Non-Violent Action in the Downfall of Apartheid". *The Journal of Modern African Studies* 37(1) (1999): 137–169

Reports

Arthur, Paige; Gonzalez, Eduardo; Lam, Yukyan; Rice, Joanna; Rodriguez-Garavito, Cesar and Yashar, Deborah J. "Strengthening Indigenous Rights Through Truth Commissions: *A Practitioner's Resource*". New York: ICTJ, 2012

Bloomfeld, David; Barnes, Teresa and Huyse, Luc, eds. "Reconciliation After Violent Conflict: A Handbook". Stockholm: International Institute for Democracy and Electoral Assistance, 2003

Bloomfield, David. "On Good Terms: Clarifying Reconciliation". Berlin: Berghof Research Center for Constructive Conflict Management, 2006

Chinkin, Christine. "Peace Agreements as a Means for Promoting Gender Equality and Ensuring Participation of Women". United Nations Division for the Advancement of Women, 2003

Danish Institute for Human Rights. "Informal Justice Systems. Charting a Course for Human Rights-Based Engagement". New York: UNDP, UNICEF and UN Women, 2013

Due Process of Law Foundation. "Victims Unsilenced: The Inter-American Human Rights System and Transitional Justice in Latin America" Washington: Due Process of Law Foundation, 2012

Equipo Argentino de Antropologia Forense. "Annual Report 2005". Buenos Aires & New York: Equipo Argentino de Antropologia Forense, 2005

Instituto Interamericano de Derechos Humanos. "Contribución de las Políticas de Verdad, Justicia y Reparación a las Democracias en América Latina". San Jose': IIDH, 2011

Inter-American Commission on Human Rights. "Situation of Human Rights in Guatemala: Diversity, Inequality and Exclusion". Washington DC: Organization of American States, 2015

Inter-American Commission on Human Rights. "The Right to Truth in the Americas". Washington DC: Organization of American States, 2014

Kurtenbach, Sabine. "Guatemala's Post-War Development. The Structural Failure of Low Intensity Peace". Project Working Paper 2, Institute for Development and Peace, 2008

Martinez, Denis; Flores, Gabriela and Rogers, Oliver. "We Struggle With Dignity: Victims' Participation in Transitional Justice in Guatemala". Research Report, Impunity Watch, 2016

Office of the United Nations High Commissioner for Human Rights. "Rule-of-Law Tools for Post-Conflict States: Amnesties". New York and Geneva: United Nations, 2009

Orentlicher, Diane F. "Shrinking the Space for Denial: The Impact of the ICTY in Serbia". New York: Open Society Institute, 2008

Riesenfeld, Camilla. "Instruments of Reconciliation?: Potentials and Risks of Reparation Measures in post-Conflict Guatemala". Uppsala: Department of Peace and Conflict Research, Uppsala University, 2008

Saferworld. "Masculinities, Conflict and Peacebuilding. Perspectives on Men Through a Gender Lens". London: Saferworld, 2014

Salick, Jan and Byg, Anja. "Indigenous Peoples and Climate Change". Oxford: Tyndall Centre for Climate Change Research, 2007

Salvesen, Hilde. "Guatemala: Five Years After the Peace Accords. The Challenges of Implementing Peace". Oslo: International Peace Research Institute, 2002

Taylor, David. "Victim Participation in Transitional Justice Mechanisms: Real Power or Empty Ritual?". Utrecht: Impunity Watch, Discussion Paper, 2014

Truth and Reconciliation Commission. "Truth and Reconciliation Commission of South Africa Report". Cape Town: Juta and Co., 1998

Vess, Joseph; Barker, Gary; Naraghi-Anderlini, Sanam and Hassink, Alexa. "The Other Side of Gender: Men as Critical Agents of Change". Washington: United States Institute of Peace, 2013

International and Regional Treaties and Documents

Agreement Between the United Nations and the Government of Sierra Leone on the Establishment of a Special Court for Sierra Leone, Lome', 16 January 2002, 2178 UNTS 138

Agreement on Identity and Rights of Indigenous Peoples, Mexico City, 31 March 1995

Agreement on Socio-Economic Aspects and the Agrarian Situation, Mexico City, 6 May 1996

Agreement on the Establishment of the Commission to Clarify Past Human Rights Violations and Acts of Violence That Have Caused the Guatemalan Population to Suffer, Oslo, 23 June 1994

American Convention on Human Rights, San José, 21 November 1969, 1144 UNTS 123

Cairo Communique 1, Cairo, 1 December 1943. In Royal Institute of International Affairs, *United Nations Documents 1941–1945*. London and New York: Oxford University Press, 1946

Cassese, Antonio (Independent Expert). "Report on the Special Court for Sierra Leone" (12 December 2006)

Convention against Torture and Other Cruel, Inhuman or Degrading Treatment or Punishment, New York, 10 December 1984, 1465 UNTS 85

Convention on the Prevention and Punishment of the Crime of Genocide, Paris, 12 September 1948, 78 UNTS 277

Declaration of Solidarity of the United Nations, London, 12 June 1941. In Royal Institute of International Affairs, *United Nations Documents 1941–1945*. London and New York: Oxford University Press, 1946

Declaration on Atrocities, Moscow, 19–30 October 1943. In Royal Institute of International Affairs, *United Nations Documents 1941–1945*. London and New York: Oxford University Press, 1946

European Convention for the Protection of Human Rights and Fundamental Freedoms, Rome, 4 November 1950, 213 UNTS 221

Geneva Convention Relative to the Protection of Civilian Persons in Time of War (Fourth Geneva Convention), Geneva, 12 August 1949, 75 UNTS 287

Human Rights Committee. "General Comment No.31: The Nature of the General Legal Obligation Imposed on States Parties to the Covenant". UN Doc. CCPR/C/21/Rev.1/Add. 13 (26 May 2004)

International Convention for the Protection of all Persons from Enforced Disappearance, New York, 20 December 2016, A/RES/61/177

International Convention on the Elimination of All Forms of Racial Discrimination, New York, 07 March 1966, 660 UNTS 195

International Convention on the Suppression and Punishment of the Crime of Apartheid, New York, 30 November 1973, 1015 UNTS 243

International Military Tribunal for the Far East Charter, Tokyo, 19 January 1946

Japanese Instrument of Surrender, Tokyo, 2 September 1945

Peace Agreement Between the Government of Sierra Leone and the Revolutionary United Front of Sierra Leone, Lome', 7 July 1999

Proclamation Defining Terms for Japanese Surrender, Postdam, 26 July 1945

Protocol Additional to the Geneva Conventions of 12 August 1949 *and Relating to the Protection of Victims of Non-International Armed Conflicts (Protocol II)*, Geneva, 8 June 1977, 1125 UNTS 609

Protocol Additional to the Geneva Conventions of 12 August 1949 *and Relating to the Protection of Victims of International Armed Conflicts (Protocol I)*, Geneva, 8 June 1977, 1125 UNTS 3

Rome Statute of the International Criminal Court, Rome, 17 July 1998, 2187 UNTS 90

Statute of the International Court of Justice, San Francisco, 24 October 1945, United States Treaty Series 993

Statute of the Special Court for Sierra Leone, Lome', 7 July 1999, 2178 UNTS 138

UN Security Council Res 1315 (2000), Un. Doc. S/RES/1315 (2000)

UN Security Council Res 827 (1993), Un. Doc. S/RES/827 (1993)

UN Security Council, *Statute of the International Criminal Tribunal for Rwanda*, U.N. Doc. S/RES/955 (1994)

UN Security Council, *Updated Statute of the International Criminal Tribunal for the Former Yugoslavia* (last amended 7 July 2009), 25 May 1993, UN Doc. SC/RES/827

UNCHR (Economic and Social Council). "Promotion and Protection of Human Rights: Study on the Right to Truth" (2006). Un Doc E/CN.4/2006/91

UNCHR. "Report of Diane Orentlicher, Independent Expert to Update the Set of Principles to Combat Impunity – Updated Set of Principles for the Protection and Promotion of Human Rights Through Action to Combat Impunity" (2005). Un Doc E/CN.4/2005/102/Add.1.

United Nations Declaration on the Rights of Indigenous Peoples, New York, 13 September 2007, A/61/L.67/Annex

United Nations, "Guidance Note of the Secretary-General: UN Approach to Transitional Justice". United Nations, 2010

National and International Jurisprudence

Case of Almonacid-Arellano et al v Chile (Judgment) Inter-American Court of Human Rights Series C no. 154 (26 September 2006)

Case of Barrios Altos v Peru (Judgment) Inter-American Court of Human Rights Series C no. 75 (14 May 2001)

Case of Bazorkina v Russia (Judgment) European Court of Human Rights, Application no. 69481/01 (27 July 2006)

Case of Cyprus v Turkey (Judgment) European Court of Human Rights, Application no. 25781/94 (10 May 2001)

Case of El-Masri v The Former Yugoslav Republic of Macedonia (Judgment) European Court of Human Rights, Application no.39630/09 (13 December 2012)

Case of Imakayeva v Russia (Judgment) European Court of Human Rights, Application no.7615/02 (9 November 2006)

Case of Radilla-Pacheco v Mexico (Preliminary Objections, Merits, Reparations and Costs) Inter-American Court of Human Rights Series C no 209 (23 November 2009)

Case of the Pueblo Bello Massacre v Colombia (Judgment) Inter-American Court of Human Rights Series C no 140 (31 January 2006)

Case of Velásquez Rodríguez v Honduras (Judgment) Inter-American Court of Human Rights Series C no. 4 (29 July 1988)

Human Rights Committee, Communication no. 1469/2006 (*Sharma v. Nepal*), Un Doc. CCPR/C/94/D/1469/2006 (6 November 2008)

Human Rights Committee, Communication no. 59/1996 (*Blanco Abad v Spain*) UN Doc. CAT/T/C/20/D/59/1996 (14 May 1998)

Ieng Sary case (Provisional Detention Order) ECCC Criminal Case File No. 002/14-08-2006 (14 November 2007)

International Military Tribunal for the Far East: Dissentient Judgment of Justice Pal. Tokyo: Kokusho – Kankokai, 1999

Prosecutor v Anto Furundzija (Judgment) ICTY-95-27/1-T (10 December 1998)

Prosecutor v Augustine Gbao (Decision on Preliminary Motion on the Invalidity of the Agreement Between the United Nations and the Government of Sierra Leone on the Establishment of the Special Court) SCSL-04-15-PT-141 (25 May 2004)

Prosecutor v Zenjil Delalić et al (Judgment) ICTY-96-21-T (16 November 1998)

Rigoberta Menchu et al v Ríos Montt et al (Judgment) Constitutional Court of Guatemala Exp 1904-2013 (20 May 2013)

The Azanian People's Organization (AZAPO) v The President of the Republic of South Africa CCT 17/96 (25 July 1996)

The Trial of German Major War Criminals. Proceedings of the International Military Tribunal sitting at Nuremberg, Germany. Published at Nuremberg, Germany, 1949

Zimbabwe Human Rights NGO Forum v Zimbabwe (Judgment) African Commission on Human and Peoples' Rights, Communication no. 245/02 (25 June 2002)

Other Sources

Allen, Tim and MacDonald, Anna. "Post-Conflict Traditional Justice: A Critical Overview". The Justice and Security Research Programme, Paper 3, 2013

Amnistia e Indulto per Reati Comuni, Politici e Militari (Amnesty and Pardon for Common, Political and Military Crimes): Decreto Presidenziale 22 Giugno 1946 No. 4, G.U. 137 (23 June 1946)

Armakolas, Ioannis and Vissou, Eleni. "Transitional Justice in Practice: The International Criminal Tribunal for the Former Yugoslavia and Beyond". UNISCI Discussion Paper 18, 2008

Bergenfelz, Linn. "On Truth and Ideology in International Criminal Law". Master diss., Lund University, 2012

Control Council Law No. 10: Punishment of Persons Guilty of War Crimes, Crimes Against Peace and Against Humanity, 3 Official Gazette Control Council for Germany 50–55, 1946 (December 20, 1945)

Duffin, Georgina. "Past Truths and Present Justice: The Right to Truth in Transition". Master diss., School of Oriental and African Studies, 2010

Futamura, Madoka. "Revisiting the Nuremberg Legacy: Societal transformation and the Strategic Success of International War Crimes Tribunals – Lessons from the Tokyo Trial and Japanese experience". PhD Diss., King's College London, 2008

Hollander, Theo. "Neglected Voices. Untold Stories of Gender, Conflict and Transitional Justice in the Great Lakes Region". PhD diss., Utrecht University, 2014

International Committee of the Red Cross, "Protocol Additional to the Geneva Conventions of 12 August 1949, and relating to the protection of victims of international armed conflicts (Protocol I), Geneva, 8 June 1977. Commentary of 1987"

International Law Commission. "Principles of International Law Recognized in the Charter of the Nuremberg Tribunal and in the Judgment of the Tribunal, 1950". Report of the International Law Commission covering its Second Session, Document A/1316, 29 July 1950

Jimenez, Ezequiel. "Hybrid Tribunals as Capacity Building: Narrowing the Impunity Gap". Master diss., University of Gothenburg, 2015

Ley de Obediencia Debida (Due Obedience Law): Ley no. 23.521, A.D.L.A XLVII-B, 1548

Ley de Pacificación Nacional (Law of National Pacification): Ley No. 22.924, A.L. J.A., 1983-B-1681

Ley de Punto Final (Full Stop Law): Ley no. 23.492, A.D.L.A XLVII-A, 192

Mallinder, Louise. "The Ongoing Quest for Truth and Justice: Enacting and Annulling Argentina's Amnesty Laws". Working paper, Institute of Criminology and Criminal Justice, Queen's University Belfast, Belfast, 2009

Mamdani, Mahmood. "When does a Settler become a Native? Reflections of the Colonial Roots of Citizenship in Equatorial and South Africa". University of Cape Town, Centre for African Studies, Inaugural Lecture, 13 May 1998

Mendez, Juan E. and Bariffi, Francisco J. "Truth, Right to, International Protection". Max Planck Encyclopedia of Public International Law, 2012

Promotion of National Unity and Reconciliation Act: Act 34 of 1995, Statutes of the Republic of South Africa – Constitutional Law, 801–854

Regan, Paulette Yvonne Lynette. "Unsettling the Settler Within: Canada's Peacemaker Myth, Reconciliation, and Transformative Pathways to Decolonization". PhD diss., University of Victoria, 2006

Rodriguez Medina, Greisy Lorena. "Transitional Justice and Enforced Disappearance: The Right to Truth and the Obligation to Search for Disappeared Persons. The Colombian Case". Master diss., University of Oslo, 2013

Sieder, Rachel and Sierra, Marìa Teresa. "Indigenous Women's Access to Justice in Latin America". Working Paper, Chr Michelsen Institute, 2010

Index

G. Girelli, *Understanding Transitional Justice*, Philosophy, Public Policy, and Transnational Law, DOI 10.1007/978-3-319-53606-4

CPSIA information can be obtained
at www.ICGtesting.com
Printed in the USA
LVOW05*2038110817
544666LV00013B/260/P

9 783319 536057